W.A.WINTER-36

THE HONOURABLE COMPANY

" The Hon'ble Company's affairs in this quarter, I am happy to say, look well: the Trade is in a prosperous state and the Natives more orderly and appear better disposed than they have been for some time past."—GEORGE SIMPSON, governor-in-chief of the Hudson's Bay territories to William Smith, of the London Committee. York Factory, August 20, 1830.

Prince Rupert, Governor of the Hudson's Bay Company, 1670–1682

THE HONOURABLE COMPANY

A HISTORY OF
THE HUDSON'S BAY COMPANY

BY

DOUGLAS MacKAY

WITH 48 HALF-TONE ILLUSTRATIONS

AND 13 MAPS BY R. H. H. MACAULAY

CASSELL AND COMPANY LIMITED
LONDON, TORONTO, MELBOURNE
AND SYDNEY

First Published . . . 1937

382/

/42,540

61239

F1060

c

Printed in Great Britain by T. and A. CONSTABLE LTD.
at the University Press, Edinburgh.
F. 1236

To

ALICE RUTH MACKAY

CONTENTS

APPENDICES

LIST OF ILLUSTRATIONS

FOREWORD

THIS book is the result of personal enthusiasm for the subject, the willingness of the publishers, and the change of heart of the Hudson's Bay Company. The last of these must be explained. For more than two centuries the Company was conspicuously indifferent to its own history, but about the end of the nineteenth century the apathy froze into a firm policy of negation. Company history was private business, and the widening interest among Canadian and American historians in the archives met with scant sympathy from the Governor and Committee. It was not until after the war, and the two hundred and fiftieth anniversary of the founding of the Company, that the work of organizing the archives commenced, and the vast, historically important records were made available for research.

Probably a great official history will be undertaken some day; at present plans are being made for the publication from time to time of some of the original material. Meanwhile, twenty-five years have passed since a general history of the Company was undertaken by anyone with more than the usual published sources to draw upon.

The Honourable Company is in no sense official. My association with the Company has not meant that any archives or resources were at my disposal that are not within the reach of any student of the subject. A lifetime of work remains to be done before a final definitive history can be written. If this book does anything to widen or stimulate interest in a remarkable story, its major purpose

13

will be served. To have worked for the Company by day
while probing into its past by night throughout several
years, has not, I trust, weighed upon historical judgment.
I believe it has made possible the examination of the past
with a keener sense of living reality. The complete freedom
of opinion I have enjoyed reflects the generous, liberal
attitude of the Company today toward the interpretation of
its own story. Those who are familiar with the extensive
library on fur trade and exploration will probably find here
more frank criticism of the Hudson's Bay Company than in
the works of many who have written from without rather
than within the service.

Where every page, almost every paragraph, might be the
take-off into stories of trade, politics, or adventure as thrilling
as man "could ever hear by tale or history," the problems
of compression and omission have been acutely present.

The bibliography is selective, listing only published works
and omitting the huge secondary field of Arctic exploration
as well as most of the literature on the Selkirk controversy,
the Red River Insurrection, and the North West Rebellion.
Of original material, the most interesting for commercial
and fur trade history is the statement of earnings and capital
structure since 1670, given in the appendix.

Having had to choose between the recounting of men and
events on one hand and capital investment and management
on the other, the tendency has been to hold close to the
former, even at the expense of neglecting some of the precise
details of fur prices and markets and the evolution of
business methods.

Footnotes and references have been deliberately discarded,
though the important authorities have been cited in the
text. To the handful of earnest and professional historians
of the fur trade who may be exasperated by this omission,
I can only say that while I am alive and able I shall be

most happy to make all my sources and references available to them by the congenial route of private correspondence.

To the Governor and Committee of the Company I am indebted for the use of much original material from the archives in London. To the Canadian Committee of the Company, Winnipeg, I am grateful for permission to reproduce all the illustrations except those acknowledged on the pages where they appear.

D. M.

WINNIPEG, CANADA.

Labels on map: Hudson Bay, Ft.Nelson, Nelson, Hayes, Severn, James Bay, Rupert, Ft.Charles, Albany, Moose, Moose Factory, Tadoussac, Quebec, Three Rivers, Ottawa, L.NIPISSING, Montreal, Boston, Mississippi, Radisson's Probable Journey 1659

THE HONOURABLE COMPANY

CHAPTER I

"WE WEARE CESARS"

BEFORE the seventeenth century was half spent the Puritans were in Massachusetts, Champlain had found the Great Lakes, and Henry Hudson had pressed through the ice into Hudson Bay. French and English were strengthening their colonial grip on those parts of North America where Europeans might hope to live and prosper. The subarctic Hudson Bay, cutting deeply into the continent from the north, held its wealth for those who had the courage of flesh and blood, and capital for speculation.

It was a freebooting sergeant-major of the French colonial

militia at Three Rivers who, with his wife's brother, reached out to this fur wealth of the north. Upon the pattern of their erratic careers the Hudson's Bay Company was created.

Médart Chouart, Sieur des Groseilliers, was the colonial sergeant-major, and with him is always associated the name of his brother-in-law, Pierre Esprit Radisson. Within the austere realm of historical research, these names have inflamed bitter scuffles during the past fifty years. The dust of these encounters has blurred the story, until today the innocent reader turns aside from Radisson and Groseilliers to more lucid history.

The exact story of the Frenchmen's expeditions in Canada will never be known. Radisson, the writer of the pair, wrote his narratives in English years after the events he described. This record makes stimulating reading, though cluttered with contradictions and sprinkled with statements not always confirmed by the more disinterested writings of the Jesuit missionaries. His journal was prepared to impress the courtier investors of Charles II, and raise capital for trading expeditions to Hudson Bay. Somehow it became the property of Samuel Pepys, and was discovered by accident after Pepys's death when his papers were being sold to London shopkeepers for wrapping paper. Even the vault and archives of Hudson's Bay House, London, though illuminating considerably the Company's relationship to the Frenchmen, lack vital minute books in a stormy period of several years of its first decade.

It matters little now, why these two Frenchmen alternated allegiance between Charles and Louis. What does concern this history is that from their bold, scheming, fearless spirits sprang the Adventurers of England Trading into Hudson's Bay.

A more daring pair of unscrupulous international promoters cannot be found in the history of commerce. Glib, plausible, ambitious, supported by unquestionable physical courage, they were completely equipped fortune-hunters. They knew more about fur trading than any men of their time, and they were artful enough to exploit their knowledge and sell their services to European powers. Fortune-hunters they were, and they made fortunes for their employers, but, true to their stamp, they never held to the wealth they brought themselves.

As a boy, Radisson was captured twice and once adopted by the Iroquois. He found a flavour in Indian life which he never lost. "I love these people well," he wrote many years later. He lived with them through alternate bestial feasts and agonizing famines, participated in their bloodiest tribal wars, watched the horror of Indian torture, without losing affection for them. It was the life he knew best, and all the efforts of his career were directed to the wilderness. Because he was the chronicler, and because of the cheery egotism of all he wrote, historians have long given him credit for the real enterprise he and the older Groseilliers displayed. But, as the history of the period becomes more closely knit by reason of the scholarly examination of material, Radisson emerges as the garrulous promoter of their projects, and Groseilliers the steady, shrewd brains of the partnership. An Indian trader by nature, the older man apparently lacked that capaqty for self-dramatization which so often has distinguished the explorer type. Radisson had it.

Radisson was in his early twenties in the summer of 1656 (early dates in his life are only approximate) when he and Groseilliers appeared below the walls of Quebec with a band of Cree and the results of two years' fur trading. To the colony of New France this was wealth, for fur trading was the Crown's business and Indian wars had brought lean times. Salutes of guns and official praise from the governor of the colony met the traders from Trois Rivières. They tasted prosperity. Médart Chouart became captain of the local militia, and purchased himself a bit of uncleared land known as Des Groseilliers—the gooseberry patch. The village sergeant-major fur trader entered the ranks of colonial gentry with acres of his own and the self-conferred honour of a title now found somewhere in the pages of every history of Canada—Sieur des Groseilliers.

Perhaps it was the seigneurial ambition, restlessness, or genuine taste for the wilderness that roused the pair to fresh enterprise.

"We weare Cesars, being nobody to contradict us," wrote Radisson of the fur trading life.

Barely two winters after their first success, they applied to the governor at Quebec for the necessary official sanction for another expedition. Officialdom bargained for a division of profits. Licence to trade would be granted if Groseilliers and Radisson would take with them two of the governor's men. The Frenchmen asked time to consider this proposal. A spring morning came at Three Rivers when villagers learned that their captain of the local militia with his bold brother-in-trade had bolted for the forests in defiance of the Crown of France. Groseilliers, the trader, was off to the forest again, with Radisson the teller of the tale.

Radisson, the true *coureur de bois* of New France, described pungently what lay ahead of them on that early summer night:

"What fairer bastion [of self-confidence] than a good tongue, especially when one sees his owne chimney smoak, or when we can kiss our owne wives or kisse our neighbour's wife with ease and delight? It is a strange [different] thing when victualls are wanting, worke whole nights & dayes, lye downe on the bare ground, & not allwayes that hap, the breech in the water, the feare in the buttocks, to have the belly empty, the wearinesse in the bones, and drowsinesse of the body by the bad weather that you are to suffer, having nothing to keepe you from such calamity."

Fur traders have never been inclined to romanticize nature, and it was Radisson's rôle when writing of his exploits for the benefit of his prospective English employers, to cast himself in an heroic part.

They doubtless believed that a second arrival at Quebec with a fortune in furs would bring official pardon, but the affairs of the colony were at a low ebb and the governor was in no mood to forgive the soldier who had deserted his post.

Upon their return with three hundred Indians and a new fortune in beaver skins in the summer of 1660, they were arrested and fined. Of the results of their season's trade, worth about £60,000 in modern values, the State left them about £4,000, and if the colonial administration of France was true to custom, bureaucracy took its pickings. Radisson's wrath over this affair explodes in his narrative where he denounces Governor d'Argenson, whose term was about to expire, as an extortionist, a corrupt administrator who was looting honest traders "that he might the better maintain his coach and horses at Paris."

It was all too much for men who had found wealth in the wilderness, only to be penalized by the avarice of colonial governments. They cut the ties of allegiance and became free agents in the world trade of their century.

It is not a matter of profound importance whether or not Radisson and Groseilliers discovered the headwaters of the Mississippi River. Radisson's erratic narrative suggests travels to the Gulf of Mexico and hearing from Indians of bearded Spaniards with their galleons. There is evidence of their having reached as far west as Minnesota and north to James Bay. These are threads of history still being unravelled. It is enough for the purposes of this history to record that they lived and travelled in the western basin of the Great Lakes and that they knew the northern watershed dividing the Great Lakes from Hudson Bay where the deepest and richest furs were found. This was the knowledge they bargained with in London, six years after they cut loose from France.

After the seizure of their furs, in 1660, the two Canadian *coureurs* engaged on the first of those searches for capital which were to sway their lives remarkably. Their singleness of purpose, acumen, energy and political cunning in seeking support from England, France and Holland for a venture into the great Bay of the north, mark them as two of the most interesting men in American colonial history.

Before finally breaking with France, Groseilliers went to

Paris to protest against the action of the colonial governor; a journey with a conclusion commonplace in the story of the colonies for the next two centuries. Returning to America, he and Radisson commenced feeling the New England colonies for support. At Port Royal, Nova Scotia, they encountered a sea captain, in 1663, who agreed to carry them to Hudson Bay. The season was late; they were forced back by ice; Radisson said their captain was frightened, "being more familiar with Barbados sugar icing" than with Labrador ice.

Then they contracted with Boston shipowners for two ships to go north. One of these was wrecked on Sable Island while fishing for supplies, and instead of in Hudson Bay the two Frenchmen found themselves in a New England lawsuit. They were acquitted, but tales of their exploits had become known to all Boston.

Thirty years later, when Radisson was petitioning the Lord Privy Seal for an increase of pension from the Hudson's Bay Company, he varied the story, neglecting to say that Groseilliers was rejected first by France, and claiming that they were on their way to France with prospect of great success when they were lured into the English service by a Colonel Nicholl, governor of New York.

The Radisson tale of the founding of the Company, given in this pension petition of 1694, deserves quotation:

"On or about the yeare One thousand six hundred sixty and two your Orator and his Brother [des Groseilliers] intending to goe into France to give the French King an Accompt of their discoverys there did goe into New England in their way to France and there discoursing with Collonell Nicoll (who was then Governour of New Yorke) and severall other English men of great Esteeme there your Orator and his said Brother made knowne to them their design of goeing to the French King and to Informe him of the great discoverys they had made in the said parts of the West Indies and of the Easinesse of setling Factorys there (which would prove very advantageous to him) whereupon the said Collonel Nicolls and the other persons there (haveing some wild Notion before of that

part of the World) hearing your Orator talke soe distinctly
and give such particular Accompts of the places persons
languages and Commoditys thereof did at length prevaile
on your Orator and his said Brother to quitt their designe
of goeing into France and instead thereof to come for
England where they assured your Orator and his Brother
that they would be as well and kindly received by King
Charles the Second as by the French King and would be
employed on the same Errand or businesse of settling
Factorys and makeing new discoverys in the West Indies
as they could expect if they had gone into France and
would be certaine of very great Rewards in case they
Succeeded in their Enterprizes. And thereupon your
Orator and his said Brother came from thence in the yeare
One thousand Six hundred Sixty and Five with very many
Letters to diverse of the Lords of the Privy Counsell and
other persons of Quality from the said Collonel Nicolls
and others giveing an Accompt of your Orators great
knowledge and Experience in that part of the World and
of his Abilitys of settling Factorys there and how they had
dissuaded him by large promises to quitt his intended
Voyage to France and to come for England to offer his
and his said Brothers Service to King Charles the Second
whereupon severall of the Lords of his said Majesties
Privy Councell did carry your Orator and his said Brother
to the said King Charles the Second who was pleased to
command your Orator to give him an Accompt of the
Manners Languages Scituacion and of the severall parts
of that Country and his said late Majestie was soe well
pleased with the relacion given him by your Orator
thereof and of the Ease and advantage of setling or
establishing Factorys there that his said late Majestie did
thereupon by his Letters Patents grant a Charter to Prince
Rupert the late Duke of Albermarle and to severall others
and Incorporated them by the name of Governour and
Company of Adventurers of England tradeing into Hudsons bay . . . and thereupon (about 1673) your Orator and
his Brother retorned to London and when your Orator
and his Brother went to the said late King to give his
Majestie an Accompt of their successes in the late Expedicion his Majestie was soe well satisfyed with what they
had done and the Good that was like to come to the said

Company and this nation thereby that his Majestie was gratiously pleased to give to each of us a Gold Chaine and Meddall as a token of his favour and particularly recommended us to the Company to be well rewarded and in pursuance of such Recommendation and the Companys sence of the great good done to them thereby they promised to your Orator and his said Brother One hundred pounds a yeare each. . . ."

This appears to be a fair statement of events, with due allowance for the special purpose the document was to serve, and the writer's now known uncertainty about dates. It would not have been in character with the Radisson-Groseilliers saga for them to proceed uneventfully from New to Old England. Their ship was battered, boarded and captured by a Dutch war vessel, and its passengers were made prisoners and put ashore on the coast of Spain. It is a typical footnote to the fantastic adventures of the pair. They came somehow to London early in 1666.

There are provoking gaps here in the chronicle, for it was two years before the project became reality, and four years before it took on the form of the corporation. Through either Colonel Nicholl or Sir George Carteret they were maintained in London that winter on an allowance of forty shillings a week from the royal purse, and later were received by Charles II at Windsor. War, pestilence, and the Great Fire composed only a part of the Restoration monarch's difficulties. It is fair to assume that Charles quickly promised the seal of royal approval on a venture promising financial returns. Slowly, from 1667, the first individual investments of twenty pounds increased until by 1675 the Company's paid up capital was ten thousand five hundred pounds, and in the meantime expeditions had reached Hudson Bay and returned with the first profits in furs.

It was two years after their arrival in 1666 before the pair sailed for Hudson Bay for Prince Rupert's syndicate. Little is known of their life in the meantime, though much may be imagined. They must have met and convinced the select group of shareholders, later known as proprietors.

The writer Radisson became friendly with the family of Sir John Kirke, soldier and member of the original Committee of the Company. His daughter, Mary Kirke, became Mary Radisson in 1668 or 1669. The elder Groseilliers had been married many years before to Radisson's sister. Both men must have been busy organizing the expedition of 1668. Pepys would have known something of them, for as secretary of the Admiralty he doubtless arranged details of the loan of the *Eaglet* of the Royal Navy for this first trading voyage to the Bay, and it was from his papers that the Radisson manuscript was rescued. This journal found its way to the Bodleian Library, and was published by the Prince Society of Boston, in 1885.

On June 3, 1668, the *Eaglet* and the *Nonsuch* sailed down the Thames from Gravesend. The story of the Hudson's Bay Company was taking form.

In the elaborate instructions to the masters of the *Nonsuch* and the *Eaglet* are significant sentences which reveal the importance of exploration for the route to the Orient. The acceptance by Rupert's syndicate of this obligation to search for the North West Passage at the very outset, and the hopes expressed, throw new light on the controversy that was to boil up round the Company with exasperating frequency for nearly two hundred years. The instructions are also important for disclosing the false inducements held out by Radisson and Groseilliers, of a tidewater south sea within two weeks' travel of the Bay.

"When it shall Please God to bring you thither to Hudson Bay you are to saile to such place as Mr. Gooseberry and Mr. Raddison shall direct you within the Bay and there endeavour to bring yor said vessells into some safe Harbour in ord^r to trade with the Indyans there and you are to deliver unto them the goods you carry by small parcells with this Caution that there be no more than fifty pounds worth at a time out of each shipp and that when they returne on board with such goods as they shall have in Exchange from the Natives you stowe the same on board the Vessells before you deliver out any more. This being according to the particular advice wee have received of Mr. Gooseberry and Mr. Raddison themselves. . . .

"You are upon yor first arrival there to raise some fortifications upon the shore for your most convenient accommodation and safety in the prepaireing whereof both your shipps Companies are to give their mutuall assistance and you are allwaies to have extraordinary Care of your vessells to prevent any surprize.

" As soone as you have gotten together of the commodityes of the Country to any considerable value you are to putt them all on board the Nonsuch ketch into wch Capt. Stannard is to remove with so many of the Company of the Eaglett Ketch as you shall Judge convenient to saile her home and shall bringe along with him Mr. Gooseberry upon the said vessell and also you are to use your utmost endeavour to bring some of the copper or other mineralls of that Country making what hast you can in the dispatch of the said Vessell that so it May be out of the streights before the Ice doth hinder. . . .

"You are to have in yor thoughts the discovery of the Passage into the South sea and to attempt it as occasion shall offer with the advice and direction of Mr. Gooseberry and Mr. Radisson, or one of them they having told us that it is but 7 daies padling or sailing from the River where they intend to trade and Harbour unto the stinking Lake and not above 7 daies more to the streight wch. leads into that sea they call the South sea and from thence but forty or fifty leagues to the sea it selfe in all wch. streight it Ebbs and flows by meanes whereof the passage up and downe will be quicke and if it be possible you are to gett so much light in this matter before the returne of the Nonsuch Ketch as may encourage us the next spring to send a vessell on purpose for that discovery. . . .

"Wee doe . . . declare that if by accident you meete with any sea horse or mors teeth or make advantage by killing of whales It is to be made good to our accompt. Lastly we desire and require you to use the said Mr. Gooseberry and Mr. Radisson with all manner of civility and courtesy and to take care that all your company doe beare a perticular respect unto them they being the persons upon

whose credit wee have undertaken this expedition. . . .
You are to keepe exact Journalls."

Signed
RUPERT ALBEMARLE
CRAVEN G. CARTERET
J. HAYES P. COLETON

Radisson was on board the *Eaglet*, commanded by
Captain Stannard. Somewhere on the Atlantic she was
dismasted in a gale and compelled to turn back. The other
ship, the fifty-ton ketch *Nonsuch*, with Groseilliers on board
and Zachariah Gillam, of Boston, for her master, won
through to Hudson Bay.

It is necessary at the outset to visualize the gigantic *U*
of the Hudson Bay coast line. The base of the *U* opens into
a lesser *u* which repeats in reduced size the same general
contours and forms James Bay. Arctic islands sprawl across
the opening of the greater *U*. In and out of this sea there is
but one route for ships, Hudson Strait, where currents, tide
and ice restrict navigation to the midsummer weeks. In
the great Bay itself there is drifting ice in August, and the
first snow flurries whip the air in September.

The eastern shore line is treeless, rocky, and offers only
meagre shelter for ships for hundreds of miles. As the curve
of the coast swings south several hundred miles into the
lower cup of James Bay, there is forest on the monotonous
shore line, but without promontories: a landscape that
seems to crouch in the brief warm summer, gathering
strength to meet the violence of each winter.

On the west coast the Bay offers little more to the eye:
long, unbroken shore lines with forest and muskeg behind,
and as the coast crosses the Arctic Circle some broken
shoulders of mountains, crushed and subdued by a glacial
age.

The glory of the Bay is in its rivers. From east, south and
west fresh water pours into the basin: fast subarctic waters
from Labrador, from the north slope of the Laurentians,
and from the glaciers of the Rockies and the shallow valleys
of the prairies. These waters from mountain and muskeg

became the arteries of the fur trade, and the shores of this harsh, unfriendly bay were to be the front line of the struggle for a fur empire for a century and more.

Master Gillam of New England and the ex-sergeant of the colonial militia of Trois Rivières were not the first there. Henry Hudson, Thomas James, Thomas Button, and Luke Foxe, of England, and Jens Munck, from Denmark, had all groped into the Bay since the start of the century, searching for the North West Passage to the Orient. But they were not fur traders with any expert knowledge of life in the Canadian north. Rejected as a route to China, and with a reputation for being haunted by scurvy, starvation and death in winter, the Bay had been deserted for twenty-five years.

It was late September, 1668, one hundred and eighteen days out from Gravesend, when the *Nonsuch* anchored in the little harbour they named Rupert's, at the southern extremity of James Bay. Winter was almost upon them and there was work to be done. Groseilliers, the veteran woodsman, put the English crew to work on a palisaded fort, and named it Charles, after the King.

The ship was drawn into the estuary of Rupert's River, and Fort Charles was a cramped hut behind log walls among the pines close to the water's edge. Since known in fur trade history as Rupert's House, men have been trading there with Indians for more than two and a half centuries. Mister Gooseberry, as the Company papers called Groseilliers, had touched the fringes of the richest beaver country of North America.

The episode is linked with the fur trading of 1937, for Rupert's House is now the headquarters of the greatest commercial beaver preserve in the world; seven thousand square miles are patrolled by the native descendants of those Indians who met Master Gillam and Mr. Gooseberry, and this territory is being nursed back into scientific beaver production by the Hudson's Bay Company.

The winter of 1668–69 was bitter. No one has put down what the bosun and the carpenter and the able seamen of the *Nonsuch* said about the climate, but it was no doubt vigorous, and Gillam observed that all the world seemed frozen into death. To the French fur trader it was the opportunity he had sought for fourteen years. Here were Indians unspoiled by competitive trading with European fur seekers. The tariff was absurdly low, and as the winter passed, with the *Nonsuch* crew huddling close to the fires, Groseilliers baled up beaver skins bought in exchange for tools and trinkets, laying the basis of centuries of Hudson's Bay Company trade.

Summer's exotic heat released the ship from the ice in June, and she sailed for the Thames with her cargo. In the State Papers of Charles is the report of the ship's return:

"Last Satterday night [October 9, 1669] came in the Nonsuch Ketch from the Northwest passage. Since I have endeavored to find the proceeds of their voyage, and understand they were environed with ice about 6 monethes first haleing their ketch on shore, and building them a house. They carried provisions on shore and brewd Ale and beere and provided against the cold which was their work. They report the natives to bee civill and say Beaver is Very plenty. Those that carryed out no Venture brought home 10 li or 12 li worth of beaver."

New wealth from a new land consolidated the enterprise. On May 2, 1670, Charles II signed the charter granting sweeping imperial powers to the Company of Adventurers of England trading into Hudson's Bay.

Fur trade was pursued as vigorously as time and distance and climate would permit, but the new company did not allow itself to be dazzled into extravagance by the prospect of sudden riches. This was not the wealth of all the Indies sought by Europe's merchants across the Atlantic, but it looked like a fair speculation. Charles Bayly, first resident governor sent to the Bay, may have been impressed by the resounding phrases of the great Royal Charter, but to Radisson and Groseilliers it was important as a good passport to more fur trading. Bayly seems to have been close to the King, and it has been suggested that a resident governorship of a remote wilderness was a form of banishment. In any event, he was the first of a long unhappy line of seventeenth-century administrators overseas who fumbled through their duties and returned to home and England without ever demonstrating the gusto of the fur traders of later history.

In 1670, the year of incorporation, the reunited Frenchmen were again at Fort Charles in James Bay with two ships, and Bayly was nominally in command as governor, representing the London proprietors. Groseilliers settled down to trade, and the younger man to explore the western coast line, prying with a trading eye into the mouths of the Moose, the Severn and Nelson rivers, all to become great depots of fur wealth from the interior. Radisson picked the right positions.

By autumn, 1671, they were in London again, preparing with Gillam for the 1672 voyage to the Bay. They probably wintered at Fort Charles in the season of 1672–73, when they abandoned their fort for coastal exploration and returned to find that a French Jesuit missionary, Father Albanel, had seized it in the name of King Louis. Moreover, Albanel had brought some communications for Radisson and Groseilliers from their Quebec relatives. The Jesuit withdrew after an exchange of courtesies, and returned south by exhausting portages over the height of land into the canyon of the Saguenay River. Master Gillam of Boston and Governor Bayly smelled a rat. All that was English and Protestant provoked suspicion of the Catholic French fur traders, and this encounter on the lonely shores of James Bay was apparently carried to London.

This may have been the year the King gave them each the "gold Chaine and Meddall" referred to in the pension petition twenty years later. Apparently Charles was cordial and impressed, and the smoke of suspicion cleared. But the Frenchmen were vacillating. Possibly the enforced periods of London life were not healthy for two Indianized travellers. Financial returns cramped their families' lives; they had expected "great rewards in case they succeeded in their enterprizes." The Company paid no dividend until 1684.

They recalled their original idea of taking their discoveries to France, their native country. In 1674, Company minutes record a pension of one hundred pounds per annum for them, with promise of further consideration "if it shall please God to bless this Company with good success hereafter that they shall come to be in a prosperous condition."

It was not enough. Radisson and Groseilliers bolted for France, where the tireless imperialist Colbert paid their debts, pardoned their past desertion, and found new services for them. Radisson served for a time in the French marine; perhaps he was mindful of the estrangement from his English wife, since he sought to re-enter the Hudson's Bay Company's service and was refused. He returned to the fur trade for New France in 1682, when he and his brother-in-law guided two small vessels from the lower St. Lawrence to the Hayes River on Hudson Bay. They had with them this time Jean Baptiste Groseilliers, twenty-eight-year-old heir to the Groseilliers acres at Three Rivers. The Hayes and the Nelson rivers enter Hudson Bay close together, and the narrowing land between their estuaries has witnessed two hundred and fifty years of fur trading, mostly under the name of York Factory.

Radisson (again from his own erratic account) eluded Danish pirates, suppressed a mutiny, and landed at the mouth of the Hayes to start fur trading for France. He had noted the spot ten years before, while exploring for the English.

Of all the fantastic episodes of fur trading, the incidents of that winter make the most preposterous. The Frenchmen found a post already established in the forest by a party of freebooting New Englanders under one Ben Gillam, son of the captain who had brought the *Nonsuch* to the Bay fourteen years earlier. A younger generation was appearing in beaver trading. This party, of course, operated in defiance of the Company of Adventurers' Royal Charter. Radisson moved cautiously. He himself was an outlaw on Hudson Bay, and here were New Englanders also poaching. Radisson opened negotiations with them. Then a Company ship arriving from Fort Charles under Gillam *père* and with the resident governor Bridgar on board, piled up on the mud flats.

Thus two outlaw parties, one from New France and one from New England, plus an armed ship with the authority of the English Crown, all converged upon the mouths of the Nelson and Hayes rivers in the autumn of 1682. All that was adroit, cunning and diplomatic in Radisson rose to this three-cornered crisis. He claims to have kept both crews separated for considerable time, and played one against the other while saving some from starvation and protecting others from Indian massacre. In the end he brought them all to terms without bloodshed by outwitting Bridgar and sailing out of the Bay for Quebec in *The Bachelor's Delight*, with the Frenchmen in command, a load of furs partly contraband, and English prisoners including Bridgar and Gillam senior. Young Groseilliers was left with seven men to continue trading.

The whole affair was typical of Radisson's story as told by himself about himself, with the hero equal to every occasion. What the captured Company Englishmen told the Committee on their return to England remained unwritten. They must have had a long, cold, dark winter, unfortified against low temperatures, at the mercy of men who had been fellow employees and also the originators of their whole fur trade.

Quebec must have gloated secretly at the sight of two crews of Englishmen brought captive on an English ship, to say nothing of the fur cargo. But there was no war between France and England, though the sovereignty of either over Hudson Bay was shadowy. De la Barre, governor at Quebec, restored the ship to Bridgar and Gillam and allowed them to go home to tell their unhappy adventures.

Somewhere on this bizarre 1682–83 expedition, Groseilliers died. How, where, or when, Radisson failed to record. He had had his own troubles manœuvring to outwit the Company and the rival New Englanders, and contriving at

King Charles II who granted the Charter of the Hudson's Bay Company on second of May, 1670

James, Duke of York, afterwards King James II, Governor of the Hudson's Bay Company, 1683–1685

the same time to destroy at least one Company fort. The Company was not informed of Groseilliers's death, though Radisson seemed to have passed on the torch of his brother-in-law to young Groseilliers by leaving him in command.

Radisson, alone now, was in bad odour with England, and news of his adventures had also reached France. Nevertheless, in 1684 Louis XIV fitted out another expedition for him, to sail for Hudson Bay on April 24. In London, the Company Committee minutes of a meeting on May 12 record the news that "Peter Espirit Radisson has arrived from France." At the last minute Radisson had bolted again, thrown up a French command and offered his services to the English, though there is evidence of English persuasion, and it has been suggested that he was an unconscious agent for the fulfilment of a secret treaty between Charles and Louis. Through all these years Mary Kirke Radisson had been living in England with their children, and with none of the great rewards her adventurous husband had anticipated.

The Company needed him, welcomed him. He was hastily presented at Windsor to the Duke of York, who had succeeded Prince Rupert in the governorship. Radisson's salary was agreed upon at two hundred pounds of stock, fifty pounds a year, and twenty-five pounds "to set him up to Proceed to Port Nelson; and his brother Groseilliers to have 20 shillings per week if he come over from France to Britain and be true." (Groseilliers was dead.) The English insisted upon "an oath of fidelity to the Company," according to the minutes. On May 15 the ship *Happy Return* was one of three ships on the North Atlantic heading for the Hayes River on Hudson Bay, with Radisson pacing the cramped deck, eager for the wilderness again.

Young Groseilliers, who had been left there to trade for France, must have been astounded when Uncle Radisson came ashore from an English ship to seize the post and the furs in the name of the Company of Adventurers. He protested, but was obliged to surrender. It was a magnificent haul for the Company of twenty thousand pelts which Radisson delivered to the proprietors on October 25, 1684.

"He was thanked, and a gratuity of 100 guineas given him," states the minute book, adding, "a promise having been made of 20 shillings per week to Groseilliers, and he not having come, the same is transferred to his son in the Bay."

Sir William Young, of the Committee, was made a gift of seven musquash skins for having brought Radisson back to the Company from France. Young Groseilliers was employed at one hundred pounds a year, and one hundred pounds was awarded to four Frenchmen left in the Bay.

Radisson had a further salary wrangle with the Committee the following year, and they reached a settlement of one hundred pounds a year salary, and three hundred pounds or one hundred pounds stock to Mary Kirke Radisson in the event of her husband's death. There is evidence that the grant to Mrs. Radisson was later raised to four hundred pounds. The ship's instructions for the year included "a hogshead of claret for Mr. Radisson, such as Mr. Radisson shall like." The Indian trade was progressing, and four hundred guns, one thousand hatchets, eighteen hundred long knives, as well as bricks, tiles, glass and timber for construction, went on board the same vessel.

Radisson, now a citizen of England, continued with the Company on more or less active service for five years; busy years with many voyages to and from the Bay, all laconically recorded in London. In 1685 sailed the *Success*, the *Owners Goodwill*, the *Happy Return*, and the *Perpetuana Merchant*. The *Success* was lost late that autumn. The *Owners Goodwill* arrived in the Downs, October 10; the *Perpetuana Merchant* was captured by the French in Hudson Straits, July 27. The *Happy Return* fulfilled her name, but the following year was lost in July, in Hudson Strait. And so it went. Each spring three or four ships sailed to the Bay; each autumn, or perhaps it would be the autumn following, they returned, though usually one or more would be missing. Voyages were fraught with hazard for employees of the Adventurers, quite apart from the perils of life on the Bay.

Younger generations of captains and employee fur traders went to and from the Bay. The old scheming originator, Radisson, was not always at peace with them. Traces there must have been of *sub rosa* dealing, the subject of stern warnings from London heads.

Radisson acquired another gratuity of fifty pounds, and one hundred pounds dividend on the two hundred pounds stock awarded him. His dividends dropped to fifty pounds the next year, and rose to one hundred and fifty pounds in 1690. Hard times came. The French and English struggled for the fur trade in the lakes and forests of America, and went to war. Radisson's annuity was cut to fifty pounds. Could the Company continue to employ a twice renegade Frenchman during a war with France? Sir William Young presented his case to the London Committee, making a substantial claim for neglect of a courageous servant who had brought them wealth. There was no friendship now from a gracious monarch or an honourable prince of the blood. Charles who had given the "Chaine and Meddall" was dead. Rupert of the Rhine was dead. Twenty-two years had passed since the *coureurs* from Three Rivers arrived at the English court.

The Committee retorted not too effectively, and refused the petition. Radisson carried his case to the courts, and English justice ordered payment of the one hundred pounds annuity with arrears in full. This was in 1694 and Radisson was sixty years of age. His case, as stated in his own petition and the previous petition of Sir William Young, was technically settled. The documents involved agree on singularly few points. It had been twenty-four years since the granting of the Charter. The personnel of the Company had altered. There had been glittering prizes some years, and again no prizes at all. In 1700 Radisson applied for the position of warehouse keeper and was refused. The stubborn attitude of the Committee through these later

years in declining to concede an inch beyond the requirements of the law suggests some depth of offence. Other
independent, courageous men were content in the service.
Radisson probably overtalked his case, a type well known
to pioneer America as the disgruntled old-timer, impoverished and garrulous on his neglected rights and high
adventures, writing interminably with faulty memory of
events beyond the knowledge of most of his contemporaries.

Whatever the cause, his "great rewards" became an
annual pension of one hundred pounds. His family, deserted
by him even as he had deserted at various times both
France and England, ended in poverty.

And yet in Radisson's case he had an authentic tale to
tell, packed with the stuff of men and ships and money,
of far-off lands and savage people, of snow and ice and
intense summer heat. He had shown the way to profits,
but he had been a Frenchman and a renegade and a
Catholic in a century when Protestant Englishmen were
finding new arrogance in their faith and their nationality.

Radisson drew the last quarterly instalment of his pension
in July, 1710.

Later historians have tried to find in his life more than
mercenary adventuring. So far as the Hudson's Bay
Company is concerned, he did a first-rate job for which
he was underpaid—not an uncommon incident in any
company's history. There are threads of the story yet to
be gathered in. The scholarship now being brought to fur
trade history will weave a fuller tapestry for Radisson and
Groseilliers. It will be a good chronicle, worth reading.

CHAPTER II

RUPERT, CHARLES AND THE CHARTER

PRINCE RUPERT, first Governor of the Company, has provided history with a glamorous setting for the launching of the Hudson Bay venture. Lely painted him in rich, sombre colours, glittering orders on his blue cloak, aquiline features framed in a wealth of dark hair, the elaborate costume a gorgeous background for the fine, strong figure of the warrior bachelor Prince of the Palatine. This fighting Royalist Rupert would intoxicate any romancer; but, in truth, the Hudson's Bay Company was not more than a profitable incident in his later life.

Writers have been inclined to wax maudlin over this royal relationship, but never with official encouragement, for if ever an historic organization was indifferent to the glamour of its past, it was this Company of Adventurers during the first two and a half centuries of its existence. The fluctuations of a business which originated in the subarctic and ended in the luxury trades of Europe were too all-absorbing to permit the cultivation of company annals, to say nothing of romantic concern over a royal prince of the seventeenth century.

Overdramatizing of the royal beginnings has come principally from those who have not even been content to give the Hudson's Bay Company its correct legal title, "The Governor and Company of Adventurers of England trading into Hudson's Bay," but have insisted on the unauthorized flourish of "Gentlemen Adventurers." It is characteristic of the romantic approach to the long story. Certainly the Company's men could not be accused of being poseurs strutting on the red carpet of tradition, unless perhaps some of the older men in the later years of the nineteenth century became infected with the mingled aura of a royal charter and Kipling's "white man's burden."

If overcoloured by well-intentioned writers, Rupert's place is secure in authentic Company history. He was fifty-one when Radisson and Groseilliers were brought to the court, not old, yet a veteran, and at the very height of his popularity with the London crowds. Old wounds pained him, and he had recently come through a serious illness. Essentially a soldier in the disciplining of his own life, his strong, masculine carriage, scorn of politicians, and indifference to the populace made him the hero of the streets. He had ridden hard, fought hard, and suffered in the lost cause of his cousin, the beheaded Charles, and he had returned from exile, booted and spurred, with the Restoration. Charles II, who had worshipped him as a boy, was happy to have him by his side again. To Englishmen of the Restoration he was that irresistible, heroic figure, "the man on horseback."

Grave, reticent Rupert, living at Windsor, experimented with chemistry (which suggested alchemy to the common mind of the day), played tennis with the King, and worked with more than ordinary talent at the art of the mezzotint. Senior in years to most of those surrounding the King, he abstained from the broader vices of the court, preferring his narrow circle of old soldiers who like himself had been schooled in the Thirty Years' War and fought on the Continent for the Protestant faith wherever a sword was needed in the cause.

De Grammont wrote of him, "He was polite, even to excess, unseasonably; but haughty and even brutal when he ought to have been gentle and courteous; he was tall and his manners were ungracious; he had a dry, hard visage, and a stern look even when he wished to please."

This was Rupert of the Rhine, twenty-five years after the dust and thundering hoofs of Edgehill, Marston Moor, and Naseby, when the offer of a speculation in the North American fur trade came unexpectedly from Quebec via New England. The prospect held out by Radisson and Groseilliers did not bring any prompt flood of capital.

Note the two years between their arrival in England and the sailing of the *Nonsuch*. Besides, money was not easy. The Royal Navy was a million pounds in debt and Sir George Carteret was keeping the fleet at sea mainly by pledging his own private credit.

The King needed funds badly. The Frenchmen's offer linked colonial enterprise with mercantile expansion and not too high a hazard. More than likely it was Charles rather than Rupert who crystallized the idea and turned it over to the courtiers and bankers to carry through. Three times the King gave audience to Radisson. Groseilliers was with him on two occasions, and the significance of the "Chaine and Meddall" gift would indicate a real personal interest. Radisson claimed it was Charles who instructed the Company in 1684 to pay him a pension of fifty pounds a year until the King should find for him "an employment or place of greater advantage." Moreover it is not entirely in character with the ageing Rupert to take up such a project. The other chartered companies of the time do not seem to have attracted him.

Even the form of the Company was not fixed at the outset. The Frenchmen came to London in 1666. Late in 1667 the first investment was made by seven original Adventurers, but the early capital of ten thousand five hundred pounds was not fully paid up until 1675. The *Nonsuch* sailed into the Bay in 1668, returning in 1669. On April 18, 1670, articles of incorporation were tentatively drawn, entitled *An Incorporacion of Prince Rupert, Duke of Albemarle, Earl of Craven . . . into one body politique by the name of Governours and Adventurers trading to Hudsons baye.* The Royal Charter of May 2, 1670, gave the names of eighteen original Adventurers, some of whom had financed that pre-Charter voyage of the *Nonsuch*, and others who had come in as a result of the success of that voyage. The total investment on May 2, 1670, was four thousand seven hundred and twenty pounds.

Rupert's group did not stir London gossip with its plans or certainly Samuel Pepys would have had a sentence in his diary about the new speculation. Unfortunately the diary stopped in 1669 or we might have had a shrewd entry about the granting of the Charter the following spring.

Most of the absorbing details of the fitting out of that one pre-Charter expedition, except those given in the preceding chapter, have been lost. It is known that tools and trinkets for the Indian trade were valued at six hundred and fifty pounds, and the *Nonsuch* on her return voyage brought to London on October 9, 1669, furs worth nineteen thousand pounds. The glowing, expansive language of the Royal Charter reflected the percentage of return. Here truly must be an empire overseas, with profits for those who came early, and with the added merit of being an English flank threat from the north towards the French colonies in the valley of the St. Lawrence for Charles to use in his diplomatic sparring in Europe.

The royally chartered company was an old formula. For more than a century it had been an accepted trading structure, growing originally out of groupings for mutual protection of merchants with ships sailing to the Far East and homeward. In the seventeenth century they took on a more rigid form of proprietorship, and included monopoly privileges as well as imperial powers under the blessing of the Crown. The Muscovy Company, the Eastland Company, the Levant Company, were examples. The Company of Merchants of London had sent Thomas Button into Hudson Bay in 1612 to search for the North West Passage to their markets of Cathay. This same London company, in 1616, raised £1,629,000 from 964 shareholders (including 15 peers, 82 knights, 13 countesses, 313 merchants, 214 tradesmen, 18 "widows and maiden ladies"). After profits and vicissitudes it combined with The Company of Merchants of England in the first years of the eighteenth century to form the Joint Company, known familiarly to the world as "John Company" and to imperial history as the East India Company. If Britain today wishes to place historical responsibility for her empire in India, it must be to the Governor and Company of the Merchants of London. The colonial empire which took form in America was founded on the Virginia Company.

"It was wonderful and unprecedented," writes David Hannay in his study of *The Great Chartered Companies*, "that bodies of traders should found empires, but it was not to be desired that they should be left to rule forever what they had won." This same writer sets the Hudson's Bay Company somewhat apart from the rest as a late maturing variety blossoming for a time as a "society pet" of Charles's court. Certainly its original investment was modest compared with the others, and the "proprietors'" names seem to indicate rather picking and choosing.

It required nearly seven thousand words of tortured English legal phrases, lettered in eye-straining characters on five large sheets of parchment, and a gigantic seal to bring the Hudson's Bay Company into corporate birth. There is museum interest in the preservation of these sheets today in Hudson's Bay House, London, but there is infinitely wider interest in the fact that the Charter of 1670 stood as a living instrument, unamended until the forty-eighth year of Victoria's reign, despite the most savage assaults upon it from generation to generation. Cumbersome and awkward as it may seem, it was well and truly drawn in the interests of self-preservation. Succeeding waves of British parliamentary inquiries, whipped up by the high winds of indignation against special privilege, rose in flood tides only to recede again, leaving this remarkable Charter unscarred through centuries until the day came "when it was not to be desired that they should rule forever what they had won."

"Whereas Our Deare and entirely Beloved Cousin Prince Rupert," states the Charter, proceeding to name the seventeen other proprietors, "have at theire owne great cost and charge undertaken an expedicion for Hudsons Bay in the north West part of America for the discovery of a new Passage into the South Sea and for the finding some Trade for Furrs Mineralls and other considerable commodityes . . . there may probably arise very great advantage to us and our Kingdome . . . wee do give grant and confirm unto them the sole Trade and Commerce. . . ."

The legal scrivener warmed to his task as he drafted this instrument inspired by all the divine rights of Stuarts and guided by the fortunes and misfortunes of a century of English merchant-adventuring into far-off places.

Charles, of course, was granting more North American territory than he or any other white man knew—"The whole trade of all those seas, streights and bays, rivers, lakes, creeks and sounds . . . within the streights commonly called Hudson's Streights together with all the lands, countries and territories upon the coasts and confines of the seas, streights, bays, lakes, rivers, creeks and sounds aforesaid. . . ."

Several generations of fur traders toiled, sweated, and froze in "the north west part of America" before the geographical significance of this giant was comprehended, and even then dimly. Before the eighteenth century was ended the Company began to understand the outlines of the territory over which Charles had made its shareholders "true and absolute Lordes and Proprietors." On a modern map the Company received those portions of the Provinces of Ontario and Quebec north of the Laurentian watershed and west of the Labrador boundary, the whole of Manitoba, most of Saskatchewan, the southern half of Alberta, and a large portion of the North West Territories; in all a great basin of one million, four hundred and eighty-six thousand square miles.

A trade monopoly over an empire to be known as Rupert's Land—"one of our Plantacions or Colonyes in America"— was not quite enough. There were powers of war and peace by which the Company might send "shippes of war men or amunicion unto theire Plantacions, Fortes, Factoryes or Places of Trade," or build "Castles, Fortificacions Fortes Garrisons . . ." while anyone with the temerity to trespass upon these rights would "incurr our Indignacion" and be seized and brought to "this Realme of England."

Time was to bring countless trespassers upon this royal

preserve. "The factoryes and places of Trade" were to be raided and burned again and again. There were to be pages of humiliation and chapters of human suffering, yet this stilted imperial gesture on five sheets of parchment was to continue as a powerful instrument, not by reason of the divine right of Stuarts laid upon the shoulders of London proprietors, but by the hard trading sense, loyalty, and force of character of the men who served the Company in Canada in the nineteenth century.

Threads of this Charter survive in the modern Company. Some are merely archaic usage but others have corporate significance. The Charter of 1670 has been supplemented by four others, 1884, 1892, 1912, 1920. All have been signed under the warrant of the reigning monarch, two by Queen Victoria, and two by King George V.

The original Charter establishes the executive operation by a governor and committee who are responsible to the proprietors who in turn are given an account of stewardship each year at a general court. This structure exists today.

Conforming to the practice of other royal charters, a payment to the Crown was provided for as a symbol of obligation. In the case of the Hudson's Bay Company it was to be "yielding and paying yearely to us our heires and Successors . . . two Elkcs and two Black beavers whensoever and as often as Wee our heires and Successors shall happen to enter into the said Countryes."

The obligation was met two hundred and fifty-seven years later, when King Edward VIII, as Prince of Wales, was in Winnipeg, the centre of "our colonye of Rupert's Land," *en route* to his Alberta ranch, in 1927. George W. Allan, K.C., a member of the London Committee and chairman of the Canadian Committee, presented two elk heads and two black beaver skins to the heir to the throne of England.

The original and the four supplemental Charters have been sustained in the highest courts of the British Empire, and they have provided an intangible yet undeniable morale to those in the Company service. The influence of this imperial association makes a curious study in loyalty to a commercial enterprise, evolving through several phases in varied forms to emerge into our own times as something perhaps pallid by comparison, yet real.

Returning to the origins of the Charter, and to those proprietors whom it was to benefit, one cannot avoid the conclusion that there was a judicious picking of royal friends and favourites for the speculation. No motley lot of London tradesmen, shipmasters and physicians; no calling for public funds in the coffee-houses; no fussing, clamouring army of shareholders to mollify from year to year if the beavers were wary or the ship went down in the ice; just a convenient group of peers, knights and gentlemen and one "citizen," who could be counted on to support the Governor and the Committee's decisions in prosperity and to take their losses with appropriate phlegm in adversity.

Here they are, the original Governor and Company of Adventurers of England trading into Hudson's Bay, showing a few changes from the original syndicate of two years before:

His Highness Prince Rupert (£100 on June 29, 1668; £100 on July 9, ; another £70 by May, 1669).

Christopher, Duke of Albemarle (£300 by March 30, 1670. He invested money in the *Nonsuch* cargo).

William, Earl of Craven (£300, assigned £150 stock to Sir Paul Neile on April 4, 1670).

Henry Bennet, Lord Arlington, created Earl of Arlington in 1672 (£200 on July 9, 1668, in cash).

Anthony, Lord Ashley, created Earl of Shaftesbury in 1672 (£200 in 1668 and another £100 by 1670).

Sir John Robinson, Knight and Baronet (£400 by 1669).

Sir Robert Vyner, Knight and Baronet (£300 by April 22, 1670).

Sir Peter Colleton, Baronet (£300).

Sir Edward Hungerford, K.B. (£300 by May 28, 1670).

Sir Paul Neile, Knight (£200).

Sir John Griffith, Knight (£300).

Sir Philip Carteret, Knight, earliest recorded investor on December 10, 1667, with £20 (increased by 1670 to £300).

Sir James Hayes, secretary to Prince Rupert, created

Knight Bachelor in 1670, paid in his first £20 on Dec. 24, 1667 (£300 by May 28, 1670, later increased his holdings).

Sir John Kirke, whose daughter Mary married Radisson (£300).

Francis Millington (£300).

William Prettyman, Esquire (£300).

John Fenn, Esquire (£300).

John Portman, Citizen and Goldsmith of London, first treasurer of the Company (£300).

Adventurers of England trading into Hudson Bay? None of these ever felt the shuddering of a vessel in the ice of Hudson Strait, or agony of insect pests in the brief scorching northern summer, or the cruelty of the wind from the Barren Lands. Yet these men were no cluster of court parasites with a few sovereigns to gamble. Of those who can be identified today, the majority were as at home in the saddle or on the quarter-deck as in a counting house committee room, or they were sound merchants as solid as their very English names indicate.

Christopher Monk, Duke of Albemarle, 1653–88, was the son of General Monk and the plebeian Anne Clarges. He must have felt the reflected glory of a father valued by Charles to the extent of a seven thousand pound pension, a fighting father who had been Captain-General of Charles's forces, who with Prince Rupert had carried destruction into the Dutch fleet, whose regiment had become the Coldstream Guards. The first Duke died in January, 1670, and his son died without an heir, in 1688, when he was only thirty-five years old.

William, Earl of Craven, had fought under William of Orange on the continent, and with Rupert had suffered imprisonment; a stout soldier and loyal friend to the Prince. In 1682 he was chief mourner at Rupert's funeral.

Anthony, Lord Ashley, first Earl of Shaftesbury and famed parliamentary leader, had assisted at the Restoration, and at the coronation was made Baron Ashley of Wimborne St. Giles, almost immediately becoming Chancellor of the

Exchequer and Undertreasurer. He was one of the grantees of the province of Carolina and took a leading part in its management. He was vitally interested in all trade questions. Not long after the granting of the Charter he lost favour at court.

Sir John Robinson had been a cavalier colonel at twenty-six years of age under Charles I, a vice-admiral, and a Member of Parliament during the Restoration.

Sir Philip Carteret was the original Adventurer named in the Charter, but he lost his life in the battle of Solebay on May 28, 1672, and his stock went to his father, Sir George, who is recorded as attending a General Court of the Company on October 24, 1671.

Sir Robert Vyner was a banker and goldsmith and Lord Mayor of London in 1674. He was close to the King, who apparently found vast pleasure in his entertainment and his loans. Pepys said of him, "No man in England lives in greater plenty and commands both king and council with the credit he gives them."

Sir Edward Hungerford was lieutenant-colonel of the Regiment of Archers. Extravagantly, he "went through thirty manors," built a market house designed by Wren on the site of Charing Cross Station, and was a Member of Parliament from 1660 to 1702.

Sir John Kirke was the father of Mary Radisson. His kinsman, Sir David Kirke, had captured Quebec with an expedition from Boston in 1608, and more than one historian has suggested that family claims against the French prevented Mary, of whom so little is known, from joining her husband during his years in the service of Louis XIV.

James, Duke of York, brother of the King, while not an original proprietor, was in on the ground floor, for on April 17, 1672, he was presented by the Hudson's Bay Company with three hundred pounds "in the Stock and Adventure." The resolution of the Committee is worded:

"Upon an humble motion lately made to his Royall Highnes by some members of this Committee by direction

& in the name of the Company, that he would bee pleased
to accept of a share in this stocke & become an Adventurer
therein; his Royall Highnes haveing bin pleased to
signifie his acceptance thereof it is ordered that his sayd
Royall Highnes bee entred in the Companyes books as an
Adventurer of one equall share with them in this joint
Stocke & that credit be given him for three hundred
poundes which is the just summe that one equall share
amounteth unto."

Of the others admitted to the new trading opportunity
we know practically nothing beyond the recurrence of their
names in the Company books. But there is enough here to
flavour the proprietorship; these were the men whose
speculations were to send men and ships and merchandise
to "so wretched a colony" as Hudson Bay.

The description is by John Oldmixon, a pamphleteer,
playwright, poet and historian of sorts who wrote a
history of the British Empire in America forty years
after the granting of the Charter. "Rich as the trade
to those parts has been or may be, the way of living is
such that we cannot reckon any man happy whose lot is
cast on this Bay." An ominous and perhaps premature
observation.

Oldmixon had been refused material for his history from
the Company records. "Notwithstanding the pressing instance I made to the concerned in the Hudson's Bay trade
for information to continue the account of it down to this
time, it not being yet come to hand, I am obliged to be
short therein." It was to be the complaint of historians
against the Company until the years following the war,
1914–18. John Oldmixon was encountering the tight-lipped
reserve with which the Company met inquirers, an attitude
which was to become second nature to the officers and
servants, and more than once carried to the point of
arrogance.

Prince Rupert became first Governor of the Company in
1670, and he was re-elected at each succeeding annual
General Court until his death in 1682. Minute books

from October 24, 1671, to July 22, 1674, and from November 28, 1679, onwards (the others being missing), show the Royal Governor's attendance at General Courts, in the Tower once and afterwards regularly in Rupert's lodgings in Whitehall. A few months before his death the Company acquired a house of its own. The great Charter was left with Prince Rupert, and at the annual General Court in 1679, a set of bylaws was approved.

The General Court occupied itself with many details of trade. On November 21, 1671, arrangements were made for paying the seamen returned from Hudson Bay on the *Prince Rupert* and the *Wivenhoe*, and orders given for an inventory of the goods brought back on the two ships. Captain Z. Gillam was told to estimate probable costs of a 1672 voyage and to decide whether it would be necessary to send one or two ships. In 1673 the General Court had the names of Adventurers and their stock printed and copies sent to all members of the Company.

On December 22, 1673, it was decided to petition Charles II for a patent of "Busse Island." This was granted in 1675 by Charles, but the island was never found!

On February 24, 1674, the General Court decreed that "Charles Bayly, the Company's Governor in Hudson Bay, be sent for home, while the choice of another Governor to succeed him and also of the officers and men to be employees on the voyage to the Bay and to remain at the Forts there was left to the Governor and Committee." It was further resolved that all private trade be vigorously suppressed.

This was more strongly censured at the May 8 meeting which resolved that no private trade in furs would be permitted under any circumstances and that all private trade in other commodities was to "bee by publicke License & brought into the Companyes warehouse to the ende that they may have cognisance thereof." At the same time commanders of Company ships were strictly enjoined to suppress all manner of "privacy that may bee in the sayd

John, Lord Churchill, afterwards Duke of Marlborough, Governor of the Company, 1685-1692

Page one of the Charter granting Rupert's Land to the Hudson's Bay Company
1670

shippes for Stoueing private trade, in order to prevente the same."

On February 11, 1681, arrangements were made for hiring a ship for that year. It was decided to make application to King Charles II "to grant ye same priviledge to this company for ye lending all manner of provisions for ye factory in Hudsons Bay wth. out paying of Custome, according to what hath been granted to ye R^ll. Affrican Company and other companys, and for order thereunto S^r. James Hayes is to prepare a memoriall wch. when prepared His Highness Prince Rupert will be pleased to Intercede with his Matie. for that favour."

At Hudson's Bay House in London are letters signed by Prince Rupert and other members of the Committee. The copy of a letter to Governor John Nixon, May 15, 1682, the year Rupert died, bears his original signature.

On July 21, 1682, at Windsor Castle, Prince Rupert, Vice-Admiral of England, issued a warrant to Captain Maximillian Keech, bound for Hudson Bay as commander of the *James* ketch, to "weare the Kings-Jack or Coullers upon the sd vessell" from his entrance into Hudson Strait outward bound and until he arrive back at the same place on the return journey.

Rupert, after a restless period of shore duty while the English and Dutch fleets pounded each other in the North Sea, withdrew more and more to the Round Tower of Windsor Castle. There he occupied himself with reconstruction of the state apartments, experiments in chemistry, and riding through Windsor Park with "a faithful great black dog." In 1682 this fearless prince died.

The Duke of York was Governor for the two following years, which are notable for the declaration of the first dividend, 50 per cent. in 1684, though there must have been earlier divisions of profits.

Charles II died in 1685. That all too human king stands definitely at the beginning of the Company's story as one who sensed the opportunity brought by the Frenchmen from New France. In this as in any great enterprise, there must always be an obligation to men who saw just beyond the horizons of their contemporaries. The *coureurs de bois* and the King had this stature.

The Duke of York became James II, and that rising young soldier John Churchill, afterwards Duke of Marlborough, enjoyed court favours and became Governor of the Hudson's Bay Company for seven years. His office terminated when he was arrested for treason and imprisoned in the Tower. It was only an incidental setback to a Churchill's career, but the Company knew him no more.

The century of Cromwell, Milton and Wren is over.

Chapter III

WARS WITH THE FRENCH

CAUTIOUSLY expanding during the first fourteen years of fur trading, blessed by peace, and fed by a series of 50 per cent. dividends, the Company built a chain of forts (or factories) at the mouths of those "rivers flowing into Hudson Bay." It was the beginning of chain

51

merchandising in North America. By 1682 the posts were:
Rupert's House, Moose Factory, and Albany Factory on
James Bay; and Fort Nelson, later York Factory, on the
west coast of Hudson Bay—a logical maritime growth
developing from season to season as the profits of London
fur sales warranted.

Life in the fur trade was taking form. Each year Company
ships worked into the Bay through fog and ice and out again,
to have their "arrival in The Downs" reported to the
Committee. The local governors were sent out armed with
their boldly worded commissions to direct trade, keep
discipline in the forts, and write "exact Journalls." It was
essentially a marine operation even in its personnel. These
were seamen trading from ship to shore. When the proprietors in London urged their servants to more vigorous
expansion and exploration, their instructions were carried
out as a coastwise effort. If the natives would come to the
sea, why push inland? The Englishmen, engaged by the
season, had no consuming desire to become intimate with
the ways of the forest. Indians were savages to be traded
with and distrusted; and the interior was full of unknown
terrors. The Governor and Committee in London might
dictate instructions about seeking out the natives and urging
them to come to the Bay, but the Governor and Committee had never seen an Indian. Their employees were
sailors and traders. The voyage into the Bay itself was a
hazard not many men would take for a very few pounds
a year, and if the proprietors could be kept content with
substantial dividends on their modest investments, why
freeze or drown for wages? Energy was applied to the
building of new forts, but the whole operation was scarcely
in the tempo of the Royal Charter.

Down in the valley of the St. Lawrence the colony of
New France had reason for alarm in the success of the
English establishments to the north. The New England
colonies south on the Atlantic seaboard were consolidated,
and now the English were reaching in from the north.
French Canada might be encircled. This led naturally to

rivalry between the Hudson's Bay Company and the French traders for the furs of those Indians who found it just as easy to reach one as the other. In 1681 the Intendant Duchesneau at Quebec complained that the English "are still at Hudson's Bay on the north and do great damage to our fur trade. The farmers [of the revenue] suffer in consequence by the diminution of the trade at Tadoussac, and throughout that entire country, because the English draw off the Ottawa nations."

France and England were not at war, but a few skirmishes in the far north might drive off these traders without serious repercussions at home. So began ten years of intermittent war in Hudson Bay—war with interludes of peace but such a confusion of captures and recaptures that, to history, the decade becomes page after page of burning forts and foundering ships. Now the English dominate. Next year the French have ousted them. Yet through it all the Company always holds at least one post, the thin thread of continuous occupation.

The few ships and small parties of men engaged in this forest and offshore fighting make them seem slight, viewed only as military and naval operations; but the spirit-breaking distances and the harsh temper of the climate sharpened the suffering and added burdens to every movement. These victories and defeats on the Bay assumed more than trifling importance when peace was weighed about the conference tables in Europe. Much of it was piracy carried on without regard for treaties, and while the amenities and elaborate gestures of continental warfare were usually observed, there were incidents of barbarous cruelty. In most of the actions the Company was on the defensive. Handfuls of men of sluggish mould who occupied the forts were incapable, even though led occasionally by some spirited person, of first-rate military performance in the face of an enemy.

Rupert's House is six hundred miles north of Montreal overland. York Factory on the Hayes River is three thousand miles from Europe. By land and sea the French struck at the English, and almost won. The simplest way to summarize these crowded years is in the form of a chronicle:

1682

England and France are at peace. It is the year Radisson, the Company, and Ben Gillam meet and spar with each other on the neck of land between the Nelson and Hayes rivers (York Factory). They each build forts for the winter, and Radisson dupes them into captivity without bloodshed.

1683

Spring comes and Radisson sends most of his men south to the Company's posts at "the bottom of the Bay," but sails off for Quebec with Bridgar, the Company governor, and Ben Gillam as his prisoners. Young Groseilliers stays at the post to trade. During the summer two Company ships appear at the mouth of the Nelson with Governor Abraham on board. There is a skirmish and two Englishmen are killed. The Company ships, not finding the establishment Bridgar was to have set up the previous year, continue south to their other posts.

1684

Radisson, again in the Company service, arrives at York, takes over fort and furs for the English. Phipps takes charge and with him is a fourteen-year-old lad, Henry Kelsey, who is to win for his name pages in Canadian history. Radisson sails for London with a cargo of twenty thousand beaver which helps to pay a handsome dividend. But the French at Quebec, believing this choice trading site to be still French, send two ships to the Hayes River, arriving in September to find the English already there. "We were more than surprised at this," writes Father Antoine Silvy, Jesuit missionary, in his gently tempered account. They build three houses and a fort on the south bank, and spend the winter trading and sniping at the Company men.

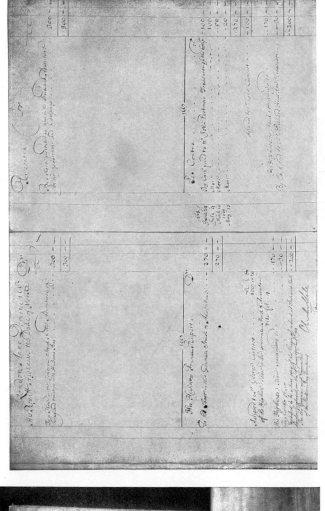

Opening sheets of the original stock book of the Company showing shares held by the Duke of York and Prince Rupert

Outward Letter Book, 1680–1687, from the Hudson's Bay Company Archives

The first public sale of Hudson's Bay furs at Garraway's Coffee House
London, 1671

1685

In midsummer they clear out for home, and in Hudson Strait have three brushes with three Company ships, the *Success*, the *Happy Return*, and the *Perpetuana Merchant*. The last they capture and carry their prisoners to Quebec.

1686

The contest warms. Chevalier de Troyes with Le Moyne d'Iberville, age twenty-four, thirty regulars, seventy Canadian militia, and a chaplain come overland from Montreal up the Ottawa and down the Moose River. (The young French noblesse have a flair for this sort of thing.) They seize Moose Factory, Rupert's House, and Albany. It is a brilliant little wilderness campaign. As each post is taken there is a waving of swords, speeches of conquest, and a proclamation of victory in the name of the King of France and Navarre; also prayers for the dead from the same Father Silvy. These men can travel; they are soldiers who know the technique of Indian fighting. The civilians at Moose, Rupert's House and Albany are easy game. At Albany the local governor, Sergeant, surrenders after a two-day siege, despite forty-three guns and log walls with four bastions. (Later in London the Company brought action against him in the courts to recover twenty thousand pounds; it ended by the Company having to pay Sergeant three hundred and fifty pounds and all London laughed.) Meanwhile England and France are still at peace; de Troyes makes a smart retreat overland to Montreal, leaving d'Iberville in charge of the captured forts. Overseas, crowned heads are trying to patch up these matters with a treaty of neutrality in Europe, but it does not hold in the Bay.

1687

D'Iberville sails out to Quebec with his captured ship loaded with captured furs, leaving his brother Maricourt in command. The Company still holds York and Severn, and trade on "the Eastmain," the east coast of the Bay, is good.

1688

Apparently it is a year of peaceful trading. Company ships *John & Thomas* and *Dering* get in and out of the Bay. The *Churchill* and the *Yonge* go out and winter there.

1689

William of Orange is on the throne, and now war is declared with France. William receives a dividend of three hundred pounds on the three hundred shares of Crown stock which had belonged to King James. Sir Edward Dering, deputy governor of the Company, waits upon the King and expresses the brave classic hope that "yʳ· majesty may be as Victorious as Cæsar, as beloved as Titus and have the glorious long Reigne and Peacefull end of Augustus," adding comments upon the Company suffering from "those common enemy of all mankind, the French." To which William replies, after accepting the purse of gold, that he will give all " protection and favour." which he can. So he sends the man-of-war *Hampshire* to the Bay with the Company ship *North West Fox* to retake Albany, but d'Iberville is there. The story is obscure, but the Frenchman seizes both ships, burns the *North West Fox*, and sails off to Quebec in the *Hampshire* loaded with furs. In this year young Kelsey is put ashore north of Churchill " in order to bring a commerce to ye Northern Indians but we saw none although we travelled above 200 miles in search of yᵐ." It is their first inland exploration.

1690

D'Iberville is in the Bay again with the *Ste. Anne*, *St. François* and *Armes de la Compagnie*. He attacks York but is beaten off, goes down the Bay to New Severn Post, takes and burns it. He winters at Albany and goes to France with his furs in the spring. Henry Kelsey writes of this year, "I was sent away [from York] wt ye Stone Indians in whose country I remained 2 years enduring much hardship and did increase ye trade considerably as may be perceived in their acct books and I returned to ye factory in '92." It is a good year at home and the

Company of Adventurers trebles its original stock from ten thousand five hundred pounds to thirty-one thousand five hundred pounds and declares a twenty-five per cent. dividend.

1691 and 1692

Fur trading goes on, the French "at the bottom of the Bay" and the English at York. Company ships get in and out unscathed. Geyer at York must have been cheered in '92 to learn from the Governor and Committee that a quantity of French brandy "which we procured with great difficulty" was being sent out.

The Governor and Committee select James Knight as "our Governor and Commander in Chief" to head the strongest expedition yet sent to the Bay. Knight is empowered to take French forts and carry out reprisals. Twenty thousand pounds are spent to outfit four ships, with two hundred and thirteen men, eighty-two guns, and supplies for twenty months. The ships are: the frigate *Dering*, the frigate *Royal Hudson's Bay* (commanded by Michael Grimington who had served on her as mate when she fought the French in 1689), the frigate *Perry*, and the pink *Prosperous*, a fire ship. The expedition arrives at York on August 27, 1692; the *Dering* lands her trade goods, takes on bales of fur and hastens home. The other three ships move south to winter at Old Factory Island.

1693

James Knight's ships sweep the winter-weakened French garrisons from the bottom of the Bay as effectively as the French had cleared the English out seven years before. Since Knight's summer raids the forts have remained with the British. Michael Grimington parades his French prisoners before the Governor and Committee in London by way of proof of victory. The Company is briefly in the ascendant.

1694

D'Iberville, the scourge of the Bay, is at sea again with the *Poli* and the *Salamander*, and Father Gabriel Marest as chaplain-missionary. They bring their ships to York in

September and land their guns in the snow. Thomas Walsh is the Company's local governor (better skilled in trade than in martial affairs, wrote Father Marest) commanding fifty men including Henry Kelsey. There are skirmishes. The Frenchmen offer no quarter to defenders. The Company men surrender in the face of the mortars against their log walls and spend a miserable winter as prisoners.

1695

D'Iberville waits through the summer to trade and to trap a Company ship, but the Adventurers do not reach York this year. In September he sails for France, leaving a garrison of sixty-seven men with the English prisoners.

1696

From the Royal Navy the *Bonaventure* and the *Seaforth*, from the Company three frigates, *Hudson's Bay*, *Dering*, and *Knight*, are in the mouth of the Hayes by August. In the face of this flotilla the sixty-seven Frenchmen surrender and go to England as prisoners along with twenty thousand beaver pelts. Kelsey is back at York. The Company enjoys its key trade position for one year only.

1697

The English traders are trying to recoup their losses when the roar of gunfire heralds the greatest sea fight in Arctic history.

From Quebec fiery Frontenac, strongest of French colonial governors, sends a squadron north in the most determined effort yet made to clear the English from the Bay. D'Iberville pauses from visiting the English colonies in Newfoundland with fire and sword, to lead the five ships. They enter Hudson Strait barely forty hours after a quartet of ships from England. D'Iberville's flagship *Pelican*, separated from the fleet, makes a speedy trip across the Bay (five hundred miles from the Strait to York) and anchors off York to wait for the others. Instead of the French, the English ships appear. D'Iberville pulls up anchor, clears his decks, takes them on single-handed,

one against three, since the fourth, the *Owner's Love*, is a
fire ship. For four hours they fight. D'Iberville's ship is
raked fore and aft but beats off all attempts to board her.
With startling suddenness the English man-of-war *Hampshire* ceases fire, lurches and sinks, taking with her two
hundred and ninety men.

Samuel Clarke, mate of the merchantman *Hudson's Bay*,
is pulled aboard the *Pelican* a prisoner. A year later he
appears before the Lords of the Admiralty in London to
make a deposition in support of the claim for a pension by
the widow of Captain John Fletcher, commander of the
Hampshire. Their Lordships listen gravely while a clerk
quills the account of gallantry in the face of death in
Arctic waters:

"And further the said Samuel Clarke Saith That he
being taken by the French; Dureing the time he continued
on Board the French Man of Warr wch. the said Monsr
D'Brevile [D'Iberville] had the Comand of in his returne
home; Hee the said Samuel Clarke having some Dis-
course with the said French Captaines brother, Who
Spoke English; He told the said Depon^t. That Capt.
Fletcher (who Comanded the Hampshire) was a brave
man, and Just before he gave his last broad Side, called to
the said Monsr D'Brevile, bidding him Strike, which he
refuseing to do, Capt. Fletcher took a Glass and drank to
him, telling him, he should dine with him immediately;
Upon which the said French Capt. Pledged him in another
Glass, And there upon his Men Fired a Volley of Small
Shott upon the Hampshire which was returned with a like
Volley to the French man; And after that the said Capt.
Fletcher was not Seen; So that it was Supposed the said
Capt. Fletcher was then killed."

Soon after, the Company ship *Hudson's Bay* surrenders
with one hundred and ninety men. The third ship, the
Dering, escapes to the mouth of the Nelson River. The
season is late, and before D'Iberville can put the *Hudson's
Bay* in order, a storm with snow howls down from the
north-east and he is compelled to beach his foundering
flagship six miles from York Factory. The *Hudson's Bay*
also piles up, and as the two crews flounder ashore in the
icy tide, twenty-eight are drowned. Captain Smithsend

of the Company ship escapes with his survivors and leads them into the feeble shelter of York Factory. Meanwhile the other French vessels come up. Mortars are landed and set up in the scrub forest, now under two feet of snow. D'Iberville commands nine hundred men. Four days of siege leave York's log bastions badly knocked about.

Bailey is in command for the Company, and he has with him men whose courage is sound, Grimington of the *Dering*, Smithsend of the *Hudson's Bay*, Kelsey and others, but in men and guns the odds are heavily against them. He haggles for terms, then surrenders on September thirteenth, marching out with some honours of war—arms, drums and flag. Grimington is allowed his ship and returns to England with Bailey and the refugees. The Company now has only Albany from which to trade. In Europe William and Louis XIV sign the Treaty of Ryswick and the Company frantically advances claims for two hundred thousand pounds damages. The Charter is publicly attacked but Parliament renews it.

1697 to 1713

No one is happy about the fur trade in Hudson Bay. The War of the Spanish Succession keeps Europe marching. The French at York have the best site for trade, but the English Navy keeps their ships from getting in and out. John Oldmixon observes in 1708, "Commerce seems not to be worth the risk that is run for it. . . . Peltry is not now the commodity it was." But there is trading in the bottom of the Bay and on the Eastmain (east coast of James Bay). One John Churchill, Duke of Marlborough, and one time governor of the Company, is emblazoning battle honours—Blenheim, Ramillies and Malplaquet—on British regimental colours. And the Treaty of Utrecht gives the Bay to Britain in 1713. There is no dividend for the Adventurers of England from 1690 to 1718—an almost unparalleled experience in any company story.

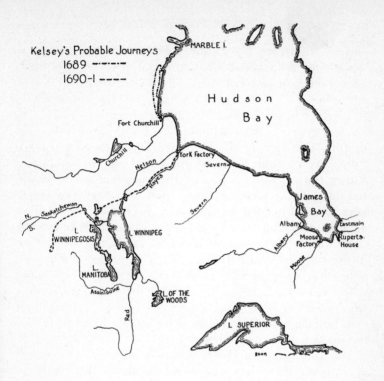

Kelsey's Probable Journeys
1689 —·—·—
1690-1 ————

MARBLE I.

Hudson
Bay

Fort Churchill

York Factory
Severn

Churchill

Nelson

Hayes

Severn

James
Bay

Albany

Eastmain

Moose
Factory

Ruperts
House

N. Saskatchewan

S.

L.
WINNIPEGOSIS

L. WINNIPEG

Albany

Moose

L.
MANITOBA

Assiniboine

L. OF THE
WOODS

Red

L. SUPERIOR

Rhen

CHAPTER IV

"DISCOVERY TO YE NORWARD"

COURAGE flowered in the wilderness, not the courage
of a score of men with firearms defending themselves
from behind log walls, but the cool, singlehanded enterprise
undertaken with an appreciation of the known hazards and
a reasonable anticipation of unknown dangers. The remarkable thing is that there is record of only one man who
struck out into the interior during the first eighty-four years
of the Company's existence, although the governor in the
Bay received annual instructions from London: "Choose
out from amongst our Servants such as are best qualified

61

with Strength of Body and the Country Language, to
travel and to penetrate into the country. . . . For their
encouragement we shall plentifully reward them."

Captains of Company ships gave a good account of
themselves in sea action, but ashore there was fear. The
resident governor from behind his palisades wrote to London
in 1685 that neither the four men whom he had selected
"nor any of your servants will travel up the Country."
Either the calibre was low or the maritime tradition was
too deep in the men. Possibly, had they been ordered to
man a vessel headed for unknown places they would have
gone gladly. But they would not go into the forest. The
same reluctance to undertake inland expansion is apparent
in the story of British India. The Committee had a legal
obligation to explore. Moreover, even three thousand
miles away in London, they knew they must have men
who could live and travel among the Indians, talking their
own language, if the trade in pelts was to flourish. So far
the ranks lacked the Radisson spirit.

The appearance of Henry Kelsey is all the more remarkable among these men who could not be prodded into the
essential work of fur trading. His place in the story has
only been established since the discovery of certain of his
papers in 1926. Until then the Kelsey story was under a
hazy shadow of half legend.

Kelsey was only fourteen when he came to the fur trade.
"Henry Kellsey is entertained in the Compa. service as
their apprentice for 4 yeares his time to commence at his
arrivall in the Bay and to terminate from his comeing from
thence who is to have £8 and two shutes of apparell,"
states the entry in the minute book of April 14, 1684. He
went out to Hudson Bay that year on the ship *Lucy* commanded by John Outlaw. Probably Radisson was on
board, for it was the year he returned to the Company.
The Indianized Frenchman, who had travelled so far into
the continent and who talked so well, may have fixed in
the adolescent mind of the boy some glimmer of the rewards
of exploration which compensate for the pains of travel.

Kelsey came first to official notice in 1687. Four Indians had been employed to carry letters from York Factory to Severn, and they returned without having accomplished the mission. Kelsey was sent with an Indian boy, and returned in a month with the answers, having made a journey along the coast of two hundred miles. The Committee noted this and directed the resident governor Geyer "that the Boy Henry Kelsey bee sent to Churchill River with Thomas Savage because Wee are Informed hee is a very active Lad Delighting much in Indians Compa. being never better pleased than when he is Travelling amongst them." There was work to be done by anyone who would travel.

Kelsey neatly summed up his carrying out of these instructions in the back of his journal:

"In '89 Capt. James Young put me and ye same Indian boy ashore to ye Northward of Churchill River in order to bring a commerce to ye Northern Indians but we saw none although we travelled above 200 miles in search of ym."

Actually it was a brief, bitter little expedition. It was June, and there was still ice along the shore. He was landed after some difficulty on the edge of the Barren Lands, mostly "ponds and hills" and "abundance of musketers [mosquitoes] and at night could not gett wood Enough for to make a smoke to clear ym," he write, ". . . ye hills being all stones with a coat of moss over ym."

July 2: "At noon it rained hard having no shelter but ye heavens for a Cannope nor no wood to make a fire."

For a month and a half in the Barrens this active lad tasted all that was hard in the subarctic, that summer of 1689. He was the first white man to see the musk ox, having on July 9 "spyed two Buffillo and we Killed one." Their horns, he wrote, "joyn together upon their forehead & so come down ye side of their head and turn up. . . . Their Hair is near a foot long." At the Churchill River he was picked up by the ship after being "forct to shoot 3 Desperate falls" on a raft.

There is a Radisson touch to all this, and it is not surprising to find Kelsey selected by Geyer, in 1690, for a larger mission, and one that was to place him first in the annals of overland travel into western Canada. The journal he wrote of this 1690–92 trip has become a concise minor classic of North American exploration. Partly in doggerel verse and partly in quaint, pointed English, it exasperates geographers who attempt to trace him from river to lake and over every portage, but the real essentials of the explorer type ring clear. It was sixty years before the Company could find his equal.

Geyer at York Factory was not slow to take advantage of this young man's willingness to look beyond the scrubby forest at the mouth of the Hayes River, and in 1690 he wrote:

"This summer, I sent up Henry Kelsey (who cheerfully undertook the Journey) up into the Country of the Assinae Poets, with the Captain of that Nation, to call, encourage and invite the remoter Indians to trade with us." A year later he reported to the Committee that he had had a letter from Kelsey asking for supplies, which were sent, along with instructions to return to the Bay the following summer. The laconic record of the fur trade post journal reported the "active lad" back at York in September, 1692, with "a good fleet of Indians."

Kelsey had kept his own journal which was turned over to his superiors. In 1749, when the Company was under galling fire before a committee of the British Parliament, this journal was produced in defence of the claim that they had tried to fulfil their Charter obligation to explore. In the flurry of pamphleteering which critics stirred up, the Kelsey journal was denounced so vehemently as a fabrication produced for the occasion by the harassed Company, that historians could never quite accept it as authentic. In 1926 came one of those discoveries which occasionally touch the work of history with exciting colour. From Castle Dobbs,

Moose Factory on James Bay, established by the Company in 1672, captured by the French in 1686 and recaptured by Hudson's Bay men in 1694. Trading has been carried on on the present site since 1730

"When the Blackfeet Hunt," from a painting by John Innis in the Historical Exhibit of the Hudson's Bay Company, Winnipeg

Carrickfergus, Ulster, came a gift of papers to the Public Records Office of Northern Ireland, and among them a manuscript book of one hundred and twenty-eight pages now known as the *Kelsey Papers*, published by the Public Archives of Canada in 1929. All that had been legendary became established in truth. The manuscript book contained not only copies made by Kelsey for his own private use, of his journal of the 1690–92 journey, but the rhymed introduction, fragmentary notes on other occasions including the surrender of York Factory to d'Iberville, and a memorandum setting forth briefly his own record of service with the Company. Skilful research has linked the material of these papers with the records of Hudson's Bay House, London, making the Kelsey story the most absorbing personal narrative of this early history, excepting only the Radisson-Groseilliers epic.

The *Kelsey Papers* from Castle Dobbs, Carrickfergus, had been in the possession of one Arthur Dobbs, whose clever and tireless attacks upon the Company led up to the public investigation of 1749. So convinced was Dobbs that it was only Hudson's Bay Company lethargy which kept the world from enjoying the trade benefits of a North West Passage, that he actually promoted two expeditions for its discovery. Whether or not he owned the *Kelsey Papers* at the time his charges were forcing the Company to disgorge the details of its affairs, is not known. Certainly, had the Governor and Committee been able to produce the more complete journals instead of the curtailed one in their possession, the Adventurers' case would have been much stronger, and it needed all the strength it could summon.

In Kelsey's crude rhymes and in his observations of native life, he disclosed a nature vastly superior to his associates. His day-to-day journal must have been kept under most trying conditions long before the Company's men learned the countless trifling details of outfitting which made northern travel possible. Kelsey had to slip completely into Indian life, and yet keep his English wits alert

E

to observe and write good records. They are not the journals a chief factor would expect from an apprentice clerk in later days when the fur trade controlled the north land, but they were good enough to become celebrated source material, and they reveal a faint suggestion of a consciousness of history.

It was June 12, 1690, when Kelsey, age twenty, started up the Hayes River into the unknown west.

> "In sixteen hundred & ninety'th year
> I set forth as plainly may appear. . . .
> And for my masters interest I did soon
> Sett from ye house (York Fort) ye twealth of June
> Then up ye River I with heavy heart
> Did take my way and from all English part
> To live amongst ye Natives of this place
> If god permits me for one two years space
> The Inland Country of Good report hath been
> By Indians but by English yet not seen . . .
> Gott on ye borders of ye stone Indian Country
> I took possession on ye tenth Instant July
> And for my masters I speaking for ym all
> This neck of land I deerings point did call
> Distance from hence by Judgement at ye lest
> From ye house six hundred miles southwest
> Through Rivers wch run strong with falls
> thirty three Carriages five lakes in all."

Before the summer was over Kelsey left the bush country for the Canadian prairie in his search for the Stony Indians. He was the first white man to see the buffalo on the Canadian plains.

> "And then you have beast of severall kind
> The one is a black a Buffillo great
> Another is an outgrown Bear wch is good meat. . . .
> He is mans food & he makes food of man . . .
> This plain affords nothing but Beast & grass
> And over it in three days time we past. . . .
> It being about forty six miles wide. . . .
> At deerings point after the frost
> I set up their a Certain Cross

In token of my being there
Cut out on it ye date of year
And Likewise for to veryfie the same
Added to it my master sir Edward deerings name."

His adolescent years at York Factory gave him the advantage over the Company's seamen-traders in the understanding of Indians. He knew the language and grasped the Indian's inherent love of speech-making so well that, with a pipe for communal smoking, a few trade articles for gifts, and a sense of rhetoric, he was able to live among them for almost two years, sharing their improvident existence. Now feasting, now close to starvation, it was a dreary life of eating half-cooked food in dim, smoky lodges and urging the natives to give up their tribal feuds and bring beaver skins to York Factory.

Kelsey's "deering's point" cannot be positively located on the map. Men of the fur trade believe it is the present site of The Pas, Manitoba. Kelsey appears to have spent the winter of 1690–91 there, and to have received from Geyer at York supplies for his second summer.

The prose part of the journal describes his start from "deering's point" in July and the subsequent fifty-nine days of travel for six hundred miles, partly by canoe but mostly through the bush and on the open prairie. He confesses to the failure of his peace mission. Reaching the Stony Indians, he undertook to mediate between them and their enemies, referred to as the "Naywattame poets."

"Septr. ye 12th. This morning having no victuals to invite ye capt. to so I filled yt pipe wch ye Governr. had sent me wth tobacco & then sent for ye Capt. So then I made a speech to him & told him yt he should not mind wt had passed formerly as concerning ye nayhaythaways killing six tents of his Country men & for ye future we English will seek for to prevent it going any further for if so be they did so any more ye Governr. says he will not trade wth ym if they did not cease from killing his friends & when I had done I presented him wth a present coat &

sash Cup & one of my guns wth knives awls & tobacco wth small quantities of powder & shott & part of all such things as ye Governr. had sent me so he seemed to be very well pleased & told me he had forgott wt had past although they had kill'd most of his kindred & relations & likewise told me he was sorry he had not wherewithall for to make me Restitution for wt I had given him but he would meet me at Deerings point ye next spring & go with me to ye factory but it happened in the winter after I had parted wth them ye Nayhaythaways came up wth ym & killed two of ym wch struck a new fear into ym yt they would not venture down fearing lest ye home Indians would not let ym up again into their own Country so when I was at Deerings point in the spring wch is ye place of resortance when they are coming down to trade upon ye arrival of some indians I had news brought me yt ye Capt. aforesd. had sent me a pipe & steam of his own making & withall ye news of their being kill'd as I have spoken of before yet if so be I would send him a piece of tobacco from ye factory upon ye return of ye same indians he would certainly come down ye next year. But if not ye beavour in their Cuntry are unnumerable & will certainly be brought down every year so having not to inlarge sir I remain your obedient & faithful Servt.

HENRY KELSEY."

With allowance for a meagre education, it is excellent reporting, revealing as it does the very essentials of the trader's problem in dealing with the Indian. The Governor and Committee might have learned much from this journal of how to handle primitive people. Here was forecast the rôle of peacemaker which Hudson's Bay men were to fill in succeeding centuries. It became clear at the very start of English fur trading that warring Indian tribes were not assets in the business of producing peltry, but it was not until Company men actually lived among the natives that any real work of spreading the peace gospel was accomplished.

In the summer of 1692 Kelsey returned to York, and the following summer the Committee welcomed him in England.

Geyer was instructed to reward him "for the service done us in travelling into the countery."

The next three stormy years Kelsey with the others at York was captured by d'Iberville (1694), witnessed the retaking from the French when the ships from the Royal Navy came to the Bay (1696), and wrote in his journal in 1697 of the great sea battle when he, with the English, "marcht out . . . and ye french took possession of ye fort this being ye end of a Tedious winter and a tragical Journal by me Henry Kelsey."

The following year he was with Captain James Knight at Albany, and in 1701 he became master of the frigate *Knight*. Back in England in 1703 he continued to rise in the service, making frequent voyages into the Bay.

The Company minute books of 1710 show £58.8.2 paid "to Mrs. Elizabeth Kelsey, wife of Henry Kelsey." But the Governor and Committee felt obliged to restrain him. "As for the discovery of mines, etc., it is noe time to thinke upon them now. In times of peace Something may be done."

However, the proprietors were eager to have their fur traders better equipped. Kelsey had spent long winter nights preparing a dictionary. That same year of 1710 the Committee sent him printed copies of the dictionary of the Indian language, with their commendation, "You doe well to Educate the men in Literature but especially in the Language that in time we may send them to travell if wee see it convenient. . . . We have sent you your dixonary Printed that you may better instruct the young Ladds with you, in ye Indian Language."

In 1714, a year after the Treaty of Utrecht brought the promise of better days, Kelsey was sent to York as deputy to James Knight for four years at one hundred pounds a year "with ye benefit of a servt." Thus, bearing a commission from Queen Anne, he came once more to aid in the peaceful taking over of York after sixteen years' occupation by the French.

"All the factory run to ruin, the covering of the houses

all rotten so there is no place fit for a man to go into . . . and so leaky that I found the best place to lye our goods was out of doors," wrote Knight.

Throughout Kelsey's journals and in the minutes of the Committee and instructions sent from London, are references to "discovery to ye Norward." Clearly Kelsey had not settled snugly into such comforts as a Bay post with servant were able to provide. Though he made more than one trading trip by coast to Eskimo country, getting "whalebon, oyle and some Sea Horse Teeth," and acquiring two Eskimo boys with a view to learning their language, the Company disapproved of plans to winter too far north "to the hazard of yr life." He was a valued officer now, governor at York since 1718 with men to command at the posts. The Company was much interested in reports of summer expeditions with descriptions of people and details of tides and currents.

Home again in 1722, Kelsey was welcomed after eight years' continuous service in the Bay. He applied for the captaincy of the ship *Hannah* in 1724, but no vessel was sent out that year. His active service was over. Some time before 1730 he died. In that year, on January 27, the minute book records:

"Eliz Kelsey Widow of Capt Heny Kelsey late Governor for the Compa at York Fort in Hudsons Bay having Petitioned the Committe to Allow her something towards puting out her son apprentice; The Comittee takeing into consideration the former Service of her Husband the said Heny: Kelsey Ordered that the Secr. do pay her ten Guineas as a Gratuity from the Compa for that purpose, £10.10.0."

One note of tragedy is the footnote of the Kelsey story. His name appears finally on February 20, 1734, fifty years from the time the boy apprentice went across the sea for eight pounds and "two shutes of apparell."

"Eliz. Kelsay Widow of Heny Kelsey formerly Govr for the Compa at York Fort in H. Bay haveing petitioned the Committee to give her Something to buy her son John Kelsey Cloths She being wholly incapable to do it herself this Committee considering the former Service of his Father the sd. Heny Kelsey Ordered the sum of £6.6.0 to be laid out for cloths for him & that ye Secr see the same laid out."

Apart from the importance of Kelsey's journey to the prairie country, his career will always survive in fur trade history. He was the first apprentice who pulled himself up from the ranks to hold a commission. He was the first to work seriously upon the Indian and Eskimo languages. He mastered the unpleasant but essential technique of living and travelling like a native. Of all the men of his time in the Bay he alone worked actively to promote peace among Indian tribes. He wrote the first account of the life and customs of prairie Indians. He became a ship captain and governor of the senior fort. Even the poverty of his widow and child seemed to forecast the legend that money made in Indian trading brought no contentment to those across the sea. While the wages and salaries appear small, they were reasonable for the time. (Christopher Wren had been content with two hundred pounds a year as the architect of St. Paul's Cathedral.)

James Knight entered Company history as a shipwright-supervisor of fort construction. He lived to be a resident governor in the Bay, a member of the Committee, and to die of starvation in the cause of northern exploration. He was the mariner-trader with a business sense which carried him to the proprietor group, and he had the personal courage for enterprise. Knight had not, like Kelsey, spent his youth among Indians, and consequently conformed to the English seaman type. But he was of the best of that breed and became, perhaps, one of the first real veterans to die on active service.

James Knight was first employed in May, 1676, for the construction and reconstruction of the factories at Moose, Rupert's, and Albany rivers. Recalling these times in a spirit of weariness forty years later, when he was governor of York Factory, he wrote:

"It has been my misfortune always to have nothing but fatigue and trouble in this country, for when I first came into it we had nothing but a little place not fit to keep hogs in, and the Company's goods all lying without doors in tents not fit to preserve them; and when I went to Moose River there I built a good house fit to accommodate ourselves and goods in; and after that I went to Albany river and did the like again."

His importance was recognized by the Company in the annual outfitting of 1682, when he was in London. The inspection of the ship *Albemarle*, the supplies of guns, powder and clothing were his responsibility, and in the same year he was commissioned as deputy governor and chief factor at Albany at one hundred pounds a year, and the privilege of a servant at his own expense. He was at Albany when Radisson outwitted the Company's men at the Nelson River, and back in England in 1683. Three years later he faced charges of having carried on a secret traffic in furs. This was "private trade," gravest of all Company offences. It was cleared up, for in 1687 he and a Robert Sandford approached the Governor and Committee with plans for more economical operation, including reduction of staff to thirty-six men distributed among Albany, Moose and Rupert's. (According to Dr. J. F. Kenney, who has studied this period closely, there were eighty-nine men in the Bay at this time, including the garrison at York.) They also proposed that the Charlton Island establishment should be abandoned; that wheat be substituted for flour in supplies; that certain supplies be obtained in New York; that oatmeal be used for Indian gift purposes; that the attempt to send Englishmen into the interior be dropped, and leaders among the Indians of the remote country be employed to persuade the natives to make the journey down to the Bay with their furs. Sandford had been at Albany when the Committee was urging inland voyages, and was probably trying to excuse himself by this proposal. The plans were shelved, and Knight was not re-engaged that year.

D'Iberville's overland raid of 1688 pinched the Company by wiping out the James Bay posts, and in 1692 the Committee roused itself to a determined effort to retake York and the posts "at the Bottom of the Bay." There is a gusto and a brisk energy about this year. James Knight was recalled, given command of four ships, and offered the governorship of the "Bottom of the Bay." He had not been idle in the meantime. He was referred to as a merchant of London and he was able to bargain for terms. He was given two hundred pounds of stock and empowered by Royal Commission to carry out reprisals against the French. Four ships, eighty-two guns, two hundred and thirteen men, and supplies for twenty months: this was the most militant effort the Company had yet produced. It was the instrument given James Knight to restore their fortunes.

The expedition reached York in August, 1692. The *Dering* loaded the year's furs and sailed back to England. The other three ships wintered at Old Factory Island, perfecting warlike plans to besiege Fort Albany. The result in the early summer was an anticlimax. Four Frenchmen, the sole garrison at Albany, surrendered with a comfortable supply of furs. Knight celebrated the profitable, bloodless victory by a distribution of beaver skins to his men. Captain Grimington took the frigate *Royal Hudson's Bay* to England with the furs, appearing before the Committee in November with the prisoners in chains, by way of proof of the conquest.

The Company gratefully voted Knight five hundred pounds in the form of an interest-bearing bond, for cash was low and the expedition had cost nearly twenty thousand pounds. A new forty-eight-ton frigate was named *Knight* in his honour.

For five years Knight clung close to Albany as governor. All the struggle and confusion of York in the north, changing hands three times, passed him by. His friend Mike Grimington had crowded a lot of naval action into those years, and when Knight did get back to England in '97, he learned that his isolated Fort Albany was the only post left in the Company's hands.

As there had been no dividend since 1690, and feeling acutely the need of men of Knight's capacity, the Committee met the problem of salary arrears by transfer to him, in 1701, of six hundred pounds stock. The transfer was from the holdings of Sir William Trumbull, who was guaranteed against loss. James Knight, shipwright, merchant of London, sea captain and fur trader, became a member of the London Committee, and for thirteen years served the Company actively and usefully while developing substantial private interests of his own.

When the Treaty of Utrecht closed the long War of the Spanish Succession, Knight returned to Company duty. He went to Holland with Bibye Lake, Governor of the Company, to press the Company claims at the peacemaking, and with splendid result, since the treaty provided for the restoration to Great Britain of the territory of Hudson Bay and cash compensation to the Company for damage done by the French.

Knight went out as governor, to take over York, and with him went Henry Kelsey as deputy. On the frigate *Union* they arrived at the mouth of the Hayes River, September 5, 1714. A few days later he received the formal surrender from Jérémie, the French commander. Knight was nearly seventy years of age, but he applied himself vigorously to rebuilding the Company's fortune—and his own. It was a type of front-line ownership and management which would have served the Company well had it been continued.

Knight turned his energy towards peace among the Indians, the expansion of trade and the rebuilding of York Factory. In the next three years he encountered a series of such heart-breaking misfortunes that he sometimes on winter nights wrote pitiful, weary entries in the York Factory journal. "For my part I am weary of having the name of Governor in this country. . . . I have not in 12 weeks time had 3 hours in 24 rest, and sometimes none at all."

Spring floods on the Hayes, in 1715, damaged their buildings and ruined a large part of the stores, the ice piling twenty feet higher than the warehouse roof. The summer was spent salvaging French cannon and erecting the new fort, with a main house thirty-six feet square and two storeys high. The ship from England that year reached the Bay but was unable to get into the mouth of the river. Poor Knight knew he was to be without fresh supplies or trade goods for another year at the shortest.

Indians coming down the hundreds of miles of fast, dangerous waters with canoes deep laden with furs, in the summer of 1716, found a handful of Englishmen house-building, but without guns, powder, kettles, axes, or brandy to barter. Desperate Indians made a desperate situation. Company men could not hunt for supplies or cut timber for fear of being ambushed by enraged tribesmen, many of whom hung about the post starving throughout the winter. Knight, with Kelsey, maintained discipline and avoided bloodshed, though the strain on the older man seriously impaired his health. Failure of the ship to arrive, with all the subsequent complication, destroyed the best-laid plans for peace missions and the building of a new northerly fort at the mouth of the Churchill River.

The geographical division of the Indian tribes and the southerly limits of the Eskimo trading country made the Churchill establishment the next logical move if new territory was to be reached. In his book *The Founding of Churchill*, Doctor Kenney briefly summarizes the native problem:

"The Indians of the country around Hudson Bay from Churchill river to the southward, were Crees and other branches of the Algonquian family; those to the north and north-west were Athapascans—Chipewyans ('Northern Indians'), Yellowknives ('Copper Indians'), Slaves and Dog-ribs. Along the coast to the north were the Eskimos who regularly came south as far as Churchill, and occasionally even further. Between these three groups continual hostilities existed. In particular the Crees, equipped with guns from the factories on the Bay, carried on an exterminating war against the Athapascans, of whom one division, the Slaves, have received their name from the large number carried off and held in servitude by the Crees. It was primarily to tap the trade of these Athapascans to the north that a trading post at Churchill was designed, for the Indian bands that came to York Factory seem to have been limited almost entirely to the Crees and their Siouan allies, the Assiniboines, Assinaepoets, or Stone Indians. To ensure that the 'Northern Indians' would come to the new factory it was necessary in the first place to get into communication with them, and in the second to satisfy them that when coming they would not be assaulted by their southern enemies. Captain Knight had no sooner become established in the recovered fort at York than he turned his attention to these two objects."

Knight persuaded a party of Cree under a Company man, William Stewart, to go on a peace mission to the Athapascan tribes north of Churchill. They wintered on the edge of the Barrens, hovering close to starvation, but succeeded in smoking a pipe of peace with the northern enemy and telling of the new fort to be built at the mouth of the Churchill for their trading. Back at York in May, 1716, Stewart estimated he had been one thousand miles north. Knight estimated six hundred. But Knight had broader plans. "I am Endeavouring to make a peace in the Whole Country Round from N to S W for a 1,000 Miles." Other Indian groups were persuaded to the propagation of the principle of less bloodshed and more trapping.

Most of Knight's work must have been dissipated by the summer of 1716, when the Indians came and he had nothing to barter. Yet he cross-examined them for geographical information. He heard of the river where virgin copper was found, of mountains which rose to the sky, thirty-nine days coming and three times as long returning from the Bay. There was talk of yellow metal. James Knight was hearing of the Rocky Mountains, and all that was merchant-adventurer in him responded. Years later, John Carruthers, surgeon under Knight at York, told of his growing obsession with the prospect of gold, "very earnest in this discovery which was always his topic."

The strain of the summer of 1716 was eased by the arrival on September 4 of the new ship *Hudson's Bay*. Knight wrote, "There was never nothing more welcome to me than the arrival of the ship for I was almost in disspair —but her arriving has put new life into our affairs here." Two days later he proclaimed, in accordance with the news brought by the ship, George I, King of Great Britain, France and Ireland, with the salute of "nine great guns" and the drinking of His Majesty's health.

It was July, 1717, before the expedition for the Churchill River was launched. Knight left Kelsey in charge at York, and his party coasted north on a mission destined to place a significant name on the map of Canada. The ice was barely out when they entered the mouth of the Churchill River on the morning of July 14 after three days in open boats.

"I never see such a miserable place in my life," was Knight's observation, and one which has found sympathetic echoes from fur traders, policemen, prospectors and surveyors many times since that day.

It was an elemental struggle which James Knight took on with his twenty-five men that summer, and from his journal it is not difficult to picture the man. Heavy, energetic, impatient, planning his men's work on the fort, portioning the rations, sending out hunters and quilling his nightly journal—which he sprinkled liberally with abuse of the captain who had failed to reach York two seasons before and so upset the entire strategy. The caribou did not appear. There were few geese, and seals broke the fish nets. One gathers that the party lived on oatmeal (mouldy), two Cheshire cheeses, and an occasional partridge or goose.

The age-old prejudice of the front-line, active-service men, against the remote headquarters steams up while these Englishmen flounder half-starved through the muskeg, nearly insane from mosquitoes.

"I have Often heard Sev'll of the Committee say as they had a good mind to Come over here: I wish they and all the rest of the Committee had took their summer campaign here. Then I believe they would set a Little more Value upon mens Lives & their goods not to expose all to this Hazard & wee to such hardships. Were they but here to see the Sculls & bones of Men as Lyes Scatter'd . . . it would put them into a feavor to think how they should Secure Themselves."

Knight built his fort on the site of the spot where Jens Munck's Danes had wintered and died nearly a hundred years before, and the spectre was a constant stimulus to the summer's work. The nearest scraggly timber was a mile from the only reasonable site for the post, and the men worked in swamp to their knees while the mosquitoes stung "like great wasps that wee are nothing in the world but knotts and bumps."

So they toiled on upon a point "as hardly contains so much ground as the Royall Exchange," painfully dragging the timber from "as farr as it is from the Hudson's Bay Company's house to Ludgate." Cockney Knight was defining his position in terms the Committee might grasp. By August the frigate *Hudson's Bay* came to relieve the tension, but September brought gales and snow. Knight concluded his journal, and among the later entries was a note of hope:

"York Fort is badd but this is ten times worse,—for here is neither fish, Fowl nor Venison but I believe it will be good for the Compys. interest in time."

Fortified by a present of eight dozen bottles of wine from the Company, Knight sailed for home, though he was not to resume the comforts and dignities of a merchant of London. The old man had the gold-hunting fever, and in the winter of 1718–19 he placed his proposals before a sub-committee of the Company directorate. By May, 1719, an agreement of discovery was sealed. Either Knight was completely convincing of the merits of his expedition or, as suggested by later writers, he threatened to go to the Crown for support if refused by the Company. Such a step could not be permitted by a Committee obliged under Royal Charter to undertake such ventures as Knight was urging.

Whatever the persuasion, Knight got his ships, the frigate *Albany* under Captain George Berley and the sloop *Discovery* under Captain David Vaughan. They sailed from Gravesend in June, 1719, with instructions to find the illusive Passage "in order to discover gold and other valuable commodities to the northward."

They found only death on a bleak Arctic island.

Curiously enough, the Committee did not attempt to co-ordinate this thrust for gold with its existing establishments in the Bay. From York Henry Kelsey operated his small ships northward for several seasons with no apparent concern for the vanished "gold hunters," as he called them, except some annoyance at finding they had touched the coast above Churchill and cut into his trade. The Committee sent out the sloop *Whalebone* under Captain George Scroggs in 1721 to supplement Knight's work and to search for him.

Forty-eight years passed without knowledge of what had happened. It was Samuel Hearne, Governor of Churchill, destined to make the most celebrated Arctic journey of the century, who secured the first authentic report of the fate of Knight. The Company's whalers in using Marble Island, nearly three hundred miles north of Churchill, and sixteen miles off the mainland, found the wreckage of the ships and buildings. Hearne subsequently interviewed old Eskimos who had visited the island while Knight's party was being rapidly reduced through sickness and starvation, probably in 1721. The whole story will never be known, but so horrible was the death of these men that to this day the tale is told among the Eskimo; and when landing on the barren friendless island, they drop to their knees and creep across the narrow beach in deference to the spirits of stout James Knight, shipwright, merchant of London, one-time governor of York Factory and master mariner, and of the Englishmen who perished with him.

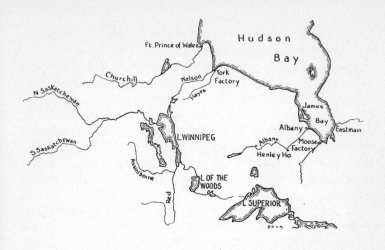

Chapter V

PARLIAMENT INQUIRES

NO profitable monopoly drawing its earnings from primitive barter on the fringes of an unexplored continent three thousand miles away could hope to flourish long unchallenged at home.

The Hudson's Bay Company had twice trebled its stock by 1720, and by the middle years of that century was bringing to England furs valued at from £23,000 to £30,000 each year, with costs averaging £19,400 per annum; this with about 120 officers and servants, and three or four vessels. It was a comfortable operation conducted by a secretive management. The Royal Charter remained a tower of strength, but there were few friends at court. The character of the proprietorship had changed remarkably in the first 75 years. By 1749 there were 98 shareholders, with only one knight and two baronets to compare with the constellation of princes, peers and lords of 1670. The investment of the original "absolute Lordes and Proprietors" had been £10,500; their 98 successors (including 11 women, a clergyman, and the estates of 22 deceased persons) held stock valued at £103,950.

This, and much more, was revealed to a highly interested London through an investigation into the Company's affairs by a committee of the House of Commons, in 1749. The Company was learning some of the costs of monopoly. A clear-cut licence to exclusive trade was a handsome instrument when supported by the Crown of England, but the eighteenth century developed a rising sense of public policy, and special privilege was coming in for considerable scrutiny.

An Irishman, Arthur Dobbs, endowed with wealth and an inquiring mind, became interested about 1730 in the possibilities of a North West Passage. It was the unquenchable flame of his enthusiasm which brought about the parliamentary investigation. From the very outset, of course, he encountered the Hudson's Bay Company's exclusive privileges in these northern waters where he would seek the route to the Far East. For nearly twenty years, as he pursued his brilliant attack on the Company, it became apparent that he too desired exclusive trade privileges, for eventually he proposed the creation of a new company with similar rights.

From its experience in coastwise trade, and from the conclusions of its captains and the reports of Indians, the Company had come to doubt the North West Passage. Yet, prodded by the Dobbs irritant, two Company ships (the sloop *Churchill* under Captain Napper and the sloop *Musquash* under Captain Crow) were sent north along the west coast of the Bay in July, 1737. Their minute instructions opened with admirable honesty of purpose, "You are hereby ordered to sail to the Northward." The sailing orders conclude reverently, "So God send the good Sloops a Successful Discovery and to return in Safety. Amen."

They found no Passage. The expedition, far from silencing Dobbs, stimulated him to a major assault. He tried to organize an expedition to be backed by the government, and sought to draw a Captain Middleton from the Company's service for the command. Middleton, content with his employment, declined at the time, but in 1741 accepted.

The Lords of the Admiralty gave him command of the sloop *Furnace* and handed him orders including instructions to govern his conduct in meeting Japanese vessels or upon landing on the coast of California. There was a second ship, the pink *Discovery*, under Captain William Moore. They entered the Bay in August and wintered at Churchill under the suspicious eye of the officer in charge of that fort. In July, 1742, they proceeded north, making elaborate observations. The search ended abruptly in August in the ice fields of Roes Welcome. Middleton went home and reported that there was no Passage.

This was no obstacle to Dobbs, who set about to prove Middleton a liar and a receiver of bribes from the Hudson's Bay interests. The Admiralty showed their satisfaction in Middleton by giving him a naval command, and later exploration substantiated all his reports. Dobbs pursued his case of claiming that Middleton had been serving the Company throughout, and that he had deliberately fumbled the expedition. Dobbs filed with the Admiralty a pamphlet known as his *Criticism*. Middleton retorted with *Vindication of the Conduct*, both issued in 1743. It was the first flutter in a gale of wordy pamphlets arising out of the Dobbs episode.

The Irishman pushed his case in a two-hundred-page book published in 1744, *An Account of the Countries Adjoining to Hudson's Bay*. It was an important book, based largely upon the account given by a renegade French half-breed, Joseph La France, who had worked his way up from Lake Superior to York Factory by way of Lake Winnipeg, some time about 1740. La France gave quite a glow to his picture of Indian life and indicated possibilities of fur trade expansion inland. Dobbs rounded out the story with his own sharp enthusiasm, and the book was widely read among all who had interests in colonial expansion

and overseas trade. He thumped hard on the drum of
Empire, contrasting all the glories of English seamanship
and exploration with this Company's smug content with
dividends while the North West Passage awaited discovery.

The Company, under Sir Bibye Lake's governorship,
took it all in silence, which only incensed the Dobbs party
and roused speculations of concealed iniquities in the minds
of those on the outskirts of the crowd. So cloaked were the
Company's affairs that it was widely believed that the
shares were all held by about ten persons.

Parliament itself was moved to post twenty thousand
pounds reward for discovery of the Passage, despite the
cost of a war with France. From this was born the Dobbs
Company with a paid subscription of seven thousand two
hundred pounds, later raised to ten thousand pounds.
Two more ships were dedicated to the search. The Governor
and Committee must have felt disconcerted, and their ship
captains doubtless smiled grimly over the news.

The *Dobbs*, one hundred and eighty tons, under Captain
William Moore, and the *California*, one hundred and forty
tons, under Captain Francis Smith, left the Thames in
May, 1746. Two Company ships, *Hudson's Bay II* and
Mary II, left at the same time in order to have the benefits
of naval protection against French war vessels.

The early-season ice in the Strait gave them trouble.
The Company ships reached York Factory first, after which
James Isham, governor at York, pulled in all the buoys at
the mouth of the Hayes River and cut down the beacon.
When the *Dobbs* and the *California* came up they were
allowed to grope into the estuary unpiloted. Isham coldly
challenged their right to be there, but later thawed and
gave them assistance in putting up winter quarters, lent
them fur coats, and, according to a subsequent account,
allowed them to dig a cellar in the factory "in which
they put some of their beer and cheese." The explorer
crews wintered wretchedly, with scurvy rampant among
them.

Arthur Dobbs was not with the party, but his agent

Henry Ellis went along and later wrote a book about it, thus lending early support to the deplorable practice of following Arctic experience with a mediocre travel book. The Dobbs expedition nosed north along the west coast of the Bay in the summer of 1747, and got safely home to England by October. Ellis was bound to confirm Middleton's conclusions, but managed to squeeze a meagre drop of hope in a style of tortured English peculiarly the property of Arctic explorers. "Thus ended this voyage, without success, but not without effect; for though we did not discover a north-west passage . . . we returned with clearer and fuller proofs . . . that evidently such a passage there may be."

The literary side of the controversy had become an avalanche.

1. Dobbs's *Criticism* filed with the Admiralty, 1743.

2. *A Vindication of the Conduct of Captain Middleton*, 1743.

3. *An Account of the Countries Adjoining to Hudson's Bay in the North-West part of America*, by Dobbs, 1744.

4. *A Reply to the Remarks of Arthur Dobbs*, by Middleton, 1744.

5. *Remarks upon Captain Middleton's Defence*, by Dobbs, 1744.

6. *Forgery Detected*, by Middleton, 1745.

7. *A Reply to Captain Middleton's Answer*, by Dobbs, 1745.

8. *A Reply to Mr. Dobbs Answer to a Pamphlet Entitled Forgery Detected*, by Middleton, 1745.

9. *A Voyage to Hudson's Bay, by the Dobbs Galley and the California in the years 1746 and 1747 for the Discovery of a North West Passage*, by Henry Ellis.

These publications indicate only the main current of the controversy which feathered off into numerous side scuffles and anonymous letters. Three fruitless expeditions proved nothing to Arthur Dobbs except the ineptitude and incompetence of the Hudson's Bay Company. The Passage was his wedge towards obtaining Charter privileges for himself and his associates, and when it could not be discovered he turned his forces into the direct attack. In the winter of 1747–48, after some eighteen years of agitation, he launched the parliamentary assault.

The minute book of the Company for March 10, 1748:

> "Mr. Sharp, the company's Solicitor, attending the Committee acquainted them that a motion was yesterday made and carried in the House of Commons to inquire into the state and condition of the countries and trade of Hudson's Bay, and also the right the Company pretend to have by charter to the property land and exclusive trade to those countries and that the committee was appointed accordingly."

The business interests of London prepared themselves for dazzling revelations. The secrets of the silent Company of Adventurers were about to be disclosed, and men would gasp over fabulous profits. They learned, instead, that the Company capital of £103,950 in thirty years had only once paid a dividend of better than 10 per cent. (12 per cent. in 1724) and that 8 per cent. dividends had been frequent. Moreover, as the Company was turned inside out during two months' investigation, the hazardous nature of fur trading both at home and abroad became apparent.

Those interested in "settlements and plantations" in America hoped to hear of lush meadowlands where the deer roamed and were hunted by noble red men. Others listened for rumours of gold, while some, no doubt, believed a taciturn Company was about to be caught guiltily concealing the secret of a seaway to the Indies and Cathay. It turned out to be pretty dull stuff; good profits when there was peace and enormous losses in time of war; it was a long-distance operation into a most intemperate climate where Englishmen did not want to go, and even in peace times the marine hazard was high.

The investigation was conducted with admirable judicial detachment. The members of the parliamentary committee maintained an attitude of honest inquiry into the minutiæ of their subject without losing the view of larger

policy. In this case the larger policy was the relationship
with France in America. The ultimate findings of the
committee were unquestionably dictated by the desire to
hold fast to such claims as Britain had upon the north half
of the American continent.

The Company made an attractive target with its relatively
small group of shareholders, few of whom were persons of
major importance, enjoying exclusive trade and administrative privileges over an area no one knew how great.
The King was no longer a patron; "His Most Excellent
Majesty" appeared only as a private shareholder. The
bitterest charges could be flung at them without offending
vested interests. The whole attack could be put on the
loftiest plane of imperial purpose.

Dobbs's allegations in his petition to Parliament have
been summed up by George Bryce in his *Remarkable History
of the Hudson's Bay Company* (1910):

"1. The Company had not discovered, nor sufficiently
attempted to discover, the North-West Passage into
the southern seas.

2. They had not extended their settlements to the limits
given them by their Charter.

3. They had designedly confined their trade within very
narrow limits:

(*a*) Had abused the Indians.

(*b*) Had neglected their forts.

(*c*) Ill-treated their own servants.

(*d*) Encouraged the French.

The Hudson's Bay Company, now put on their mettle,
exhibited a considerable amount of activity and filed
documents before the Committee that in some respects
met the charges against them. They claimed that they
had in the thirty years preceding the investigation done a
fair amount of exploratory work and discovery."

The petitioners produced twenty witnesses, mostly disgruntled ex-employees, but including several London
merchants hopeful of wider trade outlets in Hudson Bay.

Joseph Robson, surveyor and stonemason, who for six years had been employed in the construction of the great Prince of Wales Fort at the entrance to Churchill Harbour, was apparently to have been the star witness. He was called first and proved to be singularly innocuous. Some years later he joined the authors' circle with a bitter attack on the Company, justifying it on the grounds that he had not been quite himself when before the committee and had consequently neglected to say many of the things which were really on his mind.

Richard White, seven years a clerk in the Bay, told of competition from the French to the south, of the standard of Indian trade, of Indians being beaten for stealing, and of the peas, beans, turnips and "sallad" grown in the governor's garden at Albany Fort. He believed corn would grow there. The Indians grew nothing, being "a slothful people."

Matthew Sergeant mentioned the principal articles of trade: brandy, tobacco, blankets and beads. He thought corn might grow. He had seen a Company servant in irons for drunkenness.

John Hayter, carpenter for about ten years in the Bay, told of lean rations, punishment for servants attempting private trade with Indians, and said that he had seen Indians wearing copper ornaments.

Edward Thompson, three years surgeon at Moose Factory, compared the barley and oats of the James Bay country to the same grains in the Orkney Islands. He thought the trade could be extended by inland posts which would reach Indians who could not make five-hundred-mile trips to the Bay each year. He was of opinion that Captain Middleton had made no honest attempt to discover the Passage. The witness had seen copper, and said a Company ship had brought ore samples from Labrador.

Henry Spurling, merchant, showed various furs to the committee, explaining the values in European trade of beaver, squirrel, and ermine, emphasizing the superior value of the northern types such as came from Hudson Bay.

Arthur Dobbs, Esquire, was called, and briefly verified the Joseph La France narrative which was made an appendix to the committee's report.

The Company seems to have been content to reply by the filing of documentary evidence, some of which proved highly interesting and illuminating.

The beating of a servant for breaking fort rules, or of an Indian for drunkenness, gave the parliamentary committee no concern. Harsh treatment for petty offences was commonplace. The navy was kept up to strength by press gangs. Even Company ships had been stopped at sea to have their crews depleted by compulsion in order to fill the ranks on the King's men-o'-war. Nor were the Members of Parliament troubled by the sale of brandy to Indians. This aspect of fur trading had not then assumed the proportions it was to acquire towards the end of the century; and, while there was no attempt to reduce Indians to conditions of slavery, the European attitude towards uncivilized people was coloured by the acceptance of human beings as chattels. Primitive races were viewed either as potentially subject people, or as barbarians to be traded with on the most favourable terms possible. Yet even the uninspired local governors in Hudson Bay were beginning to perceive that healthy, intelligent natives held by honourable trading methods, would be necessary if the fur takings were to be kept up in the face of rising competition from the French. They had also learned that education did not improve the Indian as a hunter.

The Members of Parliament asked chiefly about the possibilities of agriculture, settlement and trade expansion, metal discoveries, and the menace of the French crowding in on territory held by Britain through the Company Charter. They were given only slight hope for "plantacions." True, some cereals were grown at the James Bay posts, but that was about all. As for gold and copper, they were only rumours, though confirmed by the ornaments worn by the Northern Indians.

Indications of French encroachment probably gave the

Members of Parliament more concern than any other evidence. It was important that the validity of the Charter should be sustained to consolidate the British claim to all that unknown territory draining into the Bay. To declare the Charter invalid would place the British at an obvious disadvantage when it came to patching up the next peace treaty with France. Certainly, the evidence showed an undiminished French aggression in fur trading in the lakes and forests to the south and out towards the plains of the west, about which the English had such scanty knowledge.

The Company's defence brought its affairs into the open for the first time. The Royal Charter was printed as an appendix to the committee's report, and its terms were examined with more than casual interest. The Company also filed papers which included a series of instructions to its captains, orders to chief factors, trading tariffs, ownership of stock, operating costs, and the *Journal* of Henry Kelsey's expedition of 1691–92. The story of this *Journal* has been told in the life of Kelsey. It was an abbreviated form of the *Journal* which came to light in 1926 from Dobbs's own residence, and it will always remain a matter for supposition whether or not Dobbs had it at the time of the inquiry.

If the case had been considered solely upon the Company's pursuit of the Passage and its unrolling of the map westward, things might have gone badly, but the fur traders produced record of impressive achievements in the face of Arctic wind and weather demanding courage and fortitude rare in commercial enterprise.

Even the laconic listing of ships sent out to search for the Passage tells a story of death in the north. It is further evidence of the essential maritime character of the Company up to that time.

1719—*Albany Frigate*, Captain George Berley, sailed from England on or about June 5. Never returned.

Discovery, Captain David Vaughan, sailed from England on or about June 5. Never returned.

Prosperous, Captain Henry Kelsey, sailed from

The Trapper—Yesterday and Today

Coat of arms of the Hudson's Bay
Company

A one shilling note, typical of H.B.C.
currency, in general circulation during
the middle years of the nineteenth
century

"Made Beaver" coins of brass,
currency in the Indian trade, in
denominations of one, one half
and one quarter, and discontinued about 1910

Gold medals worn by members of the
Beaver Club of Montreal. Each bore
the date of the member's first visit to
the Indian Country. These were the
property of James McGill, posthumous
founder of McGill University

SYMBOLS OF FUR TRADE

York Fort, June 19. Returned August 10 following.

Success, John Hancock, Master, sailed from Prince of Wales's Fort, July 2. Returned August 10.

1721—*Prosperous*, Captain Henry Kelsey, sailed from York Fort, June 26. Returned September 2.

Success, James Napper, Master, sailed from York Fort, June 26. Lost 30th of the same month.

Whalebone, John Scroggs, Master, sailed from Gravesend, May 31; wintered at Prince of Wales's Fort.

1722—Sailed from thence June 21. Returned July 25 following.

1737—The *Churchill*, James Napper, Master, sailed from Prince of Wales's Fort, July 7. Died August 8; and the vessel returned the 18th.

The *Musquash*, Robert Crow, Master, sailed from Prince of Wales's Fort, July 7. Returned August 22.

After seventy-nine years of trading into Hudson Bay, the Company establishments were: Moose Factory, Henly House, East Main House, Albany Fort, York Fort, Prince of Wales Fort. Of these, Henly House was the only inland post, and it was barely one hundred and fifty miles up the Albany River.

In the statements of revenues and expenditures over a ten-year period, the very heart of the Company's affairs was disclosed. Consolidated for purposes of clarity, the following table, for 1739–48 inclusive, shows the value of trade goods exported, operating costs, and revenue from fur sales.

Value of annual exports: 1739, £4,994; 1740, £5,630; 1741, £5,622; 1742, £4,007; 1743, £4,894; 1744, £6,736; 1745, £5,462; 1746, £5,431; 1747, £4,581; 1748, £5,102.

"Amount of the Charge attending the carrying on the Hudson's Bay Company's Trade, and maintaining their factories . . .": 1739, £12,245; 1740, £13,346; 1741, £11,757; 1742, £12,084; 1743, £12,772; 1744, £20,201;

1745, £21,702; 1746, £19,360; 1747, £16,609; 1748, £17,352.

Thus total charges were £157,432. For the ten years the amount exported of trading goods only was £36,741, leaving a balance of £194,174 or £19,417 for each year. (In all these figures shillings and pence have been omitted.)

Revenue from fur sales: 1739 ("from Michaelmas, 1738 to Michaelmas, 1739"): £23,328; 1740, £30,279; 1741, £28,877; 1742, £22,957; 1743, £26,804; 1744, £29,785; 1745, £30,148; 1746, £26,350; 1747, £24,849; 1748, £30,160.

A comfortable profit, indeed, but the cost of doing business was increasing, and the detailed statements show that beaver, most important of the furs taken, was declining. The French were cutting in, taking their trade goods into Indian territory at great effort by way of the Great Lakes and the portages to the prairies, making it unnecessary for the natives to hazard the long dangerous journeys between their hunting grounds and the Bay.

The appendix foreshadowed later years when fur trading ceased to be the only channel of business within the Company. Returns included such items as: "bed feathers, 5,433 pounds; whale fins, 300 pounds; goose quills, 12,000; deer horns, 40 pounds." Beaver pelts varied from 69,911 in 1739 to as low as 39,505 in 1747.

The standard of trade of 1748 was also published. The scale varied slightly among East Main, Albany, Moose and York, but the following twenty-five items are typical of what was called the "standard of trade" in all four posts:

For half a pound of beads, "large Milk, of colours, of all sorts," the native gave one beaver skin; a brass kettle "of all sizes" cost a beaver skin at Albany and Moose, but one and a half skins at York and Churchill. Black lead was a pound for a beaver at Albany and Moose. One beaver bought a pound and a half of powder at Albany and Moose, but only a pound at York and Churchill. Shot was five for a beaver at Albany and Moose, and four at York and Churchill. A beaver bought two pounds of brown sugar at Albany and Moose. The standard of trade at Moose of other articles follows: tobacco, Brazil, one pound, one beaver; leaf and roll tobacco, a pound and a half for a beaver; thread, one pound, two beavers; vermilion, one-half pound, one beaver; English brandy, one gallon, four beavers; broadcloth, red, white, or blue, two beavers a yard; one blanket for six beavers; flannel, a beaver a yard; buttons, a beaver for twelve dozen; ivory combs, two for a beaver; red feathers, two for a beaver; fishhooks, twenty for a beaver; fire steels, four for a beaver; twenty flints for a beaver; a four-foot gun for twelve beavers; a handkerchief, one and a half beavers; two hatchets for a beaver; eight pairs hawk-bells for a beaver; eight knives for a beaver; two looking-glasses for a beaver; twelve needles for a beaver; two powder horns, one beaver; four spoons, one beaver; one shirt, one beaver.

The conclusions of George Bryce on the subject of this trading scale are well considered and worthy of quotation:

"The charge that the Company abused the Indians was hardly substantiated. The Company was dependent on the good will of the Indians, and had they treated them badly, their active rivals, the French, would simply have reaped the benefit of their folly. That the price charged the Indians for goods was as large as the price paid for furs was small, is quite likely to have been true. Civilized traders all the world over, dealing with ignorant and dependent tribes, follow this policy. No doubt the risks of life and limb and goods in remote regions are great, and great profits must be made to meet them. It is to be remembered, however, that when English and French traders came into competition, as among the Iroquois in New York State, and afterwards in the Lake Superior district, the quality of the English goods was declared by the Indians better, and their treatment by the English on the whole more honest and aboveboard than that by the French."

Wartime instructions to local governors in the Bay were explicit for the defence of Company property. These rules were supported by compensation offered to widows and wounded men. The parliamentary committee learned, for instance, that the Company sent out orders to Joseph Isbister at Albany Fort in 1744 in these terms:

"The English and French having declared war against each other, and the War with Spain still continuing we do hereby direct you to be always on your Guard and keep a good Watch; and that you keep all your Men as near Home as possible." Trees and bushes are to be levelled within cannon shot, "which we compute to be a Mile," and "you are to keep up and repair your Palisadoes." Small arms must be cleaned regularly and kept loaded. Indians were to be employed as scouts. Secret signals between the forts and Company ships were given. "You are to fire point blank upon any ship sloop or vessel that come near the Factory unless they make the true Signal and answer yours."

Dependents of a man killed in defence of Company property would receive thirty pounds. The loss of a limb earned a similar amount, with appropriate rewards for conspicuous bravery.

Each year of war the instructions were repeated, with this special admonition in 1747:

"War still continuing with France and Spain, we renew our former Order, of being always on your Guard, and to keep a good Watch, and your Men near Home, except those that are guarding the Battery at Cape Merry; but not to hinder a proper Number to be employed in providing a sufficient Quentity of the Country Provisions; to prevent the Complaint of those Persons that murmur for want of Victuals: And we recommend Sobriety, that you may be capable of making a vigorous Defence, if attacked.

"We again recommend your keeping the Land round the Fort, and the Battery at Cape Merry, free from every thing that may possibly conceal or shelter an Enemy, that you may thereby prevent being surprised.

"We again direct, That you keep up a general Correspondence with all the Factories, and get what Intelligence you can of the Designs of the French."

There was solicitude about quality of merchandise and an earnest desire to suit the merchandise to the customer which has a curiously modern flavour. On May 1, 1740, for instance, the committee made the first reference to an article of trade still famous under the Company's brand:

"We have sent you full Indent of Trading Goods: Stores and Provisions and instead of 150 Blankets which we thought might be too few, we have sent 225. The Flannel, now sent we have chose out of a thicker Sort, but yet very fine and good." Then follows a note highly suggestive of twentieth-century merchandising. "Let us know whether the Size of the Crown of the Hats are pleasing to the Natives."

All these things the parliamentarians pondered, and on April 24, 1749, Lord Strange presented the report of the committee of investigation to Parliament.

Briefly stated, the committee suggested that if Dobbs wanted to have the Royal Charter rendered void, let him pursue his trade and explorations into Hudson Bay, carry his claim of freedom of trade to law and get "some Judgment of a Court of Justice to warrant it." The committee disposed of the charges of neglect of exploration, neglect of trade, abuse of Indians, and ill-treatment of servants, in a few words:

"We think these Charges are either not sufficiently supported in point of Fact or in a great measure accounted for from the Nature or Circumstances of the Case." Concluding, they pointed to the "great confusion" which would arise from granting privileges to the petitioners similar to those held by the Company "in those parts."

Plainly, larger policy had prevailed. The British Government was to keep a united front to the French. The Company had won its first tilt in a public arena. Its victory was complete but not conclusive. Its case had been adequate if not overwhelming, and the verbose Charter, together with the exigencies of colonial policy, had carried the day.

Dobbs, too, emerged with a minor personal victory. He was appointed governor of North Carolina where his genuine and forceful interest in overseas development gave more stimulus to British expansion in North America than he lived to know.

The Lords of Trade and Plantations in this year of 1749 asked for a map and a definition of boundaries. The Company replied, "How or where these lands terminate to westward is also unknown."

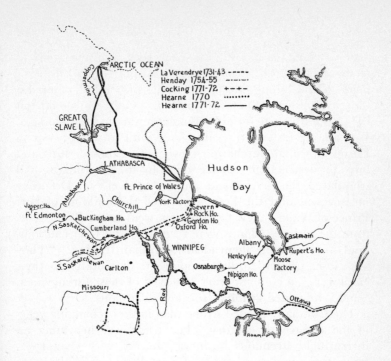

Chapter VI

OVERLAND TO THE ARCTIC

THE tempered evolution of policy that was the most
pronounced characteristic of the Company's long story
proceeded unperturbed by the parliamentary inquiry. The
conservative proprietorship and the elements of time and
distance made the entire operation a slow-motion development. The perfect illustration is Fort Prince of Wales at
the entrance to Churchill Harbour. Years of planning in
London preceded the first turning of the soil in 1732; for
thirty years men toiled at its construction; in two more
decades it was sacked by the French; within a year a log
fort replaced it.

G

Slowly and cautiously the Company adjusted itself to changing times and conditions. Years of comforting dividends had a lulling effect; operating principles acquired a sanctity it was heretical to question. Only war could jolt the Committee into the animation necessary to basic changes. War among Indian tribes interfered with trapping; war in Europe lowered purchasing power and exposed ships and forts to destruction. Peace missions to the Indians had stimulated the first inland journey of Kelsey. Defensive measures against the French inspired the building of Fort Prince of Wales. New types of men went to the Bay. Scots from the Orkney Islands were recruited, and their cautious, dour natures made them ideal for Indian trading. "They are close, prudent, quiet people, strictly faithful to their employers," a contemporary observed of these Orkneymen, "and," he added grimly, "sordidly avaricious."

The Company needed strong men in these changing years of the eighteenth century. Fur trade was becoming an increasingly strenuous business. In the very year 1732, when the foundation stones of Fort Prince of Wales were being laid, La Vérendrye came west from Three Rivers, and competition from French Canada had to be reckoned with more heavily each year. York Factory returns shrank; the Englishmen were obliged to take to the lakes and the forests of the hinterland for their fur trade. The Company ceased to be solely a sea-going venture, but moved steadily inland, establishing new posts. Wolfe's conquest of Quebec brought peace with the ancient enemy—and then came the menace of Montreal competition threatening the very roots of the old Company. It was a difficult century for the Adventurers of England.

Turning back to 1732, here was Pierre Gaultier de Varennes, Sieur de la Vérendrye, of Three Rivers, travelling west with his three sons and fifty Frenchmen. Bearing on his body sabre wounds from Malplaquet, La Vérendrye was another of the French Canadian noblesse who combined powers of leadership with an intimate knowledge of Indians. Rivers and forests were the environment of their youth, and Indian wars and fur trading were their careers.

La Vérendrye established his first post on the Lake of the Woods. For the next seventeen years this courageous man and his party endured every form of privation known to northern travellers. Dogged by debt, with political enemies in Montreal, and cramped by the regional monopoly system of French fur trading, they established a chain of posts reaching far up the Saskatchewan. In 1738 Fort Rouge had risen, at the juncture of the Red and Assiniboine rivers where Winnipeg stands today, and one of the sons pressed on westwards to see the Rocky Mountains. La Vérendrye died in 1749, but he had discovered the crossroads of the continent by establishing for the first time the true relationship of the Red, Assiniboine and Missouri rivers, and Lakes Winnipeg, Manitoba and Winnipegosis. His posts included Fort Pierre, near Rainy Lake; Fort Charles on the Lake of the Woods; Fort Maurepas at the mouth of the Winnipeg River; Fort La Reine some fifteen miles east of Portage la Prairie; Fort Dauphin on Mossy River; Fort Bourbon on Cedar Lake; La Corne's post below the Forks of the Saskatchewan.

All these menaced the Company's immediate and future trade, as well as the sacred Charter rights. The Company responded with a series of one-man expeditions up from the Bay into the prairie, the forest, and the Barren Lands. From 1754 to 1774, the Governor and Committee ordered sixty inland voyages, and in 1774 had built Cumberland House, the first interior post.

From this period came the first men who accepted the country as they found it and made it part of their lives. Men came forward who could go native and live and travel among Indians without loss of morale; men who found deep satisfaction in the new and unknown; keen observers and keepers of good journals; surveyors with inquiring, mathematical minds who plotted the contours of the waterways. Anthony Henday, William Pink, Samuel Hearne, Matthew Cocking, Malcolm Ross, Philip Turnor,

William Tomison, and Peter Fidler are some of these men
who took up where the boy Kelsey had left off, and won
for themselves that simple but complete honour which
northern men confer, the name of "good traveller."

Anthony Henday, said to have been an outlawed English
smuggler, went inland from York Factory in June, 1754,
with a party of Assiniboine Indians, "to explore the country
inland and to endeavour to increase the Hudson Bay
Company's trade." They reached The Pas after a journey
made difficult by many portages and "intolerable" mosquitoes. Henday tells of meeting the French at this
place:

"We came to the french factory on my arrival, two
french men came out, when followed a great deal of
Bowing and Scraping between us, and then we Entered
their fort, (or more properly a Hogstye) for in Short it is
no Better, they have neither victuals nor drink. Except
a little Ruhigan, they are very Lazey, not one stick of wood
anigh their house; they asked me where the Letter was,
I told them I had no Letter, nor did not see any Reason
for one, but that the Country belonged to us as much as
them; he made answer it did not, and that he would
detain me there, and send me home to france, I told him
I knew france as well as he did, and was not afraid to go
their more than himself, which Made Monsieure a Little
Cooler."

Henday and his party pressed on, and late in July
abandoned their canoes, striking out across the grasslands,
rejoicing in plenty of game, wild strawberries and Saskatoon
berries. He wintered with Indians somewhere between the
North Saskatchewan and Red Deer rivers, and during this
interval found much to admire in the Blackfeet tribe.
Their mastery of horsemanship and skill at buffalo-hunting
made them coldly indifferent to the glitter of European
goods. Henday talked of trade advantages. The chief
replied that to his people buffalo meat was essential; they
were not canoe men; they ate no fish; they could kill
enough for their needs with bow and arrow and had no

use for firearms; nor did they care to forsake their hunting grounds for the long journey to the Bay.

The chief, Henday entered in his journal, "was informed the Natives that frequented the Settlements, were sometimes starved on their journey. Such remarks I thought exceeding true."

After the winter's trapping, Henday's party built twenty canoes and started east for York Factory in April. Again they met the French near Fort La Corne.

"Ye 23rd (May) we came to a french house, where was 5 french men, the Govr. came with his hatt in his hand, and followed a great deal of Bowing and Scraping, but neither he understood me nor I him, he treated me with 2 glasses Brandy and half a Bisket, this Evening he gave the Inds 2 Gallons Brandy, for to get them for to trade, but he got but very Little trade. Ye 24th Saturday fine weather wind S Et. Lay by, this day Breakfasted, Dined and Sup'd with the french, he asked me many Questions, but I told him I know nothing but come to see the Indn. country."

Both here and as he passed The Pas again Henday was obliged to stand by while the Frenchmen debauched his Indians with brandy and took the choicest furs. He was powerless to do anything but accept the hospitality of the Frenchmen and hope to persuade some of the sober Indians to continue on three hundred miles to the Bay. He had some success and was back at York five days less than a year after his departure.

His expedition, which can be appraised today as a great achievement, was somehow discredited. That Indians should hunt the buffalo on horseback and be so content with that life as to decline to travel through hostile country to reach British goods, was apparently incredible to his less venturesome superiors at York Factory.

At the time, the Company was having great difficulty with illicit trade, described in the London minute books as "privacy." The ships' captains and even the local governors were smuggling out furs and making private profit in spirits despite the strongest efforts of the Committee. Probably Henday became a victim of some inner ring. Years later, Andrew Graham, the factor at York, made these revealing notations on the margins of the manuscript of Henday's journal (which apparently had been put aside and forgotten):

"I know this man: he was a bold and good servant. . . . The accounts of horsemen being inland were not credited. He, Henday, was misrepresented by those in the Bay who were not acting a just part to the Company, and he perceiving not likely to meet with promotion he had so deservedly merited, quitted the Company's service . . . drove out . . . by the ships gentry because he would not buy slops and brandy from them."

It was just the old, old story of the corrupt, jealous official suppressing the record of an able subordinate and blocking promotion. To complete a vicious circle in this case were the "ships gentry," the captains, coming out once each year armed with considerable authority and ready to doublecross the owners.

Henday's journal had no effect on the policies of the Company. It had been sixty-two years since the Kelsey expeditions, and now Henday had drawn aside the curtain to disclose the interior. The location of the French posts, the nature and value of their trade, were but a fragment of the priceless information the Committee might have had. Henday might well have continued his work and become one of the greatest fur trade explorers—but for these petty people "who were not acting a just part."

Before the next Company men went inland, Wolfe took Quebec for England, and the French régime in America was ended. The conquest of Canada, fought out in the valley of the Saint Lawrence, gave a fresh character to the fur trade in the north and west. The Company rejoiced at the prospect of extracting from the peace treaty cash claims for French depredations. Quebec fell in 1759, and the French system of licensed local monopolies soon crumbled, leaving only a few handfuls of free traders west of the Great Lakes. The Adventurers, though frustrated in their hopes of cash compensation from the Peace of Paris, must have warmed to the prospect of a clear field of operation. Their peace was to be short-lived.

The early appearance in the west of British traders from Montreal took the Bay men completely by surprise. Certainly the vigour and bitterness of the competition they brought, could not have been foreseen. At first, the Company merely tried to continue its practice of sending expeditions inland on missions of peace and persuasion. It was fifteen years before the first inland post was established in Cumberland House on the Saskatchewan in 1774. Here was a pronounced change in policy, a defensive measure at the time, but the forerunner of great inland expansion.

Company men dubbed the newcomers "Pedlars," a name that stuck to them through the sixty years of bloody rivalry that ended so strangely in union.

The effort to keep the Indians coming to the Bay in the face of the new and powerful competition brought out some conspicuously successful "travellers" from the ranks of the Adventurers.

William Pink, "labourer," left York Factory in July, 1766, and during the next four years made four journeys, reaching into what is now Alberta. Having traced the Beaver River to its source he must have been near that height of land west of Lac la Biche and within sight of the vital watershed which starts the Athabasca River flowing to the Mackenzie and the Arctic. Pink was the first to report the appearance in the west of a British trader: "His name is James Finley from Montreal he came up with Three Canewes to this house."

The Northwesters had arrived.

William Tomison, a "labourer" in 1760, made his first journey upstream from Severn six years later. He became a notable traveller, and in 1777 was placed in charge of the new Cumberland House. From there he organized the trade of the Saskatchewan River against the invaders from

Montreal, building posts almost beside theirs. He appears to have been the most energetic fur trader in the service up to that time, and carried the title of "inland chief." The Northwesters had no more bitter enemy.

His record, revealed in the journals, is of thirty-five years' tireless effort and occasional interludes of furlough. Oxford House, Gordon House, Edmonton House, Carlton House and Buckingham House were some of the stockaded log posts which appeared in the Saskatchewan Valley during his service. Each one involved heavy problems of labour and transportation of goods, and over all lay the harsh dictation of the seasons.

The trade struggle had not yet narrowed down to the two companies, for the Montrealers had not then consolidated themselves, and in some places three and four rival establishments crowded each other.

Tomison wanted to retire after forty years' service, but was asked to go out again as "inland master" and returned to the interior in 1806. In later years he became unpopular with the men and with the Indians, who at some posts refused to trade with him because he would not give them liquor, despite the liberal rum dispensed by his competitors. Retiring finally in 1811, he was voted fifty guineas "for his exertions in the service of the company."

Matthew Cocking joined the Company as a "writer" or clerk in 1765. In 1772 he was second in command at York when instructions came from London for him to go inland to report on the "Pedlars" from Montreal. He was also to advise on the wisdom of an inland post on the Saskatchewan. Hence the title of his journal: *Being the journal of a Journey performed by Mr. Matthew Cocking, second Factor at York Fort, in order to take a View of the Inland Country, and to Promote the Hudson's Bay Company's Interest, Whos Trade is Diminishing by the Canadians Yearly Intercepting Natives on Their Way to the Settlements, 1772–1773.* It is a journal of terse, daily notings—"paddled, dragged & carryed the Canoes & Goods at intervals amongst rocky shoals & strong currents. Course South 45 West, Distance 20 miles."

Cocking wintered on the plains somewhere between the north and south branches of the Saskatchewan River. Like Henday, he found prairie Indians far superior to those of the eastern forests, who traded at York. They were well mounted, adequately clothed, and more cleanly. They grew tobacco and cooked food in earthen pots. His gifts to the chiefs brought no promises of trade. "They said that they would be starved & were unacquainted with the Canoes & mentioned the long distance; I am certain they can never be prevailed upon to undertake such journies."

The spring of 1773 came, and on May 6 they started down to York, "musquitoes plenty & troublesome." As Cocking and his Indians went eastward, they met Montreal traders who, with four gallons of adulterated rum and gifts of coats and hats to chiefs, garnered the choice furs. "I endeavoured all in my power to prevent the Natives giving away their furs, but in vain; Liquor being above all persuasion with them," wrote Cocking. "It surprises me," he observed a few days later, "to perceive what a warm side the Natives hath to the French Canadians."

Cocking returned to York Factory that June with ample evidence of "Pedlar" presence, and the following year went with Samuel Hearne to build Cumberland House. The momentum of the coming battle was slowly gathering its force.

Those who study the material of Hudson's Bay Company history come upon the story of Samuel Hearne for the first time with pleasure. There is more specific information about Hearne than about most of his contemporaries in the service. His record as a fur trader included one of the most effective pieces of exploration in his century. He was something of an artist, studied astronomy and surveying, commanded ships and forts, was a modest and loyal servant of the Company and wrote with a clarity and style new to fur trading.

Hearne came from a "respectable family" in Somersetshire. Having given trouble at school, he was put into the navy as a midshipman, under the special care of Captain, later Admiral Lord Hood. As a boy he saw plenty of action, and years later it was recorded in his obituary that he had assigned his share of the naval prize money to his widowed mother. He came to the Company in 1766 for two years as mate of the whaling sloop *Churchill*, and then became mate of the brigantine *Charlotte*. In 1769 he wrote the Governor and Committee asking for transfer to some other branch of the service "where there is greater probability of making some returns, and giveing satisfaction to my Employers." The Committee was notably prompt in exploiting this glimmer of ambition, and commissioned him to explore. For three years he worked to a splendid failure, finding no solution to the North West Passage puzzle but giving to the world first definite knowledge of the proportions of the northern half of the continent.

There was enough backwash from the Dobbs controversy in speculation on the Passage and unexplored mineral wealth, to keep the Governor and Committee alive to their own interests and obligations. So Hearne's orders included requests for reports on alleged copper deposits and information to clear up, if possible, any remaining mystery "respecting a passage out of Hudson Bay into the Western Ocean as hath lately been represented by the American Traveller."

Hearne was to take possession of such Arctic rivers as he might discover "on behalf of the Honourable Hudson's Bay Company." The orders were issued at Fort Prince of Wales, November 6, 1769, and signed by the local governor, Moses Norton, a half-breed of none too fragrant reputation who had been educated in England and returned to the fur trade, where he maintained, according to Hearne who hated him, a rowdy cluster of native wives. Hearne, however, gave him credit for honesty in business, and in the same paragraph retells a rumour to the effect that he poisoned two of his wives.

Hearne had a timely opportunity to equip himself with knowledge of geography and astronomy, for two prominent scientists spent the winter of 1768–69 at Prince of Wales. They were William Wales and Joseph Dymond, who had come out to the Bay as guests of the Company and under instructions from the Royal Society to observe the transit of Venus over the sun on June 3, 1769. Wales was one of the foremost astronomers and mathematicians of his time. He later accompanied Captain Cook on his two voyages around the world.

On November 6, 1769, Samuel Hearne, fur trader, age twenty-four, late of the Royal Navy and ex-mate of a whaler, stepped off into the unknown under a salute of seven guns from Fort Prince of Wales. Barely two hundred miles inland his chief guide and most of the Indians deserted him and his two subordinates. They barely escaped starvation, and were literally brought home to the gates of the fort by two friendly Cree "to my own great mortification, and to the no small surprise of the governor." Hearne still had much to learn about wilderness travel and Indian character.

By February 23 he was away once more. No guns saluted this time, for the snow was too deep on the fort walls, but "the governor, officers and people insisted on giving us three cheers." Hearne had determined to take no other white men with him, and Norton made the odd error of sending no Indian women. Hearne learned quickly now the essentials of northern travel; the importance of women for cooking and clothing maintenance; how to exist on raw fish or porcupine; the improvidence and gluttony of the natives; the wisdom of light equipment.

"It may justly be said to have been all feasting or all famine," he wrote. And the title "the land of feast and famine" has been given many times since to the Barrens and their sparsely timbered fringe.

Through the spring and brief summer, Hearne's Indians took him on a clumsy circuit of the Barren Lands within a triangle of the Churchill mouth, Dubawnt Lake where the ice never completely melts, and Chesterfield Inlet. In July, after alternative diet of fish, deer meat cooked in blood, and raw musk ox, followed by periods of hunger and acute indigestion, Hearne stayed for a time in an encampment of about six hundred Indians who were living richly in that desolate land, on the passing caribou.

Early in August his quadrant, in which lay any hope of accurate geographical data, was blown over and shattered. A few days later a band of Northern Indians firmly, but without violence, looted him and his southern Indian party of everything they cared to take. They had the humanity to leave him bare necessities, including soap, razor, and, happily, his papers. Hearne started back to the fort. Game was plentiful, and he fell in with several bands of Indians going down to trade their furs. His greatest good fortune was his meeting with a southern Indian named Matonabee whose manner and bearing appealed to him from their first encounter. Matonabee sensed the English-man's plight, furnished him with "a good warm suit of otter and other skins," and upon learning of his disappoint-ment in not reaching the Coppermine River, volunteered to undertake a better-equipped expedition later in the same winter. "He was the most sociable, kind and sensible Indian I had ever met with," Hearne wrote. It is a reasonable supposition that Matonabee was the model for countless glamorous redskins who appeared in European fiction of succeeding generations. He had unquestionably many of those qualities of courage and nobility which romance attributed too freely to the North American Indian. Hearne was back within the comforting walls of the fort on November 25.

Twelve days later he was away again. One must have an intimate familiarity with northern winter to appreciate the quiet courage of this third attempt. In the fur trade, where time moved slowly and thirty years passed in the building of a fort, and policy changed only with generations, it would have been completely reasonable for young Hearne to wait another year. But he was mastering Arctic travel, and, though he was not in the true sense a geographer, those forces which possess and drive men on in exploration had apparently touched him.   Above all he had a clear-cut sense of duty.

"In order to understand Hearne's achievement," writes Professor Brebner in his *Explorers of North America*, "it is necessary to remember that Churchill stood on the dividing margin between the forest belt and the barrens. A line drawn from the mouth of the Churchill north-west to the Mackenzie delta, with slight bulges to the north-west for the basins of Great Slave and Great Bear lakes, indicates approximately the northern limit of the forests. 'And to the Eastward of the woods,' (Hearne wrote) 'on the barren grounds, whether hills or vallies, there is a total want of herbage except moss, on which the deer feed.' The surface is rough and broken, sometimes with rocky hills, and often strewn with boulders. The northern tundra is rather better watered than the slight precipitation would suggest, but the streams, when open, are too shallow and rocky to be navigable for far.   The maintenance of human life in its wastes depended on unceasing vigilance and skill in living off the scattered game, notably the herds of caribou and musk oxen.   It was much more difficult than living off the buffalo because of the migrations of these animals, but the Chipewyans and other Athapaskans could manage it, as the Eskimos, their successors, do today.   They had to do so, increasingly, for the Crees were steadily pushing them out of the more bountiful forests. Hearne could never have kept himself alive by his own resources.   We must think of him as having been guided and supported by the Indians."

It was no dash to the Arctic.   Often they moved barely four or five miles a day, and the party varied from sixteen (including Matonabee's seven prized wives, selected for stalwart stature) to several hundred migrant caribou hunters and their families.   Hearne may annoy the geographers by being somewhat out in his observations, but he was a good reporter and put down a highly interesting account of all he saw of Indian life, including birth, death, marriage, adultery, murder, hunting, fishing and war.   Month after month they moved on west and northward.   As they

neared the country of the Copper Indians, Hearne's natives
prepared for war with the hereditary enemy, the Eskimo.
The women were left behind, and they quickened their
pace through a July blizzard followed by sultry heat and
voracious mosquitoes.

They reached Coppermine River on July 13. Descending
the river on the 17th, they fell upon an Eskimo encampment
at a spot since known as Bloody Falls. Hearne's account
of the slaughter of these sleeping Eskimo is as harrowing
a passage as any in fur trade history. He had attempted
to dissuade the Indians, but quickly found they were fired
with a blood thirst which for the time changed them from
a rabble into a disciplined, murderous crew with a unity
of purpose he had never seen before. The Eskimo had no
chance to fight. Those who survived the first knife blows
rushed naked from their tents to be struck down in the
open. A girl died writhing and clutching at Hearne's feet,
transfixed with two Indian spears. He begged for her life,
and while she was "twining round their spears like an eel,"
the Indians jeered at him until he besought them to dispatch
her quickly.

"Even at this hour," he wrote years later, "I cannot
reflect on the transactions of that horrid day without
shedding tears." Exactly fifty years afterwards, on July 17,
1821, Sir John Franklin with John Richardson and George
Back, stood on this spot and observed the skulls and bones
still strewn about.

Hearne turned with relief to his duties, and on July 18
located the copper mine which from Indian legend had so
fired European imagination. This beckoning Eldorado
was "no more than an entire jumble of rocks and gravel,"
about thirty miles south east from the river's mouth. A
four-pound lump of copper was the best he could find after
some hours' search. Hearne carried the piece back to the
Bay, and after many years in Hudson's Bay House, London,
it was presented to the British Museum where it may be
seen today.

Hearne had reached the Arctic Ocean.

The lakes froze over in September as they retreated south to Great Slave Lake. Game was plentiful that winter, and they kept moving eastward, Hearne's Indians looting any weaker parties they encountered. He reached Fort Prince of Wales on June 30, 1772, "having been absent 18 months and 23 days on this last expedition; but from my first setting out . . . two years seven months and 24 days."

Hearne had no exaggerated opinion of the importance of his work. His deepest satisfaction came from the knowledge that he had carried out his orders, and from his confidence that he had settled the North West Passage mystery:

"Though my discoveries are not likely to prove of any material advantage to the Nation at large, or indeed to the Hudson's Bay Company, yet I have the pleasure to think that I have fully complied with the orders of my Masters, and that it has put a final end to all disputes concerning a North West Passage through Hudson's Bay. It will also wipe off, in some measure, the ill-grounded and unjust aspersions of Dobbs, Ellis, Robson, and the American Traveller [one of the anonymous pamphleteers]; who have all taken much pains to condemn the conduct of the Hudson's Bay Company, as being averse from discoveries, and from enlarging their trade."

Hearne's book is one of the greatest in the library of northern travel. The reticence of the Company marked most of its men, and meagre indeed are the books written from within the service. The Governor and Committee received his manuscript report with enthusiasm, and awarded him a bonus of two hundred pounds.

An increasing number of canoes were coming west, and the interlopers carried back to Montreal thousands of choice furs. By 1772 Andrew Graham, an officer of long service (whose private hobby was the collection of specimens for the Royal Society), convinced London of the vital importance of inland establishments to compete with the Montreal "Pedlars." Graham recommended Samuel Hearne, with

Matthew Cocking as his assistant, to start the peaceful offensive.

On June 23, 1774, they left York with eleven men and four Indians, moving up the Hayes River. A year later Hearne returned to York with Cumberland House established on the Saskatchewan, and bringing the year's results of fur trading. He remained barely a fortnight at York, and returned to the new post. That autumn he received his appointment to command Fort Prince of Wales.

Fort Prince of Wales, for all the strength of its walls and the power of its cannon, had a brief and uninspiring history. The Company was determined not to be caught again by the French with only log "palisadoes" for defence, and in 1732, after due deliberation, the first foundation stone had been laid for the most pretentious post the Bay had ever known at the mouth of the Churchill River on Hudson Bay. Stone and lime were close at hand; labour was cheap, and time not very important. For more than thirty years the work proceeded until the Adventurers must have felt a sense of timeless security with their subarctic fortress of stone walls thirty to forty feet thick, measuring three hundred feet by three hundred feet.

The very proportions of Fort Prince of Wales, and the casual regard for the passing of years during its construction, are significant of the Company in the eighteenth century. There was a calm assurance about its moves that completely offset such disasters as the sacking of the fort they had thought impregnable. Hearne was only thirty years of age when he took command of it in January, 1776. His orders were to continue the white whale fishery operations, extend the fur trade to the northward, and to press "Inland Discoveries as the surest means of promoting Our Trade and the Public Interest." The proprietors were leaving no loopholes for future Dobbses.

Hearne had sick leave in Europe, and returned to his command with instructions to set up posts inland from the mouth of the Churchill. His plans were violently interrupted by the appearance of the ancient enemy the French.

The ruins of Fort Prince of Wales, at the mouth of the Churchill River, established by the Company, 1731. Against the horizon is the Canadian Government's grain elevator at Churchill, Manitoba terminus of the Hudson Bay Railway

Hearne's name in stone, Fort Prince of Wales, Churchill

Within the walls of Fort Prince of Wales, on that August day of 1782, were thirty-nine Englishmen. Why the garrison was so slim has never been adequately explained. Perhaps the new energies being directed against the Canadian traders absorbed most of the personnel, estimated at that time at about five hundred men. More than forty years had passed since there had been an armed enemy in the Bay, a long period of peace; for a Company that had never acquired a militant character it was long enough to allow powder to get damp and side-arms rusty.

Hearne knew nothing of the war in Europe. La Pérouse appeared with his three war vessels at the mouth of the Churchill, and landed between three and four hundred men. The thing was grotesque. Hearne had hardly enough men to carry powder and shot for two of his forty-two cannon. He surrendered and, with his men, was taken aboard the enemy ships. Next day the French sacked and burned the elaborate buildings, and tried without much success to blow up the walls, leaving them finally, much as they are today, high against the monotonous horizon of the shore.

La Pérouse then proceeded to capture and burn York Factory. It was the last raid into the Bay, France's final touch of flame in the north.

There was public criticism. It was claimed that the French crews were ragged and starved and incapable of any sort of assault on Prince of Wales or York. Details of the captures are obscure, but history is profoundly indebted to Pérouse. He was one of the greatest French geographers; he appreciated Hearne, recognizing in him a brother in exploration, and allowed him to keep his papers, including his priceless journal and notes, on condition that they would be published.

Hearne and his men were released and allowed to return home on one of the Company's ships. Evidently under no official shadow, he was soon re-establishing Churchill in 1783. Prince of Wales was never reoccupied. Five miles upstream from its stone ruins, Hearne built a new frame fort on James Knight's original site "where the Danes had wintered." There the Company traded until 1933 when a new post building was erected in the modern site of Churchill on the south bank. Today it is possible to stand on the ruined ramparts of Prince of Wales and look across the harbour to the port of Churchill where the steel of the Hudson Bay Railway ends and a grain elevator pierces the sky.

In 1784 the results of Hearne's expeditions became public when his route to the Arctic Ocean was incorporated in the general map of the world in the *Introduction to Cook's Third Voyage.*

He returned to England in 1787, retired, and died in 1792. Three years later his book appeared in English and French editions. In 1911 the Champlain Society had the unique privilege of republishing the celebrated *Journey* with the benefit of editing by J. B. Tyrrell, Canadian explorer and geologist, who himself had made two celebrated expeditions across the Barrens in 1893–94. With his party, Mr. Tyrrell was the first white man since Hearne to explore the country between Churchill and the eastern end of Great Slave Lake.

New maps and new political alignments were emerging in Europe and America during the final quarter of the eighteenth century. But for the few hundred men engaged in the fur trade of northern Canada, life continued without major upheavals. The Company, even then old as a trading corporation, had acquired routine methods of operation so rigid that they resisted all change until it was forced upon them by the "Pedlars" from Montreal.

After the turn of the century, policy became more decisive. In the early days Indians came steadily to the Bay with their furs. Then it became necessary to send men inland to persuade them to come. The arrival of the Canadians in the very hunting grounds of the Indians, with quantities of trade goods, compelled the Company to build inland posts. Reluctantly abandoning the old formula, Hudson's Bay men moved further and further westward up the Saskatchewan Valley, following close on the canoes of their rivals into the Athabasca country and the Arctic watershed. Names of English flavour dotted the new maps of Mr. Arrowsmith, that illustrious cartographer—Cumberland House, Brandon House, Oxford House, Nottingham House.

There were other changes. With the inland expansion, officers in command of each unit could no longer be allowed to wait months for London instructions. The proprietors conceded some new measures of authority, and officers were given a graded seniority. The Bay posts became less trading centres and more warehousing depots for incoming goods and outgoing furs. Bonuses for officers and men were granted, and surveyors came to map out the fur kingdom.

Chapter VII

"THE MASTER PEDLARS"

THE lakes and the forests will not see their like again. The epic of the Northwesters moves into fur trade history like a flood released by the British conquest of Canada. In the years between 1759, when Quebec fell, and 1821, when the North West Company merged with the Hudson's Bay Company, these men from Montreal took the continent in their stride; they reached out to the Arctic Ocean; they crossed the Rocky Mountains to build forts on the Pacific Coast. Ambitious to the point of avarice and ruthless to the point of lawlessness, their reckless courage and energy brought its own destruction. But it was a magnificent effort for all that. On the front line of fur trading, where laws did not matter much, and in the courts, where law meant everything, they fought the great Company and its Royal Charter. Always on the offensive, in the end they outreached their own strength.

Washington Irving called them the Lords of the Lakes and Forests. Without that Cæsar touch they could not have won what they did, but their baronial flair was costly, and they took their winnings every year—fortunes in some years—without regard for the future of fur resources or their own corporate existence.

W. Stewart Wallace, who has carried research into the North West Company's history beyond anyone else working in this field, gives a splendid glimpse of this first great Canadian company in the introduction to his *Documents Relating to the North West Company*, published in 1934 by the Champlain Society.

"The story of the Nor'-Westers, though not without its darker pages, is a brilliant chapter in the history of Canada.

No braver or more picturesque band of adventurers ever put it to the touch, to gain or lose it all. Some of them were French-Canadian traders and voyageurs, the sons of those who had followed La Vérendrye to the rivers and prairies of the West in the dying days of the French régime. Others were American frontiersmen who had served their apprenticeship in the fur-trade in the valleys of the Ohio and the Mississippi. Most of them were Scottish High-landers, the sons of those who had come to Canada in Wolfe's army or as United Empire Loyalists in the American Revolution. The number of them who were connected with that gallant regiment, the 78th or Fraser's Highlanders, is remarkable; and it is no less remarkable that the numerous Frasers, McTavishes, and McGillivrays, who played such an important part in the history of the North West Company, nearly all came from Lord Lovat's estates. The names of the North West Company partners sound like a roll-call of the clans at Culloden. These men were hardy, courageous, shrewd, and proud. They spent a good part of their lives travelling incredible distances in birch-bark canoes, shooting rapids, or navigating inland seas. They were wrecked and drowned. They suffered hunger and starvation. They were robbed and murdered by the Indians, and sometimes by one another. They fell the victims of smallpox, syphilis, and rum. Yet they conquered half a continent, and they built up a com-mercial empire, the like of which North America at least has never seen."

The North West Company did not leap fully armed and disciplined into the fur trade. It was ten years after the British were in Montreal and Quebec that the first "Pedlars," as Company men contemptuously named them, were in the valley of the Saskatchewan. By 1774 Samuel Hearne at Cumberland House reported to his employers that more than sixty canoes had come inland from Grand Portage on Lake Superior that year. These were the men from Montreal who were bringing their canoes and goods fifteen hundred miles by river, lake, and portage to challenge the Hudson's Bay Company.

They came mostly as private traders, some backed by

Montreal merchants, others with their own capital invested in the powder, shot, muskets, trinkets and rum they brought laboriously west. They were individualists and capitalists from the start, but they were front-line men who took hazards and discomforts themselves, and, as the Canadian Company emerged from these first years, it was directed by men who knew every portage and rapids between the St. Lawrence and the Saskatchewan. The very nature of the operation barred all but men of uncommon resourcefulness. Consider the prospect of engaging upon a venture requiring a voyage of over a thousand miles by canoe into unmapped territory to trade with savage people and winter among them in a land where game might or might not exist; to turn east again in the spring over the swampy portages and down the fast water; to travel week after week in a cramped canoe, with nights of exposure to rain and the insect pests of early summer. These were adventurers working not in the interest of remote investors, but in their own right.

By 1775 the traders from Montreal had begun to pool their interests in groups. The labour of the portages and the cold, cramped discomfort of winter living often brought them together in a community of interest; not always happily, though, for Matthew Cocking in his Cumberland House journal of 1776 reported, "The Master Pedlars up above are at present at Variance, and some of them parted stocks." It was in this year that the North West Company emerged as a power. Three years later it was a sixteen-share organization, owned by eight groups of traders of celebrated name: Isaac Todd, James McGill, Benjamin and Joseph Frobisher, Simon McTavish, Robert Grant, Peter Pond, Lawrence Ermatinger and others.

Within a few years Simon McTavish, a Montreal and not a "wintering" partner, had elbowed his way to the top. It is likely that he directed the overhauling of the North West Company in 1783 by which several smaller traders were crowded out and other groups agreed to restrict their operations to the south-western area of the upper Mississippi, leaving the known and unknown north-west to the North West Company. It was an adroit manipulation. Young Simon McTavish manœuvred his own personal interests into the position of being the Montreal agent or supply house for the North West Company. By the turn of the century he was the wealthiest man in Montreal, and before his death in 1804, he had purchased an estate in the Highlands of Scotland. He had been known to the fur trade as "the Marquis," for his overbearing manner and possibly because of a taste for good living. If one cares to scramble through some underbrush on the slopes of Mount Royal today, the walls of his unfinished mansion high above Montreal can still be found. Within the gaunt walls Simon McTavish is buried.

McTavish's consolidated group in 1793 had been out for monopoly, but the west was too big and the profits too good, and rivalry broke out again. This time it came from the firm of Gregory, McLeod and Company, also of Montreal. This organization had in its ranks as a clerk, Alexander Mackenzie, destined to become the most famous of all Northwesters as an explorer, who gave his name to the greatest northern river, and was the first white man to cross the North American continent to the Pacific.

The Gregory, McLeod Company struck hard. By 1786 they had followed the Northwesters out of the Great Lakes basin, across the prairie and into the Athabasca country where Peter Pond had established the farthest outpost on the long, thin line of trade communications from Montreal. Pond was an ex-soldier from Connecticut and a veteran of the French and Indian Wars; half literate but with the explorer sense; an amateur geographer whose maps had a definite importance in boundary-making and discovery during the final years of the century. He had led a violent life, and when in the Athabasca country his party clashed with Gregory-McLeod men and killed a partner, John Ross, it was the second incident of the kind in which Peter

Pond had been involved. Back in Montreal, the Marquis
was quick to see that competition involving bloodshed
could not continue. Reprisals would follow unless there
was peace, and the colonial government would be cancelling
trading licences. Gregory, McLeod was brought into the
North West Company, now a forty-six-share organization,
with McTavish and Frobisher still in the key position as
Montreal agents, taking substantial commissions on all the
business of the pool, while the "wintering partners" lived
and directed the business in the interior.

The North West partners met each summer at the field
headquarters, Grand Portage, at the head of Lake Superior.
It was the great depot where trade goods from the east
were unloaded from the large canoes and packed over the
nine-mile portage to be loaded again into the smaller
canoes for the Rainy Lake, Lake of the Woods, and

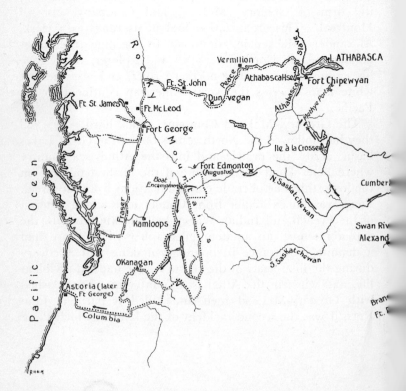

Winnipeg River route to the Saskatchewan and Athabasca country. After 1800, when the international boundary placed Grand Portage in United States territory, the headquarters were shifted north to Kaministiquia (Fort William, Ontario) and a new portage route chosen.

At this palisaded fort, several acres in extent, on the shores of the greatest of the Great Lakes, the Lords of the North met each summer to wrangle for days over rights and privileges of partnerships, to dine well in the great, portrait-lined mess room, and somehow to evolve policies and unanimity which brought them each year closer to the final test of strength with "the English" on Hudson Bay.

Fortunes were made by the wintering partners between 1787 and 1795. Some returned to Scotland to purchase great houses and acres on their native hills, while others bought French seigniories in Lower Canada. Their fortunes

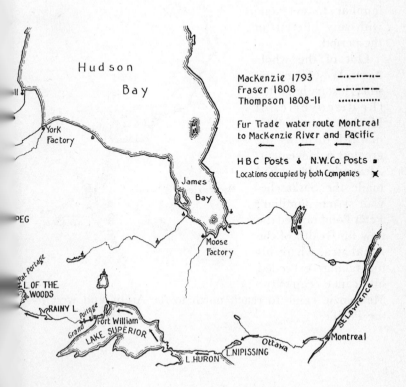

failed to become the cornerstones of powerful families, and for generations it was a commonplace observation that wealth made in the Indian country would not flourish on foreign soil. It has more truth than most generalities, for, with one or two exceptions, the second generation of fur trade families was hounded by lawsuits, debts, and bankruptcy, and the number of former partners, even those of Scottish birth, who died in penury is familiar to everyone with any interest in the period.

Out of the whole North West Company story, history has lifted the discoveries of Mackenzie and rightly marked them as the greatest achievement. Alexander Henry had made the Saskatchewan system familiar; Peter Pond tapped the new fur wealth of the Athabasca, where his fur takings exceeded his canoe capacity;

Mackenzie 1789----·-
    "   1793 ----

Mackenzie came to reach north to the Arctic and west to the Pacific.

Alexander Mackenzie, thoughtful, ardent young Scot from Stornoway, who had a sound apprenticeship of five years as a clerk in a Montreal merchant's office and three years in active fur trading, was sent at the age of twenty-four into the Athabasca country to relieve the veteran Peter Pond. They wintered together at the post near Chipewyan known as the Old Establishment, and the younger man drew much advantage from the association, for Pond had absorbed information from Indians and had many reasonable theories about the unknown contours of the continent.

Mackenzie was a leader of men, handsome, powerful, and intelligent; he was a thruster who drove himself as relentlessly as he drove his men. His active mind made him dislike the enforced isolation of fur trading and the natural outlet for his energies was exploration. Unlike Hearne he had no instructions to explore. On the contrary, his plans had to be made and his expeditions launched with some precautions of secrecy to avoid the displeasure of his partners at Grand Portage.

Mackenzie arranged to have his cousin Roderick McKenzie, the "Dear Rory" of his letters, as a lieutenant. Roderick came ostensibly to build a new Fort Chipewyan, but in reality to command the district while Alexander explored northward during the summer of 1789. The cousin built the fort, and made it more comfortable than most posts of the time. He had books, and each year he sent out for more books which were packed by canoe and portage across half a continent to establish a collection of such proportions that in the nineteenth century it achieved the dignity of a separate building and a catalogue and a fame through the entire north-west. "Little Athens," the fur traders called Chipewyan. A substantial portion of the library is preserved today in Hudson's Bay House, Winnipeg.

Alexander Mackenzie had mastered canoe travel, and in one hundred and two days of that summer he covered three thousand miles, mapped the longest river on the continent, and added substantial evidence against the existence of a

North West Passage. He had found some of the richest fur country in the world, but was disappointed in having found only the Arctic Ocean and not the Pacific at the estuary of the waterway which bears his name. On the very day, July 14, 1789, that the mobs in the streets of Paris were storming the Bastille, Mackenzie set up a post on Whale Island on the Arctic Coast to mark the limit of his endeavour. He had with him an Indian, "English Chief," who had been with Hearne to the Coppermine. When Mackenzie's partners back at Grand Portage learned of the journey, they dismissed the effort as unimportant, and the young man was not surprised.

On a day in June, 1791, on a lonely lake in the far north-west, Mackenzie met a party from the Hudson's Bay Company. They camped side by side, and the Englishman, Philip Turnor, surveyor for the Hudson's Bay Company *en route* to the Athabasca country on a map-making expedition, wrote in his journal:

> "At 7 P.M. Mr. Alex Mackensie the Master of the Athapiscow Lake Settlement and its dependances arrived with one Canoe in which he had 20 Packs of furs besides his own things which is not common for a Canadian Master to have as they mostly keep their own canoe for their own things. He informed me he had Fourteen Canoes more following him. . . . he likewise informed me they had a new settlement up the Peace River. . . ."

Mackenzie the next morning wrote to Roderick back at Chipewyan:

> "Entrance to Lac des Beoufs, June 1, 1791, I met Mr. Turner here this morning. I find the intention of the expedition is discoveries only. I also find the party ill prepared for the undertaking. Mr. Ross wishes to obtain storage from you for some baggage, should the expedition proceed further than your place where, they say, they intend to pass the winter."

Mackenzie was going east to Montreal and England on furlough to study surveying and astronomy in preparation for his second attempt to reach the Pacific. Turnor was the first Company man in the Athabasca, and the kindness he and his party, including Malcolm Ross and Peter Fidler, received from Roderick, made the following winter endurable.

It was the Company's preliminary and typically cautious probing into the far north-west, and Turnor's very presence there gave additional incentive to Mackenzie's ambitions. The relationship between the parties during this chance meeting was not typical of the Pedlars and the English, and it reveals the essential humanity of Mackenzie.

By October, 1792, Mackenzie had returned from England and was at his new establishment just above the juncture of the Peace and Smoky rivers which gave him a starting point two hundred and fifty miles west of Chipewyan for his westward attempt. On May 9, 1793, he pushed off in a twenty-five-foot canoe containing three thousand pounds of gear for ten people: his lieutenant, Alexander McKay, six voyageurs, and two Indians. Up the Peace River Canyon, poling, climbing, portaging, he was on the Parsnip and the Fraser, finally abandoning the canoe to lead his party on a fifteen-day march to the sea. Only determination could have carried it through. "Distressed and distracted," as he admits he was many times, he never failed to command the confidence and loyalty of his party. With seventy- and ninety-pound packs on their backs, they struggled through the tangled forest in heat, mosquitoes and gnats, changing Indian guides almost daily, and moving into hostile country where the leader had to exercise the utmost tact. They were impressed by the advanced culture of the coast Indians, and interested in the signs of trade with the Russians of Alaska. At last, in a condition which did not allow for vigorous celebration, they reached the sea at the outlet of the Bella Coola River.

In vermilion mixed with grease, Mackenzie wrote on a rock, "Alexander Mackenzie, from Canada, by land, twenty-second of July, one thousand seven hundred and ninety-three." Had he been there on June 3 he would have met the crew of one of the ship's boats of Captain Vancouver of the Royal Navy, engaged upon their admirable survey of the British Columbia coast.

Returning, the party more than once nearly collapsed from the strain of constant travel and open threats of natives. Mackenzie never gave a sign of hesitancy or fear, and had his party back at the fort on Peace River by August 24 (seventy-four days out and ninety-three days returning), completing one of the most important commercial and geographical expeditions in the history of Canada.

North West Company partners were still breaking away in disgruntled groups from the central pool. They were too occupied to be impressed by Mackenzie's discoveries. He never returned to the interior country, and retired in 1799 to live in England, where his *Voyages* was published in 1801. It is one of the great travel books of the language, and enjoyed prompt success in several translations. Even Napoleon studied it closely in the hope of discovering some means to strike at the British Empire indirectly.

Mackenzie was knighted, and quickly became a personality in London, but he soon returned to Montreal. His prestige and power were too great now for him to continue in the North West Company. He formed his own syndicate, sent his traders west, and threatened to eclipse the Marquis, Simon McTavish himself. So the opening years of the nineteenth century found the North West Company fighting once more, this time with an enemy known successively as Sir Alexander Mackenzie and Company, the New North West Company, and the X Y Company.

It was the last great struggle between Montreal factions, and the Marquis extended himself. He sent a party to the Pacific Coast, another to the English stronghold in Hudson Bay, and he acquired from the Crown the lease of the King's Posts, the group of establishments the British had taken over from the French on the lower St. Lawrence. The structure was dangerously near over-expansion when Simon McTavish died in 1804, and the old and new companies in Montreal came together, with McTavish's original group dictating severe terms by which Sir Alexander "was excluded from any interference" in the fur trade, despite his shareholder interest. Mackenzie withdrew to his estate in Scotland, but his holdings were large and he continued to make financial bids for control, even buying some Hudson's Bay Company shares.

The North West Company now stood alone, meeting all opposition with harsh, relentless efficiency. It is in these fifteen years before the absorption by the Hudson's Bay Company that fiction writers have found extremes of villainy and heroism. Rum flowed freely; Indians were debauched; some areas were depleted of fur-bearing animals. Wages were trimmed. The half-military structure of clerkships and junior partnerships took rigid form. The partners travelled in light canoes with picked crews and personal servants. Freight went from Lachine to Grand Portage in great canoes thirty-five feet long and six feet wide, capable of carrying five tons including provisions for ten men. The north canoes were about half the size of those paddled below Grand Portage. The transportation system in the interior had only the driving force of the arm and leg muscles of voyageurs, but it achieved astounding efficiency. On the Great Lakes the company had schooners. On salt water its ships carried trade goods from England around the Horn to the Oregon coast and the markets of China.

It was the period of the North West Company's greatest success. With fifteen hundred to two thousand men employed, the profits of fifteen years were estimated at one million one hundred and eighty-five thousand pounds. Dividends of four hundred pounds per share were not uncommon.

The acclaim with which the world had received Mackenzie's discoveries had opened the eyes of the Northwesters, and with the tightening up of their whole organization they came to a new appreciation of the value not only of discovery beyond their immediate fur-bearing areas, but of accurate map-making of their own domain. One David Thompson, of the London Blue Coat School, served their purposes for sixteen years, and has been described as "the greatest land geographer the British race ever produced." His apprenticeship was with the Hudson's Bay Company, but the slow deliberation of their plans could not hold his energies. He served from 1784 to 1797 and then joined the North West Company, becoming a partner in 1804. With that authority and a marvellous freedom of action, this quiet, courageous man travelled tirelessly from the Great Lakes and the headwaters of the Mississippi to the mouth of the Columbia River, surveying and mapping. When he retired in 1812, he prepared a great map of the Canadian north-west upon which all the seventy-eight posts of the Montreal company were marked. This huge map hung for years in the mess hall at Fort William. It survived to become the basis of all subsequent maps of the Canadian west.

He married a half-breed woman of the west, and they had sixteen children. After being employed on surveys of the Canada–United States boundary, he died at Longueuil near Montreal in extreme poverty and neglect.

Only with great reluctance, one leaves this biographical side of the North West Company history to move on with the chronicle of the Hudson's Bay Company. The rich diversity of their origins, their careers, and their destinies, continues to hold deep satisfaction for those who explore fur trade history. Five Camerons, fourteen Grants, eight McGillivrays, seven Frasers, and fifteen McKenzies were Northwesters during the five decades of its rise and fall. If there is a shred of colour in the history of Scottish people, surely it will be here.

Professor Wallace, in the Champlain Society volume, has assembled by brilliant research the essential biographical material on two hundred and sixty Northwesters, many of whom later became commissioned officers of the Hudson's Bay Company. Here, one can only examine in passing the parts they played, and hope that some day a Scott or a

Sir Alexander Mackenzie (1764–1820)

John Stuart (1779–1847).

m McGillivray with his wife and child.
(1764–1825)

Joseph Frobisher (1740–1810).

FOUR NORTHWESTERS

Chief Factor (Dr.) John McLoughlin (1784–1857), North West
Company partner who, after the Union, ruled the Oregon for the
Hudson's Bay Company

Dumas who knows prairie skies and mountain canyons, who has felt the death threat of western blizzards, and seen the ice go roaring out of the great rivers in spring, will come upon the life stories of these Scots and stir men's minds with heroic tales.

A fluency which is quite extraordinary in the light of their occupation has given added zest to fur trade annals. In an age of stilted writing, their journals and letters are often pungent, nearly always lucid, and those who settled down to the writing of memoirs are rarely dull. Even the minutes of the North West Company meetings could break into salty sarcasm from time to time. The writings of their men were scattered beyond all hope of recovery when the company lost its identity, and only during the last forty years has any serious work been done in gathering up and publishing North West material. Most of the books published have been by learned societies or universities.

It was not entirely a story of canoes and counting houses. In Montreal the full-blooded lives of these men found outlet in the Beaver Club where hospitality was famous. The club was founded in 1785 with nineteen members who qualified by having wintered in the north-west, "the *pays d'en haut.*" Later the membership numbered fifty-five men. The club met fortnightly in winter; fines such as six bottles of Madeira were imposed for neglect of exacting rules and ritual. Members wore large gold medals on club nights, and on the unvarying toast list were: "the fur trade in all its branches," and "voyageurs, wives and children." Pemmican, the dried buffalo meat mixed with berries and fat which was the staple food of the fur trade, was brought from the Saskatchewan to be served in the unfamiliar atmosphere of mahogany, silver and candle glow. After hours of dining and drinking, the climax of the evening was "The Grand Voyage." Members and guests sat on the floor in a row as if in a great canoe. With fire tongs, swords of soldier guests, or walking sticks, for paddles, they dipped and swung to the rhythm of voyageur songs. It was all very brilliant, expensive, and probably extremely noisy.

I

One September night in 1808, thirty-one members and guests sat down to dine. The bill has survived.

32 dinners	£12
29 bottles of Madeira at	6/
19 bottles of Port at	5/
14 bottles of Porter at	2/6
12 quarts ale	8/
7 suppers	8/9
Brandy and gin	2/6
Cigars, pipes, tobacco	5/
Three wine glasses broken	3/9
Total	£28.12/

The club that night had a notable list of rollicking fur traders. Presiding was Joseph Frobisher, then sixty-eight years of age. Alexander Henry, the elder, was vice-chairman. The "Cork" was William McKay, a recently retired partner. His brother Alexander, who had crossed the mountains with Mackenzie and was later murdered on the ship *Tonquin*, was also present. About the table were such fur trade celebrities as William McGillivray, James McGill, whose fortune established McGill University; Isaac Todd, Josiah Bleakley, John Gregory, George Gillespie, Roderick McKenzie, Thomas Thain, who died insane after bankruptcy; General Drummond, who succeeded General Isaac Brock in command of the Montreal garrison; Sir John Johnson, Bart., superintendent-general of Indian Affairs; Colonel Sheaffe, who assumed command after Brock was killed at Queenston Heights; John McDonald of Garth, builder of Rocky Mountain House; Archibald Norman McLeod, active in the later feud with Lord Selkirk; Alexander McKenzie, cousin of Sir Alexander Mackenzie; John Jacob Astor, that rising citizen of New York, who had just established the American Fur Company and was on his autumn buying trip to Montreal.

On other occasions the dinner list included Sir John Franklin, Lord Selkirk and Washington Irving. Not all the North West Company partners were active on these spirited

occasions, but most of them were members of the club.
From the fragmentary records of its life, one thing is
abundantly clear: the Beaver Club was an animated
expression of the *esprit de corps* of the North West Company.

The partners lived and worked intensively, as men who
relished power for its own sake. Within the circle of their
lives, they applied themselves so closely to the consummation
of ambition that they ultimately miscalculated the power
of the forces they were to fight. The very sweep of their
success in the first years of the nineteenth century carried
them beyond their power to recover, and close profit-taking
left no reserves to meet the prolonged test of strength with
the Hudson's Bay Company. Moreover they could not,
in their most visionary speculations, have anticipated the
nature of the attack which was gathering inevitably against
them.

Chapter VIII

THE CONTEST

WITHOUT a map sense and some judgment of distance, the heroic scale of the fur trade's nineteenth-century history becomes a jumble of place names. It was essentially a geographic conquest. The wringing of wealth from fur trading allowed no temporizing with the elements. The extremes of summer and winter in the north swing swiftly, inexorably through their annual cycle, demanding from all who would travel there a sureness of timing. It has always been so. Weather is the final arbiter, and profits could only be won by intelligent men who could adapt themselves to its dictates and seize upon its concessions to exploit the resources of the remote places.

Look at the maps to grasp the position of the fur companies at the beginning of the last century. Start from Montreal and trace the long thread of the canoe route to the north-west by the Ottawa River, on across the upper Lakes to Fort William. Over this tenuous way came all the Canadian trade goods; hundreds of men, hundreds of canoes, and tons of goods in summer. Then follow on west by the waterways of the prairies, and the routes fan out west, north-west, and south to the posts of the North West Company. Trace the line on up the prairie rivers, over the northern watershed, and down to Athabasca Lake and the Peace River, where the waters of the Rockies start to the Arctic in the great valley of Mackenzie's River, as the fur traders called it. This is not all; the trail crosses the Rockies, for in 1812 the North West Company bought out John Jacob Astor's Astoria at the mouth of the Columbia River. Outgoing goods and returning furs; an expensive operation, and ever expanding under the pressure of the partners at Fort William.

Consider now those waters draining into Hudson Bay mentioned in the Charter of the Hudson's Bay Company. On the east coast of the Bay are a few posts, only moderately successful, for the great fur-bearing area is not there. South, within the circle of James Bay, are the old original posts, Rupert's House, Moose Factory and Albany House, with the later sprinkling of interior posts to mark resistance to the men from Montreal: Mistassini, Brunswick House, Osnaburgh House, and others with temporary outposts. Good territory this, where the Company appears to have held its own against the invader.

Now look to the south-west and west of Hudson Bay. The Company is still snug on the Bay, but these forts are becoming depots or factories now. More and more trading is done inland. The Company has been forced into the interior to survive. Despite double transportation costs, the Northwesters have threatened their existence. The Company puts its trade goods ashore almost in the heart of the continent; the Montrealers have fifteen hundred expensive canoe miles between them and the Indian country.

When Hearne built Cumberland House in 1774 near The Pas, the rival traders had already been established there for six years. During the next thirty years the Canadians had passed through bitter rivalries and dissensions among themselves, and emerged as a single, fighting, flexible company with posts being established (and abandoned) wherever trade justified it.

During these same thirty years the Hudson's Bay Company roused itself slowly. Travellers returning to York Factory, Moose Factory, or Churchill brought warning reports of the Canadians' inland trade. The Company clung long to the belief that the Indians would continue to come great distances to their posts, even after the Montrealers had set up permanent posts. Then in the ranks a new aggressiveness appeared. No longer did a Governor and Committee have to beg and bribe its men to make inland journeys. On the contrary, volunteers were sufficient, though the proprietors would not concede authority to its men to meet their competitors with the full force of their fighting power. Robert Longmoor, C. T. P. Isham, William Tomison, Philip Turnor, Malcolm Ross, and Peter Fidler were as alert and intelligent as the average of the North West partners, but they worked under the constant restraint of decisions arriving from London two years after a condition was reported demanding immediate action. The entire machinery was retarded, with the consequent dulling of fighting qualities.

The Eldorado of the fur trade was the Athabasca country, reached by the Churchill River to Ile-à-la-Crosse Lake, then north-west over the high ridge, Methye Portage, of thirteen miles, down to the Clearwater River. That racking portage, ultimate test of the voyageur, also known as Portage la Loche, was to become perpetuated in folk song and story. Every traveller and fur trader who wrote of his adventures has an account of its gruelling demands on the legs and backs of men, and most of them are lifted into at least a moment of excitement by the thrilling view across the valleys to the north at the peak of the portage. This was the rampart which separated the Saskatchewan Valley from the river system of the Mackenzie. Peter Pond went over in 1778, and it has been estimated that half the profits of the North West Company came over Methye Portage.

It was 1803 before the Hudson's Bay Company got a fur trading post there, though Philip Turnor explored it in the summer of 1791–92, and saw the potentialities of the country. At the conclusion of this expedition he volunteered to return to set up a permanent establishment, but the little council of his superiors at York Factory ruled against it. They shrank from the responsibility of such a decision without consulting London. Turnor's journal entry on the final day of his two years' travel reveals the restraining hand that was ever upon bolder spirits:

July 17, 1792: "Thursday continued on and the Musketoes came of the shore in such clouds that they nearly blinded us at 9 AM we arrived at the Factory found all well and not a single Canoe set of for any of the Inland Settlements. In the evening I made an Offer to Willm Tomison Mr. Joseph Colen and Counsel to return to the Athapiscow Country but my offer was not accepted as will appear by the York Factory Correspondence One objection that of the Mens unreasonable demands I am not acquainted with the method used to come at that necessary information I have made some enquiry but could not learn that a Single man had been asked either to return or the terms they expected in case they should be wanted to return to the Athapiscow Country but as my duty I made an inquiry of those that had been before and whose example many was ready to follow when the difficulty of procuring men was talked of I informed the Counsel that the men which had been with me was ready to return and that of course two Canoes was ready Mr. Tomison desired to know which of them had proposed it I said Robert Garrock was the first that spoke of it but they would all agree to return with me and Mr. Ross upon which Mr. Tomison went and engaged him as Steersman of his own Canoe so that I was fully convinced he had set his face against any undertaking to the Northward shall conclude with my wishes that the greatest Success may attend the Honourable Company and remain their

Dutifull and Obedient
Humble Servant to Command
PHILIP TURNOR."

London might suggest more aggressive action from time to time, but with local governors on the Bay competing against one another from York, Moose, and Churchill, and the inland parties being victimized and inadequately equipped, and with corruption among ship captains, there was small hope for powerful, concerted action. Besides, no Company man in Canada had authority to make bold decisions. With little appreciation of geography, climate or native character, it was the merest fumbling and groping for a group of London merchants to direct the minute details of the exploitation.

The speed and distance of the North West Company drives could be comprehended only with a grasp of (1) the freight-carrying canoe as it was evolved by the Canadians, and (2) the capacity for canoe labour of the French Canadian and half-breed voyageurs. In *The Fur Trade in Canada*, Professor H. A. Innis has said that the North West Company was "built on the work of the French voyageur, the contributions of the Indian, especially the canoe, Indian corn and pemmican, and the organizing ability of Anglo-American merchants."

Sir Alexander Mackenzie conceded to the Hudson's Bay Company a strength which most historians have been reluctant to admit. Describing the competitive position of the two companies after 1774 in his famous *Voyages*, published in 1801, he noted that although the Hudson's Bay Company had followed the Canadians post by post up the Saskatchewan, they were overtaking their rivals in trade:

"The traders from Canada succeeded for several years in getting the largest proportion of their furs, till the year

1793, when the servants of that company thought proper to send people amongst them (and why they did not do so before is best known to themselves) for the purpose of the trade and securing their credits, which the Indians were apt to forget. From the short distance they had to come, and the quality of goods supplied, the trade has, in a great measure, reverted to them, as the merchants from Canada could not meet them upon equal terms."

History and fiction have justly given at this period the front of the stage to the Northwesters. There was moneyed success and splendid arrogance about their half-century; a pace was set which the older company could not quite pass, and which they themselves could not maintain indefinitely. In the literature on the race between the two companies, the remarkable vitality of the Hudson's Bay Company has been disregarded. While the Company was not conditioned to meet the opponent on equal terms, it had gathered through a century of operation a certain toughness of fibre which substantially compensated for its lack of speed in operation.

The dividends paid the proprietors in the eighteenth century are a record of stability any corporation might envy. From 1721, when the capital stock was increased to £103,950, until 1783 the Hudson's Bay Company never missed a dividend, and in those sixty-two years the dividend only twice went as low as 7 per cent., and for thirty-six years it was 10 per cent. This period, it should be noted, included the Seven Years' War and the American Revolution. There were no dividends for 1783, 1784 and 1785, "on account of the heavy loss sustained by the destruction of Prince of Wales and York Forts in Hudson Bay by a squadron of French ships of war," according to the minute book. In those years, also, smallpox ravaged the Indians. A 5 per cent. dividend was resumed in 1786, rising to 8 per cent. in 1792, 1793, and 1794, but dropping to 4 per cent. in 1801 and continuing at that level until 1808. These were not spectacular profits, but they represent a consistent return to shareholders over twenty-three years during which some historians have variously described the Company as exhausted and on the verge of ruin. The Napoleonic Wars closed the markets of northern Europe, and the warehouses became congested with unsold furs, so no dividends were declared from 1809 to 1814, though the Governor and Committee were able to tell the proprietors that "affairs at their Factories and Settlements" continued to prosper. Four per cent. dividends were resumed again, and continued for the remaining seven years until the union of the North West and Hudson's Bay Companies in 1821. It is worth noting in advance of the chronology of events, that dividends were paid regularly for the next fifty-six years. A century of fur trading and only eight years without profits to shareholders. No one could complain. Throughout the century from 1720 to 1820 the number of shareholders varied from fifty to one hundred and nine.

Another measure of trading strength, which discounts any generalization on the Company's disastrous loss of trade to the Canadians, is found in the British customs imports from Hudson Bay. While customs valuation has no bearing on the prices furs brought at auction, it gives a fair basis for comparison over the years. Between 1799 and 1807 the Company shipped into England furs valued at from ten thousand pounds to twenty thousand pounds each season, and only in the four years before the companies merged did the customs valuation go below twenty thousand pounds. In 1808, a dividendless year, they appealed to the government for relief from customs duties.

Clearly the fur trade was not being entirely lost by the Company. Trade was increasingly costly in exported goods and in wages, but the English gave no indication of surrender, and dividends were interrupted only by acts of war.

The building of inland posts was the most drastic departure from the century-old policy of maritime trading which the rivalry forced upon the Hudson's Bay Company. Remembering the one or two years necessary for orders in London to be translated into action in Canada, this inland

expansion assumed the proportions of a substantially
energetic campaign. "Their Honours" in London had no
intention of allowing any of their officers in the Bay to run
away with their investment by frenzied building of forts
on rivers and lakes which they had not yet seen even
pinpointed on their maps.

By 1778 the old Company was stirring itself. Gouty old
Humphrey Marten, chief at York Factory, with his second-
in-command, William Stephenson, the surgeon, dispatched
William Tomison to Cumberland House with the following
letter of instruction:

> "We the chief and Council for the Honorable the
> Hudson's Bay Company at York Fort having taken into
> our most serious Consideration the Situation of the
> Companys Affairs Inland are greatly alarmed at the
> Information We have received from You and Other
> Persons of the greatly increased numbers of Canadian
> Traders that now overspread almost this country and
> have absolutely blocked up every Passage to their Honor's
> Inland Settlement, as most of those to York Fort. In
> Order to prevent as much as possible the apparent
> approaching increasing Evils from intirely destroying the
> Natives and consequently the Company's Trade, We think
> it necessary to You to send off from the Inland Settlements
> as soon as possible after Your arrival at that place Robert
> Longmoor with what men can be spared and an assort-
> ment of Goods that may be requisite for the Indians tribes
> that now are hindered by the Canadian Traders from
> coming to You; Robert Longmoor hath faithfully prom-
> ised to go as far as any of the Canadians shall Inland, and
> to do his Utmost for his Master's Interest; in Considera-
> tion of his known abilities, Fidelity and Courage, We have
> agreed to his signing a Contract for one Year at 30£ Per
> Annum, but as it was impossible either to get Goods from
> hence Inland or to supply Robert Longmoor with Men
> sufficient to assist him in his intended Journey; We have
> entertained Willm. Oman one Year at 12£ with this
> Clann, that should the Honorable Committee agree to
> give their other Servants whom are now at William
> Oman's Wages a higher Salary, He shall receive an equal

benefit; James Banks two Years and on the same Conditions, James Spence late Servant to Mr. Martin is engaged to serve the Company two Years at 10£; Isaac Batt having desired to have a quantity of Goods delivered to Him in trust to trade for his Masters benefit, Should You think it prudent so to do, We desire You will supply him in any Quantity that may be requisite to enable him to promote their Honors Interest; should any other Persons be willing to go on the like Service that You think are fit to be trusted You will please to assist them as farr as is necessary."

The inland move had started. A month later, young Philip Turnor, fresh from England, carried to Cumberland House a further letter from Marten to Tomison:

"By the safe arrival of the Company's ship King George Captain Jonathon Fowler, I received command from the Governor, Deputy Governor and Committee of the Honorable Hudsons Bay Company. . . . It would be highly pleasing to their Honors to have the House in the Buffalo Country settled as soon as possible, and I hope long since Robert Longmoor with sufficient hands and materials have been sent on that Service. I intend next year to augment your number to 26 men, that is if you should think that number requisite, three of whom may be left if convenient at the new Settlement which for distinction sake, you may call Hudson House. I beg Sir you will exert yourself to the Utmost and assure the Companys Servants of having their deserts laid before the board; the building of Canoes should be a primary Object with You; have inclosed three filled up Contracts, which You are to see dated and duly Executed, which you will please to return by the first Conveyance . . . Should you find any thing in the Mineral or Vegetable way worthy their Honors attention You will be carefull to send it; I would advice You to trade full to the York Fort for Prime Wolves or Otters and should any Indian bring You a considerable Number of fine skins, make him a suitable present rather than alter the Standard."

The listing of some of the posts set up about this time

suggests the energy brought to the contest. While some of these have survived as trading posts to this day, many were merely a hut, a stockade, and perhaps a tiny warehouse erected only to be abandoned to meet the shifting demands of the trade. Many were built within sight of the opposition post, and all were the result of competition from Montreal.

1776—Brunswick House.

1778—Grand Rapids House, Lake Winnipeg, at the mouth of the Saskatchewan River.

1779—Hudson House, eighty miles above the Forks of north and south Saskatchewan River.

1783—Frederick House on the Abitibi River.

1786—Manchester House, on the north branch of the Saskatchewan River, forty-two miles above Battleford.
Osnaburgh House, Lake St. Joseph.

1790—Carlton House, on the Assiniboine.
Swan River House on Swan River.
Island House, three miles below Manchester House.
South Branch House, sixty-five miles above the Forks of the Saskatchewan River, on the South Saskatchewan.

1792—Buckingham House, Beaver River.
Nipigon House, on Lake Nipigon.

1793—Brandon House, on the Assiniboine six miles above the Souris.
Marlborough House, on the Assiniboine.

1795—Green Lake House, upper Churchill near Reindeer River.
Fairford House, on the Churchill.
Edmonton House, on the upper Saskatchewan River.

1799—Jasper, or Rocky Mountain House, on the upper Athabasca.

1802—Nottingham House, on Lake Athabasca.

In 1821, when the companies united, the Hudson's Bay

Company had seventy-six posts, the Northwesters ninety-seven.

The erection of each fort was a matter of gravest deliberation. The journals of the men, the fort journals, the minute books in London, and outgoing letters to the Bay all attest to the inherent caution which ultimately saved the Company and the fur trade. "Their Honours" played for security of capital and continuity of dividends, and realized both. The Northwesters played long odds for fortunes, and only latterly came to feel any regard for the ultimate survival of their organization as a corporate entity.

The very formal style of letters from subordinate to superior in the Hudson's Bay Company service reveals men who did not quite own their own souls. The loyalty that was to be the supreme glory of the Company was in its infancy. This was an old London Company at the end of the eighteenth century; it could not operate otherwise. Scottish and American traders might be able to make rapid grabs for quick, fabulous profits, but not the Hudson's Bay Company with its hundred-odd shareholders, including a generous number of estates of deceased persons and infants.

An attempt to purchase the Company outright for one hundred and three thousand pounds was made by the North West Company in 1804. Many years later Edward Ellice, then North West agent in London, said the reason the transaction was not completed was because "part of the stock was held by infants and other persons incapable of giving title or making transfer," which would have made Chancery Court action necessary.

It seems curious that the North West Company wanted complete ownership when control would have been enough for their purpose. Lord Selkirk bought control in 1811. Where the competition between the two methods of operation would have led, had Selkirk not seized and shaken up the whole Hudson's Bay operation, is a nice speculation in commercial history. Until Selkirk planted his agricultural settlers in Rupert's Land on the banks of the Red River,

the relationship between the two companies had not
reached the violence which had marked the Northwesters'
feud with the X Y Company. Sharp, unethical practices
were frequent, but actual physical violence was uncommon.

In the Northwesters' writings there is a common note of
contempt for the English, probably born of their own sureness of action, independence, and easy familiarity with
wilderness life learned from their French-Canadian voyageurs. Yet when rivals met on the fur trade routes, they
were friendly enough. Daniel Harmon, a New Englander
of the North West Company, whose published journal is
one of the best of the period, tells of coming down the
Assiniboine with furs, and arriving at Fort Alexandria on
May 27, 1805:

> "Last evening Mr. Chaboillez (manager N. W. Com-
> pany) invited the people of the other two forts to a dance;
> and we had a real North-West country ball. When three-
> fourths of the people had drunk so much as to be incapable
> of walking straight the other fourth thought it was time
> to put an end to the ball, or rather bawl. This morning
> we were invited to breakfast at the Hudson's Bay House
> with a Mr. McKay and in the evening to a dance. This,
> however, ended more decently than the one of the pre-
> ceding evening."

Another Harmon entry, of 1807:

> "Two of the Hudson's Bay people arrived from Fort des
> Prairies, who were so obliging as to bring me letters from
> several gentlemen in that quarter. The greater part of
> the North West and Hudson's Bay people live on amicable
> terms; and when one can with propriety render a service
> to the other, it is done with cheerfulness."

At Christmas all barriers were dropped, and amenities
of the season observed. John McKay, of the Hudson's Bay
Company, writes on December 25, 1799, "I had the
honour of my Neighbours (from the North West fort)
company to dinner; your Honours has the honour of
bearing the expences."

James Sutherland reported hospitality at Brandon House in his journal, December 26, 1796. "Had dinner with Mr. McDonell (of the North West Company) was treated with good Madeira Wine and had a grand Dinner."

Years earlier, in the very beginning of Canadian inroads on the west, there had been many pleasant encounters. One of the earliest meetings mentioned was when Alexander Henry and the Frobishers paused at Cumberland House and were greeted by "a Mr. Cockings, by whom, though unwelcome guests, we were treated with much civility."

The way of life was to be changed by conditions which the fur traders never anticipated. By 1811 a policy had been formulated in London which brought upon the fur trade ten years of violence, recrimination, and incidents of bloodshed more savage than the north-west had known since white men came. With all the immediately disastrous effects of the new policy to which the Hudson's Bay Company found itself committed, there survived the foundation stones, though the structure was crushed for a time, of the ultimate agricultural settlement of western Canada. The new policy, also, for all its distress, became the basis of the Hudson's Bay Company's greatest fur trade power.

Chapter IX

A GENTLEMAN UNAFRAID

THOMAS DOUGLAS, fifth Earl of Selkirk, was a personable young Scottish peer with the best that ancestry, Edinburgh University, and a grand tour on the Continent, could give. He married well, managed his estate admirably, and turned up in London for the season. Walter Scott was an intimate friend, and Byron a nodding acquaintance. He had seven centuries of fighting blood in his veins, and he was a Whig with advanced humanitarian sensibilities. His marriage to Jean Wedderburn Colvile, in 1807, brought him happiness at a time when his career was giving promise of brilliant heights not far ahead. But Selkirk's marriage brought him shares in the Hudson's Bay Company, and so turned his footsteps into a strange bypath of empire destined to lead him on and on into ten years of struggle with the North West Company in far-away America; and finally he was to die, shattered in body if not in spirit, from this encounter of a truly gallant soul with the Lords of the Lakes and Forests. Lord Selkirk, a gentleman unafraid, never seemed to comprehend the full fighting strength of the Scottish-Canadian fur traders, and poured out his energy and personal fortune in an attempt to shatter their organization, which he firmly believed to be a vicious association and a menace to law and liberty. The story of Selkirk and his settlement on the banks of the Red River is one of the strangest in the history of British colonization.

By the time he was thirty, the furthering of emigration to the British colonies had become the great philanthropy to which Lord Selkirk had committed himself. To find new homes in America under the British flag for the thrifty, sturdy Scottish crofters who were being turned out of their cottage in the notorious Highland "clearances" was a worthy cause for an enlightened young Scottish peer. Selkirk, after years of examination of the prospects, succeeded in placing on Prince Edward Island eight hundred of his countrymen, and the enterprise was regarded as successful. A second attempt in southern Ontario, near Chatham, was a failure, but the circumstances were such that Selkirk's belief in his cause was unshaken.

The Wedderburn-Colvile family circle brought wealth and political support to the young peer's overseas colonization plans. Visiting Montreal in 1804 to arrange for the establishment of his Prince Edward Island settlement, Selkirk, as guest of the Beaver Club, heard much about the fur trade and the "Indian country" of the west. His writings of these years also indicate an interest in the possibilities of settlement in the upper Mississippi country.

By 1808 a plan had taken form. The Hudson's Bay Company was to be the instrument of policy and of a new settlement of Irish and Scottish people on the banks of the Red River. When Selkirk set out to purchase sufficient additional Hudson's Bay stock to give him a place on the Committee, he found Sir Alexander Mackenzie interested in the same property. In his *Voyages* Mackenzie had suggested a union of the two companies. When he had returned to Canada, formed a rival company to the North-westers, and in turn amalgamated with them and retired to Scotland, he soundly advised them to buy out the Hudson's Bay enemy in London rather than fight it out in the fur trade in Canada. They did not take the advice, and Mackenzie bought Hudson's Bay stock on his own account. For a time Lord Selkirk and he pooled their interests in buying Hudson's Bay shares, but the purposes of the prospective buyers were so divergent that they soon parted, with the ex-fur trader threatening suit for some of the stock. Then young Selkirk purchased enough stock to control the Company.

In May, 1811, the Hudson's Bay Company granted Selkirk in fee simple one hundred and sixteen thousand square miles, which today includes parts of Manitoba, Minnesota and North Dakota. Mackenzie and one or two other North West men who had acquired Hudson's Bay shares, attended the General Court that year and denounced the whole enterprise as "wild." Realizing that here was a new enemy and that they had been beaten on the first move, North West partners then in London met to decide the next move. This colony "would strike at the very existence of our trade," they wrote. The man with the plough was to be placed across the vital route by which all North West transportation moved. The forks of the Assiniboine and Red rivers (Winnipeg today) was the very crossroads of their highways, and now it had been given like a town lot to a "Bible peer" who had never been west of Lake Ontario and did not know a beaver from a musquash. They wrote to the Montreal partners about the new opposition and a "year of trial" which might be expected. The express canoes carried the news west, and in a few weeks the partners in far Athabasca had been warned to expect trouble.

Selkirk had hoped for the full support of the Governor and Committee for his colonization plan, but beyond the security of capital and maintenance of dividend they did not care to go. It became the Selkirk family's own venture, though that did not keep Lord Selkirk from moving actively into Company affairs, and he complained of "the jog trot mode in which the Company's concerns have hitherto been carried on." Within a year the men in the isolated log forts became aware of new energies at work in the service and a crisper note of command in the annual orders from London. Selkirk realized that his colony must have the sympathetic support of the fur traders themselves, and already he felt North West opposition. "I have every reason to expect that every means the North West Company can attempt to thwart it will be resorted to," he wrote in December, 1811. An ominous forecast.

Six months earlier, his advance party of seventy had left Stornoway, Scotland, but only after encountering every imaginable obstacle from terror propaganda, customs delays, and desertion, all directly traceable to North West Company influences in London. These were not strictly emigrant settlers, but men employed by Selkirk personally to prepare the way for the permanent colony. After a crossing of sixty-one days, they were coolly received at York Factory and sent up the Nelson River to make their own winter quarters. Their commander was an ex-soldier, Miles Macdonell, whose energy and resourcefulness were sorely taxed between internal dissensions and discontent sown among the newcomers by the Hudson's Bay men at York. The Company's officers even recruited openly for fur traders from the settlers' ranks. "The old hands have done their utmost to corrupt all my people," Macdonell wrote to Selkirk.

The spring of 1812 came, and while far to the south on the frontier Canadians armed to repel United States invaders, Miles Macdonell led twenty-three of Selkirk's men seven hundred miles inland from Hudson Bay, and on the banks of the Red River set up the first building of the colony. This was no bedraggled, spiritless party of squatters, but the advance guard of an agricultural colony, proceeding under instructions from the proprietor of the land. Accordingly, the legal ceremony was carried out with a flourish on September 4, 1812. On the east bank of the Red River, Macdonell, as Selkirk's deputy, with an armed guard and colours, took seizin from Hillier, of the Hudson's Bay Company. A few half-breeds, some Indians, and three of the "N. W. Co. gentlemen" stood by to watch the bit of ritual which made the young Scottish lord the owner of one hundred and sixteen thousand square miles in the valleys of the Red and Assiniboine rivers. The North West men returned to their Fort Gibraltar on the other side of the Red, and sent dispatches to their Fort William headquarters with the news. Macdonell moved his people out to the buffalo pasturing grounds on the prairie, where

half-breeds could be employed to provide food for the
winter. He left a few men near the Forks to establish
Fort Douglas, named after Selkirk, on the west bank of the
Red, and the headquarters of the colony.

The act of taking over the property irrevocably completed the transaction in Selkirk's mind. There could be
no possible question of his rights under British law. What
he described as the "unimpeachable validity of these rights
of property," became the rock upon which he anchored all
his aspirations, and upon which he fought for the next
nine years. If the Royal Charter of the Hudson's Bay
Company was worth a pen scratch, his title to this land
was beyond challenge. These claims, he wrote, "are
universally considered as clear and indisputable." On
them he was to stake his fortune and his life.

Selkirk disliked fur trading. "It is a business that I hate
from the bottom of my heart," he wrote. If the Royal
Charter granted a theoretical monopoly, it also granted
land title, and Selkirk was prepared to accept the one to
achieve the other in the interests of his colonization plans.
He was prepared to assert the rights of the fur trade by
force if necessary, if that was essential to the furtherance
of his settlement, though force was repugnant to his
nature.

The second party of settlers set out from the homeland
in June, 1812, and arrived in September to spend an uncomfortable winter at Red River colony, which now contained one hundred settlers. The first harvest had failed,
and buffalo-hunting was unfamiliar work in the depths of
winter. Macdonell was hard put to keep his colony content
and at the same time restrain his militant nature in the
face of growing irritants from the North West fort. "Even
some in the employ of the H. B. Co. acted with more
hostility than friendship," he reported to Selkirk.

Selkirk was too sure of his legal position to throw open
a case by demanding the ejection of Northwesters from
his property. He was certain of the jurisdiction of the
Charter, except for some points under a law (George III)

known as the Canada Act.   Under this statute, criminal
cases in the "Indian Territories" could be tried in the
courts of Upper or Lower Canada.   That was the eventuality he must avoid.   He wrote to Macdonell on this
point:

> "Means will be found of bringing our legal rights to a
> fair trial before the Supreme Tribunal of England. . . .
> it would not yet be advisable to attempt forcibly to dis-
> possess the N. W. Company of the posts which they
> occupy.   The only point at present to be attended to is
> that they be not allowed to acquire any prescriptive right."

For the third party of settlers there were seven hundred
applicants from the Highlands.   All the subversive propaganda and undercover obstructionist tactics of the Northwesters in London could not retard the eagerness of the
evicted Highland crofters to seek new homes abroad.   The
limited number of boats for transportation from York
Factory to Red River made it necessary to select only a
hundred.   Typhoid broke out on shipboard, and death in
the cramped quarters apparently terrified the captain, for
he put the immigrants ashore at Churchill instead of York.
After a cruel winter in tiny log huts, followed by an overland journey to York, they took the old water route up the
Nelson.   Fifty-one persons reached Fort Douglas on the
Red River in June, 1814.

For the Selkirk Settlement, 1814 was the decisive year.
Macdonell began to feel more strength in his position.
There was encouraging unanimity and contentment in the
colony of which he was governor.   In January he asserted
his authority by issuing a proclamation forbidding, in the
interest of his people, the export of pemmican from Selkirk's
territory of Assiniboia.   Pemmican was the concentrated
staple food of the fur trade, and Assiniboia was the richest
pasturing ground of the buffalo.   From these plains the
half-breeds hunted for both companies, and the food supply
of the entire fur trade had become dependent upon the
area.

To the North West Company it was a challenging blow, and they chose to ignore the embargo. Threats and seizures followed. The Canadian brigades assembled at Fort Gibraltar in the spring, and Macdonell's eighty-three effective men were confronted by about one hundred and twenty of the opposition. There were negotiations, and a compromise seemed to ease the situation for the summer.

At Fort William, on Lake Superior, in the summer of 1814, the North West partners learned of the latest move with indignation. Behind locked doors they talked it over, sharply criticizing those at Fort Gibraltar when the pemmican proclamation was issued. "It is the first time the North West Company has ever been insulted," said William McGillivray. Talk of "the old North West spirit" and "the compromise of honour" ended with a formulated policy. Selkirk and Macdonell "must be driven to abandon it." The Montrealers took the pemmican embargo as an act of war, but they were smart enough not to commit their full purposes to official paper. The hints and suggestions of the senior partners became active policy in the interior. Only in some surviving personal letters can be discerned the deep drift of affairs.

Alexander Macdonell and Duncan Cameron returned from the meeting to the Red River with instructions to shatter Selkirk's settlement. Macdonell, the Northwester, who was a cousin of Selkirk's governor, Miles Macdonell, wrote that he was about "to commence open hostilities against the enemy in Red river. . . . Something serious will undoubtedly take place. . . . Nothing but the complete downfall of the colony will satisfy some by fair means or foul. . . . So here is at them with all my heart & energy." The battle spirit that had fought the X Y Company was decidedly alive. Processes of law meant nothing, if terrorism would be cheaper.

The colonists were not their only concern. In the North West minute books of 1814, a new stiffening towards the Hudson's Bay Company appears. "It is probable some changes may be made for the strengthening of Division

Posts and those threatened by the Hudson's Bay Company."
Of Fort Dauphin the Council observed, "This Department
was too short of men to cope with the Hudson's Bay
Company." In the same year it was agreed that "none
of the Hudson's Bay servants should in future be received into any of the Company Forts except in cases of
Starvation."

Selkirk in three years had made his influence felt throughout the entire Hudson's Bay Company. He was neither
governor nor deputy governor, though he might have been,
because of his thirty-five thousand pounds holdings, but
these offices did not interest him. He went daily to
Hudson's Bay House, toiling from ten to six o'clock to
master the details of the business. If by improving the
trading organization he could further his settlement's
welfare and meet the opposition on fighting terms at every
post, no labour was too great. But there was to be moderation. All his instructions firmly warned his men not to
exceed their legal rights.

It was simple for the Northwesters to set the machinery
of the law in motion. Several partners were justices of the
peace in Upper and Lower Canada; a warrant for the
arrest of Miles Macdonell on charges of illegal seizure of
pemmican was duly arranged. Cameron and McLeod
returned to Red River with this fragment of colonial
authority. They proceeded to rouse the half-breed people
against the settlers, employing Cuthbert Grant and Peter
Pangman for the purpose. Both these half-breeds were
bold, intelligent young men, the sons of wintering partners.
Grant was particularly able, had been educated in Montreal,
and already held a position of some authority in the half-
breed race, who numbered several hundred and made up
the voyageur-buffalo-hunting services of the North West
Company. These people felt a very real proprietorship in
the land in which they had been born, and appeals to
patriotism could stir them. At the same time, McLeod
and Grant undermined the morale of the settlement by an
attitude of assumed sympathy for colonist hardships, made

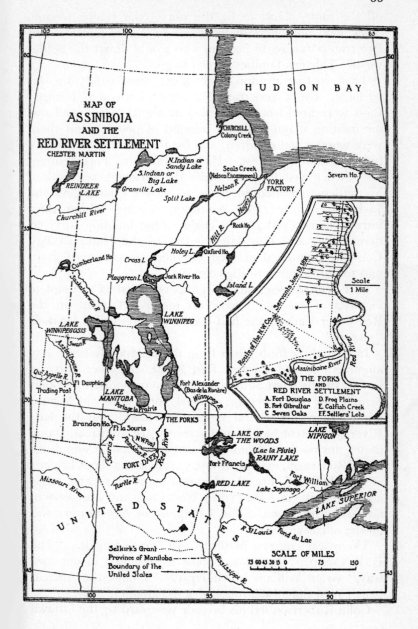

MAP OF
ASSINIBOIA
AND THE
RED RIVER SETTLEMENT
CHESTER MARTIN

all the more plausible by the use of the Gaelic tongue. They held out offers of free land in Upper Canada and free transportation to families who would desert the Settlement. Thirteen families agreed to go.

Then, in that autumn of 1815, organized vandalism was let loose. Crops were trampled down; barns were burned; shots were fired from the bushes at night. Macdonell was for fighting it out with his handful of people; but there were women and children, and for the safety of the colony he submitted to arrest. He was taken to Fort William and thence east for trial while the surviving remnant of his settlers retreated in boats to winter quarters on the Jack River near Lake Winnipeg, leaving behind their burned homes and ruined crops. One building survived destruction, and four Highlanders of the Hudson's Bay Company remained at their fort and salvaged seed grain and tools belonging to the colonists.

Fort William celebrated; it was regarded as a complete victory. They would hear no more of farming in the Red River Valley; the half-breeds were rewarded for their "victory."

In 1815 three fresh forces from the Selkirk–Hudson's Bay alignment moved towards Red River. Another party of settlers mostly from Sutherlandshire commanded by Robert Semple, the new governor, reached York Factory in August, paused there for several weeks, and heard that the Red River Settlement had been destroyed. In Montreal, acting under instructions from the Governor and Committee, Colin Robertson, ex-Northwester, organized a shock brigade of one hundred French Canadian voyageurs and trade goods to strike into the North West Company's preserve in far-away Athabasca. The Company of Adventurers was on the offensive at last.

There was concern in the North West councils. "The H. B. Company intend to oppose us seriously, in our own way," wrote William McGillivray. "I hope the Ancient North West Spirit will rouse with indignation."

Colin Robertson led his brigade westward by the Ottawa

River–Lake Superior route. This indeed was not only carrying the war into the enemy country but over the enemy's own highway, and with Canadian voyageurs. It was the first time Hudson's Bay goods had not come into the west by Hudson Bay.

At Jack River Colin Robertson gathered up the refugees and brought them to Red River, remaining with them while the fur traders pressed on to the Athabasca under command of John Clarke. The four stalwarts who had remained at Red River had done their work well, and the returning colonists were able to reap a generous harvest. Semple brought his new party of settlers the long seven hundred miles from York; prospects at the Selkirk Settlement seemed brighter than at any time in its eventful history.

"The colours were hoisted," Semple wrote. "The guns were fired, at night we laughed and drank and danced and now the serious Calculations of the Colony commenced."

The third force converging upon Red River was Selkirk himself. He had hoped to come out with the 1814 party, but business had prevented. With Lady Selkirk and their two daughters he arrived in Montreal via New York, in September, to learn of the breaking up of his settlement the previous year. At once he undertook to open negotiations with the North West partners in their own stronghold. But every move he made towards negotiation was rebuffed; he became more and more resolved to fight it out. By the spring of 1816 he moved up the Great Lakes with a party of one hundred ex-soldier settlers, recruited to strengthen the colony as farmers and to be available on call for military service. They were mostly Swiss mercenaries from the de Meuron Regiment brought to Canada to serve in the War of 1812, and recently disbanded. While Selkirk travelled westward in June, 1816, the Northwesters struck once more at the Red River Settlement, and with a blow so calculated and savage that it turned their course towards the extinction of their name.

Private letters reveal the brutal spirit of the plan made

at Fort William. This was written to two partners in the interior:

"You will as soon as possible assemble as many Indians as you can by any means induce to go to the Red River to meet us there. . . . We shall be in Red River about 17th of June." It was signed by three partners. Other letters that month refer to coming troubles, indicating plainly the Canadian Company's determination to push terrorism to new extremes. "You will see some sport in Red River before the month of June is over," wrote one. "It must end in some sickly work in the long run," wrote another. "I would not be surprised if some of us leave our bones there," was yet another forecast of events.

There had been some provocation. Semple, governor of the Settlement, foresaw the strength of the approaching storm. Colin Robertson had seized the North West express canoe, and the letters found confirmed all fears; but the seizure of their northbound mails was the final spark that inflamed the Fort William partners. "A more complete disclosure of plans of deliberate villainy has never yet met my eye," Semple wrote. Other aggravations that spring were the arrest of Duncan Cameron, North West partner, at their Fort Gibraltar, and the destruction of the fort itself.

It all boiled over on June 19. Cuthbert Grant, who had led a party of half-breeds in sacking the Company's post, Brandon House, rode on along the banks of the Assiniboine at the head of seventy men to keep the rendezvous appointed by his North West masters. About two miles above the forks of the Red and Assiniboine, armed for war and painted hideously like Indians, they left the river bank and started across the plain in the general direction of Fort Douglas, the centre of the Selkirk Settlement.

Warned of their coming, Semple quickly raised thirty volunteers and led them out on foot across the fields to meet the half-breeds. The mounted half-breeds spread into a semicircle, forestalling an attempt by the settlers to deploy in a loose, open order. The colonists were being manœuvred around until their backs were to the open river. A Frenchman named Boucher rode out from the half-breed ranks, shouting unintelligibly in broken English. Governor Semple strode forward to meet him, and boldly seized the bridle of Boucher's horse. An angry interchange followed; Semple seized the man's gun. A shot was fired. In an instant the shooting became general.

"In a few minutes," wrote an eyewitness named Pritchard, "almost all of our people were either killed or wounded."

The murderous treachery of the Indian blood sent the half-breeds among the wounded to kill with second shots and to mutilate the dead with knives. Semple had gone down wounded in the thigh in the first fusillade. Cuthbert Grant spared his life, but in the mêlée an Indian shot him fatally in the breast. Twenty-one settlers were killed; the others were nearly all captured, though a few escaped by swimming across the Red River in the gathering darkness. The bodies lay on the plains, to be preyed upon by wolves during the days and nights that followed.

This was the massacre of Seven Oaks, hard by Main Street of the city of Winnipeg today. This was the culmination of fur trade arrogance from Montreal. All that was feudal and lawless found vent on that June evening in 1816. But the cunning political methods of the North West Company had overreached themselves, and the happenings of the next four years were only manifestations of a dying Machiavelli reduced to clumsy street brawl methods and political corruption.

Fort Douglas surrendered to the half-breed Cuthbert Grant. The North West partners from Fort William to the east and Portage la Prairie to the west arrived at Red River judiciously late for their planned rendezvous with the half-breeds. They knew there was to be ugly work and came on the scene only in time to stop the boats of the nerve-shattered settlers who were once more retreating north to Lake Winnipeg, and to search these survivors for papers. They took over Fort Douglas amid the primitive celebrations of a "victory." Salutes of guns were fired.

The half-breeds were given rewards for valour and publicly praised by wintering partners.

William McGillivray, leader of the Northwesters, was losing his grip. It is hard to understand how a man whose political sense had carried the company to such heights of power not only in the Indian country but in the civil life of Upper and Lower Canada, could have allowed this disastrous breach of the peace to come about. Too late, he realized the ruinous consequences, and a month after Seven Oaks he wrote in a private letter, "I really wish I was decently out of it, although I shall never submit to being kicked out of it by any Lord or Commoner of the King's Dominions." He spoke also of "this too famous trade."

News of Seven Oaks reached Lord Selkirk at Sault Ste. Marie. Instead of proceeding to Red River by way of Fond du Lac (Duluth), he struck out for Fort William, stronghold of the North West Company. He coasted the rocky north shore of Lake Superior, entered Thunder Bay, and camped within sight of the enemy fort. Before leaving Lower Canada, he had himself appointed a justice of the peace, and he promptly exercised this authority by arresting William McGillivray, Kenneth McKenzie and Dr. John McLoughlin, all of whom submitted at once, though there was a bloodless scuffle between the de Meurons and the voyageurs before the fort was seized.

Hudson's Bay Company furs were found as evidence of stolen goods; papers came to light which definitely implicated the North West Company in the Seven Oaks slaughter. Under guard, the Canadian partners were sent east for trial by Canadian courts.

For Selkirk to press on to Red River, where there were no supplies for his hundred-odd soldiers and canoe men, would have been madness. To return east would be to lose the effectiveness of his expedition. He decided to winter at Fort William, and in arranging for this stay he committed the first of the technical legal errors which were to entangle him hopelessly in the machinations of colonial courts. To get supplies for his party, he entered into an arrangement with Daniel McKenzie, a North West partner who for a few days had been under arrest along with the other Fort William officers. McKenzie, though a partner, was not in good standing. He had written critically of some of his colleagues as being "McGillivray's geese," and he had sneered at the "Froth, Pomp and Ostentation" of the Montreal partners as opposed to the winterers. The ruling McGillivray group regarded him as a garrulous drunkard. This was the man from whom Selkirk bought Fort William's food stores for three thousand pounds. Selkirk was right when he sensed that the sale might later be declared invalid, and not long afterwards wrote of the business as "ill-judged and imprudent."

By the end of 1816 a party of his veterans proceeded to Red River under command of Miles Macdonell, capturing Fort Douglas from the Northwesters on a winter night with no shots fired. The year also ended with Selkirk's second error. The North West Company could also play the warrant-and-arrest game, and when an express canoe with a constable arrived at Fort William from the east in November, Selkirk was unprepared. The constable carried no credentials except the warrant for Selkirk's arrest. It was, of course, instigated by the North West Company, whose control of Canadian legal machinery far outweighed Selkirk's rights as a citizen. Selkirk declared the document spurious, and declined to submit.

The winter dragged on. News of the resisted arrest was made official with all the speed that Selkirk's Montreal enemies could command. By February, 1817, Lord Bathurst in the colonial office in London had advised the Canadian colonial authorities that Lord Selkirk had "by resisting the execution of the Warrant issued against him . . . rendered himself doubly amenable to the Laws." The Colonial Governor Sherbrooke was told to issue a true bill against Selkirk, and as the subject to be arrested was surrounded by a military force, it was suggested the officer making the arrest be advised to approach Lord Selkirk prepared for trouble. Selkirk was enmeshed in a weighted net. As he wintered at Fort William, pondering and planning the consolidation of his ill-starred colony and writing long letters to Lady Selkirk in Montreal, his enemies in the east followed up their success over the resisted warrant by laying more elaborate legal traps.

Lady Selkirk in Montreal worked constantly in her husband's interests. She had succeeded in rousing substantial sympathy and even support for his cause. By the exercise of her social charm, she created a following among the enemies of the North West Company, and by active correspondence she pressed the case with Sherbrooke. Her letters to her husband are brave, cheering incidents in the whole dark controversy. Through the tedious, exhausting two years which followed, she never faltered in courageous, high-spirited support.

Selkirk left Fort William in May for his Red River colony, and in June he saw for the first time the tiny settlement on the edge of the prairie in which all his hopes and aspirations were now centred. Once more the settlers had been shepherded to the sites of their homesteads, and the Hudson's Bay men who had remained had again kept the faith, for grain had been planted and the flourishing green fields brought that hope and confidence to Highland hearts which has somehow never entirely failed among the people who have lived upon those plains.

In the four months at Red River, in 1817, Selkirk was in the rôle for which he was completely fitted by temperament and training. It is the tragedy of his life that only in these fleeting summer weeks was he able to exercise freely the qualities of the enlightened colonial administrator. His long study of agriculture, his understanding of the people, and his practical political sense, made the brief visit almost a complete vindication of the enormous expense and effort put into the project up to that time. Generous, clearsighted, yet with a sense of immediate reality, he planned roads, bridges, set aside sites for churches and common

he York boats were unique craft created by the Company for inland water transport. They have been displaced by power boats.

Thomas Douglas, Fifth Earl of Selkirk (1771–1820), whose attempt to establish an agricultural settlement in the valley of the Red River profoundly affected the destiny of the Hudson's Bay Company

schools, and sprinkled liberally over all the familiar place names of the Highlands.

Commissioners from the Crown authority in the east arrived to investigate and report on the circumstances surrounding the outrages of the previous summer, and were welcomed by Selkirk as impartial inquirers who could only vindicate his cause. He watched their work for some weeks, and soon lost hope of support from that source.

Autumn came, and he turned east through the United States to face the charges against him in the colonial courts. Frost killed the settlement crops that year. So little was his character understood, and so effectively had the North-westers blackened his motives, that in Montreal and York (Toronto) it was widely believed he would forfeit the fantastic bail of six thousand pounds and leave the United States for some foreign land rather than face his accusers.

The rest is misery and an utter chaos of tortuous legal proceedings. The controversy was the sensation of Upper and Lower Canada, and before Selkirk died in 1820, thirty books had been published on the affair. Against Selkirk and the Hudson's Bay Company were directed thirty charges, ranging from riot and larceny to false imprisonment and assault. Countercharges against the North West Company totalled one hundred and fifty, for murder, arson, robbery, malicious shooting, burglary and grand larceny. Out of the latter charges emerged one verdict against a confessed murderer, and not one of those who massacred Governor Semple and twenty-one colonists was ever brought to justice.

From Sandwich, Ontario, to York and to Montreal, Selkirk was compelled to move with his counsel and witnesses from court to court at ruinous expense, fighting every inch of the way against all the designs of men whose dominance over the entire colonial machinery made it a battle against overwhelming odds. Selkirk seems never to have doubted his ability to expose the North West Company. His confidence was absolute and unshakeable. Lady Selkirk wrote during the darkest days, "If we are to be poor for

three generations we must absolutely fight this out." All
through 1818, from one courtroom to another, the struggle
went on, and Selkirk's health broke completely from utter
exhaustion. In November he sailed from New York for
England. Two months later verdicts totalling two thousand
pounds against him were brought in, and the Northwesters
proclaimed a victory.

A year in England, when friends rallied to his support
in demanding justice from the British Government, brought
some hope. But the government was already giving tacit
encouragement to certain preliminary moves towards union
between the two companies. Letters edging towards a
merger were passing between Ellice, senior North West
partner in London, and the Governor and Committee.
The Northwesters even offered protection for the Red
River settlers. It had all got beyond Selkirk's hands.
Besides, it had already cost the Hudson's Bay Company
forty thousand pounds. There were dividends to be considered. The loss to the Selkirk family was to be more
than one hundred thousand pounds.

Lord Selkirk died in Pau, France, on April 8, 1820,
aged forty-nine. A month earlier Sir Alexander Mackenzie
had died. In these two Scotsmen had been the very anti-
theses of the conflict. One the hard trader-explorer,
grasping wealth, untrammelled by humanitarian principles
on far horizons; the other the student-philanthropist, born
to wealth, endowed with moral courage, sensitive, generous
and well-meaning. "I never knew in my life a man of
more generous distinction," wrote Sir Walter Scott of
Selkirk.

The way was clear at last for the coming together of
the companies. While the Selkirk colony lingered on for
fifteen years until the Hudson's Bay Company took over
its administration by purchase of the territory from the
Selkirk heirs, and fur trading became a source of vast new
wealth, the inherent clash between trade and settlement
remained to be settled strangely by later generations.

CHAPTER X

DEEDS AND COVENANTS

LORD SELKIRK'S attempt to transplant Highlanders
to the prairie had never received any wholehearted
encouragement from the British Government. To some it
had been romantic, ill-conceived, and doomed from the
start to expensive failure. To others it was a gigantic
device to transpose feudal practices across the Atlantic and
create a landed estate on a scale never known before.
Still others saw in it a colonial disguise for a death-blow at
the North West Company. The Seven Oaks killings stirred
the colonial secretary Bathurst into a see-here-this-won't-do
position, and from the dim recesses of his office dispatches
were written to set moving the machinery of investigation
in Canada. The report of W. B. Coltman, one of the
commissioners of inquiry, suggested in 1818 the possibility
of compromise between the companies. Sir Alexander
Mackenzie had written of it in 1801.

Seven Oaks, in 1817, made union and peace more
remote than ever, and the three years following the massacre
were the most bitterly competitive of all.

The Hudson's Bay Company's first serious plan to wrest
the Athabasca trade from the North West Company was
a severe test of its men. Colin Robertson had organized
the brigade in Montreal and accompanied it to Red
River in 1815. There John Clarke took over command
and led it on up the Saskatchewan over the long Methye
Portage.

The Northwesters at Chipewyan prepared to receive the
Bay men by scattering the Indian hunters, after buying up
all available provisions. It was a lean winter even for

them, and the newcomers (fifty men and six clerks) nearly starved. One party did perish, and another group at Great Slave Lake got food from the North West men only by surrendering their year's stores of trade goods.

While Selkirk struggled in colonial courts, he still kept his hand in the fight for the fur trade. At his instructions, Colin Robertson left Montreal in April, 1819, with a second brigade of nineteen Hudson's Bay canoes, and landed one hundred and thirty armed men at Chipewyan. It was the most spirited attack his Company had yet made. They succeeded in winning most of the Indian hunters to their fort, named Wedderburn after Lady Selkirk, but Robertson was tricked into captivity and held prisoner in the North West fort for eight months by order of William McGillivray and Samuel Black. In the spring he was being taken east, still as a prisoner, but at Cumberland House on the Saskatchewan he escaped to the Bay fort and invited attack. The Northwesters, who later claimed that he had broken parole, refused the challenge and went on downstream with their furs. At the foot of Grand Rapids where the Saskatchewan River finally empties into Lake Winnipeg, the North West brigade was swept by the final descent of the river into an ambush. William Williams, governor-in-chief of the Hudson's Bay Company territories, had brought de Meuron soldiers from the Red River and anchored an armed barge midstream, waiting there to capture the season's furs from Athabasca as well as a handful of North West partners including Benjamin Frobisher. They had expected to rescue Colin Robertson, but his earlier escape made that main purpose of the ambush unnecessary. While the captured Northwesters were being taken to York Factory on Hudson Bay, Frobisher escaped and died from starvation in the forest.

Such passages added fuel to the flames even after Seven Oaks.

Colin Robertson became a hunted man. He was in the Peace River country the winter of 1819–20. Three duels were fought in the wilderness that winter between men of the rival companies. The Montrealers reversed the ambush game at the Grand Rapids bottle-neck, and caught Robertson a second time. On the way to Montreal he escaped his guards, and knowing there were North West-inspired warrants awaiting him in Montreal, he fled across the border to New York and embarked for England in November, 1820, to report to Hudson's Bay House.

It was a strange voyage. On the same ship were two North West partners, Angus Bethune and Dr. John McLoughlin. Only Robertson's version of the encounter has survived, and that high-spirited fur trader rather delighted in his position, largely because he guessed the truth about their visit to London. For the wintering partners had seen the end approaching; they mistrusted their Montreal partners, and they were going to London to open negotiations with the Hudson's Bay Company on their own account. Events had crowded fast, since 1815, but there is nothing to indicate that the wintering partners realized the hopeless mess of their position until they met at Fort William in the summer of 1820. Then they appointed Bethune and McLoughlin their emissaries of peace.

In London, with official urging from the colonial secretary, Lord Bathurst, Edward Ellice opened negotiations. Ellice was partner in a firm which acted as London agents for the North West Company, and he was a shareholder. His father, before the American Revolution, had been a partner in the fur trade firm of Phyn Ellice & Company, of Schenectady, and for a time represented the firm in Montreal. Ellice took his master's degree from Marischal College, Aberdeen, went to Canada in 1803, and a year later was involved in the union of the X Y and North West Companies, securing a partnership in the latter. In the next forty years after the union with the Hudson's Bay Company, Ellice was a tower of strength through all the adjustments and expansion. At the moment he was an admirable negotiator. A Member of Parliament of increasing prominence in Whig circles, a brother-in-law of

Earl Grey, and a man whose fur trade interests had not involved him in violence, he was excellently fitted to approach the Governor and Committee with merger proposals.

Also in London were William and Simon McGillivray, representing the Montreal faction of the North West Company and consequently closer to Ellice than the Fort William delegation.

Who first moved towards union is perhaps an academic point, but it has some importance here if only to clarify the true position, which most writers on the period have glossed over with the hasty conclusion that the two companies collapsed into each other's laps only a few steps ahead of bankruptcy. Though the Hudson's Bay Company was under terrific strain to keep up the struggle, they had sustained a successful offensive since Selkirk had prodded the "jog trot" methods into a gallop. Moreover, since the Napoleonic embargo on European markets had been lifted and furs were once again selling abroad, the Company maintained its 4 per cent. dividend, which meant a comfortable if not spectacular position. After Seven Oaks the widows of slain Company men were pensioned. In 1820 the shareholders numbered only seventy-seven, and the Governor and Committee had been setting up reserves.

On the other hand, the North West Company, by the structure of its partnership groups and individuals grasping for quick wealth and early retirement, was drained each season by the complete division of all profits. There was no apparent provision for reserves, and no accurate system of accountancy.

Four influences sought union with the Hudson's Bay Company: the colonial office, Edward Ellice, the McGillivrays, and the wintering partners. The English Company's position was strong. The decisions against Selkirk in the Canadian colonial courts had been empty victories. London was the only place where finality could be sought. The Canadians had dissipated their energies by fighting Selkirk at a time when the Hudson's Bay Company remained intact and active.

Andrew Colvile, member of the London Committee, acted for the Hudson's Bay Company in receiving the various overtures.

The first moves in the coming together of the two proud organizations were hesitant, suspicious, and, because of division in the North West Company, secretive. Edward Ellice had been in private communication with Colvile months before the McGillivrays, McLoughlin and Bethune arrived. Ellice offered to buy a controlling interest, probably with new London capital, and assured protection to the Selkirk colony or free transportation of settlers to Lower Canada if desired. This offer, with variations, was rejected scornfully by the dying Selkirk. After his death the appearance in London of the spokesmen for two factions of the North West Company raised the scale of the bargaining.

Glimpses of the principal actors as they move about lodgings and bank parlours and counting-houses of Georgian London, emerge from letters and diaries of the winter of 1820–21. The McGillivray brothers, wealthy, energetic, ambitious men, fur traders for forty years and leaders of the Montreal wing, knew the end had come, but they were out to fight for terms. Their private affairs in Montreal were destined to hopeless bankruptcy. William died in 1825, and Simon laboured on over the debris, and later found employment in Mexico.

Edward Ellice, M.P., the careful merchant-statesman with business experience in Montreal, had inherited from his father a London supply house for fur traders. His public career was marked by consistent support of the liberal movements of the next forty years. As a grand old man of the Hudson's Bay Company, he was to provide the most powerful evidence in favour of the renewal of the exclusive trading rights, when these privileges were under fire in Parliament thirty-seven years after the union.

Colin Robertson, the ex-Northwester, who had given

bold leadership to Selkirk's shock brigades to Athabasca, wrote letters revealing sidelights on the negotiations. Cordially hated by the Montrealers for his attacks on their preserves and for his escapes from their clutches, he was able to provide Colvile with intimate knowledge of the fur traders in London at the time. After it was all over, Robertson was able to make his peace with the late enemy, and he lived to serve the Hudson's Bay Company for twenty more years.

Dr. John McLoughlin, physician and fur trader, was a large, stern person who, though elbowed to one side in the actual settlement between the companies, later rose to the senior ranks of the Hudson's Bay fur trade, and is honoured today as the father of the Oregon. Yet the eighteen powers of attorney which he carried to London from his colleagues, and all his arguments, were not enough to win his case during the negotiations.

Colin Robertson, writing on shipboard in November, 1820, describes with relish his encounter with McLoughlin and Bethune:

"Who do you think accompanies me to England in the Albion but Messrs. McLaughlin and Bethune? The latter I found in the steam boat at Burlington, he wished to be very polite, but I kept him at a distance—the doctor I found at this place."

And later:

"The cloth being withdrawn and the land in sight, the wine went about rather freely, when a subscription was set on foot for the stewards and other servants. Our friend the Doctor had put down his name, and I took up the pen for the same purpose, but perceiving Bethune writing I turned to Abby Carriere—'Come, Abby, put down your name, I don't like to sign between two North Westers.'

"'Never mind, Mr. R.,' replied Monsr. Carriere, 'remember our Saviour was crucified between two thieves.' The Doctor was in a dreadful passion, but being an honest

Catholic did not like to quarrel with one who stood so high in the Church."

Robertson, fresh from the trails, took a dislike to Edward Ellice, the young parliamentarian, who again acted as go-between. In January, 1821, Robertson wrote indicating that Ellice was making progress, and the McLoughlin-Bethune representations were being disregarded.

"I know not what the Doctor is about but the negocia-tions have commenced. . . . The Receiver General (Sir John Caldwell, of Lower Canada) and his friend Mr. Edward Ellice called at my lodgings & I had a good deal of conversation with the latter. He talked a good deal of the influence of himself and his friends and as to the Charter of the Company he seems to think it hung on his nod. . . . he would be very happy to meet Mr. Colvile half way. I replied that I should have much pleasure in communicating his sentiments to Mr. C. . . ."

On the subject of the Charter, Ellice was sparring for terms. Years later he told the parliamentary committee of 1857 that he had:

"taken the opinion of every lawyer against the Company when I was opposed to them and for the Company since I have been connected with them. We have the opinions of Lord Mansfield, Sir Dudley Ryder, Sir Richard Lloyd, Lord Erskine, Gibbs, Romilly, Cruise, Bell, Scarlett, Holroyd; and the law officers have been consulted upon every occasion by the Colonial Office when this question has come under discussion and I think the universal opinion without exception, of these eminent lawyers is, that the proprietory rights of the Company cannot be disputed."

So much for the Charter. For Ellice to suggest to Robertson that he and his influential friends might upset the Charter was sheer bluff.

Robertson's letter continues:

"Mr. C. is willing to listen to any moderate proposition, but seems to think they must lower their terms. . . . He appears to have taken pretty high ground, which the present situation of our affairs in some measure authorizes. . . .

"Now, my good Sir, with regard to our friend the Doctor . . . he is too honourable a man to expose the actual state of the N. W. Co.'s affairs unless he makes an agreement for himself and friends which I understand he is averse to. . . . Messrs. Ellice & McGillivray talk as if the Bank of England was at their disposal, and when they come to touch on the business of the interior, they will be equally ostentatious in stating their advantages, so that when Mr. C. comes to weigh these matters, I would not at all be surprised if Simon makes a better bargain than he has a right to expect."

A few days later in January, Robertson wrote from Boulogne:

"I had a long conversation with Simon (McGillivray) a few days previous to my departure from England. The old story of Grand Rapids was smoothed over as prelude to other matters, when my two voyaging companions were brought on the market, their powers of Atty. etc. . . . all of which Simon treated with the utmost contempt. . . . I confess candidly I like Simon much better than his friend the Member of Parliament: there is a sort of highland pride and frankness about the little fellow. . . . He seems bent on union, and after all his claims and advantages are thrown out, he comes back to that point."

From Paris Robertson wrote on January 25:

"I had letters from London the other day reporting the negociations as being broken off by Simon but I think he will return to the point, he was too eager in pursuit to give up the chase."

Simon returned to the point, for Robertson wrote again from Paris before the end of February, 1821:

"I learn that a reconciliation is nearly completed between the two companies. The whole trade is com-

prised under one concern to be carried on from the first
of next June under the name and charter of the H. B.
Co. . . . What a dreadful blow this must be to the Montreal
agents."

Robertson returned that midsummer to the heart of the
fur trade empire, writing from Fort William, where he had
been a prisoner the year before, on July 12, 1821, "The
wintering partners dissatisfied with the Union? Any terms
would have been acceptable in the present state of their
affairs."

Simon McGillivray, addressing the clamouring creditors
of his bankrupt Montreal business in 1825, makes some
significant statements upon the moves approaching the
union.

"Before the commencement of this unfortunate contest,
the concern had been a profitable one. Large fortunes
had formerly been made in the House; and, but for the
competition of the Hudson's Bay Company and Lord
Selkirk, it was not doubted that the trade would continue
to yield large profits. The effects of the impending contest
were not duly appreciated; and the Partners had got too
much into the habit of regulating their expenditure rather
according to their own inclination and convenience, than
to their actual income.

"With reduced means, with a losing trade and with
credit in jeopardy—with disunion in our councils, and
defection among our Partners, if not direct treachery in
our camp—with some Partners of our House not only
useless, but burthensome to us, and whom we yet feared
to cast off, because they had the power to injure us—it
was under these almost desperate circumstances, that in
the month of December 1820, I opened a negotiation with
the Hudson's Bay Company, for a general arrangement
upon a new basis; which, with the cooperation of my
friend Mr. Ellice, was in three months concluded, and
which in course of the following summer, I carried into
effect throughout the interior country. It was effected
just in time to save the whole concern from destruction;
and our circumstances not being known to our opponents,

and they also having their own reasons for wishing to terminate the contest, I obtained liberal, and even advantageous terms for all parties connected with the North-West Company, and yet not one was satisfied."

The Northwesters considered themselves well out of the "too famous trade."

Edward Ellice has a third version which deserves quotation if only to show how varied are men's opinions of their relative importance in great affairs. It appears in his evidence before the committee of the House of Commons, meeting in 1857:

"I think about 1819 or 1820 Lord Bathurst, then Secretary of State for the colonies, sent for me to consult me whether it was possible to do anything towards promoting a union between the companies. I undertook that matter not only at his request, but from obvious considerations of interest, having come under considerable engagements from one of the companies; and after very difficult negotiations, I succeeded in uniting the interests of the various parties, and in inducing them to agree to carry on the trade after that agreement under the charter of the Hudson's Bay Company."

Obvious, and perhaps pardonable discrepancies appear in these accounts, but it is quite clear that imperial policy fostered the union. Only the incentive of the British colonial office, and later the official sanction of Parliament by statute, could have moulded the Hudson's Bay and North West companies into the powerful corporate body, armed with authority and endowed with prestige, which it was to be during the ensuing fifty years.

Ellice, the McGillivrays and McLoughlin and Bethune knew that the only alternative to union was chaos. They all recognized that the North West Company was forever shattered. Without union, the fur trade in Rupert's Land and the Indian territories would revert to a state of unlicensed, unprofitable traffic with the natives far worse than that land had ever known.

To the Hudson's Bay Company union was vitally important. It could not afford further recurrence of such years as 1815 to 1821. Monopoly was the very bedrock of its existence, and in these years the Charter privileges of exclusive trade in Rupert's Land had been at best theoretical in execution. From the shareholder point of view, and from the executive angle, amalgamation was the logical solution of major problems. The clear reasonableness of union probably led Colvile, on behalf of the Governor and Committee, to agree to terms substantially more favourable to the Canadian Company than would have been acceptable if he had known the true state of their affairs.

The final agreement, called "a deed of co-partnership," was between The Governor and Company of Adventurers of England as one party, and William and Simon McGillivray and Edward Ellice as the other. The second group acted, though with questionable authority, for the North West Company.

The old Royal Charter, cornerstone of the Adventurers for a century and a half, was the sheet anchor of the amalgamation. The fur trade was to be carried on under a clear-cut monopoly, asserted not only in the Charter of 1670 but endorsed in a statute of the British Parliament of 1821. Where the Charter monopoly had been limited to the drainage basin of Hudson Bay, the new "licence to trade" for twenty-one years specifically gave exclusive right to trade with the Indians in all that territory east of the Rocky Mountains. This had not previously been granted to the Hudson's Bay Company; it was a sort of no man's land belonging neither to the colonial provinces nor to the United States. The Company held sole British right of trade in the Oregon country west of the Rockies. Parliament guaranteed the continued sovereignty of the Royal Charter, and no rent was asked. Hitherto, the administration of criminal and civil law had been transferred to the courts of Upper and Lower Canada, where cases involved costs of more than two hundred pounds. Now the onus was placed on the Company and all cases were to be settled within the territory. The Company agreed to set about regulating and diminishing the sale of spirits to the Indians.

It was, in effect, the control of nearly half a continent: today's Dominion of Canada, except the Great Lakes-St. Lawrence basin and the maritime provinces. With many blank, unexplored fringes on the map, the Company partitioned British America into four great departments:

1. The Northern Department of Rupert's Land, embracing the area between the United States boundary to the south, the unknown Arctic on the north, Hudson Bay on the east, and the Rocky Mountains on the west.

2. The Southern Department, extending from James Bay southward to the provinces of Upper and Lower Canada and east to include East Main, the eastern coast of Hudson Bay.

3. The Montreal Department covering the Company's business in Upper and Lower Canada, and, later, Labrador.[1]

4. The Columbia Department covering the valley of the Columbia River, and, after 1825, the Canadian Pacific slope called New Caledonia.

The net profits of the Company were to be divided into one hundred equal shares to be apportioned as follows:

Twenty shares to the proprietors of the Hudson's Bay Company; twenty shares to the proprietors of the North West Company; forty shares to chief factors and chief traders; five shares to the executors of the late Earl of

---

[1] This is exclusive of the King's Posts extending down the St. Lawrence to beyond Anticosti, leased in 1831, and the posts opened thereafter on the coast of Labrador. The King's Posts originally belonged to the King of France, but on the conquest of Canada in 1760 they passed into the possession of the British Crown. The North West Company acquired the lease from 1802 until 1822—the year after their union with the Hudson's Bay Company. The Hudson's Bay Company held the lease from 1831 until 1859. They continued, however, to occupy posts which they had themselves established.— *A Brief History of the Hudson's Bay Company*, London, 1935.

Selkirk; five shares to Simon McGillivray and Edward Ellice as compensation for the loss of their agency and commission in London; ten shares to be invested in parliamentary stocks or Public Funds of Great Britain.

To the Hudson's Bay men, the union brought new status. They were admitted to true partnership, cementing an invaluable bond between London proprietorship and Canadian management which endured almost half a century and then was destroyed by shareholder greed.

The new partners, twenty-five chief factors and twenty-eight chief traders, were the Commissioned Gentlemen, the very fibre of the Hudson's Bay Company. They were the men who set traditions of loyalty, courage, and personal integrity which gave prestige to the Company throughout the nineteenth century. Had they been the motley handful of unscrupulous men "without a soul above a beaver skin," as someone later charged, the destiny of British North America would have been different.

Here they are, as their names appear in the Deed Poll of 1821, that document governing their duties, rights and privileges, and divided to show the company from which they came:

CHIEF FACTORS:

Hudson's Bay Company: Thomas Vincent, James Bird, Colin Robertson, James Sutherland, John Clarke, John Charles, Alexander Kennedy, John Davis, Joseph Beioley, Alexander Christie.

North West Company: John Thomson, John Mcdonald, James Leith, John Haldane, Alexander Stewart, John George McTavish, George Keith, John Dugald Cameron, John Stuart, Edward Smith, John McLaughlin, James Keith, Angus Bethune, Donald Mackenzie, John McBean.

CHIEF TRADERS:

Hudson's Bay Company: Jacob Corrigal, John Peter Pruden, James Clouston, John Spencer, John Lee Lewes, Roderick Mackenzie, William Brown, Robert McVicar, John McLeod, Alexander McDonald, Andrew Stewart.

North West Company: William Mackintosh, Thomas McMurray, Donald Mackintosh, Allan Macdonnell, Hugh Faries, Roderick Mackenzie, Daniel Williams Harmon, John Warren Dease, Angus Cameron, Simon McGillivray, Joseph McGillivray, William Connelly, Peter Warren Dease, John Rowand, Joseph Felix La Rocque, James McMillan, Alexander Roderick McLeod.

Thirty-two of these fifty-three commissioned officers were Northwesters. The reasons for this predominance were several. The Canadian company, operated by partners, had produced a more aggressive type of men; the North West "winterers" had been discontented with the state of their affairs and their delegates to London had been elbowed aside; it was necessary in the interests of unity to placate them. By actual numbers the North West Company probably had more men in the fur trade than the London Company, and hence more of the officer type. It is significant, however, that the first local governors appointed after the union to the Northern and Southern departments were Hudson's Bay Company men.

The 40 per cent. of profits to be set aside for the officers was divided into eighty-five parts, of which each chief factor then would receive two and each chief trader one part. Upon retirement each officer was to keep his share or shares for one year; then for six years he was to receive

Nicholas Garry, Deputy Governor of the Company, 1822–1835

Fort Garry Gate, in the city of Winnipeg, preserved as memorial
to the old fur trade capital

one-half the profits of his holdings. This Deed Poll lasted for fifty years, and under its benefits many Company officers retired with fortunes.

The Deed Poll established the machinery of government by council in the fur trade. The chief factors were to meet annually in each department under a local governor. While the supreme executive control remained with the Governor, Deputy Governor and Committee in London, the councils were given wide powers. This form was borrowed from the annual Fort William meetings of the North West partners, and it was a radical change from the old tight-reined grip Hudson's Bay House, London, had previously held over its overseas men, although under Selkirk something resembling this form had been set up. The councils, each comprising the local governor and chief factors, assembled from the wilderness each summer to meet and establish regulations, examine the results of each outfit's trading, determine furloughs, mete out discipline, and recommend promotion and retirements to the London board.

While it prepared the way for a clear-cut operation on the other side of the Atlantic, the union of 1821 was less successful in London. At first the two parties were to find equal share of capital and to divide losses equally under the deed of co-partnership. A joint board of management was created for a period of twenty-one years, the majority of its members appointed by the Hudson's Bay Company. By 1824 this arrangement broke down, the capital stock was increased to four hundred thousand pounds, and the McGillivrays and Edward Ellice were given blocks of shares instead of the division of profits arranged in 1821. The financial affairs of the McGillivrays were in such confusion that it was necessary to crowd them out. Ellice was appointed to the Committee, but he and the Mc-Gillivrays had to put up fifty thousand pounds of their stock to meet possible claims against the Company because of the precarious state of their affairs in Montreal.

The story of the Northwesters in these final days has

M

been skilfully pieced together by Professor Wallace. It is his conclusion that the joint advisory board had been a means of insuring easy absorption of the wintering partners and also of sparing the pride of the McGillivrays. By 1824 a master hand in Rupert's Land had effected the welding of the old enemies in that quarter. But in Montreal and in London, Wallace writes:

"the affairs of the McGillivrays had probably reached a point where it was dangerous to consider their feelings any longer. Henry McKenzie, one of the partners of McTavish, McGillivrays and Company, had protested against the high-handed action of the McGillivrays in agreeing to the union of 1821 without consulting the partners, and was threatening action in the courts. At the same time the financial affairs of the firm approached a crisis. Early in 1824 Simon McGillivray was so embarrassed financially that he was compelled to sell at auction in London his valuable collection of paintings. In these circumstances, it seemed no doubt only common prudence for the Hudson's Bay Company to protect itself against possible litigation, and incidentally to throw the McGillivrays to the wolves."

The empty shell that had been the North West structure collapsed shortly afterwards, and in 1830 Ellice was obliged to settle with the McGillivray trustees to the tune of one hundred and ten thousand pounds while creditors received but ten shillings in the pound. So the North West Company disappeared for ever. There is no note of farewell more completely expressive of proud weariness in the finality of the story than a letter from the old stronghold of Fort William. It is William McGillivray writing in July, 1821. He has come back to the shores of Lake Superior from the London negotiations. He is clearing up the debris of the struggle and pauses to write to the Reverend John Strachan, of Toronto, who was to become the fighting bishop of Upper Canada, fighting always in strange and impossible causes just as his perverse nature had found some grounds to support the North West Com-

pany's cause. McGillivray is tired, but he writes with all
the news sparkle of other days:

"I avail myself of the opportunity of Mr. Alexr
McDonell going down by York, to tender you my
devoirs.—I have been at this place since the 1st inst:
settling a most important Business—the carrying into
effect the various Deeds and Covenants entered into on
the part of the North West Company in London with the
Hudson Bay Company;—these arrangements are happily
completed, and I part with my old troops—to meet them
no more in discussions on the Indian trade—this parting
I confess does not cause me much regret—I have worked
hard & honestly for them, and I am satisfied that I have
at least, done my duty. I have been an Agent or Director,
since 1794—and Chief Superintendent since 1799, the
management has not been easy, for we had too many
storms to weather from without, and some derangement
in the Household. But thank God! the whole is closed
with honor—and the trade will be productive if well
managed, after the Country shall have been restored to
order, which it will require a couple of years to effect,—
thus the Fur trade is forever lost to Canada! the treaty
of Ghent destroyed the Southern trade—still the Capital
and exertions of a few individuals supported the Northern
trade, under many disadvantages, against a Chartered
Company, who brought their goods to the Indian
Country at less than one half the Expence that ours cost
us—but it would have been worse than folly, to have
continued the contest further. We have made no sub-
mission—we met & negotiated on equal terms—and
rating the N. W. Co. collectively—they hold now 55 out
of 100 shares. . . .

"My own fortunes have been singular as connected
with the N W Fur trade—I was the first English Clerk
engaged in the Service of the N. W. Co., on its first
Establishment in 1784, and I have put my Hand and
Seal to the Instrument which closes its career—and name
in 1821——

"The loss of this trade to Montreal & the immediate
district in its vicinity, will be severely felt among a certain
class of the People—the yearly disbursements in cash

from the office in Montreal to the people employed in
various ways, as well as for provisions and stores, was not
less than £40,000 pr annum—a large sum taken out of
circulation—and combined with the present distressed
state of the trade in the Province is a matter of regret—
the anti-northwesters of our City have got rid of us, but
not exactly in the way they wished.   But I am prosing——

"My Brother Simon left this for York Fort in Hudsons
Bay on the 21st—he is to inspect the Depots and Inventories of Property belonging to the H. B. Co. (to form
part of the Stock)—and this duty performed, he will
make the best of his (way) to Montreal—I think by way
of Timiskamingue.

"I beg my respectful regards to Mrs. Strachan, and am
my dear Sir

ever yours most faithfully
W. McGillivray.

HONBLE & REVD
DR. STRACHAN."

Chapter XI

SHAPING THE NEW MONOPOLY

CAPITAL interests could be altered by signatures and seals in Hudson's Bay House, London, but in Rupert's Land, in the valley of the Mackenzie, and on the Pacific Coast lived the men who could make or ruin the Hudson's Bay Company. The veterans in the service presented no problem. Their new status of partnership meant better working conditions and increased earning power. In contrast, the wintering partners of the North West Company whose proprietary interest had literally been sold out without their consent, might make the final consummation of union extremely difficult. They were mostly men of pronounced character and firm decision, and as the news of the final settlement sped from fort to fort by the first express canoe packet in the spring of 1821, these traders and clerks spent long hours of discussion and argument. When summer came and the brigades set out for Fort William for the last time, the partners came down to the council sceptical and suspicious.

Anticipating danger, the Governor and Committee looked about their own numbers for one in authority who could go to Rupert's Land, confer with the Northwesters, placate them if necessary, present their commissions under the Royal Charter, and bring them into council with the old Hudson's Bay men.

Nicholas Garry, aged thirty-eight, Deputy Governor of the Hudson's Bay Company, was chosen for the difficult mission. If Garry's word is to be accepted, and he was a transparently honest person, the choice fell upon him because he was the only unmarried member of the Committee, a

181

strange enough qualification for the undertaking of an important assignment in a distant country. "It became imperative on Me that I should not hesitate to undertake this long and tedious Journey," he wrote in his diary in March, 1821.

The Garry diary is one of the absorbing documents of the period, highly informative, and at the same time excessively annoying for its omissions. An English gentleman travelling abroad with his personal servant, Raven, engaged on a mission of great consequence, he apparently never unbent. A keen sense of duty, a simple clarity of thought, a curious, wide-eyed but always gentlemanly inquisitiveness into the new world enlightens his observations. There was more than a suggestion of the prig about him. He could shudder over finding fur traders living in an unmarried state with native or half-breed women, and reflect upon their "debasement of mind," and at the same time make presents of gallons of rum to friendly Indians his party met *en route* west.

Above all he had courage, and in the light of his performance he can be forgiven for his somewhat Pecksniffian attitude towards the manners of Americans he met in New York, and his missionary zeal for meetings of the Auxiliary Bible Society among fur traders. He spent less than four months in the fur trade, a stranger coming into a group of proud, hard men whose lonely lives nourished suspicion, and he left behind him the foundations of a strong, unified company.

Nicholas Garry reached Montreal via New York where he had been agreeably dined by "Mr. Astor, the son of J. J. Astor, the Head of the American Fur Company." After seeing the younger set of Manhattan, in 1821, celebrating a wedding, he consoled himself by recording for posterity his unswerving conviction of "the Superiority of British Females over every other," by reason of their "Delicacy and Refinement of mind."

In Montreal, two days before leaving for Rupert's Land, he took communion at the Church of St. Paul's and found

himself seated next to a "Mr. Henry, an old gentleman
of 85" who proved to be Alexander Henry, the first
Englishman from Montreal to enter the Hudson's Bay
territory after the Conquest of Canada in 1759.

They started west in a great north canoe on June 13
from Lachine, nine miles from Montreal; the party numbered twenty—Garry, the two McGillivrays, their three
servants, guide, and voyageurs.

Garry was a lonely Englishman, weighted not a little
by the solemn importance of his purpose, and alive to his
disadvantages as a stranger to fur trade life. His diary
is meticulous in its notes on all manner of things, from
canoe construction to voyageur habits, wild life, and the
inescapable misery of mosquitoes. Up the Ottawa they
went, an old and familiar route to the McGillivrays making
the journey for the last time, but a way of lively interest
to the Deputy Governor.

Garry writes down the technique of the portage and the
camps for the night:

"The manner of carrying the Canoe:—She is first
turned over. Four men then go into the water, two at
each End, raise the Canoe and then two more place
themselves about midships of the Gunwhale on the
opposite side. The weight of our Canoe was about
6 cwt. The Goods are carried on the Shoulders of the
men and in this manner; each Canoe Man is provided
with a leather Sling broad in the middle; the Ends he
fastens to a Package, this is placed on his shoulders, the
broad part of the Sling placed across his Forehead. On
this Package a second is placed and in this manner they
generally carry two Packages of 90 lbs. each and sometimes a third. There is a second Portage of the Chaudiere
to which we walked and encamped. The Ceremony of
Encamping is, that the moment we land a Fire is made,
the Tent raised, the kettle put on the Fire and in the short
space of a quarter of an Hour your Inn is prepared. Our
Tent is about 30 Feet by 15, of Canvas, handsomely
striped in Paint on the Top. An oil cloth is placed as a
Carpet at the Bottom, this forms the covering of the Tent

when packed up. Our Boxes and our Casettes become our Chairs and Tables. After Supper all this is cleared and our Beds are spread. First, Canvas which forms the Cover of the Bed and our Seat in the Canoe. Then a Bed of Blankets sewn together which form an Article of Trade in the Interior; on these two fine Blankets as Sheets and above this a coloured Blanket as a Coverlid. The Fire is kept up all Night for the Purpose of boiling the Men's Dinner which consists in Indian Corn and Pork, from which they are called Pork Eaters."

This is an express canoe, and by three o'clock in the morning they are away. Each portage is described, the detail of rock formation, nature of trees and rapids. Some days are glorious with sunshine and scenery, and some nights made wretched by rain and insects. At Sault Ste. Marie, Garry pays ecstatic tribute to Lake Superior whitefish, and notes the Indians playing lacrosse with a ball and "bat four feet in length and terminating in a sort of racket."

They entered Lake Superior in fog so dense that he could not see the bow of the canoe. "It required good deal of Philosophy to bear up against Rain, Fog and Musquitoes which are in travelling real Miseries." Nicholas Garry was receiving an education which should bring the realism of the fur trade to the board room of Hudson's Bay House. He remarked the uncommon ugliness of Indian women. On Sunday, July 1, they entered the magnificence of Thunder Bay; Fort William was before them. "We were received with the firing of guns and the shouts of Indians and Canadians!!! Timeo Danaos et dona ferentes."

For the first time Garry came to grips with the purpose of his journey. The McGillivray brothers, it appears, were not entirely generous in their support. So far as active fur trade management went, they had finished, and their presence at Fort William, confronted by their late partners whose interests they had sold out, was only

the fulfilment of a final obligation assumed with the London
deal. Nicholas Garry carried the burden of fifteen days of
querulous wrangling. The diary at this point is most
exasperating. A few swift sentences on the biting comments the wintering partners must have made, or a paragraph on the defensive position taken by the McGillivrays,
would make stirring reading. But the diary passes for
days with no entries, or merely gives baffling "discussions
without end."

This much emerges during the second week of the
negotiations. Twenty-three partners had signed the Deed
Poll and received their commissions from the Deputy
Governor as chief factors or chief traders. The real obstacle
was encountered when it came to assigning these men
to their posts, a delicate task, alive with potential jealousy
and resentment because of the wide variety in living
conditions and climate of the posts from Oregon to
Ungava. Garry's ascendancy emerged at this acute crisis.
In his own odd, self-effacing way he concludes his
paragraph on the subject, "The whole Body of Chief
Factors declared that I had only to express my Wishes;
thus they were appointed and every difficulty here thus
removed."

Garry issued the list of appointments on July 17. Here
are some whose names are found today on the map of
the Dominion of Canada, marking fast rivers, crystal lakes,
and ice-crowned peaks. Unarmed and with no beating
of drums they went by express canoe to their posts in the
farthest reaches of British North America, almost un-
consciously engaged upon the bloodless conquest of an
empire. Had they led red-coated soldiery on punitive
expeditions against savages, and planted flags over burned
villages, their names might today be cut deep and large
upon stone in high places. But they were only fur traders
going about their business, and as the years rolled on and
the Company of Adventurers of England trading into
Hudson's Bay became inseparably involved in imperial
purpose, they and those who followed immediately after

them became somewhat alive to the parts they were playing in British affairs.

Athapascan Department: James Leith, Chief Factor, Chief of Department; Edward Smith, Chief Factor; Chief Traders—William Mackintosh, Joseph McGillivray, Peter W. Dease, Hugh Faries, A. R. McCleod.

New Caledonia: John Stewart, Chief Factor.

Cumberland House: William Kennedy, Chief Factor.

Columbia: Chief Factors John Haldane and J. D. Cameron; Chief Trader James Macmillan.

English River: Chief Factor James Keith; Chief Trader J. F. LaRoque.

Saskatchewan: Chief Factor James Sutherland; Chief Trader John Rowand.

York Fort: Chief Factor J. M. McTavish.

Moose Factory: Chief Factor Angus Bethune.

Lesser Slave Lake: Chief Trader William Connolly.

Red River: Chief Factor James Bird.

Upper Red River: Chief Factor John McDonald.

Fort Dauphin: Chief Trader Allan McDonell.

Pic: Alexander McTavish, Clerk.

Michicopoton: Chief Trader Donald McIntosh.

Fort William: Chief Trader Alexr. Stewart.

Lake Huron: Chief Factor John McBean.

River Winnipic: Chief Trader Thomas McMurray.

Timmiskamain: Chief Trader Angus Cameron.

Churchill: Chief Factor John Charles; Chief Trader John Lee Lewis; A. McDonell, clerk.

This merely completed the first phase of Garry's task, and on July 21 he left Fort William for Rupert's Land. "Never in my life have I left a place with less regret," he wrote. The party now travelled in two canoes, one manned by a sextet from the Montreal–Fort William route, commonly called porkeaters from their rations, the other one paddled by six voyageurs of the north country. These last looked down on the porkeaters, thinking themselves vastly superior, and forcing the pace to prove their mettle. Their rivalry added spice to Garry's trip. Up over the tedious height of land portages they passed into Rainy

Lake, the layman observing in his diary the narrow swampy trails and shallow streams, the traffic way of thousands of tons of goods and millions of dollars' worth of furs.

Through the Lake of the Woods and down the Winnipeg River; with all the haste of the express canoe Garry took time off to bathe in and admire the beauty of those waters which today are summer retreats for city-bred Canadians. Dining beside a rapids of the Winnipeg River, he muses in his stilted manner about Fact and Folly and the Want of Happiness in this Life, and the Dissatisfaction with the Present and a Longing or Desire for Something in the . Future. The beauty of flowers and "the Waterfall, wild, romantic, bold" quiet his spirit. The sentences reflect the artificial cult of nature worship which flourished in Europe at the time.

They stopped for two days at the Red River Settlement, and Garry interviewed the Scottish settlers, and formed a low opinion of the de Meurons. He could see the problems on the spot, and appreciate Lord Selkirk's efforts. It had been barely five years since Seven Oaks, and the wounds were not yet closed in spite of the settlement reached by the companies. Here was a task for the Hudson's Bay Company. The colony still belonged to the Selkirk heirs. The Company's moral obligation to support it was recognized in London, yet the ultimate incompatibility of colonial settlement and fur trading was also appreciated. Nicholas Garry was the only Committee member except Selkirk to have stood on the banks of the Red River; his moderate and tempered views unquestionably bore substantial weight in the Company's attitude during the ensuing years until the Selkirk grant was purchased in 1834 for fifteen thousand pounds of Company stock.

On August 5 the two canoes left Fort Douglas for Norway House on Lake Winnipeg on their way to York Factory and more conferences to name commissioned officers. Garry rode a borrowed horse along the Red River from Fort Douglas, joining the canoes downstream. "Rode about 9 miles today through the most beautiful meadows,

excellent grass, uncultivated and producing such Abundance
as to be almost inexhaustible." They had a bad few
hours on treacherous Lake Winnipeg when they were
caught in a sudden gale five miles from shore. At Norway
House Garry met and talked with old Hudson's Bay men
from August 9 to 16, but wrote only terse entries in the
diary. He resumed meticulous notes a few days later as
they journeyed downstream to Hudson Bay. On the
rapids of Hill River Garry's canoe struck a rock and sank;
the party clinging to rocks midstream was rescued with
difficulty by McGillivray's men; they even managed to
salvage some of their goods and spent a day drying out.

They arrived at York on August 23, having swung in a
great semicircle from Montreal to Red River and to Hudson
Bay. Garry had entered the west by the North West
Company route and he was leaving by the Hudson's Bay
Company way. The weeks of travel in close intimacy
had not nourished a friendship between Garry and Mc-
Gillivray; by the end of the journey irritations on both
sides were apparent. The proud, sensitive, little Scottish-
Canadian and the cool, remote, somewhat priggish Englishman were not on the best terms, though neither was petty
enough to endanger the interests they represented by an
open breach.

Garry needed all the diplomacy and strength he had to
carry him through his stay at York. Just before they
landed there had also come a shipload of one hundred
and seventy Selkirk colonists from Switzerland. The habit
of years made McGillivray's French voyageurs play the
old North West game of terrorizing the arrivals with
accounts of the misery and death by starvation which lay
ahead of them. Garry heard about it and acted immediately, ordering the voyageurs out of the colonist camp.
The voyageurs defied him; he appealed to McGillivray,
who declined to be firm and even took the part of the
agitators. A weaker man might have found reason to
compromise, but Garry ordered the offenders to be seized
and put on board the ship still lying at anchor off York,

and he won his point. The handling of the Red River Settlement work depressed him. He saw that the co-operation of the Company in receiving the settlers at York was inadequate, and that the Swiss immigrants he met had been poorly chosen and badly led.

While Garry was at York, a letter came from Captain John Franklin, then wintering far in the north-west at Fort Enterprise near the headwaters of the Coppermine River. It was the first winter of gallant Franklin's first overland expedition. In his letter he reported all well and supplies adequate. The expedition was destined to end the next year in misery for all and death for some of the party.

Of the granting of commissions to the Hudson's Bay men in their own headquarters base of York Factory, and of the meetings of the council newly formed under the Deed Poll, Garry writes nothing. His most intricate prob-lem, that of appointing the local governors, was un-expectedly ironed out. In order to provide amicably for all the North West wintering partners, it had been necessary to give them superior numbers in the ranks of the com-missioned officers. To offset this inequity again, the governors of the two largest and most important depart-ments, the Northern and the Southern, were to be Hudson's Bay men. The Northern Department of Rupert's Land was the dominant command, and with its governorship went the lion's share of prestige and power.

William Williams, head of the Hudson's Bay men in the last days of the fur war, had prior claim upon the post of honour. Garry says that had it not been for Williams's "firm manly conduct" in fighting the North-westers "at the Hazard of his Life," the Hudson's Bay Company would have been driven completely out of the trade. This is somewhat hard to credit in the light of the known records, yet it may be one of those many incidents in the Company's history which only advanced research into the archives can solve. In any event, Williams had won the respect of the Governor and Committee and the enmity of the North West party who had warrants out for him in Montreal and had attempted to take him there by force.

Simon McGillivray had advised Garry at Fort William that the appointment of Williams to be head of the Northern Department would not be acceptable to the Montreal interests. At the time Garry had resented this intrusion on his prerogatives, but had held his peace. When they reached York Factory, Williams was there and McGillivray demanded a settlement of the matter. "Much altercation took place between us," wrote Garry, who privately favoured appointing Williams to the Southern Department, but refused utterly to have McGillivray dictate the selection. While Garry had not a very high opinion of the average of Hudson's Bay traders, he had a wholehearted admiration for Williams, and was anxious not to injure his feelings. He approached Williams "with some fears." To his delight Williams was happy to take the Southern Department; his commission was signed one day earlier than that of the governor of the preferred Northern Department, thus giving him seniority over all other officers.

To the governorship of the Northern Department of Rupert's Land and the far Columbia was appointed a Scot, aged thirty-four, George Simpson, who had been in the Hudson's Bay fur trade barely a year. History has found large space for his name; Nicholas Garry gave him scarcely a reference in the diary.

Garry's work was finished. It was frosty at York Factory in mid-September, and the officers of the council must be away to their posts before the freeze-up. Simon McGillivray in his express canoe had already left for Montreal. The Company ship *Prince of Wales* stood out from York with Garry aboard, immensely relieved that it was all over, and recalling his depression and fear before he undertook the task.

"I was not insensible to the kind, flattering manner in which the gentlemen of York Fort took leave of me, nor shall I ever forget Governor Williams' strong expression of feeling towards myself . . . so long as I continue in the Direction their Interests will be uppermost in my Thoughts. . . . Their hearty warm cheers on my embarking. . . . Thus has terminated my Mission to Rupert's Land, the last gun fired from the Fort putting an end to the president of the council . . . all parties satisfied except those who have sinister & sordid views . . . having had it in my Power to protect so many people who otherwise would have suffered. . . ."

So Nicholas Garry leaves the fur trade scene better than he found it, having set into motion a new monopoly with potential power and authority greater than he ever imagined. This honest, pious man—he succeeded in holding a meeting of the Auxiliary Bible Society at York and actually got one hundred and thirty pounds subscribed by the astonished fur traders—left behind him a feeling of cordiality between officers and proprietors which was a large part of the Company's strength in future years. Garry was Deputy Governor until 1835, when he retired, his mind clouded by some unnamed affliction, lingering on to die in 1856, accompanied to the end by his loyal servant Raven.

The Mr. Simpson who cheered and waved farewell to Garry from the officer group on the shore of Hudson Bay that autumn of 1821, was to become "the little Emperor" of the fur trade, the ruler of a territory Bonaparte himself might have envied.

THE JOURNEYS OF SIR GEORGE SIMPSON, 1820-1860

Based upon his letters now in the Archives of the Hudson's Bay Company.

FROM—TO	APPROXIMATE ROUTES	YEARS TRAVELLED (Years underlined mean the return journey was made the same year)
New York—Lachine	–x–x–	1820, 1826, 1839, 1847
Boston—Lachine	●●●●●	1841, 1844, 1845, 1847
Lachine—Lake Winnipeg, en route to either Red River or Norway House (via Toronto and Detroit in 1848 and 1857)	——	1820, 1826, 1827, 1828, 1829, 1830, 1833, 1834, 1835, 1836, 1837, 1839, 1841, 1843, 1844, 1845, 1846, 1847, 1848, 1849, 1850, 1852 to Sault Ste. Marie only, 1853, 1854, 1855, 1856, 1857, 1858, 1859
Red River—Norway House	+-+-+	1820, 1822, 1824, 1826, 1828, 1829, 1830, 1831, 1832, 1834, 1836, 1837, 1846, 1847, 1848, 1849, 1850, 1853, 1854, 1855, 1856, 1858, 1859
Norway House—York Factory	–·–·–	1821, 1822, 1823, 1824, 1825, 1826, 1827, 1828, 1830, 1831, 1832, 1834, 1846
Norway House—Athabasca and Great Slave Lake	–o–o–	1820, 1821, 1822, 1823
Norway House or Red River—Columbia	–o–o–	1824, 1825, 1828, 1829, 1841
Moose Factory—Lachine, Red River Route	xxxxx	1827, 1829, 1834, 1836, 1837, 1839, 1843, 1844, 1851
Lachine—Lake St. John	+++++	1839
Ft. Vancouver—Sitka	–··–··–	1841
Lachine—St. Paul	x·x·x·	1860
Red River—Detroit, via St. Paul	x·x·x·	1858

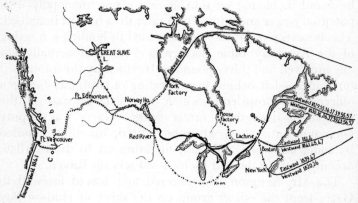

CHAPTER XII

GEORGE SIMPSON

MORE than one historian has elaborated upon the perfect combination of the man and the moment. George Simpson was such a man. A series of coincidences placed him among fur traders. In the very last year of the bitter North West war he terrorized the enemy yet collected a magnificent supply of furs. He stepped naturally into the important vacancy as governor of the Northern Department; and the way finally became clear to the very throne of the fur trade empire.

George Simpson was born at Loch Broom, Ross-shire, Scotland, in 1787, the illegitimate son of George Simpson. A kinswoman raised him, and he received a sound education. Of these early years little is known, and though his own letter and journal writing was prodigious, he never wrote of his young days. In 1809 he was a clerk in the London mercantile house of Graham, Simpson and Wedderburn, engaged in overseas trade. His uncle, Geddes McKenzie Simpson, was a partner in the firm, and father of George Simpson's future wife. Simpson's work in the firm was noticed by Andrew Colvile, a member of the Committee of the Hudson's Bay Company, Deputy Governor from 1839 to 1852, and Governor from 1852 to 1856. As a middle-aged man Simpson made whole-hearted acknowledgment to Colvile. "To you," he wrote, "I am solely indebted for my advancement in Life." Colvile introduced Simpson to the Hudson's Bay Company.

Competition by starvation, ambush and arrest had so shattered the normal course of fur trading by 1820 that the Governor and Committee were obliged to prepare for strange emergencies. The Company's local governor, William Williams, was threatened by a Lower Canada warrant for his arrest because he had seized the North West partners at Grand Rapids. The Company was thus in imminent danger of losing its local governor, and on February 9, 1820, prepared for the emergency: ". . . in consequence of the Indictments which have been found against Governor Williams in Lower Canada and the consequent risk of his being carried down to Canada, it is expedient to send out a person to act as Locum Tenens in the event of Governor Williams's absence from the Territory of the Company."

George Simpson was chosen to be the locum tenens, and he reported to Williams at Norway House, Lake Winnipeg, in June, 1820. Simpson was then thirty-three years of age. The orders were that he was to take temporary command if Williams was "carried down" to Montreal; but it was also arranged that if Williams continued to forestall arrest,

N

Simpson was to return to England the following autumn, unless his superior was satisfied that his "Services in the Country would be of essential importance."

Williams, living in constant expectation of raid and capture, was directing a fang-and-claw fight with great courage. The one thing he needed above all else was an energetic, intelligent young man. With fine generalship, he took the newcomer's measure, and sent him to take command of the Athabasca country, the very storm centre of the fur trade battle and the last stronghold of the enemy. It is to Williams's undying credit that he saw in the young man from the London counting-house the qualities of a fighter who could take the offensive against the shock troops of the North West Company.

On July 30, Simpson led a brigade of fifteen canoes up the Saskatchewan, over Methye Portage, and on to Fort Wedderburn, where he settled down to administer the final blows to the Canadian Company's forces at Fort Chipewyan a mile away. It was a fighting apprenticeship to fur trading and a baptism of fire he never forgot. Before the next year was over, he commanded the whole north-land. At Fort Wedderburn he was stepping into Colin Robertson's shoes. That enterprising adventurer had carried the Company's fur trade even beyond Athabasca and into the Peace River country. The opposition was led by Samuel Black, the very personification of a reckless North West trader. (Years later when an officer of the Hudson's Bay Company, Black was murdered by Indians.) Black by 1820 had a record of aggressive action known only too well to the Hudson's Bay men. He and Peter Skene Ogden had driven "the English" from the Ile-à-la-Crosse district, and he had been recalled from the Pacific Coast to lead the Northwesters in Athabasca.

From the stranger, Simpson—"reputedly a gentlemanly man," one Northwester wrote—they did not anticipate "much alarm." It turned out to be as strenuous a season of competitive fur trading as any Canadian party had ever encountered. Long afterwards, when Simpson was head of the Northern Department and Black was a Hudson's Bay officer, the two met, and Simpson wrote, "Black could, at first, hardly look me in the face. He remembered my Athabasca campaign and never will he forget the terrors in which he was kept that winter. We parted excellent friends."

Simpson has left another of the few glimpses of that winter which history has been allowed. "In the year 1820 our provisions fell short at the establishment, and on two or three occasions I went for two or three whole days and nights without having a single morsel to swallow, but then, again, I was one of a party of eleven men and one woman which discussed at one sitting meal no less than three ducks and twenty-two geese."

Suffering there certainly was, and there was also victory. In the spring of 1821 Simpson brought out his canoes loaded with furs, and it can safely be assumed that his accounts were in order. At Norway House he learned of the union of the two companies earlier that year. Through the following summer of truce, when the warring factions paused, restlessly waiting the arrival of Garry and Mc-Gillivray to bring authoritative news of the peace terms, George Simpson had time to reflect upon his own career and calculate the opportunities around him. He had seen in the Red River and Saskatchewan countries the wreckage of unbridled competition; he had met and lived among fur traders, toughened by the years of conflict— the genteel Nicholas Garry thought them "a pusillanimous, heartless Set of Men"—and he could look forward to potential profits of the monopoly now crystallizing.

In September came the ticklish meeting of council, and that series of convergent circumstances which made Simpson governor of the Northern Department. That was not all. Williams in the Southern Department retained his technical seniority only until 1826, when he returned to England. Then Simpson became governor-in-chief of the Hudson's Bay Company's territories.

For nearly forty years Simpson, a civilian administrator

of a commercial enterprise, ruled his benevolent monarchy. Under the authority of the British Crown and responsible only to the London Committee, who held the reins lightly, he moulded a form of economic-political government around the framework of the Company's exclusive licence to trade endorsed by the British Government. The architecture of this unique structure was Simpson's life work. Sensitive to the wishes of proprietors, who were never over-exacting in their demands while dividends appeared, and cautiously playing the hand of imperial policy for a government whose support could be counted on in any tight corner, he won a commercial and political triumph. His story as a study in business and diplomacy will some day be told at length. It is known now only as an important phase of fur trade history, but when his record is recounted in its entirety, together with the absorbing biography of the man himself, Simpson will appear as a composite of fur trader, merchant prince, Machiavelli and statesman.

In the history of the Hudson's Bay Company, he is the central figure not only in his own time but in the whole long story. He strode into office and set a tempo of management such as fur trading had never known, and he maintained the pace almost to the end of his days. "The North West is now beginning to be ruled with a rod of iron," wrote a trader in 1824, for even then Simpson was vigorously stripping down the Company into a smoothly operating business mechanism.

In the beginning his main task was the incorporation of the old enemies into the new organization. His position as a comparative newcomer free from the old rancour strengthened his hand, although Simon McGillivray had planted parting seeds of dissension by warning his old colleagues to distrust Simpson as "a more dangerous man than the other [Williams] altho' not so violent." The real test of his authority came at the meetings of the Council of the Northern Department each summer at Norway House or at Red River. For the first few years Simpson sat with his men and played a bland, compromising rôle, winning the support of both factions, but steadily guiding the whole structure into the somewhat painful path of economy. With the passing of years his grip on the council became absolute, and his decisions were unchallenged.

As soon as snow fell in 1821, the new governor moved off on the first of his many trips of inspection, making a circuit of fifteen hundred miles from York to Norway House, Cumberland House, Swan River, Qu'Appelle and Brandon House, to arrive at Red River's newly named Fort Garry early in March, 1822. In a private letter to Colvile from Fort Garry in May, 1822, he estimated the prospects of the district he had just covered. Indians, spoiled by the recent extravagant competition, were now reluctant to trade. "Mild and cautious measures" would be necessary here. The winter buffalo hunt had failed again, and the Selkirk colony, augmented by the Swiss whom Garry had met at York, barely escaped starvation. Simpson thought little of a mission-school plan for the education of Indian children which apparently had originated in the Committee. In his opinion an educated Indian meant an indolent Indian, and the only benefit would be in "filling the pockets and bellies of some hungry missionaries and schoolmasters." He made it clear to Colvile that while the Rev. John West, chaplain to the Hudson's Bay Company, was a worthy, well-meaning man, he should keep his fingers out of the Company's trade affairs and not expect to be transported freely about the country in Company canoes which should be loaded to capacity with trade goods or furs.

His letter, crammed with business details for Colvile's guidance in Committee affairs, tells of new and shorter river routes to the Bay which he proposes to explore personally, despite the veiled sneers of the old hands, in the hope of saving days and hours of costly transportation.

This was young Simpson of 1822. Years mellowed his judgment, and before a decade passed he was an active supporter of native schools, a contributor to the missionary cause, and pressing upon the Northern and Southern councils resolutions consistently restricting the use of spirits in various districts, working towards complete elimination of liquor in the fur trade.

The autumn of 1822 found him planning another inspection trip, this time by snowshoe and dog team to the upper Saskatchewan, the Athabasca and the Peace River country. "The object of this immence Journey," he wrote Colvile, "is, if possible, to check abuses which nothing but my own presence can effectually stop; and to get rid of several Establishments which are a heavy burden on the concern . . . this will not only relieve us of heavy expences but Enable exhausted tracts of Country to recruit." The last phrase is one of his first references to his policy of conservation of fur wealth which marked his administration.

A year passed, and the young governor, tirelessly applying himself to his enormous task, writes once more to his benefactor in London. The Red River colony, or Assiniboia, as it was called, continued to irritate the commissioned officers who felt that its administrative costs as borne by the Company reduced their fur trade profits. There was the problem of bringing the former North West men into conformity with Hudson's Bay accounting methods. Simpson also planned his first exploration by sending Samuel Black into unknown northern Caledonia. The management of the half-breed race would require study. Simpson hoped to cross the mountains to the Columbia. The letter to Colvile is quoted for its wealth of revelation of the difficulties Simpson faced, and his own clarity of purpose:

"I . . . shall therefore now take the liberty of drawing your attention to the feelings of the Council in respect to Colony affairs. Nearly every member thereof is hostile to the Settlement, both Hudson's Bay and North West, and this principally arises from the expense it entails on the concern and the continual fever in which the Colonists keep us. By the Deed Poll or rather the Original Deed between the Contracting parties it is provided that no expense relating to Colonization will affect the Fur Trade. The salys [salaries] to the Governor and Clergyman therefore gave them a handle to break out violently; it kept them in a ferment the whole season, and altho' I used every means to bring them into good humour it was for a length of time impossible; they looked upon me with suspicion, had private meetings in Councils day after day, and were about to have written the Committee in a strain which must have given offence. Robertson [Colin] was one of the leading malcontents, but his blustering folly knocked the whole on the head, and in order to make himself pass for a man of weight came out with all their secrets which gave me an opportunity of bringing them to their senses; in short I found it necessary to show my power and authority and in full Council gave them a lecture which had the desired effect, made them look on each other with suspicion and restored their confidence in myself. Instead of writing themselves they left the whole to me and attended to their other business. No man ever took greater pains or labour to please and give satisfaction than I have done but some of our Chief Factors are so much accustomed to grumble that a Saint could scarcely keep them in humour. This last season however I found it necessary to act with firmness, convinced them that I could talk loud also, and made an example of Robertson to begin with. He was more noisy about the Colony than any other, talked of rights and previledges, getting Councils opinion on the Deed Poll, in short wished to be a Leader, but I have made such an exposure this season of his maladministration in the Saskatchawine and told him so many home truths in presence of the whole Council that he is quite crest fallen and will I think give no more trouble. McDonald (one eye) was likewise inclined to be violent about the expenses incurred on account of the Colony, and was to have given me a set down or prepared speech thereon at the close of the sittings, but the lecture to Robertson had the desired effect, none seemed inclined to enter the Lists with me again, and on the whole we all separated on excellent terms and I believe they have now a greater respect for me than ever. It is extremely desirable to keep our Factors and Traders in good humour until the accounts look a little better than they at present do. . . . With these men I find nothing does so well in the long run as candour and plain dealing, it may not be palatable at times, but must ultimately prevail, and finesse should never and will not be resorted to by me except in extraordinary cases. . . .

"A great number of discharged servants with their Families have this season gone to the Settlement which will relieve our Establishments greatly, but I imagine it will be necessary for us to assist many of them this winter.

"I have requested leave of absence of the Committee agreeable to your kind suggestion, but have left it to Mr. Garry privately whether I go to England or to the Columbia next season, and it is probable he will consult you on the subject; in this I have no choice or request to make; you know the object of my visit to England and I have pointed out where my services and presence may be useful, and have no desire that my private views should interfere with the interests of the service. . . ."

The object of the visit to England was marriage to his cousin Frances Ramsay Simpson, but the event had to be postponed seven years in the interest of the Hudson's Bay Company's efficiency. In the early years of his administration, the Governor and Committee through Colvile directed Simpson much more closely than later. Thus Colvile, answering this letter from Simpson, suggests delay for one or more years as there will be long and hazardous journeys for the governor of Rupert's Land. As for the animosity of the officers towards the colony, Colvile declares that the Governor and Committee will act at all times with justice towards the chief factors and chief traders, but it is to be understood that London will not tolerate any return to the old oppression of Selkirk's colony. The settlers have the rights and privileges of British subjects, and the commissioned officers as partners in the Company have obligations in the maintenance of the settlement. Colvile puts his young governor right upon the exasperating subject of missions, pointing out that if there were no colony at Red River the Company would still be obliged to keep a chaplain. "Indeed it wd be extremely impolitic in the present temper & disposition of the public in this Country to show any unwillingness to assist in such an object. By uniting with the Missionary Society & the Settlement these objects are obtained safely, conveniently & cheaply."

Colvile outlines two or three years of travel and exploration to be accomplished. First, to put the settlement in good order; then off across the prairie and the Rockies to the Columbia River; a season "perhaps in McKenzie's river & near Caledonia" where "active and discreet" officers were to be sent to explore north and west into new passes of the mountains. It is the old call from London for more discovery, as in the Kelsey days, but now the men of the Company are ahead of the management, for already under Simpson traders are reaching into the blank spaces of the maps.

By 1824 Simpson had put new life into the fur trade, from Hudson Bay to the Rockies. West of the mountains there was still work to be done. The northern part of that vast and mostly unexplored land was known as New Caledonia, and the southern was called the Department of Columbia; both were unprofitable legacies from the North West Company. Bold and enterprising as the opening of the Pacific Coast had been, the costly operation of this peak of North West ambition had contributed to that company's distress. For Simpson it offered a very different problem from Rupert's Land. The sovereignty of the Pacific slope was a question of international uncertainty. California was Spanish. Alaska was Russian. The central part, which today is British Columbia, Washington and Oregon, at that time was only vaguely outlined and there was a ten-year treaty of joint occupation between the United States and Great Britain. This compromise had been arranged in 1818; under its terms citizens of both countries were free to engage in trade. The British

Government, by the exclusive licence to trade, had granted the Hudson's Bay Company a monopoly over the territory so far as British subjects were concerned. Thus the Hudson's Bay Company's competitors in that part were "free traders" from the United States. The position was delicate, requiring a keen trading sense and a capacity for high statecraft. The joint arrangement was renewed in 1827, and it continued until the Oregon Treaty of 1846 finally determined the Canada–United States boundary.

The Northwesters had opened their Pacific slope venture by building posts at McLeod and Stuart lakes, the latter named after John Stuart, uncle of Donald A. Smith, who was to rise from an apprentice clerk in the Simpson régime to be governor of the Hudson's Bay Company from 1889 to 1914. The post on Stuart Lake, Fort St. James, trading with the Indians to this day, is the oldest permanent settlement in British Columbia. In 1808 Simon Fraser had descended the river bearing his name, to seek a practicable outlet to the sea, but its waters were too turbulent for a trading route. Between 1808 and 1811 David Thompson in his dogged, orderly way had explored the entire circuitous length of the Columbia River, building posts in the present states of Washington, Idaho and Montana. New England captains had been in the Pacific Coast trade since Robert Gray of Boston had named the Columbia River after his ship, in 1792. Lewis and Clark had come overland to the southern valley of the Columbia in 1805, and John Jacob Astor's American Fur Company had established Astoria at the mouth of the river, with outposts as far north as Kamloops. The Northwesters bought him out, and then could make no profit in the trade. They had tried to sell their furs in Canton, China, but there had encountered another British monopoly, the East India Company which allowed them to sell their furs in China but not to take back the precious tea.

The Hudson's Bay Company viewed with a dubious eye its newly acquired Columbia rights after the union. In 1822 the Governor and Committee advised Simpson that they were prepared to withdraw from the country if he recommended it. Colvile urged him to inspect that department before coming home on leave so that the Company could either pull out promptly, or install a new organization there.

It was 1824 before Simpson could leave the other departments to cross to the Columbia. August of that year found him at York Factory. The Council had met and the governor had toiled days and nights over his correspondence, for he must soon be away to the west—to cross the Rockies before winter seized the water routes.

York Factory on Hudson Bay was no longer a mere trading post at the mouth of the Hayes River. It had become the great depot for imported goods and exported furs. Only a few local Indians traded there now, but the brigades of canoes, deep laden with furs, landed there each summer from all the territory between Montana and the Arctic and as far west as the Rockies. Warehouses, officers' and servants' quarters, a carpenter's shop, a smithy, and other buildings were grouped in orderly arrangement within the palisades. When the brigades were at York in summer the nights glittered with hundreds of campfires along the shore where voyageurs gambled, sang and fought (Hudson Bay style—kick, bite, scratch). Offshore the Company ship swung at anchor, the trade goods having been lightered ashore and the bales of furs stowed below. In the officers' mess and in Bachelors' Hall where the apprentice clerks gathered under the yellow lantern light, there was long talk of the year's adventures, of solitary travel, of the buffalo hunts, and of homes across the sea. Lonely, hardworking York, no longer armed to the teeth against marauding Frenchmen, her guns fired only salutes for arriving and departing dignitaries. Mosquito-ridden in early summer, torn by north-west winds from the Barren Lands in winter, York's white buildings were the ultimate luxury to the fur trader from up country; to the dour apprentice lads fresh from the Orkney Islands it was the end of weeks on the North Atlantic and the port of entry to a career.

George Simpson waited there, toiling over the Company's business, until August 15, 1824, hoping each day for the ship from England bearing the Governor and Committee's latest instructions.   At length he could wait no longer. Accompanied by Chief Trader James McMillan, a veteran of the Columbia Department, eight voyageurs, an Indian guide and his personal servant, Simpson started for the Pacific in a north canoe.   Chief Factor Dr. John McLoughlin, whose appointment to command the Columbia District had been approved by the council at York, had started west twenty days earlier.

Characteristically, Simpson set himself the double objective of exploring a new route from Hudson Bay to the Saskatchewan, and also overtaking the doctor.   He started up the Nelson instead of the Hayes River route, travelling west by Split Lake and Frog Portage.   By September 5 he was at Ile-à-la-Crosse, "having performed the Voyage from York in 22 days or 18 Working Days, the quickest passage ever made," he wrote in his journal.

This journal of the 1824–25 crossing from York Factory to the Columbia and back to Fort Garry is utterly self-revealing.   Simpson says he kept it only for his personal use, but at the end of the journey he sent it promptly to London for the perusal of the Committee, and one cannot avoid the suspicion that it was written from the outset with a view to its ultimate examination at Hudson's Bay House.   It was capably edited by Frederick Merk and published by the Harvard University Press in 1931.   Into it Simpson crammed all manner of trenchant observation so skilfully that there is scarcely an extraneous sentence. Details of every description relating to fur trading were entered; portages, navigability of waterways, weather, the business ability and character of traders and clerks at inspected posts, the trade prospects for various districts, and notes on economies to be effected.   He is the driving executive, concentrating on the work in hand with keen application.

Simpson found that one of his chief factors commanding

a brigade destined for Lesser Slave Lake from York, had sent his four canoes on ahead while he swung off in a light canoe to enjoy a few hours' diversion at Norway House before rejoining the slower freight canoes. Simpson had expected to overtake his chief factor considerably farther on.

"He did not explain the cause of this detention satisfactorily, and I consider his conduct to be highly reprehensible. This Gentleman left York on the 28th of July but on losing sight of the Factory he started ahead taking the precaution of being lighter and better manned than the other Canoes, pushed on to Norway House with his own Canoe leaving his Brigade to make the best of their way after him which is in direct opposition to the established regulations as p Resolution of Council 1823 and as might be expected when Craft and property are thus left to the charge of careless Servants, due diligence was not observed and one of the Canoes was upset in Jack river where several of the pieces were lost and others much damaged. I shall not say what induced all this haste on the part of Mr Clarke and the neglect of his duty yet will hazard an opinion that this accident and delay would not have taken place had he bestowed more attention to the charge with which he was entrusted and less to Domestic affairs. This breach of one of our most important regulations I mean to bring under the consideration of the Council and to move that the loss and expence occasioned thereby shall be placed to his private account."

This was done.

At Ile-à-la-Crosse the inventory of the post was all wrong; the Indians were hunting furs instead of provisions, which were so necessary to supply the brigades in transit. The clerks and servants here were accordingly to be reduced by two-thirds next season at a saving of three hundred and fifty pounds.

On July 26, at seven in the morning, Simpson overtook John McLoughlin's party in River la Biche, and was privately delighted with the big doctor's discomfiture at being caught still in camp at that hour. John McLoughlin was one of the strong characters rising in the fur trade. In the empire of the Columbia District he was to win power for himself, which brought a clash with Simpson and entanglement in international affairs. On this July morning he was a chief factor leading a brigade across a continent, meeting his governor who noted "his Surprise and vexation at being overtaken in River la Biche notwithstanding his having a 20 days start of us from York."

Simpson described him:

"He was such a figure as I should not like to meet in a dark Night in one of the bye lanes in the neighbourhood of London, dressed in Clothes that had once been fashionable, but now covered with a thousand patches of different Colors, his hands evidently Shewing that he had not lost much time at his Toilette, loaded with Arms and his own herculean dimensions forming a tout ensemble that would convey a good idea of the highway men of former Days."

On the Athabasca River, Simpson visited the establishment where he had been a clerk leading a trade war against Samuel Black. He makes no sentimental reference to the past, but plans for the future to save one thousand pounds a year by a redivision of canoe routes, eliminating the slow English River–Beaver River course to the Athabasca, using instead the North Saskatchewan to Edmonton and cutting a wagon road north from there. He is sure the Committee will approve. There is a note on the fluctuations of the trade. An old man alone on a raft drifts downstream. He is "Poor Burleigh" who, twenty years before, had retired from the fur trade with seven thousand pounds, "but so enchanted was he with the roving life of a Freeman and the charms of some half Doz Wives (natives of the soil) that he could not sit down quietly at Home and enjoy his good fortune but must revisit the Indian country since which time he has met with nothing but reverses;

his Money disappeared, his talent as a hunter forsook him and as he advanced in Years Wife after Wife deserted him."

Simpson "upbraided him with his folly," and offered to send him to Lower Canada without expense in Company canoes. With all his intolerance of opposition in his own ranks, and his unyielding enmity towards Company opponents, Simpson always offered practical sympathy to the poor in distress.

The governor's party was at Jasper House in the Rockies by October 10, and met Thomas McKay, son of Alexander McKay who had accompanied Mackenzie across the mountains. His father had died in the service of the Astor Company; he himself had been with Astor, the North West Company, and was at this time at the outset of twenty-five years in Hudson's Bay's service. Simpson makes further observations here on the handling of difficult Indians and the meeting of competition from the free men, independent white men or half-breeds engaged in fur trade in contravention to the Company's monopoly rights.

With a cavalcade of twenty-one horses they started across the Rockies on October 10 by the defiles of the Athabasca Pass:

"Wild & Majestic beyond description; the track is in many places nearly impassable and it appears extraordinary how any human being should have stumbled on a pass through such a formidable barrier as we are now scaleing."

Sunday, October 17: "At the very top of the pass or height of Land is a small circular Lake or Basin of Water which empties itself in opposite directions and may be said to be the source of the Columbia & Athabasca Rivers as it bestows its favors on both these prodigious Streams, the former falling into the Pacific at Lat. $46\frac{1}{2}$ north and the latter after passing through Athabasca & Great Slave Lakes falling into the Frozen Ocean at about 69 North Lat. That this basin should send its Waters to each side of the Continent and give birth to two of the principal

Rivers in North America is no less strange than true both
the Dr. & myself having examined the currents flowing
from it east & West and the circumstance appearing
remarkable I thought it should be honored by a distinguishing title and it was forthwith named the
'Committee's Punch Bowl.'"

Today the line separating British Columbia from Alberta
divides this tiny lake.

After two days in quagmire, quicksand and dense brush
the trail came out at Boat Encampment on the Big Bend
of the Columbia River. Here water communication to
the Pacific began, and the boats from the Lower Columbia
met the pack brigades from Edmonton and the east.
Simpson was now almost two thousand miles from York
Factory. This old Athabasca trail between Jasper House
and Boat Encampment was used by the fur trade for
thirty years after Simpson's crossing in 1824; then it was
abandoned for more southerly passes. Only surveyors,
Indians, and big game hunters have known it for three-
quarters of a century, and its name is recurrent in 1936
as the probable route of a trans-Canada highway.

Simpson was busy speculating on more economical
transportation routes and drafting plans for exploration.
He examined the boats used on the Columbia and found
them overmanned. These batteaux required crews of
eight and had a capacity for thirty-five pieces of ninety
pounds each. They were extravagant and employed one-
third more men than necessary. "I shall however take
care that this evil is remedied before my departure."
Through rain, fog and snow they swept downstream,
sometimes one hundred miles in a day.

Wednesday, October 27: "Got to the Forks of Spokane
river where we found Chief Trader Ogden and Mr Work
with about 30 men who had come up from Fort George
with the outfits for the interior. He [Mr Ogden] repre-
sents the Country to be in a state of Peace and quietness
and the Compy's affairs going on as usual which is not
saying a great deal as if my information is correct the

Sir George Simpson (1787–1860)
For thirty-four years Governor-in-Chief of the Hudson's Bay Company
territories

*Scottish Emperor of
the Fur Trade, 1821.*

Sir George Simpson.

An after-dinner sketch of Sir George Simpson
by James Alexander Grant

Hudson's Bay House, Lachine, near Montreal, bought by the
Company in 1833 as a residence for Simpson. He died there
in 1860 and in 1888 it was demolished

Columbia Deptmt from the Day of its Origin to the
present hour has been neglected, shamefully mismanaged
and a scene of the most wasteful extravagance and the
most unfortunate dissention. It is high time the system
should be changed and I think there is an ample Field
for reform and amendment."

The governor was now in the Columbia Department,
and a complete reorganization was taking place. The
party left the boats, to ride sixty miles overland to Spokane
House. This was the base for the celebrated Snake Country
expeditions. These were itinerant brigades of Company
trappers and freemen sent out each year into the Indian
country. It was dangerous work, trapping among hostile
savages, and Simpson removed the leader Ross ("full of
bombast and marvellous nonsense") and replaced him
with a volunteer, John Dease, ex-Northwester, a "commissioned gentleman," and one of four brothers in the
fur trade.

Simpson denounces those in authority for extravagant
importations of European luxuries. Five and sometimes
six boats have been brought up the Columbia with "Eat-
ables Drinkables and other Domestic Comforts." They
have been consuming the profits of the department in a
country which should be cultivated to produce all their
food requirements. "I mean to send some garden and
field seeds across next season to be tried at Spokane
House."

Back to the Columbia and down the rapids to Okanagan.
More reflections on linking up local farming with fur
trading to reduce expenses. "In these savage regions
Gentlemen sometimes imbibe the exalted notions of Indian
chiefs . . . and are not satisfied unless they have a posse
of Clerks Guides Interpreters and Supernumaries at their
disposal while they look on with a pair of gloves in their
hands."

A note on trading—"An Indian trader who cannot
obtain personal influence and secure himself the respect
and esteem of the Indians he has been dealing with for

o

three years successively is unworthy the title he bears and unfit for the situation he holds."

The very basic principles of Hudson's Bay Company power were being sounded by Simpson as he penned these observations in his journal in his tent by tallow light, or upon his knee as he sat in the boat. The whole journal is more than fifty thousand words in length, and the discomforts and inconveniences under which he wrote have not dulled a sentence of keen reporting nor robbed a paragraph of a clear statement of sound commercial practice.

This Columbia Department, he was convinced, could be brought to profitable production, but there were domestic complications. Too many squaws. "The Honble Committee would scarcely believe that their business is frequently a matter of secondary consideration compared to the little family affairs and domestic arrangements." Too many boats were employed transporting women and children, involving extra men and extra wages. The commissioned gentlemen were going to be held more closely to fur trading.

The western end of the journey was prepared for with traditional flourishes. It was the custom for the boatmen or canoe men to put ashore a few miles from an important fort and change to the gaudy finery of gay shirts, brilliant sashes, ribbons and beaded moccasins. On this journey Simpson had pressed his men hard, and though he encouraged the practice, he had the dressing up done the night before, and kept the men at their paddles all night. Head winds held them back the next day, and it was late afternoon on November 8 before they arrived at Fort George, "having performed the voyage from Hudson's Bay across the continent of America to the Northern Pacific Ocean in 84 days thereby gaining Twenty Days on any Craft that ever preceded us." He interjects the significant comment that on arrival he found the officers in charge of Fort George, Chief Factor Kennedy and Mr. McDonald, "amusing themselves Boat Sailing."

The governor plunged at once into his observations.

"The Establishment of Fort George is a large pile of buildings covering about an acre of ground well stockaded and protected by Bastions or Blockhouses, having two Eighteen Pounders mounted in front and altogether an air or appearance of Grandeur & consequence which does not become and is not at all suitable to an Indian Trading Post. Everything appears to me on the Columbia on too extended a scale except the Trade and when I say that that is confined to Four permanent Establishments the returns of which do not amount to 20,000 Beaver & Otters altho the country has been occupied upwards of Fourteen Years I feel that a very Severe reflection is cast on those who have had the management of the Business."

He forecast the coming of Americans to the Columbia and the possibility of the Company having to move north to the Fraser River country. With this in view a party was sent north to explore, but the Fraser waters proved too fast; and twenty years later, when the influx of settlers obstructed the fur trade, and when the international boundary was defined, the Company went north to establish Victoria on Vancouver Island. Simpson anticipated, as well as local agricultural development, a coastal trade with Spanish California and South American ports. He looked ahead to the time when coastwise shipping would mean business with the Russians in Alaska.

The amiable disposition, verminous condition, absence of chastity and prevalence of venereal disease among the Indians of Fort George were carefully noted. He conceded that here the zeal of the Missionary Society might be crowned with success, and drew up a budget for their guidance. The use of spirits was to be discontinued. The North West Company had been giving as a present, over and above the trade tariff, a bottle of rum to Indians for every ten skins. The Indians were being ruined as hunters, and they must be brought back to sobriety.

The governor spent the winter of 1824–25 at Fort George

setting the new machine in motion. Among the major
changes was the shifting of the department's headquarters
to the north bank of the Columbia in case a boundary
settlement should define the river as the international
border. Fort George was abandoned and Fort Vancouver
established. In March Simpson visited the new fort on
his way east. Having himself chosen the site, he grows
expansive over its setting:

"The Fort is well picketted covering a space of about
¾ths of an acre and the buildings already completed are
a Dwelling House, two good Stores an Indian Hall and
temporary quarters for the people. It will in Two Years
hence be the finest place in North America, indeed I have
rarely seen a Gentlemen's Seat in England possessing so
many natural advantages and where ornament and use
are so agreeably combined. This point if situated within
One Hundred Miles of London would be more valuable
to the proprietor than the Columbian Trade. . . ."

Saturday, March 19th: "At Sun rise mustered all the
people to hoist the Flag Staff of the new Establishment
and in presence of the Gentlemen, Servants, Chiefs &
Indians I Baptised it by breaking a Bottle of Rum on the
Flag Staff and repeating the following words in a loud
voice, 'In behalf of the Honble Hudsons Bay Co. I hereby
name this Establishment Fort Vancouver God Save King
George the 4th' with three cheers. Gave a couple of
Drams to the people and Indians on the occasion. The
object of naming it after that distinguished navigator is to
identify our claim to the Soil and Trade with his discovery
of the River and Coast on behalf of Gt. Britain. If the
Honble Committee however do not approve the Name it
can be altered. At 9 o'clock A.M. took leave of our
Friend the Dr. embarked and continued our Voyage.
Put up for the night about 20 miles below the Cascade
Portage."

Poling and paddling often sixteen hours a day, the
Simpson party laboured up the magnificent stretches of
the Columbia through miserably wet days and nights,
with rare intervals of feasting when a deer fell to their

guns, or pauses to meet and make goodwill gifts to important native chiefs. On April 22 they were at Boat Encampment, where news came that the horses they had expected would not be over from the east side of the portage until the end of the month. Two men were promptly sent ahead to get the canoes ready, while the rest of the party, carrying baggage averaging sixty pounds per man, started on foot through three miles of icy swamp, across two fords and six miles of slippery trail. A mutinous Indian tapped the rum keg and lightened his burden by throwing some baggage into the river. Simpson, enraged, thrashed him publicly and shattered the rum keg with an axe. They forded the river forty-one times one day and seventeen times the next.

On April 26, with blistered, lacerated feet, and every man leaning heavily on a stick, they waded through the glacier-fed water twenty-seven times before ten o'clock in the morning, when they met the horses.

At Mountain House letters were waiting. Norway House had been burned; the crop had failed again at Red River; the season's outlook east of the mountains was not good as the demands for supplies made by the Franklin Arctic expedition had been excessive, "but must be met whatever inconvenience the Service may experience." More annoyance over costly luxuries being transported by horse pack over the mountains. "My wardrobe does not exceed 20 or 30 lbs. which my servant can carry on his back and I do not see why theirs should be more weighty." Instead of gentlemen spending a fortnight crossing the mountains "studying their own comfort," five days should be sufficient. "I have done it . . . and am ready to do it again and our Chief Factors and Chief Traders ought to learn to do as I do or if incapable through age or infirmity . . . withdraw and enjoy their retired Shares."

At Edmonton, on May 2, he found "Mr. Rowand up to his ears in business as usual and without exception he is the most active and best qualified person for the troublesome charge he has got of any man in the Indian Country."

Stalwart John Rowand, founder of Fort Edmonton where he spent most of his life, became one of the great men of the fur trade.

Simpson wrote from Carlton House on May 12 about beaver conservation in the Saskatchewan Valley:

> "Altho this river has been unremittingly hunted for nearly 100 Years, it is still tolerably well stocked with Beaver and if it was possible to let it have 5 Years rest or respite it would be as Rich in Beaver as ever. In all parts we saw cuttings or other vestiges of that most industrious & valuable animal."

The Council of the Northern Department of Rupert's Land had been summoned by Simpson to meet at Norway House in 1825, but as he came eastward he grew increasingly apprehensive of the Red River colony affairs. He knew of their crop failure, and that the winter must have been miserable. A vigorous transportation and provisioning programme would probably have to be put into operation.

The Selkirk land grant, Assiniboia, was now a separate colonial entity administered for the Selkirk estate by the Hudson's Bay Company. It had its own governor and council and its proceedings were subject to review by the Governor and Committee in London. Simpson, as governor of Rupert's Land, had the right to attend the meetings of the Council of Assiniboia and to preside. In practice he made the appointments. Later, as the population of the colony increased, the Company tried to make appointments to the council as representative of the colony as possible, but was always careful to have the paramount interests of the fur trade firmly in power. It grew to be a subject of bitter discontent.

The likelihood of distress at Red River so weighed on Simpson at Carlton House on the Saskatchewan, that he struck out five hundred miles overland to the colony, instead of going on by canoe to Norway House. It was a wet spring on the prairie and the Indians were restless, but three hours after the decision was made, the party of ten started out with twelve horses. Only Simpson and McMillan were mounted, and the horses were in such poor condition that they could stay in the saddle only three hours a day. The other horses were led, and for food they depended on their guns. Tortured by mosquitoes and thirst as they were on the salt plains, the greatest discomfort came when they tried to cross the Assiniboine River. Because of high water and depth of mud on the banks they had to retreat up the Qu'Appelle to try a crossing there.

"The last 24 hours I think have been the most uncomfortable I ever passed. . . . The Water was too Deep to Wade; there was no wood of any kind to make a Raft several of our people could not Swim and the bottom & banks so soft that there was the utmost danger of drowning or miring our Horses; in this dilemma we had nearly resolved on killing our Horses & making Skin Canoes of their Hides for the purpose of going down to the Settlement by Water I however being more at home in the Water than any of my fellow travellers and anxious to save the lives of the poor animals, stripped & Swam across with a few things 3 others followed my example and by making several crossings in this way we got the whole of our little Baggage over; the Horses were driven across those people who could not Swim holding on by their Tails and with the assistance of Cords we hauled the poor Animals out of the Mud; in like manner we got across the Assiniboine River having been occupied 5 hours in effecting our passage over these two Rivers nearly the whole of which time myself and those with me being naked in the Mud & Water exposed to the blood thirsty assaults of Miriads of Muschetoes, in short I believe there never was an unfortunate Govr in such a Woeful plight as that of the Northn Deptmt of Ruperts Land this Day."

May 28, the final day of the journey, commenced after a night of shivering in the rain, continued through nine miles of swamp wading, and ended with Simpson, far ahead of the rest of his exhausted party, knocking on the gates of Fort Garry at midnight. There is more than a slight swagger in the Little Emperor's account of his lonely night ride and the final pounding on the gates of the sleeping fort and his hearty welcome from the garrison. "Here I purpose taking a rest of Eight Days after having performed one of the most dangerous and harassing Journeys ever undertaken in the Country."

Red River affairs were not so desperate as Simpson had feared, but there was much to occupy him. On June 5, by express canoe from Montreal, came the dispatches from the Governor and Committee bearing news of a gratuity of five hundred pounds and a salary increase of two hundred pounds a year for Simpson. Into his journal the Scot poured effusive thanks and pledged his abject devotion to his masters. "My heart overflows with gratitude and while I have health and Strength if I know myself they will not have occasion to alter their Sentiments towards me."

George Simpson knew himself well enough never to underestimate his own capacity, and the Governor and Committee had never any reason to regret their choice.

The capital stock, after a century at £103,950, had been increased to £400,000 in 1825, and a dividend of 10 per cent. was being paid, the highest in forty-seven years. By 1828 the dividend was 20 per cent., and George Simpson was governor-in-chief of the entire Hudson's Bay territories.

Chapter XIII

THE LITTLE EMPEROR

THE stars hang sharply glittering over the great plains, and the motionless air holds a deep frost. So still is the night that the smoke from the chimneys of Fort Garry's buildings feathers straight upward. So subtle and swift is the cold that the people of the fort and the meagre settlement outside the walls are staying close to the fires. Only occasionally a muffled figure hurries across the creaking snow.

The fort gates are shut. Most of the ten buildings within the enclosure are in darkness, but from Bachelors' Hall, the clerks' quarters, there are lights and the sound of someone scraping cheerfully on a fiddle. There is light also in the Officers' Mess. The men's quarters are in darkness, and the workshops and storehouses stand silent and unlit.

From a window in the governor's residence a light gleams, for George Simpson is wintering at Red River and tonight he works late. He has been married two years now to his cousin, Frances Ramsay Simpson, and their first child was born in the fort in August, 1831. Now it is January 10, 1832, and the child has just been baptized by the Rev. D. T. Jones, with the name George Geddes Simpson. He is a frail baby, destined to die on Easter Sunday of this year, but there will be four more children, one born in London and three at Hudson's Bay House, Lachine, which is to be the official residence for nearly thirty years. There will be other children bearing the name of Simpson, but born of swarthy, half-breed mothers in far-off posts. The records are fragmentary,

217

but the legendary tales of these affairs, passed on in fur trade gossip for more than a century, will become gargantuan. George Simpson may or may not have had the capacity for extramarital relations on the heroic scale attributed by the common talk of his colleagues and successors, but he acknowledged his obligations in these matters by contributing to the maintenance of the children. He could hardly do less. As the governor, spending most of his time in travel or in transient living within the cramped confines of palisaded forts, his relationships can scarcely have passed unchallenged or the paternity of his bastards be denied. Moreover, he himself had been insistent on having the Council set penalties for any commissioned gentleman who left the country without providing for his children born of native or half-breed mothers.

Tonight Simpson works at Company business with his desk drawn close to the fire and papers tied in neat, orderly bundles piled high about him. He is writing in a notebook. The candlelight quavers and the quill scratches. He writes:

"No. 10 About 48 Years of Age.—A very bustling active man who can go through a great deal of business but is wanting in system and regularity and has not the talent of managing the few associates and clerks under his authority: has a good deal of influence with Indians and speaks the Soulteaux tolerably well.—Very zealous in the discharge of his public duties and a man of strict honor and integrity but a great stickler for rights & privileges and sets himself up for a righter of wrongs. Very anxious to obtain a lead among his colleagues with whom he has not much influence owing to his ungovernable violent temper and turbulent disposition, and would be a troublesome man to the Comp'y if he had sufficient influence to form and tact to manage a party, in short, would be a Radical in any Country under any Government and under any circumstances; and if he had not pacific people to deal with, would be eternally embroiled in 'affairs of honor' on the merest trifles arising I conceive from the irritability of his temper more than a quarrelsome

disposition.—Altogether a disagreeable man to do business
with as it is impossible to go with him in all things and a
difference of opinion almost amounts to a declaration of
hostilities, yet a good hearted man and a pleasant
companion."

This, George Simpson writes, in a private, pocket-size
notebook. It is his opinion of Dr. John McLoughlin, his
chief factor in the Oregon country. He does not enter
McLoughlin's name boldly at the head of the paragraph.
As a safeguard from prying eyes, the character study is
concealed by a number. On a separate sheet of paper
Simpson enters the name and number.

The quill scratches on, recording his shrewd conclusions.
The governor has lived and worked ten years among fur
traders, and now he is putting into rich, compact sentences
his conclusions about his men. This is no laboriously
dictated communication to be read aloud by the secretary
to the Governor and Committee in London; this is George
Simpson, Scot, aged forty-five, born under a bar sinister,
who has risen to high office, writing secretly for his own
guidance. With no affectations of style or need for evasion
or flattery, the Little Emperor rings true. He brings to
this analysis of his subordinates a fine judicial temper.
We, who have a century spread out before us since that
winter night, and know the destinies of the men about
whom he wrote, are able to valuate the penetration of his
understanding, and perhaps attribute to him more of
human kindliness than his public character reveals.

Again he bends over the little notebook writing. This
time it is about a clerk, James Douglas, who is to become
a great fur trader, a knight, and the first governor for the
Crown of British Columbia.

"A Scotch West Indian: About 33 Years of Age, has
been 13 Years in the Service.—A stout powerful active
man of good conduct and respectable abilities:—tolerably
well Educated, expresses himself clearly in paper, under-
stands our Counting House business and is an excellent

Trader.—Well qualified for any Service requiring bodily exertion firmness of mind and the exercise of Sound judgement, but furiously violent when roused.—Has every reason to look forward to early promotion and is a likely man to fill a place at our Council board in course of time.—Stationed in the Columbia Departmt."

The observation in the *Character Book* on Cuthbert Grant of Seven Oaks is interesting for its description of the control of half-breeds, but more particularly for a generous willingness to forgive and forget:

"A halfbreed whose name must long recal to mind some horrible Scenes which in former Days took place at Red River Settlement in which he was the principal actor—About 38 years of Age, during 20 of which he has been more or less connected with the Service—A generous Warm hearted Man who would not have been guilty of the Crimes laid to his charge had he not been driven into them by designing Men—— A very stout powerful fellow of great nerve & resolution but now getting unweildy and inactive. Drinks ardent spirits in large quantities, thinks nothing of a Bottle of Rum at a Sitting but is so well Seasoned that he is seldom intoxicated altho it undermines his constitution rapidly—— A sensible clear headed man of good conduct except in reference to the unfortunate habits of intemperance he has fallen into. Entirely under the influence of the Catholic Mission and quite a Bigot.—The American Traders have made several liberal offers to him, but he has rejected them all being now a staunch Hudsons Bay Man and we allow him a Saly. of £200 P. Annum as 'Warden of the Plains' which is a Sinecure afforded him intirely from political motives and not from any feeling of liberality or partiality. The appointment prevents him from interfering with the Trade on his own account which he would otherwise do in all probability; it moreover affords us the benefit of his great influence over the half breeds and Indians of the neighbourhood which is convenient inasmuch as it exempts us from many difficulties with them. He resides at the White Horse plain about 16 miles up the Assiniboine River where he has a Farm and only visits the Establishment [Fort Garry] on business or by Invitation; but is always ready to obey our command and is very effective when employed as a Constable among the half breeds or Indians—is perfectly satisfied with what has been done for him which is quite Sufficient and has no prospect of advancement."

Today, in a basement room of Hudson's Bay House, in London, where the rumble of the traffic of Bishopsgate is heard faintly, this *Book of Servants' Characters* can be examined leisurely. All about on high shelves are the archives of the Company of Adventurers; the logbooks of ships, the journals of the posts, the account books and the letters; the paper accumulations of over two and a half centuries of "Trading into Hudson's Bay." Throughout the passage of these years, and among the thousands who have served, there is no more vital, arresting person than George Simpson. His is the complete "success" biography. He is the supreme vindication of maxims of the times producing the man. Intelligent self-interest will never find a more glittering example than Simpson. While his methods would not be applicable in the twentieth century, he is revealed in this *Book of Servants' Characters* as a leader who retained the power to command by reason of a profound understanding of men.

The finding of the key to the character book is one of the interesting footnotes to modern research in Company history. The actual notebook had been known for several years, but as the identities of the subjects were concealed by numbers it was of little use, until a single sheet of paper was discovered among Simpson's personal documents, when suddenly the whole fascinating picture of the fur trade personnel was clear.

The absolute and unswerving loyalty which Simpson retained for the Company as an institution, and for his own superiors, set an exacting standard, and gave the personnel a traditional and enviable *esprit de corps* which has survived to this day. The strength of Simpson's bond with London was based on complete frankness. His dispatches to the Governor and Committee are lucid, outspoken, and without reservations. If, in his first years, there is a flavour of undue, perhaps sycophantic deference, it was a phase that soon passed, and the Governor and Committee were well rewarded for the high authority they vested in the governor of the Hudson's Bay Territories.

In physical and mental buoyancy lay Simpson's strength as an administrator, but in 1832, the winter of the *Character Book* and the death of his child, even these qualities temporarily failed. He wrote to Chief Factor J. G. McTavish, "I myself am become so melancholy and low spirited that I scarcely know what enjoyment is, in fact . . . I feel that my health and strength are falling off rapidly. I am most anxious to get away from this Country of which I am sick & tired but my means do not enable me to shake off the Harness."

Even the local clergy had reason to note a change. "The Governor is become decidedly religious," wrote John Pritchard. The accuracy of the statement must be left to the future biographer of Simpson.

The fur trade was far from sweet unanimity. The very quality of the discipline Simpson imposed bred malcontents among the older men who had enjoyed special privileges under former régimes. Cabals were formed among minorities for the purpose of digging themselves into the comfortable berths where commissioned rank carried dignity, and there were tastes of such fleshpots as frontier life offered. Inevitably the strong man had enemies, but his control of his councils was never seriously challenged. With the majority of the chief factors and chief traders to support him, and all the vast northland at his disposal, it was not hard to find important, strenuous work and even promotion for dissenters in Ungava or the northern interior of British Columbia.

Control over these annual councils of the field partners is the clearest example of Simpson's authority. Assembling each summer, when trading was slack and river routes open, at Norway House, Fort Garry, or York Factory, a council consisted of all the chief factors of a department. Chief traders present at the fort were invited to attend, and had full voting privileges. The council decided the rules, regulations, tariffs, and general conduct of the fur trade. It considered the results of the previous season's operations, and planned the outfits, staff, and transport arrangements for the next year. Delinquents were disciplined and fines imposed. The rotation of furlough was fixed. Simpson presided, and two clerks were present keeping independent minutes, one representing the commissioned officers and the other the governor. The minutes were copied into stout leather-bound books to be consulted as commandments during the year.

As in all Simpson's public affairs, there was a calculated dignity in the conduct of councils. The actual sessions were held behind closed doors, but an apprentice clerk who travelled west in the governor's canoe in 1854 was present at the assembling of the Northern and Southern councils that year, and long afterwards he wrote his recollections of these occasions in the book *When Fur Was King*, by Henry John Moberley in collaboration with W. B. Cameron, Dent, 1929. The Southern Council is gathering at Fort William:

"As we drew near the mouth of the Kaministiquia River the old flag of the Hudson's Bay Company broke out, guns were fired and a crowd—gentlemen, Indians and halfbreeds—gathered on the wharf outside the pickets to welcome the Governor and the officers from Moose Factory, Albany and posts between that place and Sault Ste. Marie, who had joined us on our way up Lake Superior. As Sir George stepped ashore he turned to the head Iroquois guide and announced: 'At ten minutes past six o'clock we start'; adding to the chief factor in charge: 'Council meets at one o'clock. Just two and a half hours for feasting and talking; then to business.'

"Before the council began, however, we sat down to dinner. Rather, a banquet—one such as, I think, could scarcely be provided today at any price; smoked and salted buffalo tongues and bosses, moose noses and tongues, beaver tails from the wooded country, the choicest venison, wild ducks and geese, fresh trout and whitefish, and a lavish spread of delicacies from the old world, brought by the Governor himself. Sherry and old port wine, with champagne, were all the beverages allowed, discipline being very strict in those days. Each person knew his place at table. The Governor sat at the head; next, ranging on each side, came the chief factors, then the clerks in order of their standing, the apprentice clerks from above and below the Sault, the post managers and the interpreters.

"Sir George, who loved a quiet joke, played a good one at the expense of the officers and my unworthy self. Suspecting that I did not know the difference between a chief factor and an apprentice clerk, first posting the officers we have travelled with, he introduced me as the new chief factor of Saskatchewan. Those not in the secret were convinced that a youngster like myself, to have acquired such exalted rank, must be the son of one of the largest shareholders of the Company who, dying suddenly, had left me all his shares. I was seated among the 'big bugs,' and to carry off the joke Sir George took wine with me before anyone else. That settled it, though I myself thought it was merely an act of courtesy toward a stranger. This joke he carried through at all the posts we touched until we reached Norway House, at the north end of Lake Winnipeg. Incidentally, I benefited by it considerably, for it gave me opportunities for becoming friendly with a number of the commissioned officers whose acquaintance, owing to the strict discipline observed, it might otherwise have taken me some years to make.

"At one o'clock all the officers belonging to the district rose and entered the council room, but I remained in company with the men on their way east, one of whom had been in charge of the Peace River for a number of years and was retiring. The other two were going out on furlough. One had been in British Columbia, the other at Athabasca. I gathered much information from these men, besides hearing some racy yarns.

"At five o'clock the council rose. General conversation followed until five minutes after six, when Sir George shouted: 'All aboard!'

Fort Garry (1835–1884)

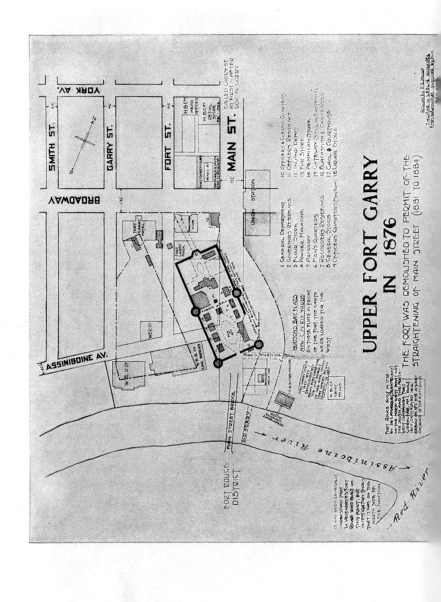

UPPER FORT GARRY
IN 1876

THE FORT WAS DEMOLISHED TO PERMIT OF THE
STRAIGHTENING OF MAIN STREET (1881 TO 1884)

1 GENERAL DEPARTMENT
2 GOVERNOR'S RESIDENCE
3 FLOUR STORE
4 POWDER MAGAZINE
5 ARMOURY
6 MEN'S QUARTERS
7 DESCORDING RESIDENCES
8 GENERAL STORES
9 OFFICERS' QUARTERS (MESS ROOM)

10 OFFICERS' & CLERKS' QUARTERS
11 OFFICERS' RESIDENCE
12 INLAND DEPOT
13 FUEL STORE
14 PEMMICAN STORE
15 GATEWAY (STILL IN EXISTENCE)
16 BLACKSMITH & CARPENTER
17 GAOL & COURTHOUSE
18 LIQUOR STORES

SMITH ST.
GARRY ST.
FORT ST.
MAIN ST.
CALLED GARRY ST. AT FIRST. AFTER GOV'N GARRY

YORK AV.
BROADWAY
ASSINIBOINE AV.

HUDSON'S BAY LAND
NOW C.N. EN YARD.
ON THESE FLATS IN FRONT
OF THE FORT THE CARTS
WERE LOADED FOR THE
WEST.

UNION STATION

FORT ROUGE
DISTRICT

MAIN STREET BRIDGE
OLD FERRY

Assiniboine River

Red River

FORT ROUGE BUILT IN 1738
BY DE LA VÉRENDRYE (IMPORTANT)
WAS THE FORT SOUTH OF THE
FORT AND TOWARD THE FORT IN
WEST. GARRISON WHICH WAS
CONSTRUCTED AND TAKEN
THEN. IT WAS SUPPOSED REAL-
LY THAT IT WAS LOCATED THE
ENTRANCE OF THE ASSINIBOINE.

IT HAS BEEN GENERALLY
UNDERSTOOD THAT
LA VÉRENDRYE'S FORT
ROUGE WAS BUILT ON
THIS POINT, BUT
INVESTIGATION SHOWS
THAT IT WAS ON THE
NORTH SIDE OF
THE JUNCTION.

Reduced by R.H.G.E. Winnipeg.
Traced as by Engineers
from Measured Original Supplied by him.

"At the wharf we found the Iroquois ready with the loaded canoes. Each man took his place and at exactly ten minutes past six we pushed out."

The party followed the old familiar Lake of the Woods–Winnipeg River route to Lake Winnipeg and on to Norway House for the meeting of the Northern Council. Young Moberley gives a vivid picture of the governor on tour at the very height of his power:

"We re-embarked as usual at one next morning, the weather still disagreeable, mixed snow and rain, so that at breakfast I hoped I should be safe from the consequence of an extremely reprehensible habit of the Governor's. Every morning at that hour it was his practice to strip and take a plunge in the cold water, and being loth to be beaten by an old man I had kept him company. This morning proved no exception to the rule, and I could not help feeling that I was a martyr to my chief's pernicious custom, though I was bound to admit it was a wholesome-enough one.

"We remained at Fort Alexander for dinner, and here I was made the victim of another joke. The Governor passed me a dish which I promptly declined. He urged me to try it, but I still refused. At length he asked me why I would not touch it.

"'Sir George,' I replied, 'I may be a green man, but you won't catch me eating bear's drippings.'

"This brought a roar of laughter from all sides. The Governor then ate a portion of the delicacy himself, upon which I made bold to test it and to my surprise found it extremely good. It proved to be berry pemmican of the best quality, made of dried pounded buffalo tongues, marrowfat, sugar and dried Saskatoon berries. In appearance it was exactly what I had called it.

"Amid the firing and the shouting we landed at Norway House, the post at which was to be held the council for the Northern Department. Here were gathered officers from Saskatchewan, Athabasca, Peace River, Mackenzie River, Isle-à-la-Crosse and Churchill River, with their followers to the number of at least five hundred men of various nationalities, including Scotch,

French-Canadians, Shetlanders, Norwegians, Indians, halfbreeds and heaven knows what else. On landing we were so overwhelmed with handshakings and questionings that we were glad to escape into the house.

"Council was called for 9.30 a.m. It was composed of the Governor, Sir George Simpson, and the chief factors in charge of Norway House, Lac la Pluie, Saskatchewan, Mackenzie River, Athabasca, Peace River, Isle-à-la-Crosse, Red River, Cumberland and York Factory. It sat behind closed doors, and, with an hour interval for dinner, lasted until five in the afternoon. Everything was discussed and arranged for the coming year for the Northern Department, which reached from the United States border along the Rockies to the Arctic Ocean and east to Hudson Bay and Fort William.

"By noon of the third day the deliberations of the council were concluded, when Sir George immediately embarked on his return to Montreal. We watched the great canoes, the flag of the Hudson's Bay Company proudly floating at each stern, the Iroquois crews chanting their boat songs, until they had turned the first point; then the men of the brigades became active in loading provisions and manning their boats."

This was the conduct of the executive side of the business for nearly forty years of George Simpson's rule. In council his policies may have been criticized but his decisions were never reversed. Not that his officers were cowed; on the contrary they were men of pronounced individualism. Sharp measures of economy, however harsh in application, won them as Scotsmen and partners, while the orderliness of good accountancy was welcomed by all who recalled the personal losses to the partners of the North West Company.

The governor made enemies. Some of the disgruntled wrote books about their fur trade days, and of these John McLean was the most articulate. McLean was, perhaps, not one of the politically strongest men in the fur trade, but he came to hate Simpson. He had joined the Company in 1821, the winter of the union, and in twenty-five years of service he had lived and travelled in the Ottawa Valley, Ungava, Labrador, the Saskatchewan Valley, the Mackenzie River and New Caledonia. His extraordinary record was marked by such achievements as having been the first white man to travel overland from Chimo on Ungava Bay to Hamilton Inlet, and he discovered the Great Falls of Labrador. He resigned in 1845, protesting bitterly that Simpson had not given him promised promotion. He settled in Guelph, Ontario, and found a publisher for his two-volume account *Notes of a Twenty-five Years' Service in the Hudson's Bay Territory*. It is a satisfying description of fur trade life in the nineteenth century, but marred by a manifestly ill-judged denunciation of Simpson which even McLean's late colleagues felt to be quite unfair.

The governor was "cold and callous," favoured by fortune, guilty of favouritism and disregard of merit, combining with "the prepossessing manners of a gentleman all the craft and subtlety of an intriguing courtier." His knighthood had been earned not by himself but by the Dease and Simpson Arctic expedition to which he (Sir George) had contributed only about half an hour's desk planning. His fur trade success was only the result of application of North West principles.

The picture has not true colours, and the disgruntled ex-employee loses perspective in his closing pages. In the secrecy of the *Character Book* twelve years earlier, Simpson had said that McLean had a florid literary style and was full of pompous conceits. John McLean is condemned by his own works. As a Hudson's Bay man, believing his career was assured, he worked happily, found adventure for many years until the break came. Then he turned upon the Company and its governor, denounced them both as vicious. He paints a picture of the North West Company, which he never knew, as the ideal fur trading organization. He is utterly wrong in his facts about the North West Company, but the phrases with which he describes the North West–Hudson's Bay struggle have been taken by incautious writers and moulded into the stereotyped account of the affair. It is unfortunate, because McLean wrote an excellent narrative of life in the service, despite Sir George's opinion of his style.

Many years later, A. C. Anderson, who had served in the Company with McLean, made this observation:

"I feel assured that on reconsideration he would at this day wish much of what has evidently been written under feelings of anger and disappointment, were unwritten. As regards his individual affairs with the Company, I will only say that he was considered in the wrong by all his colleagues in the country who were cognizant of the circumstances."

Another enemy, a kinsman, wrote a book in which Sir George was the villain. Alexander Simpson, in a biography of his brother Thomas the explorer, published in 1845, accused their cousin George of blocking promotion and exploiting his subordinates' careers for his own personal honour. Thomas Simpson's discoveries are told in another part of the Company's story, and his name occurs here only as one whose affairs became entangled with the life of the Little Emperor.

The strongest man who broke with Simpson was Chief Factor John McLoughlin—the "Big Doctor" who ruled the Oregon like a benevolent feudal baron. His quarrel with the governor and with the Company arose from a confusion of causes, but principally his own excessively liberal attitude towards the immigration of settlers from the United States. His openhanded hospitality to the covered-wagon landseekers from the central States has made his name revered in the history of the northern Pacific States. It was not, however, in accordance with Company policy, and as the story of the Oregon boundary dispute becomes clarified by research, it would seem likely that John McLoughlin's sympathies will be shown to have been with the United States quite early in the controversy. By 1845 he found he had extended credit totalling

thirty thousand dollars to the new settlers. He was the
senior representative of the Company in a territory where
agriculture was rapidly taking root. He was weary of
Simpson's domination from afar, and he resigned, became
an American citizen, and threw in his lot with the new
Oregon. The citizens promptly forgot his kindness and
hospitality in the days when they straggled hungry and
exhausted across the mountains to Fort Vancouver. The
old Northwester died in 1857, embittered against his adopted
country.

Simpson's life was enriched by the friendship of his own
men. If he was imperious and exacting with subordinates,
he was also loyal to those who did not fail him. In a
business where colleagues met rarely, letter-writing was
cultivated, and Simpson was an accomplished corre-
spondent. Wintering at Montreal or Fort Garry he wrote
prodigiously long lucid letters to his officers, full of infinite
detail of the trade, and rarely without intimate news and
gossip of men and events. About 1841, his eyesight began
to fail so that most of his work had to be carried on by
having documents read to him and by dictation. Neither
the fullness nor frequency of his correspondence seemed
to suffer. Now he writes to Donald Ross at Norway House
about the practice that has grown up of officers sending
preserved buffalo tongues to their friends in England.
If buffalo tongues are so desirable they should be part
of the trade. There are smart penalties for making gifts
of furs; why not the same for buffalo tongues? He urges
his officers to keep on good terms with the missionaries,
especially these "gentlemen of the Wesleyan Society."
The reverend gentlemen maintain an agitation for Sabbath
observance in the fur brigades, so there are letters to
missionaries placating them and pointing to the vice of
idleness and the brevity of the transport season. Now
he writes to Scotland for "a young man fully qualified for
a piper." This Highland youth is to be part of the
governor's entourage for many years and many thousands
of miles. Again he writes to Donald Ross about the

meeting of the Northern Council the next year at Fort Garry, suggesting that a responsible person must be left in charge of Norway House if Ross goes down to Red River, for "the young apprentice clerk Ballantyne now with you is not sufficiently steady nor experienced to take charge in your absence." This was R. M. Ballantyne, who later found a career as a writer of books for boys.

"Has the allowance of wine regulated by fixed system succeeded at York?" he asks Chief Factor Hargrave. He does not see any necessity for brandy-and-water parties for the benefit of the ships' captains when they are there. "Let them take their 'whack' at the dinner table like other people." The first Church of England bishop of Rupert's Land is to arrive at York Factory from England in June. The warning goes out, "Pray take care that there be no drunken scenes at York at any time, more especially when the Bishop passes, or during the visits of missionaries or strangers, and do not let brigades start on Sundays."

Day after day, throughout the years, he was for ever writing letters of encouragement, criticism, flattery, and news to his men. It was part of his power of command. Even when fur traders were groping from the Mackenzie River into the unknown interior of Alaska and sending out reports of their discoveries, Simpson's letters, enclosing the latest coastal maps, would reach them by carrier. He would compare their reports of rivers with the latest Admiralty charts and advise and encourage them, always ending up with some gossip and news of wars in Europe, or perhaps a report of the death of Sir Walter Scott, or the return of the Whigs to power.

Under his régime the Company flourished. After a dreary stretch of eleven years of 4 per cent. dividends, the capital stock had been increased in 1825 from one hundred and three thousand pounds to four hundred thousand pounds, and a 10 per cent. dividend declared. By 1828 there were bonuses which brought the earnings to 20 per cent. In 1838 the stock was earning 25 per cent.

Thereafter the dividends declined, but never below 10 per cent. in Simpson's administration. The proprietors who in 1820 had numbered seventy-seven persons, were two hundred and sixty-eight in 1856, and two hundred and eighty-six in 1863.

Simpson had been twelve winters in the fur trade when he anticipated modern business methods by setting up in the little notebook of *Servants' Characters* his own personnel system. He had spent the summers in constant travel and work, and most winters in the Red River colony. By 1832 he was the dominant personality of the entire north-west. He had won the complete confidence of the Governor and Committee, and without relaxing his grip on the trade he was extracting from the life all that it could provide in the way of honour and glory. With Russian boundary problems to the north, and American boundary difficulties looming in the south, and flag plantings in the Arctic becoming almost annual occurrences, he felt his place in Imperial affairs. The Red River colony was not an adequate stage, and in 1833 Simpson took up residence in Lachine, the village on the St. Lawrence River just above Montreal. There the Company acquired the largest house, a modest stone mansion sixty feet long and fifty feet wide. This became Hudson's Bay House in Canada, combining executive headquarters and residence. Here Simpson's family grew up; here his delicate wife died in 1853; and here he died in 1860 in his seventy-third year.

Hudson's Bay House, Lachine, faced the old Lachine Canal which circumvented the fastest rapids of the St. Lawrence. In North West Company days, Lachine had been the great base depot for supplying the Indian territories, but with the dominance of the Hudson's Bay Company, the Hudson Bay route for transportation of goods and furs took away most of the traffic. Still the supplies for those Southern Department posts in the basin of the Great Lakes were loaded into canoes each spring in the old canal. There was the same colour and confusion and the same problem of sobering up the voyageurs. Simpson must have watched these scenes from the tall windows of his office, and each spring he would say good-bye to his family here and start west with his own express canoe and red-shirted Iroquois paddlers from Caughnawaga, his secretary and the piper.

Commissioned officers and many of the clerks enjoyed the hospitality of Hudson's Bay House, Lachine, between 1833 and 1860. Coming from the north-west for their year of furlough they would be dined and entertained and would meet the leading citizens of Montreal under circumstances calculated to impress these quiet men from the interior with the prestige of their governor-in-chief. A young Scotsman reported there in 1838 with a letter of introduction from his uncle, Chief Factor John Stuart, who with Simon Fraser had been one of the boldest explorers of the Rockies. To this young Donald A. Smith, then seeking a career in the Company, his uncle wrote advice punctuated by keen observations on Simpson:

> "The only, or at least the chief drawback is that you are dependent upon the goodwill and caprice of one man who is a little too addicted to prejudices, for speedy advancement; but this is probably true in many other spheres of commercial endeavour. . . . There is, I may say, no man who is so appreciative of downright hard work coupled with intelligence, or one more intolerant of puppyism, by which I mean carelessness and presumption. It is his foible to exact not only strict obedience, but deference to the point of humility. As long as you pay him in that coin you will quickly get on his sunny side and find yourself in a few years a trader at a congenial post, with promotion in sight."

Not all the stories of Hudson's Bay House, Lachine, are fur trade tales. Surviving on faded paper is a Victorian jingle written appropriately by "A Lady," in appreciation of a children's party in the grey house by the river. She called it *The Children's Rout*:

Come, call out your sleighs, and away let us run
To the Hudson's Bay House, for an evening of fun,
For Sir George has agreed, with his blandest of smiles,
That the children shall wake all the echoes for miles.
See, from Upper and Lower Lachine how they pour,
While a sleigh from the Square dashes up to the door,
Now little hearts bound, and small feet trip about,
And Mammas are well pleased—'tis the Children's own
　　rout.

Here comes Florence, the fairy, with laugh-loving eyes,
And Edith, the pure, looking fresh from the skies;
Next Isobel comes with poetic sweet face,
Her arms round Eliza, in tender embrace;
Eliza, her Cousin, the good and the kind,
With dear Sister Mary close tripping behind.
Next two little darlings, in jackets of red,
With pretty Lawrence, by Governeur led.

Then a tiny young Sailor, so smart, one would think
He had just stepped ashore, with his Sister in pink.
Then came the fair Flanagans, hearts all a-glow—
Three charmers in blue—with their Brother, a beau;
The Ferrisses next, just the sum of the Graces,
With long flowing ringlets around their young faces;
Misses Hamilton, Anderson, Fraser and Miles,
Enter radiant in happiness, ribbons and smiles.
Papas and Mammas in a train trooping after;
The rear well brought up by Sir George's gay laughter.

　　　　　　　　(Montreal, January, 1860.)

Simpson had been knighted by the Queen at Buckingham
Palace, in January, 1841. At the same time John Henry
Pelly had been created a baronet for "his acknowledged
worth and long and meritorious service as Governor of the
Hudson's Bay Company." At Moose Factory, York
Factory, Cumberland House, Chipewyan, Kamloops and
Fort Vancouver, the late winter packet brought the news,
and the fur traders liked it. The Little Emperor had come
into his own. As men living close to the realities of a harsh
wilderness existence, they prided themselves on an aloof

indifference to these honours and baubles; the gossip writers commented cynically, but in their letters is a vein of pride that one of their own had been honoured. Simpson's real support of the Crown cause in the Papineau Rebellion in Lower Canada in 1837 and his material assistance to the series of Arctic expeditions being conducted by the Admiralty were probably the principal basis for his elevation to knighthood.

In March Simpson left London on his somewhat celebrated journey around the world. The official record of this nineteen months of travel can be found occasionally today in second-hand book shops in two stout volumes. Only here and there is the true Simpson style discernible, and it is generally conceded to be a rather flagrant example of Victorian "ghost writing" attributed to Adam Thom, a Montreal lawyer who, under Simpson's appointment, had been the first Recorder of the Red River Settlement. The two volumes published in 1847 as *Journey Round the World* are important contributions to fur trade history only in the compressed descriptions of his hasty push across his own domain. The style varies from florid to turgid, and the whole effort reflects the self-made merchant playing to the current fashion of travel books by gentlemen.

Leaving Hudson's Bay House, Lachine, Sir George was sublimely happy at having two young peers as his guests. Lord Caledon and Lord Musgrove were going to the plains to kill buffalo, and with one or two Hudson's Bay officers the party proceeded up the Ottawa route in two express canoes. From Fort Garry Sir George went overland a thousand miles across the prairie. It was five o'clock on the morning of July 3 when they left Fort Garry, but it was not too early for the traditional flourishes:

"While we defiled through the gates into the open plain with an horizon before us as well defined as that of the blue ocean, the scene resembling the moving of an eastern caravan in the boundless sands of Arabia—a medley of pots and pans and kettles, in our single vehicle, the unruly pack horses prancing under their loads, and every cavalier

armed to the teeth, assisting his steed to neigh and caper
with bit and spur. The effect was not a little heightened
by a brilliant sunrise, the firing of cannon, the streaming
of flags and the shouts of spectators."

Averaging eleven hours a day in the saddle for six weeks
and five days, they reached the Columbia and descended
to Fort Vancouver by boat. At Fort Nisqually, Puget
Sound, Sir George went aboard the Company ship *Beaver*,
the first steamship to operate on the Pacific Coast, and
proceeded north to Sitka, Alaska.

Salutes from the ship answered salutes from the fort as
Sir George went ashore to pay respects to the Russian
Governor Etholine and his "pretty and lady-like wife."
The Russian American Fur Company was a substantial
purchaser of Hudson's Bay furs, and the Adventurers paid
two thousand skins a year rent for the lease of a strip of
Alaska. One of the curiosities of commercial history is
the placid neutrality which these two companies agreed
upon a few years later when Britons and Russians were
fighting each other in the Crimea. Sir George dined well,
confirmed the existing agreements, and agreed with
Etholine to discontinue the use of spirits in all dealing with
the Coast Indians.

In California that same winter Simpson visited the
Company establishment at Yerba Buena on San Francisco
Bay, and there were prelates and Spanish colonial governors
to be called upon at Monterey and Santa Barbara. The
decadence of the administration had not reduced the scale
of the hospitality, but the fur trader was not dazzled by
the tarnished splendour of these petty courts. With the
eye of a nineteenth-century imperialist he foresaw the
collapse of overseas Spain; he noted the perfection of the
harbour, the wealth of the valleys, and the glory of the
climate. Was this land destined to be British or American?
Simpson records meeting Francis Ermatinger, a Hudson's
Bay man, riding in the disguise of a Spanish caballero.
Ermatinger was a scout sent overland from Canada to
report on the country. Alaska, Labrador or California

were not too remote to be outside the interest of the Company.

At Honolulu that winter Sir George inspected another outpost of his Company, and on his ship, the *Cowlitz*, the governor entertained a king no less, though brown, and met the native rulers of the Sandwich Islands.

Crossing the north Pacific again, and completing one year since he left London, the governor returned to the Canadian coast and heard at Stikine of the murder of John McLoughlin, Junior, by Indians during a drunken brawl. This confirmed his earlier determination to eliminate spirits from the trade. Sir George's unwillingness to agree to the wholesale reprisals against the natives, which Dr. John McLoughlin demanded, completed the bitterness between him and his chief factor in the Oregon. Sir George knew, as all the fur trade knew, that the son was erratic and that his Indian blood did not equip him to deal as a trader with natives where rum was involved.

From Alaska the governor went to Okhotsk on the coast of Siberia, a low, stark, rocky point where a Company post was to be inspected. Over the wilderness of Siberia, with Cossack escorts, welcomed by local governors on behalf of the Tsar himself, entertained with strange foods and exotic drinks; sleeping night after night in jolting coaches, Irkutsk, Tobolsk, Kazan, Novgorod, Moscow, and St. Petersburg were rolled into seven thousand miles of overland travel. He had seen, he notes on his next to last page, "more of this colossal empire than any foreigner living or dead." On the final page is this significant record: the prettiest girl seen on the entire journey was at Stitichaun on the Island of Gothland. The book, evidently, was not entirely ghosted.

The place of the Company in a rapidly expanding colonial world began to give the Governor and Committee some concern. As early as 1841, Sir George, in a private letter to Chief Factor Donald Ross, of Norway House, had conceded the possibility of ultimately selling to the

Crown the title to the land, and taking up the new rôle of private traders without the obligations to maintain peace and good government. There was no public admission of any such eventuality, though the settling of farm lands south of the international boundary and the growing interest and agitation by a Toronto group for the opening up of the north-west must have made it clear that the Company could not for ever monopolize the prairies and British Columbia. The periodical renewals of the exclusive licence to trade in the Indian territories (those lands outside the Hudson Bay drainage basin mentioned in the Charter) became occasions for concern. In 1857 a parliamentary committee literally and without prejudice held up the Company for all the world to see, and put the Little Emperor, aged seventy, under a cross-examination which tried his temper sorely.

Sir George did not live to see the passing of the monopoly, and up to the end of his administration he directed the Company as though it was to remain for ever in possession of all the powers and privileges of Prince Rupert's Royal Charter of 1670. In his final years Simpson was interested in industrial ventures in Montreal. Among other investments was a substantial holding in the Quebec, Montreal, Ottawa and Occidental Railway. Sir George was president of this railway, and while it was only a paper road, never getting beyond the charter-owning stage during his life, it ultimately became a link in the Canadian Pacific Railway main line. There was leisure, wealth and dignity in the life Sir George created about himself in the last years, though he rarely failed to make the annual canoe voyage west, for the meetings of the councils.

Albert Edward, Prince of Wales, visited Canada under a heavy escort of parentally chosen guardians in the summer of 1860. Late in August he was in Montreal, a cheerful, rather handsome boy of eighteen, who accepted gracefully, and with apparent pleasure, the adulations of Canadians. It was an opportunity to which Sir George's heart warmed. After a military review in Montreal on August 29, the young Prince, with his suite, drove out to Dorval, about three miles above Lachine, where on a park-like island in the St. Lawrence Sir George had a country home. As the Prince's party was rowed out to the island they were escorted by one hundred painted and feathered Iroquois in decorated canoes. The *Montreal Gazette* described the reception:

"The Prince of Wales was received on landing by Sir George Simpson and soon afterwards luncheon was served to a select party invited to meet H.R.H. by Lieutenant-General Sir Fenwick Williams who at present occupied the island as the owner's guest. We understand there were about forty at the table.

"Sir Fenwick Williams, as the host, had the Prince on one side of him and Sir George Simpson on the other. Among other guests were the Duke of Newcastle [Secretary of State for the Colonies], Lord Lyons [British Minister at Washington], the Marquis of Chandos, the Earl of Mulgrave [now Governor of Nova Scotia], Lord Hinchinbrook, General Bruce of the Prince's staff, Admiral Sir Alexander Milne, Mr. H. McKenzie, of the Hudson's Bay Company and Mr. Hopkins, Sir George's Secretary.

"About 4.30 the party embarked in canoes and proceeded in great style and at a rapid pace toward Lachine. One bearing the Royal Standard and carrying the Prince, the Duke of Newcastle, and General Williams taking the lead while the remainder in line abreast followed close behind it. About the centre of the brigade we observed Sir George Simpson (accompanied by the Earl of Mulgrave and General Bruce, both old fellow voyageurs of Sir George's) directing the movements in person."

Three days later Sir George, while driving from Lachine to Montreal, was seized by apoplexy. It was a second attack, for in the spring of the year, while on the way west to Fort Garry, he had been stricken and obliged to turn back; a deep blow to the pride of this old man who only three summers before was breaking through the ice of northern rivers for his morning plunge.

At Hudson's Bay House, Lachine, he lay for six days

suffering intensely, and on the morning of the seventh day
he died.

"The Little Emperor's light has gone out just after he
basked in a final blaze of glory," wrote Chief Trader
Dugald MacTavish.

CHAPTER XIV

SPIRITS

IN their relations with primitive people the merchant traders of London in the eighteenth century were not restrained by a public conscience. No waves of horror or indignation moved the nation to restrictive measures because British colonies in America and the West Indies imported more than two million slaves between 1680 and 1780. At the end of the eighteenth century more than half the African slave trade was in British hands, and only after forty years of heroic parliamentary crusading were slaves liberated within the Empire, in 1833.

Aborigines in possession of wealth sought for by Europeans were enemies if they attempted to stand between white races and their treasures. To tap the fur resources of America the merchants from across the seas could not sweep aside the Indians with the sword, and loot secret places of the continent. Indians were necessary to the fur trade, and their skill had to be utilized. Here were people whose mode of living was to be exploited and who were in a position to barter the products of their hunt for new treasures brought to them from abroad. Questions of morality did not intrude upon the simple economics of barter, and if the Indians of North America enjoyed having their minds and bodies inflamed by diluted brandy or rum, that was no concern of the fur traders of the eighteenth century. The England of James, William and Mary and the Georges felt no obligation to guide the morality or restrain the drinking habits of savages.

The French had traded in spirits from their first occupation of the St. Lawrence Valley. The Adventurers of

England trading into Hudson's Bay were importing spirits by 1692. Fifty-seven years later, when Parliament inquired deeply into the conduct of the Company and its methods of carrying on business, the use of spirits was hardly mentioned except by former servants who suggested that more brandy might help to bring the Indians from the interior to the coast with their furs, or who complained about their own rations at the Bay being six pounds of flour a week, three-quarters of a goose, a half-pint of small beer, "with what brandy the Governor pleases to give."

Precautions for the defence of themselves and the Company property were the only positive reactions of the English to the bestiality and murderous fury aroused in the Indians by alcohol. The exclusion of Indians from the stockaded enclosures of the forts and the conduct of trading through a small wicket were practices which survived many years, and arose from the necessity of protection from drunken natives.

In its first thirty years the Company's use of spirits was slight. The earliest reference in the correspondence is in a letter from the Governor and Committee to Governor Geyer at York Factory on June 17, 1692. "Whereas wee have sent you a very Large Quantity of New French Brandy which we procured with great difficulty our desire is that what you shall not have emediate use for in ye Factory to trade either with the Natives or our Servants. . . ."

A year later, a letter from London to Geyer indicated that the brandy had not been used. "We have said before that there was sent to you some spirits about 2 yeares Since wch we understand you make noe use of therefore if they are not for your service pray returne them by these ships in tite well bound Caskes as allsoe all other goods that are unvendible with you and put them into your Invoyces the Quentyty and Quality that we may discharg the Factory of them. . . ."

During the years of the French ascendancy in Hudson

Bay (1697-1713) when the Company clung to Fort Albany as the only symbol of their Charter powers, and their ships were harassed by enemy men-o'-war as well as ice and fog, references were made to the presence of spirits for cheerful occasions. Anthony Beale commanded Albany in these difficult years, but was not too molested by the French to neglect celebrations. "It being the birthday of our Sufarean Lady Quene Ann wee sallomized it having the flagg abroad and gave ye men where withall to Drink to her Majesty halth and prosperety to her forses by Sea and Land, Nott forgetting our Honarble Mastar ye Hudson's Bay Company."

In 1713 the first note of warning appears in a letter from London to Beale. "Trade as little brandy as possible to ye Indians, wee being informed it has Destroyed severall of them." A kindly thought, but a sentiment which was soon extinguished by the expediency of competitive fur trading. The French were cutting into the business with brandy and more brandy, as those Company servants who ventured inland reported to their superiors.

The inevitable and ugly problem of illicit trading appeared, and captains of Company ships going to the Bay were found guilty of carrying on private trade, forcing by extortion the sale of their "slops," as one servant called them, upon the men of the forts.

Close statistics on the volume of the liquor traffic during the North West–Hudson's Bay rivalry are elusive and frequently unreliable, and, as the ethics of debauching Indians did not enter into it, any attempt to place moral responsibility is futile. It is clear, though, that the North West Company and the X Y Company, as the more aggressive traders, imported substantially more spirits than the Hudson's Bay Company.

About 1770 the Hudson's Bay Company began importing rum instead of brandy, probably because of the heavy taxation on the French product, and also to meet the competition of the Canadian companies who found Jamaica rum cheaper and more dependable than brandy from

France, torn as that country was by revolutions and wars.

The North West Company historian Davidson, and Innis in his *Fur Trade in Canada*, give figures on the traffic in spirits from Montreal in the years of heaviest competition:

1793 to 1798 an average of 9,600 gallons a year; 1799 —10,181 gallons; 1800—10,098 gallons; 1801—10,539 gallons; 1802—14,850 gallons; 1803—16,299 gallons; 1804—12,168 gallons; 1805—13,500 gallons; 1806—9,500 gallons; 1807—9,000 gallons; 1808—10,700 gallons. From that time until the union of the companies in 1821, the average quantity brought to the Indian territories by canoe and portage from Fort William for the Montreal company was 10,000 gallons a year. To these yearly figures can probably be added 4,000 to 6,000 gallons imported through the Bay by the Hudson's Bay Company. There is one estimate of 19,000 North West Company gallons in 1814, the year before the Seven Oaks massacre, and if the English total is added it would mean that approximately 25,000 gallons were used in the fur trading areas of Canada among about 120,000 natives and whites.

As early as 1803 there were murmurs of protest in the British House of Commons, the first intimation of a public conscience. The North West partners in council at Fort William the next year, sensing the possibility of restrictions, agreed that if they were obliged to satisfy the "saints in Parliament in their mistaken notions of philanthropy," they might be able to get along with five thousand gallons annually, but no less.

It is strange that more fur traders did not turn in utter revulsion from the business, for though most of them were adventurers of the free-lance, mercenary soldier type, many were thoughtful, reflective men. It is true that David Thompson deliberately jettisoned his rum while crossing the Rockies to take command on the west coast for six years, but such protests were rare. The transient nature of the trading may have dulled the sensibilities of men.   The fortunes made in some years by Montreal merchants lured men to the wilderness, hoping to capture quick wealth and retire.   The Canadian Company men were bent only upon immediate profits and early retirement to spend their money;   they did not build for ensuing generations.

Quite different was the position of Hudson's Bay Company men; until 1821 they were not partners; it was not for them to question policy, but only to trade successfully in the interests of the proprietors and take their wages. Throughout the years of this frantic rivalry, certain orderly methods prevailed in the affairs of the forts, and daily journals were maintained as part of the routine.   These terse chronicles record, as no statistics can, the horrors of drunkenness among Indians.   The monotony of the repeated phrases "Indians still drunk," or "Indians drunk and troublesome," appearing only incidentally among journal references to weather, work or hunting reveals the complete acceptance of a normal state.   Drunken Indians were among the casual inconveniences of fur trading.

To stand today on the bank of a smooth, swift northern river when the forest is luminous in a September sun, one does not have to be fired with imagination or undue sentiment about the glory of the wilderness, to reconstruct the contrasting scenes of debauchery.   Here in the undergrowth, marked by moss-grown, rotted logs, are the outlines of the stockade, and here close by was the clearing where the Indians camped when they came to trade.   Here for days when the trading was over and the gates of the stockade closed, they drank their diluted rum; men, women and children, fighting, sleeping, drinking, and fighting again. Murder and mutilation, death from drowning, and obscenities better undescribed were part of this woodland scene.   Within the fort some young clerk goes about his duties, sorting his furs, instructing the carpenter, making entries in his journal.   Next year the fur-bearing animals of the district may be so depleted that the post will be abandoned and the hunters will be without their rum in this district. If the clerk whose sleep was disturbed by the brawling had been questioned about the right or wrong of the practice, he would probably have argued that the Indians were free men and not obliged to trade their furs for spirits. Were they not better off than the slaves in the West Indies, or the ten-year-old children in the coal mines of Britain? They were not seized and carried off to sea to serve guns in naval battles. Their homes were not burned by invading armies.

At home in England official opinion was slowly formulating against the use of rum in the trade. The excesses of the mad years from 1802 to 1821 became generally known across the seas. When the Deed of Covenant came to be written between the Company and the McGillivrays and Ellice, the colonial office specified that a clause was to be incorporated in the agreement; the new proprietors must provide the Crown with rules and regulations to be applied "for the gradual diminishing and ultimately preventing the sale or distribution of spirituous liquors to Indians."

This was the first restrictive measure, and the Governor and Committee promptly clamped a limit of four thousand eight hundred to five thousand gallons for the outfit of 1821. It was a sharp cut of probably two-thirds the average for the two companies in the immediately preceding years. It is unlikely that the total volume ever again exceeded this figure, but it was nearly forty years before the persistent efforts of the Committee were completely effective in withholding rum from the natives.

Under Hudson's Bay trading methods, spirits were not commonly traded for furs, but used for "regales" at the end of a journey or for treats to Indian Chief hunters after the year's trading was finished, or for the purchase of meat. Exceptions were the territories where the Company were exposed to competition from United States fur traders. Whisky was the basic article of trade among these itinerant and elusive adventurers, and the Company met the attack upon its preserves with rum. For years

following the union, and after spirits had disappeared
from the interior, the use of rum persisted along the international boundary and on the coast of northern British
Columbia where the English met both Russians and
Americans.

To men settling down to the service of a great monopoly,
the eminent reasonableness of the curtailing of spirits
appealed at once. If the Hudson's Bay Company had
planned to evacuate the country within ten years, the
continuance of the rum trade on the old North West
scale might have served as an effective means of speeding
up revenues. But the fur trade depended on Indian
hunters, and a rum-sodden Indian with underfed children
was no effective unit in the sequence of fur production.
The Company planned to remain as fur traders for a
long time, and it would have been the blindest stupidity
to continue the profligate dissipation of their basic asset,
the Indian hunter.

Even George Simpson, shrewdest of traders, did not
at first grasp the potential havoc of the rum business.
Fresh from London, his sudden elevation to authority
hardly provided him with an opportunity to gain a more
rational perspective, and at first he was inclined to take
the "mistaken philanthropy" stand in his letters to Colvile.
Two or three years in office with months of intensive
inspection and observation persuaded him to accept the
principle that the use of spirits must cease, though he
qualified that acceptance. Competition in liquor must
be met with liquor, and generations of Indians accustomed
to the "regale" were not to be cut off abruptly. "I have
often heard them reason thus," he wrote Colvile. "It
is not for your Cloth and Blankets that we undergo all
this labour and fatigue, as in a short time we could reconcile
ourselves to the use of Skins as our forefathers did, but
it is the prospect of a drink in the Spring to enable us
to communicate freely and speak our minds to each other
that carries us through the Winter and induces us to
Work so hard." Moreover, Simpson argued, the Plains

Indians still dressed in skins, and the English had vital need of the buffalo meat which they killed for the provisioning of forts. The Company had little to offer these people in barter but spirits and tobacco. "A quart of Mixed Liquer will at times produce more Pounded Meat and Grease than a Bale of Cloth . . . if Provision were paid for in Dry Goods they would eat up all the Gains of the Fur Trade." This was the young governor's view in 1822, when he felt that the restriction of forty to forty-two puncheons of rum was much too drastic. His attitude changed as he gained more experience.

By 1825 Simpson reported to London with pride that in the Oregon, "we have put a stop to this traffic," adding that it was a shortsighted policy to have introduced it. In 1830 he was offering to co-operate with Astor's American Fur Company to stamp out the business at border points where the companies met. In 1835 the Council of the Northern Department specifically excluded all spirits either to officers, servants, or Indians in the English River, Athabasca and Mackenzie River districts. At Norway House in June, 1838, the same council set down a more comprehensive regulation, though it still evaded complete abandonment of rum: "That liquor be not made an article of trade or barter with Indians for furs in any part of the country and that not more than 2 gallons of spirituous liquor and 4 gallons of wine be sold at the Depots throughout the year to any individual in the Company's service of what rank soever he might be."

A tinge of casuistry runs through this. The Governor and Committee had been pressing for constant contraction in fulfilment of the terms of the Deed of Covenant of 1821, while the commissioned officers in Council were reluctant to concede everything and the way was left open to continue the regales or actual barter for buffalo meat. But it was progress, and Simpson assured Governor Pelly that the situation respecting spirits was in hand, except on the north-west coast and in the valleys of the Ottawa and the St. Lawrence where practices of centuries were not easily broken. The British Columbia Coast rum trade was wiped out in 1842 when Sir George, after witnessing a revolting scene of drunken violence and soon after having one of his own men murdered by rum-inflamed natives, concluded a treaty of prohibition with the Russians.

When, in 1857, the time came to renew the Company's Charter, and a committee of the House of Commons opened all the doors and windows and let the breeze whistle through the old Company, the rum-and-Indian matter was thoroughly aired, in sharp contrast to the public indifference to the subject of the parliamentary inquiry of 1749. Some of Sir George Simpson's replies to questions on the use of liquor were evasive; at seventy years he was an imperious person with no relish for his rôle as leading witness in the inquiry.

"To what extent have you been able to prevent the introduction of spirits among the Indians?"

"Spirituous liquors have never been used as a medium for barter for furs within my knowledge."

No spirits had been used north of Cumberland House or in the Saskatchewan since 1822, Sir George declared, and in some districts there were no allowances for officers. Liquor might have been used at the close of a deal in the lower St. Lawrence country where "we are in competition with every shipmaster, pilot and fisherman," but never for trade.

Sir George summed up the use of spirits during the ten years before the investigation (1847–57). The average annual importation had been less than 5,000 gallons, of which two-thirds was taken by the 8,000 inhabitants of Red River. The remaining third, or 1,630 gallons, was for servants of the Company, or "an occasional dram to the Indians who are employed in transport with our own servants, or for the purchase of provisions in parts of the country where we cannot get them otherwise."

At one point in the Simpson régime as governor-in-chief spirits provoked an international incident. The American fur traders along the prairie boundary line, whose hands were wet and dirty from liquor business, took an exalted stand as good citizens and protested to Washington against the monstrous iniquities arising from the use of spirits by the Hudson's Bay Company. The protest reached Viscount Palmerston from the United States Legation in London, in 1850, and his Lordship was told that the English Company in the north-west was corrupting the Indians and endangering the peace. It was a smug document. The traders south of the border knew that if spirits were forbidden by the Crown north of the border they could draw the Indians south like bees to honey. The lofty note of the indignant, injured citizens was really a screen for an attempt to secure an unrestricted field for their own operations. As for endangering the peace, the Hudson's Bay Company's record for maintenance of peace among savage people would certainly bear comparison with the history of those costly and unhappy Indian wars of the United States which had their origins in the un-scrupulous practices of unrestrained free traders.

Earl Grey, colonial secretary, directed an inquiry to the Company. Sir John Pelly's reply of March 9, 1850, contained an "unqualified denial." The regale after the hunt was a custom of long standing, but it was a highly diluted beverage. The Company, wrote Sir John, had repeatedly tried to suppress the traffic in spirits at Pembina on the boundary, but their efforts had been offset by apparent indifference of United States authorities.

"I am not sorry this subject has been brought under your Lordship's notice," he continued, "as it affords me an opportunity of correcting the erroneous statements which have been made in parliament and promulgated through the press, respecting the quantities of spirits imported into their territories by the Hudson's Bay Company.

". . . From the year 1842 to 1849 inclusive the average quantity annually imported by the Company into the whole of the territories under their control to the east and west of the Rocky Mountains is only 4,396½ gallons; a quantity which if distributed only to the men employed in the service in daily allowances would amount to less than two tablespoonfuls to each man. It is to be observed too, that out of the above mentioned quantity the troops stationed at the Red River Settlement in 1846, 1847, 1848 (whose consumption in daily rations alone was upward of 4,500 gallons) had to be supplied, and also the corps of pensioners who succeeded them. There cannot, therefore, have been much left for the demoralization of the natives.

I have, etc.

(Signed) J. N. PELLY."

This correspondence was filed with the parliamentary committee of 1857, when nearly all witnesses were asked questions about the use of spirits. Colonel J. F. Crofton, who had commanded the infantry and engineers at Fort Garry referred to by Sir John Pelly, told the committee it was only when he returned to England that he heard any complaints about the Company in the matter of liquor. Dr. David Anderson, eight years Bishop of Rupert's Land, on the other hand urged the complete discontinuance of the use of rum and believed that if the Company took the lead in this, the free traders would follow.

Gradually and firmly the use of spirits was diminished. The practice of the centuries, stimulated by the flagrant abuses of 1800 to 1821, did not yield readily, and though the fur traders were anxious to avoid impairing the efficiency of the hunting Indian, they were reluctant to give up their practice of treating when the trade was done or providing water-weakened alcohol for the feasts and high occasions. The insistence of the London Committee, the tireless agitation from the Church of England Missionary Society, and the questioning, if unspecified, view of the colonial office were the principal forces in the final suppression.

By 1860 spirits were no longer given to Indians, though

in old letters and notebooks of the next ten years half-veiled references appear now and then, written by some veteran who has dropped back to the old game in the face of fly-by-night competition which had appeared in the mountain passes. Isaac Cowie, who came into the Saskatchewan country in 1867 as a clerk, and who lived to write a highly readable book of prairie recollections, observes that in the years of his apprenticeship liquor was a memory, the subject of bold tales by the old hands.

Chief Trader William Cornwallis King, who in 1936, at the age of ninety-one, is the last survivor of the commissioned officers who held partnership privileges under the Deed Poll, has said that in his years in the service from 1861 to 1904, mostly in the Mackenzie River country, he never saw a drop of spirits given to an Indian.

Yet during the 1850's there were scenes at Company posts in the districts where provisions were procured which recalled the life of thirty years before. Henry John Moberley, who joined the Company in 1854, with a flair for adventure and a consequent erratic career in the service, has left his reminiscences. Taken into history with the qualification that they are the recollections of an old man conscious of the romantic qualities of his career, he contributes an interesting glimpse of liquor in the fur trade before 1860:

"Early in the winter Chief Factor William Sinclair wrote me from district headquarters at Edmonton that provisions were likely to be short that year in the north, and I was to spare no effort to secure a good supply from the Blackfeet and other tribes in constant touch with the buffalo, and who frequented the winter post of Rocky Mountain House. . . .

"The rum trade had at this date become increasingly in disfavour with the Company, although spirits were still an important part of our outfits. In fact, without liquor we should have been at a serious disadvantage. 'Free traders,' mainly from Montana Territory, overran the region to the south, and, while the Blackfeet preferred to trade with us, they would forthwith have transferred their patronage to these men had they been unable to procure from the Company the coveted firewater which was the chief stock-in-trade of our opposition. By hook or crook provisions must be obtained if privation—starvation possibly, even—was to be avoided.

"Mountain House was surrounded by the usual 28-foot pickets, with a block bastion at each corner and a gallery running all round inside about four and a half feet from the top, each bastion containing a supply of flint-locks and ammunition. Within, was a square formed by the officers' houses, men's houses, stores and general trading-shops, a square between this and the pickets for boat-building, with forges and carpenter-shops, another square for horses and a fourth for general purposes.

"There were two gates, the main gate on the north and a smaller one on the south side leading through a narrow passage the height of the stockade into a long hall. In this hall, amid much speech-making, the Indians were received, the calumet passed and two glasses of rum of medium strength were given to each Indian. They were then turned out and the gates closed against them, the only means of communication being through two portholes some 20 inches square opening through the stockade into a small blockhouse through which the trade in rum was conducted.

"Dried and pounded meat, cakes and bladders of grease, buffalo hides, dressed leather, wolf skins and other things were taken in exchange for rum, and in a short time the effects were plainly visible. Horses were often pledged for rum and were always duly delivered after the drinking was over. The rum, being 33 percent over proof, went a long way when mixed liberally with Saskatchewan water. After the first two glasses the rum was diluted—one of rum to seven of water—and for this mixture a stiff price was obtained in 'made-beaver,' the currency of the country; dollars and cents or pounds, shillings and pence were unheard of."

Liquor, brought to Indian trading as a commercial

expedient, disappeared in response to a growing sensitiveness of British public conscience, supported by a recognition of the business sanity of the policy. Viewed from the eighteenth century it was a case of supplying a demand and making a profit. Viewed from the twentieth century it was morally indefensible.

Chapter XV

SOME COMMISSIONED GENTLEMEN

THE Hudson's Bay Company story could be told vividly and accurately in the biographies of those who served it, and no company was ever better served in all the history of commerce.

The stalwarts of the North West Company were middle-aged men by the time of the union in 1821, and by 1850 all but one or two had retired or died in the service. Of the Northwesters who had been clerks at the union, a few lived on as commissioned officers past the half-century. The infusion of new blood which Simpson introduced was from the Highlands of Scotland and notably from the Orkney Islands. For generations the Company drew the finest of these lads from the isles and glens. Equipped with a very sound Scottish elementary education, often a smattering of the classics, sturdy bodies, and unwavering knowledge of the Shorter Catechism, these boys in their teens were superb material for life in the north.

These apprentice lads had thrift and frugality. They were honest and ambitious. The majority of them joined the Company ships at Stromness and went directly to the Bay without ever having been exposed to the glitter of a great city. Their religious training and traditional unbending pride of race saved them from slipping carelessly into the squalor of native life as an escape from solitude. In this there were exceptions, and though the half-breed race did not wane in numbers for their coming, the paternal generation retained a poise and dignity quite remarkable in the light of the conditions under which they lived and worked. What they may have lacked in high spirits and joie de vivre they gained in fortitude and ambition. Among them, of course, were occasional English- or Canadian-born boys who animated the ranks with wild pranks and laughter.

Of the North West partners who entered the commissioned ranks with the union, none achieved a place in history comparable with Dr. John McLoughlin. He was born in 1784 at Rivière-du-Loup on the lower St. Lawrence, of Scottish seigneurial stock with French and Irish strains, and after an Edinburgh medical education he became a surgeon in the North West Company. His uncle, Alexander Fraser, was a retired Northwester who owned the seigneury of Rivière-du-Loup. By 1814 John McLoughlin was a partner and an active trader in charge of the Rainy Lake district. In the Selkirk troubles he was one of the partners arrested and acquitted. With Angus Bethune he had gone to London in the unsuccessful attempt to secure better terms for the wintering partners when McGillivray and Ellice negotiated the union in 1821.

George Simpson sent him across the mountains as chief factor commanding the Columbia Department in 1823, and for many years he readily agreed with the new governor's drastic reforms. The span of his life had curious associations. The blood of Wolfe's Highlanders ran in his veins, and he married the half-breed widow of Alexander McKay who had crossed the Rockies with Mackenzie in 1793. He had two sons and two daughters.

The Columbia District had never been satisfactory. Spurred on by Simpson, John McLoughlin worked it slowly into a profitable arm of the Company. He built Fort Vancouver on the Columbia River, and remained there until 1846 when he resigned from the service. In the years between, this giant of a man, known variously as "the big doctor," "the White Headed Eagle," and the "Father of the Oregon," disclosed at times the Rhodes touch of imperial vision. Unlike many of his colleagues, McLoughlin's slice of empire was not cramped into deep valleys or exposed on the plains to extremes of wind and temperature. His was a veritable lotus land, and the baronial years of his rule unfolded a prospect infinitely wider than pelt bartering. The sea, the forest, and the rivers in a soft, pleasing climate, were all his. Small wonder that he broke with his superiors and threw in his lot with the Americans who were coming by land and sea. In the days of their misery and distress he had fed and sheltered the newcomers with such profligate generosity that the Company protested. He resented this. Moreover his son was murdered by Indians, and McLoughlin never forgave Simpson for allowing the murderers to go unpunished. The fur trade held nothing more for him, and letters written late in life reveal the long-nourished grievance over the failure of his London negotiations in 1821. When he turned to new citizenship in the United States expecting to give leadership to the people in a new land, the reverend missionaries whom he had kept at his own mess table and assisted in their church building, turned upon him as a Roman Catholic, and led the settlers against him. It is a tragic story of a man who had power, intelligence and human kindness, but who collapsed from shattered illusions —a big man who just missed greatness.

The career of James Douglas might have been designed for history textbooks and empire-building oratory. There can be few parallels to this story of virtue triumphant and industry rewarded. James Douglas had been barely a year a North West Company clerk at the time of the union. He served more than ten years at posts in the mountains, chiefly McLeod Lake and Stuart Lake. Simpson, in the *Character Book* of 1832, marked him for early promotion. By 1835 he was a chief trader and by 1840 a chief factor in the Columbia District, enjoying the complete confidence of his immediate superior, John McLoughlin. Anticipating the drawing of an international boundary that would place the lower Columbia within the United States, Simpson had instructed McLoughlin to look north for a new Company headquarters. Fort Vancouver with

Sir John Henry Pelly, Bart., Governor of the Hudson's
Bay Company, 1822–1852

..., on the Red River was, for most of the nineteenth century, the great inland depot. To ... ...see with walls and

its lush pasturage might have to be abandoned, so James Douglas and six men went to Fort Nisqually, boarded the schooner *Cadboro*, and set out to explore the southern part of Vancouver Island in 1842. He chose the site, and a year later took fifteen men on the Company ship *Beaver*, the first steamship on the north Pacific, to build Fort Victoria, named after the girl queen. Douglas spent sixteen years under McLoughlin at Fort Vancouver, and more than a little of the big doctor's stern dignity became part of his own character. But Douglas never wavered from the British connection, and his later career was the reward of fidelity.

The stockades of Fort Victoria were barely finished when British occupancy of the Oregon became a political issue in the United States. The patriotic Methodist missionaries who had come west to evangelize the Indians of the Oregon, found these nomads elusive. The missionaries had turned their attention to farming and politics, and succeeded in reaching the ears of land-hungry thousands with praises of the Oregon. It was evident that the Columbia Valley was going to be American. How far north the boundary would be, no man knew. The Democratic party went into the election of 1844 howling "fifty-four-forty or fight"—the present southern boundary of Alaska, or war. The Democrat James Polk was elected president; the furore died down and Britain agreed to the boundary on the forty-ninth parallel of latitude.

The claims of the Company and its subsidiary farming corporation, the Puget's Sound Agricultural Society, for compensation for their commonlaw rights in the fields and forests south of the international boundary became a political-legal battle of a verbosity and fury which only a frontier community feeling its patriotic oats could produce. The whole affair was a crisis of sorts. Its solution did not remove the likelihood of a further rush of settlers from the United States to Vancouver Island, with the awkward possibility of another provisional government rising up to embarrass both British and United States

R

Governments.   To forestall this eventuality, the British
Government assigned to the Hudson's Bay Company the
task of founding a colony on the island in 1849.   The
Company was made trustee of the natural resources and
these were to be used in the formation of the settlement,
the Company being allowed a profit of 10 per cent.   The
effort was not a spectacular success.   The object was to
create a predominantly British colony, but there was a
long, unpleasant journey round Cape Horn between
Britain and the colony.   The Company offered the land
on terms which could be attractive only to Englishmen wishing to become gentlemen farmers.   Even these
meagre beginnings were arrested by the California gold
rush of '49.

Fort Victoria was the centre of the enterprise, and it
was James Douglas's first command.   He had been agent
for the Company when the colonial office sent out the
first Crown governor, the unhappy Blanshard, who later
told his story to the parliamentary committee.   When
Blanshard resigned, Douglas was appointed governor,
holding the unique positions of chief factor for the Company and Crown colony governor.   With a council of his
own appointment, Douglas carried on comfortably, but as
the governing body was made up almost entirely of Hudson's
Bay officers (John Tod, Roderick Finlayson, John Work)
the interests of the Company were never subordinated.
Even in 1856, when Douglas was instructed by the colonial
secretary, Labouchere, to set up a representative legislature
on Vancouver Island, five of the seven representatives
were Company men.   There was a property qualification
for members, of three hundred pounds in fixed property
and ownership of twenty acres of land.   The little government had its farcical aspect, since the Hudson's Bay
Company was still the administrator of the Island and
held all public revenues.   The legislature carried on,
somewhat amused by its own dignities, with its only source
of money the sale of licences for the vending of spirituous
liquors.   Popular government was all very well, but the

hand of the Company was still firmly on the public business.

It was a condition that could not continue, and Douglas's dual rôle brought entanglements. The discovery of gold on the Fraser River and the subsequent rush of 1858 placed him in the position of a servant of the Crown whose business it was to control the thousands of Americans who poured into British territory, while as an officer of the Company he issued proclamations and set up licence fees for the miners on the mainland.

Douglas leaves the Company's story after forty years of fur trading. On the narrow state of frontier colonial statesmanship he rose far above the minor scuffles of pioneer politics. His devotion to order and his respect for the conventions of office, even the flavour of autocracy which he brought to his administration of public affairs, were in the Simpson-McLoughlin tradition of the old Company. Once he had severed his connection with the Company, he became strictly impartial, often under difficult circumstances. In 1863 he was knighted, and he resigned a year later, to enjoy thirteen years of patriarchal retirement, living to see his colony become part of the Dominion of Canada at Confederation in 1867.

Thomas Simpson, age thirty-two, Master of Arts of King's College, Aberdeen, was killed by an unknown hand on the plains of Iowa in 1840. His death was more tragic in that he had just finished three years of spectacular Arctic exploration in the interests of the Hudson's Bay Company. Nearly a century has passed, and the mystery of his death remains unsolved.

Thomas Simpson was a cousin of Sir George. In his veins was the blood of Duncan Forbes of Culloden who, as Lord Advocate, was largely responsible for the defeat of the Jacobite Rebellion of 1745. When George Simpson first returned to England in October, 1825, he visited his aunt and offered to find places in the service for his cousins. Æmilius and Alexander Simpson accepted, but Thomas continued his education, which was leading to either medicine or the Church. In 1829, though, he accepted the offer, and arrived at Lachine by way of New York. With his advantage in education and age over most of the clerks, he was under an apprenticeship contract of only two years instead of the customary five. He served for a time as private secretary to the governor-in-chief at Red River, and travelled with him on an inspection tour of the southern department. After a year he was given command of a brigade of one hundred men from Lachine to Lake Superior. In February, 1831, he made a winter journey of seven hundred miles from York Factory to Red River, and found zest in the vigorous life. Like so many who have overcome delicate health in childhood, he revelled in the new strength of hard outdoor work.

With all his ambition Thomas Simpson was extremely self-confident of his own righteousness, and his letters reveal more than a little of the intellectual snob. The youthful pedant conceived a sharp dislike for his kinsman the governor. The young man, fresh from university, acting as secretary to the successful, self-made leader, secretly despised his master.

"His Excellency," wrote Thomas of the governor, "miscalculates when he expects to get more out of people by sheer driving; it only puts everyone in an ill humour. . . . By assuming a harsh manner towards me, he should have known—who lays claim to so much tact and knowledge of human nature—that the necessary effect on a young generous mind would be a reciprocal repulsiveness, perhaps hatred; but I know his real sentiments and forgive his apparent though unnecessary unkindness." Thomas complained he had lost much of his earlier respect for the governor, who had grown capricious and changeable, nervous and crabbed. With the ultimate note of priggishness Thomas remarked that George Simpson was "guilty of little meannesses at the table which are quite beneath a gentleman and, I might add, are indicative of his birth."

It was during this same winter when young Thomas sneered at his cousin that George wrote one of the few letters in which he admitted his weariness of mind and body and a hearty dislike of the country. It was a mood induced by the exhaustion of travel and toil, and apparently it never returned. In that same year the *Character Book* was compiled, and while Thomas wrote unpleasant things of the governor, the latter made the following observation about Thomas:

> "A Scotchman 3 years in the Service 24 Years of Age; was considered one of the most finished scholars in Aberdeen College: is handy & active and will in due time if he goes on as he promises be one of the most complete men of business in the country; acts as my secty or confidential clerk during the busy Season and in the capacities of Shopman, accomptant & Trader at Red River Settlement during the winter—perfectly correct in regard to private conduct & character."

The placid tenor of life at Red River was shattered one day when Thomas Simpson gave a black eye and a bruised jaw to a half-drunken half-breed who refused to leave the Company's store at Fort Garry. The half-breed leaders were indignant, and demanded that the governor should have his kinsman publicly flogged. The governor temporized, offered the half-breeds a keg of rum and an assurance that Thomas would be sent elsewhere. Thomas, fired with indignation, threatened to resign and the tension was high for several days. But the governor knew the Metis people better than his clerk did, and the affair quieted down, although it was remembered when Thomas was found with half his head blown off a few years later.

It was the Homeric age of Arctic discovery. The hearts of the British public beat faster as they read each new account of how Englishmen struggled across icy wastes to plant the flag upon a northern coast line. In the interlude between the Napoleonic Wars and the Crimea, the search for the North West Passage became a Holy Grail for the

British Admiralty. Learned societies brooded upon the infinite details of wind and tide and flora and fauna of the far north. Public committees raised thousands of pounds to support expeditions. Alderman Felix Booth, eminent distiller of London, by his generosity had his name fixed for ever on Boothia Peninsula.

The Hudson's Bay Company had given generous support to expeditions crossing its territories in overland attempts to solve the mystery of the Passage. Samuel Hearne believed he had settled the matter in 1771, and Company men since James Knight's day had been very dubious about the existence of any northern route to the Orient. Hearne had reached the Arctic Ocean by way of the Coppermine River in 1771; Mackenzie reached the same body by descending the river of his name in 1789; Franklin's first expedition in 1819 went down the Coppermine and explored one hundred and seventy miles of Arctic coast line; his second expedition of 1824 split at the mouth of the Mackenzie and explored the coast line east to the Coppermine mouth and west to within one hundred and sixty miles of Point Barrow, Alaska. Meanwhile, John Ross was groping for the Passage by sea, and roused public interest to fever pitch by disappearing into the unknown for four Arctic winters. George Back, one of Franklin's men, went overland to look for him and descended to the sea by the Great Fish (Back's) River, but added little to coastal exploration.

It was all very heroic. Knighthoods, promotions, pensions and medals were distributed liberally to commanders and men, while the presses were busy printing their works (which have a curious sameness about them). For all the human suffering and huge expense, there is an inescapable aura of adult boy-scoutism about these epics. They seemed to move in upon the Arctic in seaboots and cutlasses, carrying the etiquette of the quarter-deck with them.

The Hudson's Bay Company, having supported expeditions with little credit beyond a note of thanks in the inevitable book, felt moved to get into the game. Possibly some sense of the obligation to renew the search for the Passage may have prompted the Committee, but certainly the impending renewal of the exclusive licence to trade in the Indian Territories was recognized as a proper time to display some exploratory activity beyond their fur-bearing areas. As the licence was to come up for renewal in 1838, some move to win government goodwill as well as public sympathy would be appropriate.

Vast white spaces remained on the map of the north in 1836 when the Company made its offer to the Crown to organize an expedition which would round out the work of the earlier parties. George Simpson's faith in his cousin was high, for he named his young relative to lead the party. The jealousies of older officers, however, made it necessary to divide the command with the elderly, popular Peter Warren Dease, who had served with Franklin's second expedition.

Thomas Simpson spent the summer at Red River studying surveying and astronomy to equip himself for the undertaking. He brushed up his classics so that his reports would not reflect too much what he called "the stiff ungraceful style of Rupert's Land correspondence." He joined Dease at Chipewyan, February 1, 1837, after an overland trip by dog team from Fort Garry averaging 28 miles a day on the 1,277-mile journey.

By September the expedition had completed the first phase of its programme. They had descended the Mackenzie and gone west along the Arctic Coast. The last leg of the journey was made by Simpson and five of the men. He reached Point Barrow and planted the Union Jack and the Company ensign on that point, linking the western Arctic with the Pacific on the maps of the world.

The party retreated up the Mackenzie and wintered on the shores of Great Bear Lake at a post they named Fort Confidence. In reasonable comfort there, Simpson worked over maps and reports of the previous season, and plans for the next summer, while Dease organized the hunting and equipment.

"When fatigued with writing, chart drawing & astronomy," wrote Simpson, "I have a resource which you would hardly have expected here in an excellent little library which besides scientific books contains Plutarch, Hume, Robertson, Gibbon, Shakespeare, Smollett, and dear Sir Walter. . . . Mr. Dease and I live together on the happiest footing." Simpson added, though, that Dease was an indolent fellow and lacking in enterprise. When the dispatches reporting their first success reached London the Committee voted four hundred pounds to each of the commanders and two hundred pounds to be divided among the men of the party.

In June, 1838, they left Confidence, descended the violent waters of the Coppermine, and struggled east in an epic of desperate marches, fatigue and privation through blizzard, fog and rain some distance beyond Franklin's farthest east to Cape Alexander.

Again they retreated to Fort Confidence for the winter, and in June, 1839, Simpson undertook his last and most important Arctic journey. This time, and again working westward, they reached Rae Strait after great perseverance. It was the most consistent Arctic discovery recorded by any party up to that time. Simpson was within ninety miles of the Magnetic Pole. Only a narrow gap of coast line remained blank, and he was able to write in October, 1839, to the Governor and Committee:

"Honorable Sirs,
"We have the honour to report the completion of all the primary objects of the expedition."

On February 2, 1840, Thomas Simpson arrived back at Fort Garry; nineteen hundred miles with dogs in sixty-one days, including all stops. It was the end of three years and two months of persevering Arctic work, and while the results were being praised officially and in the London press, Thomas waited impatiently for the Governor and Committee to designate him as sole commander of a further expedition. "I feel an irresistible presentiment that I am destined to bear the Honourable Company's flag fairly through and out of the Polar Sea," he said in a letter to his brother.

George Simpson, at Lachine, withheld his approval, and when the express canoes arrived at Red River from Montreal with no news for him, Thomas was exasperated and discouraged. Knowing nothing of the one hundred pounds per annum pension conferred upon him by the Crown, nor of the long-awaited letter coming by ship to the Bay from the Governor and Committee in London endorsing his project, Thomas Simpson abandoned hope and started home to England by way of the United States. Three days before setting out for the south, he wrote of the deep depression that was upon him and of his "destiny" being settled. Accompanied by a party of half-breeds, he rode out from Fort Garry, heavily armed for the passage through the Sioux country. The rest of the story is the evidence of two of the half-breeds who swore that after eight days' travel Simpson said he was sick; while two of the men were putting up the tent Simpson shot them, declaring they had intended to murder him. The two remaining half-breeds left Simpson and rode up the trail for assistance. They met a larger party of Metis from Red River who returned to camp with them and found Simpson dead.

Simpson's own account of his Arctic work was published in 1843. Two years later his brother Alexander wrote a life of Thomas, claiming that his brother had been murdered by illiterate, suspicious half-breeds who thought he had in his papers the secret of the North West Passage. The book was bitterly critical of George Simpson, on the ground that the governor withheld preferment from his cousin through jealousy of his exploration. Alexander bombarded Sir George and the London Committee, accusing the former of having tampered with Thomas's papers after death and claiming from the Company such income as would have come to Thomas had he lived to receive a commission. He also sought from the Crown an extension to the estate of the one-hundred-pound pension.

Alexander Simpson had been at Red River at the time Thomas had the altercation with the half-breed. After Thomas's death he resigned, in great indignation against his cousin George. The other member of the family, Æmilius, had died in 1831. He had a successful career in the service, rose to be chief trader, and after 1826 was superintendent of the Company's marine department on the Pacific Coast. He was first buried at Fort Nass, and later his remains were brought to Port Simpson, named in his honour, and buried there in 1834.

The mystery of Thomas's death will not now be solved. A close reading of young Simpson's personal letters, written in the last year of his life, give unmistakable evidence of a rapidly mounting and almost uncontrolled egoism, the culmination of unbounded ambition and the lonely Arctic winters. The blow to his consuming pride in the apparent disregard of his further ambition might well have dislocated the mind of the courageous young fur trader.

The search for the North West Passage in the nineteenth century added to the world's sum of Arctic knowledge, but the search for missing explorers added infinitely more. Dr. John Rae, a handsome Scotsman from the Orkney Islands, of Viking build and with a flair for strenuous living, spent six years looking for the Franklin expedition, and with his men was awarded the ten thousand pounds offered by the British Government in that long Arctic patrol for trace of the missing Englishmen.

John Rae joined the Hudson's Bay Company as surgeon and clerk at Moose Factory in 1833 and remained there ten years. He held a medical degree from Edinburgh University and was barely twenty-one when he came to Moose Factory. Physician, scientist, and fur trader, he contributed more to the technique of Arctic travel than any man since Hearne. He took up Arctic exploration for the Company where Thomas Simpson had left it. Already his name was great among Company men, and the legend of his one-hundred-mile snowshoe journey from

Moose to Albany in twenty-four hours is told to this day in the service.

In his book *Hudson's Bay* R. M. Ballantyne gives a vivid glimpse of Rae in 1845 during a chance meeting on the Winnipeg River:

"In the afternoon we met another canoe, in which we saw a gentleman sitting. . . . Both canoes made towards a flat rock that offered a convenient spot for landing on; and the stranger introduced himself as Dr. Rae. He was on his way to York Factory for the purpose of fitting out at that post an expedition for the survey of the small part of the North American coast left unexplored by Messrs. Dease and Simpson, which will then prove beyond a doubt whether or not there is a communication by water between the Atlantic and Pacific Oceans round the north of America. Dr. Rae appeared to be just the man for such an expedition. He was very muscular and active, full of animal spirits, and had a fine intellectual countenance. He was considered, by those who knew him well, to be one of the best snow-shoe walkers in the service, was also an excellent rifle-shot, and could stand an immense amount of fatigue. . . . He does not proceed as other expeditions have done—namely, with large supplies of provisions and men, but merely takes a very small supply of provisions and ten or twelve men. . . . The whole expedition is fitted out at the expense of the Hudson's Bay Company. The party are to depend almost entirely on their guns for provisions; and after proceeding in two open boats round the northwestern shores of Hudson's Bay as far as they may find it expedient or practicable, are to land, place their boats in security for the winter, and then penetrate into these unexplored regions on foot. . . . How long he will remain exploring among these wild regions is uncertain, but he may be two, perhaps three years. There is every reason to believe that this expedition will be successful, as it is fitted out by a company intimately acquainted with the difficulties and dangers of the country through which it will have to pass, and the best methods of overcoming and avoiding them. Besides, the Doctor himself is well accustomed to the life he will have to lead, and enters upon it not with the vague and uncertain notions of Back and Franklin, but with a pretty correct apprehension of the probable routine of procedure, and the experience of a great many years spent in the service of the Hudson's Bay Company. After a few minutes conversation we parted, and pursued our respective journeys."

In 1846 Dr. John Rae was given formal command of this first of his five Arctic expeditions. In many respects it was the most remarkable of all. Sir George Simpson drew up the plans: Rae was to explore the coast "from the Straits of Fury and Hecla to Dease and Simpson's farthest." Sir George wrote on the instructions:

"We look confidently to you for the solution of . . . the final problem in the geography of the northern hemisphere. The eyes of all who take interest in the subject are fixed upon the Hudson's Bay Company; from us the world expects the final settlement of the question . . . your safe and triumphant return will, I trust, speedily compensate the Hudson's Bay Company for its repeated sacrifices and its protracted anxieties."

Rae set out from York Factory in two open boats with a party of twelve men, two of them Eskimo, and four months' supplies. They sailed nine hundred miles to Repulse Bay, wintered there in a house they built of stone (the ruins are still to be seen) without fuel. They lived literally off the land, Rae himself killing more than half the caribou upon which they depended. In the spring, sledge journeys were made of over twelve hundred miles, delineating the coast of Boothia as instructed. Rae brought the party back to York Factory in September, 1847, without a single case of illness. The entire expedition, including Rae's salary, cost less than fourteen hundred pounds, as compared with Parry's two-year, two-ship effort which cost nearly one hundred and twenty thousand pounds without conclusive results.

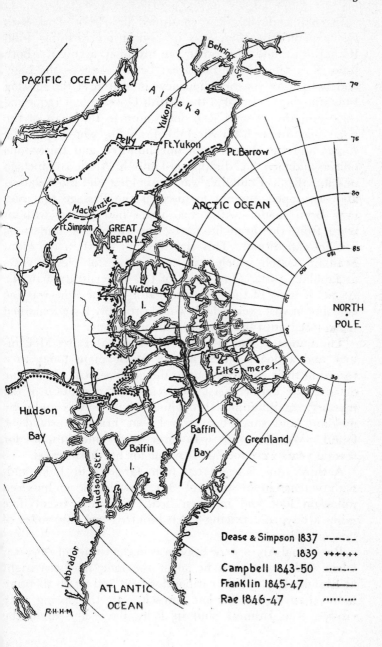

PACIFIC OCEAN

Behring Str.

Alaska

Yukon

Pelly ··· Ft.Yukon

Pt.Barrow

ARCTIC OCEAN

Mackenzie

Ft.Simpson

GREAT BEAR L.

NORTH · POLE.

Victoria I.

Ellesmere I.

Hudson Bay

Baffin I.

Hudson Str.

Baffin Bay

Greenland

Labrador

ATLANTIC OCEAN

R·H·H·M

Dease & Simpson 1837	------
" " 1839	++++++
Campbell 1843-50	—·—·—·—
Franklin 1845-47	————
Rae 1846-47	··········

In 1848 and 1849 Rae continued his Arctic work with two expeditions. One was in association with Sir John Richardson, and the other on his own account. Both times Fort Confidence on Great Bear Lake was the base, and both were coastwise journeys in search of the missing Franklin ships. In 1850 the British Government requested the Company to send Rae once more to the coast of the polar sea to search for Sir John Franklin, whose ships the *Erebus* and the *Terror*, with one hundred and thirty-nine officers and men, had disappeared into the Arctic archipelago in July, 1845. Franklin's was the boldest and most elaborately equipped attempt to discover the Passage that had ever been made. After two years had passed without word from the Franklin party, the Admiralty undertook a relief expedition. This was the first effort in the great Franklin search which was to continue for eleven years at fabulous cost. One result of this concentration in the Arctic of some of the great navigators of the time was the charting of vast areas which would probably have remained unexplored until the advent of the aeroplane.

The names of Rae, Richardson, Ross, McLure, McClintock and a dozen others are on Arctic maps today as a record of their contributions to the great search. John Rae devoted the better part of six years to the solution of the mystery, maintaining throughout that it was only by overland and small boat travel that Franklin would be found. Wooden ships with large crews and supplies for several years were too cumbersome for northern travel.

A third time Rae set out from Great Bear Lake and, with two men in the spring of 1851, travelled eleven hundred miles on foot and in open boat, averaging twenty-five miles a day, and tracing seven hundred and fifty miles of new coast line.

Rae's final Arctic expedition was in the winter of 1853–54, when with seven men he spent the long northern night at Repulse Bay, killing caribou for food and again shooting more than half the game himself. In the spring they crossed Rae Isthmus, and in Pelly Bay came upon the first authentic trace of the Franklin tragedy. Rae learned from Eskimo of a boat party of thirty white men who had died of starvation four years earlier near the mouth of the Great Fish (Back's) River. He also purchased from the natives pieces of tableware and a silver plate bearing the name of Sir John Franklin. Rae returned to England in the same year and submitted his report to the Admiralty.

The Crimean War had broken out by this time, and the British Government, having lost four good ships already in the Franklin hunt, could not resume the work to confirm Rae's discovery. He had, it was pointed out, accounted for only thirty of the missing men. The government again recruited the assistance of the Hudson's Bay Company to confirm Rae's report. Sir George Simpson agreed, and ordered James Anderson and James Stewart, officers of the Company, to descend the Great Fish River and examine the ground carefully for trace of the missing men. The orders were carried out in 1855, and on Montreal Island they came upon the wreckage of the last miserable camp where death by starvation had overtaken the party from Franklin's abandoned ships. A year later the Admiralty gave to Rae and his men the ten-thousand-pound reward of the British Government.

Rae retired from the fur trade, went to London, and enjoyed both public acclaim and membership in scientific societies. He was honoured by McGill and Edinburgh Universities. In 1864 he was re-employed by the Company when the Governor and Committee became interested in a proposed telegraph line from America to Europe via Alaska and Siberia. Atlantic cables were uncertain and the overland route seemed to offer a solution. The scheme did not survive.

John Rae, fur trader, physician, and explorer, died in London in 1893.

A young Scot named Ballantyne entered the service of the Company in 1841 as a clerk, at twenty pounds a year.

He served seven years at York Factory, Norway House, and Seven Islands, and returned to Scotland to find an unexpected career as a writer of books for boys. But for the success of his first book, *Hudson's Bay*, he would have no part in this history.

R. M. Ballantyne had printer's ink in his veins. His uncle was Sir Walter Scott's publisher, and it was reasonable that he should find author's material in the fur trade life. *Hudson's Bay* was published in 1847, the first of his eighty books. Early in the list were *The Young Fur Traders*, 1856; and *Ungava* in 1857. These yarns, the first largely autobiographical, met a phenomenal response which scarcely flagged for fifty years, and some of the titles are still available in reprints. They have an authentic place in Company history, for they told the reading world of romance in fur trade life. In spite of high colour, the tales were authentic enough to fire English and Scottish schoolboys with yearnings for the north. To this day scores of men in the service admit that they were first attracted to Canada by Ballantyne's books.

Hudson's Bay men read the author's first books with scorn, failing completely to recognize the daily adventure in their own lives. But the seeds were sown, and as imitators took up the same locale for their fiction in succeeding years, the fur trade became uncomfortably aware of unsuspected heroics in their ranks. At the time the morale of the service did not suffer. Just as the Royal Canadian Mounted Police in this century have remained undamaged by all the banalities of irresponsible fiction, so the fur trade went about its work perhaps a little self-consciously, but still uncontaminated.

John Rowand was the complete fur trader. In the closely guarded pages of his *Character Book*, George Simpson wrote of his chief factor at Fort Edmonton:

"No. 19. About 46 years of Age.—One of the most pushing bustling men in the Service whose zeal and

Sir James Douglas (1803–1877), Chief Factor of the Hudson's Bay Company and first Governor of the Crown Colony of British Columbia

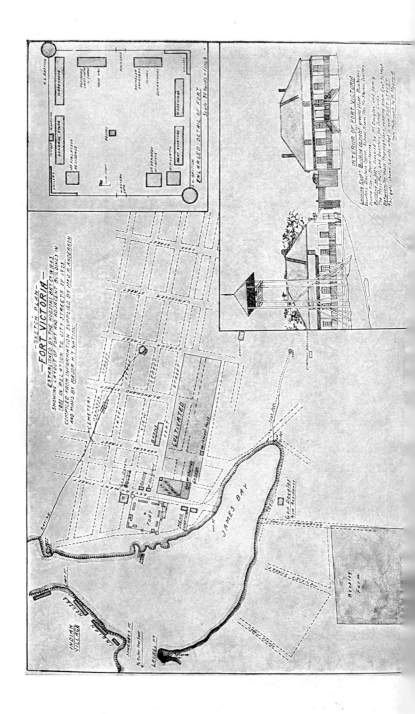

ambition in the discharge of his duty is unequalled, rendering him totally regardless of every personal Comfort and indulgence.—Warm hearted and Friendly to an extraordinary degree where he takes a liking, but on the contrary his prejudices exceedingly strong. Of a fiery disposition and bold as a Lion.—An excellent Trader who has the peculiar talent of attracting the fiercest Indians to him while he rules them with a rod of Iron and so daring that he beards their chiefs in the open Camp while surrounded by their warriors: has likewise a Wonderful influence over his people.—Has by his superior management realized more Money for the concern than any three of his colleagues since the Coalition; and altho' his Education has been defective is a very clear headed clever fellow.—Will not tell a lie publick is very uncommon in this Country but has sufficient address to evade the truth when it suits his purpose; full of drollery & humour and generally liked & respected by Indians Servants and his own equals. . . ."

When Rowand died, twenty-two years later, while visiting his son, Chief Trader John Rowand, Jr., at Fort Carlton, Simpson wrote, "The old race of officers is extinct. . . . Mr. Rowand had been conspicuous as the most influential white man among the wild tribes of the plains." Simpson was deeply attached to him, and as Rowand's last wish was that he should not be buried in the Indian country but should rest finally among his own people in Lower Canada, Sir George had the body placed in a keg of rum and carried in his own canoe to Red River. Rather than risk it being dropped overboard by superstitious voyageurs *en route* to Montreal, he had the remains shipped from York Factory to England and thence to Canada for burial.

Fort Edmonton, where John Rowand ruled, was the dominant establishment in the Saskatchewan district. On a cliff two hundred feet above a great bend in the north Saskatchewan River, it was hexagonal, and its twenty-foot palisade, bastions, flagstaff and great studded gates gave

it a martial appearance. The walls enclosed an area about
three hundred by two hundred feet, with workshops,
warehouse, residence, store and stable.

Edmonton was more than a trading post; York boats
were built there; vast quantities of pemmican were packed
in leather sacks for the Mountain and Mackenzie River
brigades. On cultivated land by the fort were raised
wheat, barley and vegetables. Another service was the
breeding of pack horses, and Rowand had a two-mile flat
race-course laid out on the prairie for sporting occasions.

The York boat industry deserves description because the
York boat was first developed, about 1826, by the Company,
for heavy transportation on inland waters. Until fifteen
years ago they were still used on the lakes and rivers of
the north, lineal descendants of the Viking galley and the
Orkney boats. They were painstakingly built of selected
spruce, in two sizes, one twenty-eight feet long, and a
larger type, forty feet by ten feet, with bow and stern posts
cut in at an angle of forty-five degrees so as to be more
easily moved off obstructions met in rapids. This larger
size of York boat was manned by a crew of eight middle-
men, a bowsman and a steersman, and would carry one
hundred pieces of baggage of ninety pounds each. The
boatmen hauled heavy sweeps twenty feet long, rising to
their feet with every pull on the oars, and completing the
stroke by sitting down. The bowsman guided the boat
through fast waters, warding off rocks with his long pole.
The steersman controlled the direction with a sweep
attached to the stern. A square sail was carried for favourable winds, and each boat had three duck covers, kettles,
frying pans, axe, hammer, tool chest, ropes for hauling
the boat over portages on rollers. Efficient freighters that
they were, the York boats replaced the great north canoes
of lovely lines.

The centre of life at Fort Edmonton was John Rowand's
Great House, sixty by seventy feet, three storeys high,
with generous windows of real glass instead of the skin
parchment used in most dwellings in the interior country.

It was the most imposing building west of Red River, and there Rowand extended traditional Hudson's Bay hospitality to all travellers, including several celebrities of the day who recorded appreciation in the books they wrote. Paul Kane, the artist, spent a Christmas there and left a description of the Great House. On one side of the central entrance was the officers' mess; on the other an immense room where Rowand held court for the Indian chiefs or balls for the festive season. Kane wrote of this room, "The walls and ceilings are boarded, as plastering is not used, there being no limestone within reach; but these boards are painted in a style of the most startling, barbaric gaudiness, and the ceiling filled with centre pieces of fantastic gilt scrolls making altogether a saloon which no white man would enter without a start and which the Indians always looked upon with awe and wonder." Here on Christmas Day Rowand presided over the feast and dance when all the one hundred and fifty people of the fort gathered in their beaded and ribboned finery.

Rowand's authority over difficult Indians was in the Company tradition. The story is told of a day when he stopped at noon to rest, while travelling on the plains. A party of two hundred Blackfeet, mounted and in full warpaint, swept down with fearful yells. Rowand jumped to his feet, ran out to meet them with arm erect, shouting, "Stop, you villains." One of the chiefs recognized him and stopped the rest. The Indians, according to Colin Fraser, the Company officer who described the incident, were abject in their apologies. "Many of them actually cried with vexation," saying they had mistaken the party for Americans and would certainly have shot and scalped them had they not recognized Rowand. The chiefs asked permission to camp beside the whites and gave assurances of no horse-stealing.

Father Lacombe, most celebrated of French Catholic missionaries to the Indian country, loved Rowand and told many tales of the generosity beneath his hard-driving methods: the days and nights on the trails and in the canoes, the personal courage among dangerous Indians, and each of the priest's stories ended with, "Ah, he was a grand little man."

Certain sectors of the Company sphere of influence in North America were in varied conditions of social and economic change by 1835. The republican destiny of the Oregon was taking form. Vancouver Island was a questionable fur trade asset, and on the other side of the continent those isolated log forts at Murray Bay, Tadoussac, Chicoutimi, and Seven Islands, leased by the Company from the Crown and known since the days of the French régime as King's Posts, were less profitable than the proprietors desired. Simpson, having first whipped the Company into a new efficiency, caught up the old North West policy of expansion where it had been dropped nearly twenty years before in the fever of the fur war.

On the maps of British North America of a century ago, the great knob of Alaska protruding off the northwest extremity of the continent held the richest possibilities of fur wealth. The Russians owned Alaska, but the boundaries were uncertain, and their fur trading was a coastal operation. George Simpson sent out his men north and west. Thomas Simpson and Dease defined the coast line to Point Barrow, while a handful of Hudson's Bay men, each reporting direct to Simpson, spent perilous years in the valleys and passes of the almost impenetrable country between the Mackenzie River and the Pacific.

An adequate account of the lives of these men, whose work can be only briefly mentioned here, would make them romantic heroes in any country. Some day their stories will be told; their journals now in the Company archives will be published, and biographers will piece together their letters. The literature of adventure will have no more stirring pages than the lives of these men who traded, starved, and travelled; who "took their wages and are dead."

Robert Campbell, Alexander Hunter Murray, John

McLeod, and John Bell are a few of those who served the
Company in exploration in the Yukon.

Robert Campbell came to Red River from Perthshire,
Scotland, to assist in the management of the Company's
new experimental farm. He was one of a party sent south
to Kentucky to buy sheep. The attempt to herd thirteen
hundred sheep from Kentucky to Manitoba, in 1833, was
not a complete disaster since a few sheep did arrive, but
it has its place in the history of western agriculture. A
year later Simpson sent Campbell to the Mackenzie River
district. It was the beginning of seventeen years of subarctic life and exploration. With the Bible and a copy
of Hervey's *Meditations* for spiritual nourishment, Robert
Campbell maintained a continuity of endeavour probably
unequalled in the north. Winter after winter when the
hunt failed, he and his men were on the verge of starvation,
and each summer they travelled on unexplored rivers so
fast and treacherous that men avoid them to this day.
Campbell's explorations took him among sullen, hostile
natives who had never seen white men and whose first
instinct was to kill the stranger. Again and again he
met natives who stood with bows drawn and arrows pointed
at his heart; Campbell would lay down his weapons and
hold up his hands in the sign of peace. His action is
duplicated in hundreds of such incidents in Hudson's Bay
journals. Coming as traders whose livelihood depended
upon peace, the Company men's chief resource in the
edging back of the frontier was their own courageous
pacifism.

Some of Campbell's adventures held the very essence of
Rider Haggard or Jules Verne. With Mackenzie River
posts for a base, in 1837 (the year Thomas Simpson planted
the flag on Point Barrow) he ascended the Liard River
of treacherous reputation (by 1852 it had taken the lives
of fourteen fur traders) and established Dease Lake post,
pressing on across the mountains to identify the Stikine
River. There, in a forested valley, he came upon a huge

Indian camp, the largest he had ever seen, ruled firmly by a native queen of superior intelligence who welcomed him, though her warriors kept the party in a state of constant alarm. Campbell retreated to Dease Lake and fought off starvation for another winter.

Two years later he discovered the Pelly River. "For three days on this trip," he wrote, "we had neither the luck to kill nor the pleasure to eat. . . . On the sixth day we had the satisfaction of seeing from a high bank a large river in the distance flowing North West. I named the river Pelly River after our home governor Sir J. Pelly. Descending to the river we drank out of its pellucid waters to Her Majesty and the Hudson's Bay Company."

It was eleven years before Campbell found that the Pelly was really the upper branch of the Yukon River, and the interval was marked by annual letters from Sir George urging him to greater efforts and promising promotion, but never allowing the glories or miseries of exploration to overshadow the basic interest of fur trading. Exploration had to pay its way in pelts.

In 1842 he wrote to Campbell: "Your exertions have been exceedingly creditable . . . we have determined on extending our operations in that direction." Sir George added that he believed Campbell's new-found Pelly would flow into the Pacific. Campbell was to press further and send his reports to London where Simpson would be two years hence. The next year Sir George wrote asking for reports on the beaver. "I trust your exertions will not be relaxed . . . hold your ground . . . persevere until you succeed in occupying that new and promising country."

Campbell persevered and succeeded, and in 1851 explored the Pelly hundreds of miles, partly by raft and partly in a boat built without tools, to its confluence with the Porcupine where both streams become the Yukon. There, at the Juncture, he found Fort Yukon, established for the Company four years before by Alexander Hunter Murray. Campbell's great work was done. He went to London, where he aided those eminent cartographers,

Messrs. Arrowsmith, in preparing new maps of the north-west. He was given a chief factorship and appointed to the Saskatchewan district where he served until his retirement in 1870, a devout Presbyterian and a loyal servant of the Company.

The lives of scores of Company men in the last century were as animated with adventure and as closely woven in the course of nations as those of these brief sketches.

Chief Factor Peter Skene Ogden, a former Northwester who spent almost forty years on the Pacific Coast, was a strong-armed, vigorous trader of the old school. He headed the famous Snake River trapping expeditions, which were made up of motley bands of freemen frontiersmen numbering up to one hundred, who travelled and hunted in that dangerous part of the Oregon country and sold their furs to the Company. Peter Skene Ogden with James Douglas succeeded to the joint command of the Columbia territory after McLoughlin's retirement.

One incident from Ogden's career delineates his character. On the night of December 6, 1847, a French Canadian arrived at Fort Vancouver with the news of the massacre by Indians of the Whitman mission on the Upper Columbia. Chief Factor Ogden might have shrugged his shoulders and expressed regrets. Eighteen months before, the international boundary had been fixed, and the murders had been committed in American territory. The victims had been Americans and the few survivors being held prisoner by the Indians were citizens of the republic. It was not a Company affair. The new provisional government at Oregon City, twenty-five miles away, was incapable of armed measures without Company aid. Should the Company remain aloof and allow the Americans to take their own punitive measures? False steps would incite a general uprising of the Indians, and in native affairs Americans had a tendency to shoot too soon.

The morning after the news came, Ogden headed north. Twelve days later, from Walla Walla, he sent out word summoning the chiefs to meet him. All day on December 24 he held council with them. The veteran, white-haired trader drew upon all his knowledge of Indians, standing alone among the savage chiefs.

"We have been among you for thirty years without the shedding of blood," he told them. "We are traders and of a different nation from the Americans, who are of the same colour, speak the same language, and who worship the same God as ourselves and whose cruel fate causes our hearts to bleed. Why do we make you chiefs if you cannot control your young men? . . . If the Americans begin war (it) will not end until every man of you is cut off from the face of the earth! . . . I can only give you advice. The Company has nothing to do with your quarrel. If you wish it, on my return I will see what can be done for you, but I do not promise to prevent war. Deliver me the prisoners to return to their friends and I will pay you a ransom. That is all."

The chief of the Cayuse tribe replied, "We have known you a long time. Your words are weighty, your hairs are grey. You have had an unpleasant journey to this place. I cannot therefore keep the families back. I make them over to you which I would not do to another. . . ."

Five days of acute suspense followed before the prisoners were turned over to Ogden. "For two nights I have not slept," he wrote. "Thank God they are all safe." It was just in time, for Oregon volunteers were already moving up the Columbia, and the United States was about to engage in another Indian war.

Peter Skene Ogden did not found colonies, explore new empires, or receive titles, but he was a loyal officer of the Company, a great-hearted gentleman whose name will live in the story of the north-west. He died in 1854, leaving many descendants and an estate of fifty thousand dollars.

Alexander Hunter Murray, of Argyllshire, Scotland, entered the service at Fort Garry at the unusually advanced age of twenty-eight. He was a son of Commodore

Murray, R.N. Sir George gave him a senior clerkship
for he had served an apprenticeship with the American
Fur Company. He was sent at once to the Mackenzie
River district. *En route* by canoe and portage he met and
loved Anne, daughter of Chief Trader Colin Campbell,
of the Athabasca District. They were married by contract in the manner of the country, with Murray's superior
officer, Chief Trader Murdoch McPherson, officiating; a
Bible, a spoken and a written pledge were enough, for
there were no clergy so far north. These active service
marriages of fur traders were recognized by courts in
eastern Canada.

Murray and his bride spent their honeymoon descending
the Mackenzie River almost to its delta, then turning up
the Peel River to Fort McPherson where they wintered.
The next season, 1847, he left his wife at La Pierre's House,
and under instructions descended the Porcupine to its
juncture with the Pelly. There, in Russian territory, he
built Fort Yukon and raised the Company flag. His
journal of that expedition was published in 1910 by the
Dominion Archives, and it is unique for a strain of quizzical
humour, so rare in fur trade records. Murray damns
the mosquitoes with cheery fervour and complains about
the Porcupine River having so many "confounded turns"
that he was kept too busy charting it to shoot the geese
flying overhead.

Murray was an artist, and his writings are animated by
sharp, clean, informative sketches of Indians, river scenes,
forts and native costumes. Having also a feeling for
architecture, he built the first Fort Yukon with an eye to
form as well as to more than ordinary defensive measures,
for he fully expected the Russians to come up from the
sea and attack him. Indians came to trade with an abundance of furs, and the country looked good. "I have determined on building a fort worthy of it," he wrote.

The palisade was to be no mere row of pickets, "but
good sized trees, dispossessed of their bark and squared
on two sides to fit closely and $14\frac{1}{2}$ feet in height above the

ground and three feet underground. The bastions will be made as strong as possible, roomy & convenient. When all this is finished, the Russians may advance when they damn please."

In that spirit Alexander Hunter Murray established the Company's most remote fort. So far from the markets of the world were these trading posts of the lower Mackenzie and the Yukon that there was a lapse of seven years between the purchase of trade goods in London and the arrival in London of the furs for which the merchandise was exchanged—a long strain on invested capital.

Murray, with a young family, was back at Fort Garry in 1852. Until his retirement he held commands of Pembina, Fort Alexander, Lac la Pluie and Lower Fort Garry with the rank of chief trader. When Upper Fort Garry was undergoing some alterations, Murray suggested a decorative gateway to improve the north entrance, and sketched on the back of an envelope the design of the gateway which has survived today to mark the site of the fort in modern Winnipeg. A Murray daughter married Chief Trader W. J. (Big Bear) McLean, and a son, Chief Trader A. C. Murray, served the Company for many years at Fort St. James, British Columbia.

The stories of these men, their characters, and their exploits could be told throughout the length of many volumes; of James Leith, a partner in the X Y and North West Companies, and a chief factor in the Hudson's Bay Company, who left ten thousand pounds for the propagation of the Protestant faith among the Indians (the Company continues to be a trustee of this fund); of Peter Warren Dease, said to have declined a knighthood offered to honour him for his Arctic work; of the clan of Finlayson, the eleven McTavishes, the generations of Sinclairs, the McFarlanes, the four Hardistys, the McKays, and the Fletts.

There were weak as well as strong men, but the less virile quickly found the level of their limitations. The family trees of the fur trade and the frontier genealogy of western Canada are subjects which await the examination of those who would learn the effects of advancing civilization upon pioneer society.

These men were more than pioneers; with all the individualism of frontiersmen they had orderliness, a high sense of discipline, and the feeling for command. Their authority carried the north and the west of Canada through the transition from a primitive to a civilized state without the bitter, painful fumblings which have been the common experience of the history of territorial expansion.

Chapter XVI

PUBLIC SCRUTINY

THE restless movements of population in the United States in the 1840's and '50's, stimulated by immigration, railways, the opening of the north-west, and the California gold rush, had been watched enviously by Canadians in Upper and Lower Canada. These two colonies had come through the adolescent pains of their first tussles for popular government with some bloodshed and a high consciousness of new strength. They had shaken off the worst elements of colonial office absentee control and united into one government. Still, the growth north of the Great Lakes and the St. Lawrence lagged far behind the pace in the United States. In Montreal and Toronto the epic of the North West Company was not forgotten. That company had brought fortunes out of the west to be spent in the cities of the east. Now the west had become a private preserve, exploited for a handful of English shareholders. While in the United States settlers streamed towards the Pacific in covered wagons, and steel rails thrust out to the great plains, Canadians looking north and west could see on their horizon only a chartered company, endowed with nearly two centuries of privilege and monopoly, endorsed by successive British Governments.

The Hudson's Bay Company held the west in three divisions:

1. Rupert's Land, the lands draining into Hudson Bay, by title under the Charter of 1670. 2. The Indian Territory, all the wilderness not under colonial rule, by an exclusive

licence to trade renewed in 1838 for twenty-one years.
3. Vancouver Island, a Crown colony administered by the
Company.

Agitation from Canada, especially from Toronto, for
the throwing open of the west, together with a thriving
opposition to monopolistic institutions in British parliamentary circles, made the renewal of the exclusive trade
licence in 1858 an opportunity to challenge the Company's
position. By 1857 the whole subject became public business
and once more the Company of Adventurers was obliged
to expose itself to parliamentary scrutiny.

The Company was in an uncomfortable position; it
had to defend monopolistic practice at a time when political
and social liberties were expanding rapidly; and it had
to defend its own government at Red River and on Vancouver Island. Primarily a trading organization, its maintenance of colonial government within its territories had
been an unavoidable obligation. Government had become
part of its work, and though it could not be called a democratic administrator, neither was it as utterly autocratic
as some of the restless settlers at Red River and on
Vancouver Island would have the British Government
believe.

Every fur trader knew that where agricultural settlement
came, fur trading ended. The most elementary self-interest
dictated a policy of opposition to agricultural expansion.
Moreover, the Company argued, farming on the Canadian
plains could not succeed. They had spent thousands of
pounds in experimental farming operations, and had proved
to their own satisfaction that frost, flood, and grasshoppers
were ruinous and unpredictable. The fur traders' opinions
on farming possibilities in western Canada read strangely
today when millions of people depend on the produce of
these plains; but within the limits of their experience the
fur traders were right, for it was only with the later scientific
development of early ripening grains that farming reached
the volume and continuity of production which enabled

Canada to become a great grain-exporting nation. Disastrous floods in 1809, 1826 and 1852, as well as plagues of "locusts," as they were called, in 1818, 1819, 1820 and 1857, had been adequate evidence for the Company. And if the fur traders tempered their evidence before the committee to the advantage of the fur trade, as did Sir George Simpson when he declared the entire British Columbia coast unfit for agriculture, certainly the Company's critics went equally far in the opposite direction with their glowing and extravagant forecasts of the country's future if only the monster monopoly could be ousted.

There were few friends to rush to the defence of the claim for a renewal of the exclusive licence to trade. The settlers in the west resented the monopoly operation; eastern business interests wanted the fur trade to be openly competitive; the government of Canada regarded the Company as an obstacle to western expansion.

In England the shareholders, now about two hundred and fifty in number, had a few powerful friends, but the general public viewed the Company as a prosperous, specially privileged monopoly. The close-lipped policy had not been relaxed since Prince Rupert's time. It had, in fact, become exaggerated by the dour qualities of the Highlanders who filled the senior posts. The English public's attitude was fairly if melodramatically described by one Andrew Freeport in an open letter to Lord Palmerston in 1857. "The management of their affairs is inscrutable . . . it is like a commercial tomb, closed with the key of death to all except a favoured few . . . its councils unfathomable and its secrets unknown . . . its revenues are acquired in secret and distributed in silence."

Still, the Company's affairs never became a matter of widespread public interest. It had none of the stuff on which elections are won; there was not much career-building material for ambitious young Members of Parliament to cut their teeth on. Yet the parliamentary committee of nineteen, appointed by the House of Commons on February 5, 1857, "to consider the state of those British Possessions in North America which are under the administration of the Hudson's Bay Company, or over which they possess a Licence to trade," went about its work with that conscientious application and inquiring judicial spirit which is the supreme virtue of British parliamentary investigations.

On the committee were some of the most distinguished men of the century. Henry Labouchere, secretary of state for the colonies, was chairman. Other members were: Sir John Packington, secretary of state for war and for the colonies under Lord Derby's government; Lord John Russell, the great Whig leader who had held the colonial office and had been Prime Minister from 1846 to 1852; Lord Stanley, a member of the House for nearly thirty years; William Ewart Gladstone, then forty-seven years of age, who had already been colonial secretary under Peel, and Chancellor of the Exchequer for three years under Aberdeen; Robert Lowe, Viscount Sherbrooke, one of the brilliant speakers and classicists of his time, and later Chancellor of the Exchequer for Gladstone; John Roebuck, the radical lawyer, free trader, and friend of John Stuart Mill, who later became chairman of a committee to investigate the conduct of the Crimean War. From February to July the committee met eighteen times and examined twenty-five witnesses. The verbatim report of the evidence fills five hundred and fifty printed pages.

Soldiers who had served at Fort Garry, disgruntled settlers from Red River and Vancouver Island, the governor of the territories, sea captains, Arctic explorers, ex-fur traders, a British merchant, an American trader, and the representative of the Canadian Government were all heard.

The first witness was John Ross, member of the Canadian Parliament and head of the Trunk Railway, who testified that the Hudson's Bay Company had done great work in keeping peace with the Indians. Therefore in the Indian Territories, he thought, the Company should be allowed to carry on. Where settlement was possible, a change should be made. Fur trading and agriculture were incompatible, and arable land should be acquired by Canada from the Company in blocks of twenty or thirty townships. He advocated a railway from the head of Lake Superior to Red River and then across the continent, to open trade with China. "But perhaps it is taking rather a long flight," concluded Mr. Ross.

Lieutenant-Colonel J. H. Lefroy, R.A., who had spent two years in the Hudson's Bay territories making magnetic observations for the Royal Society, gravely doubted any real agricultural possibilities on the prairies or the desirability of settlers being persuaded to go there. Asked about the danger of travel in the country of the Blackfeet Indians, he replied, "Under the protection of the Hudson's Bay Company it could be done with perfect safety." Colonel Lefroy approved the Company's measure to discontinue the use of spirits. Of Company officers he said, "I have never mingled with a body of men whose general qualities seemed to me more entitled to respect."

"You think, upon the whole, that their conduct was that of men who were doing their duty and acting in a considerate manner toward the Indians?"

"I think so, most eminently."

John Rae, M.D., a former chief factor and physician in the service, and one of the most celebrated Arctic travellers of the century, told the committee there were certain arable lands in the west but even so there was no ready market. Settlement would come eventually, but slowly, and then from the south as the lands in the United States filled. He believed fur trading must be a monopoly. A free fur trade would kill off the animals, introduce spirits again, and demoralize the Indian. Doctor Rae was examined at length on details of Indian trading, and he undertook to make it clear that it was to the Company's advantage to keep the native well clothed and well supplied with ammunition, "because the better they are fed and the better they are clothed, the better they will hunt."

Thomas Simpson, clerk of the Company, who explored extensive lengths of the Canadian Arctic Coast. He was killed under mysterious circumstances while travelling to Montreal in 1840.

The Dease and Simpson cairn as it stands today in the Canadian Arctic.

Chief Trader Alexander Hunter Murray who established Fort Yukon for the Company in Russian Alaska in 1847.

Chief Factor (Doctor) John Rae, physician, fur trader and celebrate
Arctic explorer, who was the first to establish the fate of Sir Joh
Franklin's expedition

The crusty doctor became exceedingly impatient with
Members of Parliament who could not be made to grasp
the principle of trading which fixed one beaver skin,
"Made-Beaver," as the unit of trade and graded all other
skins accordingly.   Thus, a gun price might be fixed at
ten beaver skins, but could be purchased with fox or
musk-rat skins in the proportion of their value to the beaver
standard.

Mr. Roebuck, of the committee, pursued tariffs trying
to establish the existence of exorbitant charges.   He read
from an old account:

> "Thus, an Indian arriving at one of the Company's
> establishments with a bundle of furs, which he intends
> to trade proceeds, in the first instance, to the trading
> room; there the trader separates the furs into lots, and
> after adding up the amount, delivers to the Indian a
> number of little pieces of wood, indicating the number
> of made-beaver to which his hunt amounts.   He is
> next taken to the store-room, where he finds himself
> surrounded by bales of blankets, slop-coats, guns, knives,
> powder-horns, flints, axes, &c.   Each article has a
> recognised value in made-beaver.   A slop-coat, for
> example, is 12 made-beavers, for which the Indian
> delivers up 12 of his pieces of wood; for a gun he gives
> 20; for a knife, 2; and so on, until his stock of wooden
> cash is expended."

Mr. Roebuck asked Doctor Rae if he had seen that
process.

> "Certainly; but a coat generally costs five or six
> skins.   The process is true; but the details are not true."
> "I will now read to you from the *Indian tariff of the
> territory embraced within the Royal Licence, situated east of the
> Rocky Mountains.*   I find that a gun which in England
> cost 22s., is charged to the Indian 20 beavers, equivalent
> in market value of 32£.10s.; is that anything according
> with your experience?"
> "It was true many years ago, but it is not true at
> present."

T

"Have you wonderfully reformed of late?"

"No, but the price of beaver is not that; it is 13s. in the market at the present day."

"Then the Indian would have to give more beavers?"

"No, it would still be the same; and the gun might rise to 30s. or 40s."

"In marten skins he gives for the same gun, costing 22s., 60 skins and their value is 46£.10s.?"

"I never saw more than two martens go to a beaver since I have been in the service."

"He gives five silver fox skins for the same gun, and their market value is 50£?"

"Yes, it is true."

"Do they descend to musk-rats, which form half the stock?"

"At some places."

"They do not say anything about musk-rats?"

"No; that is just the thing; there is little or no gain upon them. Let me give my side of the tariff: ten rats go to a beaver; for a gun it would be 200 rats, and the price in the market, some years ago, was 3d. or 4d. a skin."

Mr. Grogan: "How many beavers to a gun?"

"Twenty by that count, and that is the MacKenzie river tariff; that is the very highest tariff that we have to the Indians. If you are paid for that gun in rats, you have scarcely the profit that a London merchant would take, even in the City, instead of going to the Saskatchewan, and those musk-rats form one half of the bulk of the returns of the southern department, and a great portion of the northern."

Doctor Rae told of his own care of the sick and old Indians without charge. He answered at great length questions about the geography of the Company's territory, on which the committee was remarkably well informed.

Sharper and deeper probing marked Sir George Simpson's appearance on the witness stand on February 26. Simpson became the central figure of the inquiry and all the committee members attended throughout the two days he testified. Thirty-seven years of absolutism had not fitted the governor of the territories for a defensive rôle in a public investigation. The single great loyalty of his life was the Company, and suggestions that his management of affairs might have been better goaded him into indignant retorts. The Little Emperor was seventy years of age, but active and vigorous, though his eyesight was seriously impaired. His deliberate assumption, through the years of his rule, of an authority quite viceregal was revealed when he explained to the committee the machinery of governing by council of commissioned officers.

"They could outvote me but it has never been so," Sir George said, calling it "my own government."

Although not a good witness, Simpson gave the committee more information on the western part of British North America, its people, government, trade and geography, than any other man of his time could have done. On the increasingly annoying question of agricultural settlement he was adamant, and on old, internal political controversies, revived for the occasion by his inquisitors, he claimed difficulty in remembering. But he admitted with some pride that the Hudson's Bay Company was the greatest fur company in the world and that the takings of furs from Canada had never been larger than at that very time.

He explained the organization in Canada: sixteen chief factors, twenty-six chief traders, five surgeons, eighty-seven clerks, sixty-seven postmasters, twelve hundred permanent servants, fifty-five voyageurs, a total, counting temporary labour, of some three thousand men employed each season.

The Company estimate of the Indian population in the west was one hundred and thirty-nine thousand, of whom eighty thousand were west of the Rockies.

The committee pressed hard for precise information on agriculture. Mr. Labouchere, the chairman, asked:

"Will you have the goodness to give to the committee an account of your impressions of the character of the territory of the Hudson's Bay Company with reference to its adaptation for the purposes of cultivation and colonization?"

"I do not think that any part of the Hudson's Bay territories is well adapted for settlement; the crops are very uncertain," replied Sir George.

"Would you apply that observation to the district of Red River?"

"Yes."

"Why so?"

"On account of the poverty of the soil, except on the banks of the river. The banks of the river are alluvial, and produce very fair crops of wheat; but these crops are frequently destroyed by early frosts; there is no certainty of the crops. We have been under the necessity of importing grain within these last 10 years from the United States and from Canada, for the support of the establishment."

Sir George had an even lower opinion of the potentialities of the Saskatchewan Valley, but conceded that there might be hope for agriculture on a "mere slip of land" on the right bank of the Rainy River.

"Are you acquainted with the coast near Vancouver's Island and above it?"

"Yes. I have gone along the coast from Puget's Sound to the Russian principal establishment at Sitka."

"Do you believe that coast to be altogether unfit for colonization?"

"I believe it to be quite unfit for colonization."

Sir George told of the crop failures from grasshoppers and flood, and the need for importation of flour to feed troops in 1847. The population of Red River was about eight thousand persons, of whom more than half were engaged in hunting or fishing. Approximately eight thousand acres of land were under cultivation.

While it was not in the Company's interest to promote colonization, Simpson's sweeping conclusions were unquestionably honestly based on his own observations and expensive experience with experimental farming. However, he was made to squirm with discomfort when a Mr. Gordon of the committee confronted him with fulsome, florid extracts from his own two-volume book on his trip round the world.

"If I understand you rightly," said Mr. Gordon, "you think that no portion of Rupert's Land is favourable for settlement, but that some portions might be settled?"

"Yes."

"In your very interesting work of a *Journey Round the World*, I find at page 45 of the first volume this description of the country between the Lake of the Woods and the Rainy Lake: 'From Fort Frances downwards, a stretch of nearly 100 miles, it is not interrupted by a single impediment, while yet the current is not strong enough materially to retard an ascending traveller. Nor are the banks less favourable to agriculture than the waters themselves to navigation, resembling, in some measure, those of the Thames near Richmond. From the very brink of the river there rises a gentle slope of greensward, crowned in many places with a plentiful growth of birch, poplar, beech, elm, and oak. Is it too much for the eye of philanthropy to discern through the vista of futurity this noble stream, connecting, as it does, the fertile shores of two spacious lakes, with crowded steamboats on its bosom and populous towns on its borders?' I suppose you consider that district favourable for population?"

"The right bank of the river is favourable, with good cultivation; that is to say, the soil is favourable; the climate is not; the back country is a deep morass, and never can be drained, in my opinion."

"Do you see any reason to alter the opinion which you have there expressed?"

"I do see that I have overrated the importance of the country as a country for settlement."

"It is too glowing a description, you think?"

"Exactly so; it is exceedingly beautiful; the bank is beautifully wooded, and the stream is very beautiful. . . ."

Mr. Gordon: "Will you allow me to remind you of

one other sentence in your interesting work. It is at page 55 of volume 1: 'The soil of Red River Settlement is a black mould of considerable depth, which, when first tilled, produces extraordinary crops, as much, on some occasions, as 40 returns of wheat; and even after twenty successive years of cultivation without the relief of manure or of fallow, or of green crop, it still yields from 15 to 25 bushels an acre. The wheat produced is plump and heavy; there are also large quantities of grain of all kinds, besides beef, mutton, pork, butter, cheese, and wool in abundance.' Do you adhere to that statement?"

"I do."

"And yet you think it unfavourable for cultivation?"

"Yes. I there referred to merely a few small alluvial points occupied by the Scotch farmers."

Simpson was hard pressed, but found himself more at ease in answering questions about missionary establishments, of which there were forty-two generously supported by the Company. The Anglican bishop of Rupert's Land received three hundred pounds a year salary from the Company and one hundred pounds for support of schools; the chaplain at Red River received one hundred and fifty pounds; at York Factory fifty pounds; at Moose Factory fifty pounds; at East Main fifty pounds; at Victoria two hundred pounds. The Roman Catholic Mission at Red River was given one hundred pounds a year, and similar amounts went to the support of religious work in Oregon and on the lower St. Lawrence, with free passage on Company ships to most missionaries.

The somewhat primitive government of Rupert's Land, Assiniboia and the Indian territories left some of the literal-minded legal gentlemen of the committee quite aghast. The Royal Charter was the authority; from this came the proprietors with their Governor and Committee. They in turn appointed a governor-in-chief of their overseas affairs. He and his councils, Northern and Southern, were the masters of Rupert's Land. But within Rupert's Land was Assiniboia embracing the Red River Settlement.

Assiniboia was the nucleus of the Selkirk colony, but for purposes of government it was now a circuit of fifty miles by the compass, and its capital was Fort Garry, the petty metropolis of the west. It was ruled by a local governor appointed by the governor-in-chief, and supported by a council of "leading citizens." There was a recorder to fulfil the magisterial function, owing his appointment to the Company and "following the laws of England." The complete absence of any basic statutes or legal precedents for this machinery was a matter of no concern to Sir George, who explained its operation. It was all utterly simple, and its rightness lay in the fact that it worked. The colony jail was nearly always empty. Crimes of violence were extremely rare, and the perpetrators always brought to justice. The Company sold land at five shillings an acre to retiring officers or voyageurs at Red River, but a majority of the eight thousand inhabitants were squatters. There was no export market for farm products, it was true, but on the whole it was a contented community.

Sir George was asked about the Indian Territory, which was British property occupied by the Company, not under its Royal Charter but under an exclusive trading licence. Suppose a crime is committed in that country, is the criminal brought through Rupert's Land to Assiniboia for trial before a magistrate appointed by the Company? If so, by what authority? Sir George could only answer that his chief factors were regarded as magistrates in the wilderness, and that they did somehow keep the peace. If more settlers came to Red River and took up land, the Company would not object so long as hands were kept off fur trading.

"I do not think they would do any harm," said Sir George, "if they were restrained from interfering with the fur trade . . . provided the Company were satisfied; they consider themselves lords of the soils, proprietors of the country in their own special territory."

If Sir George seemed an unwilling witness, it cannot all be put down to the Napoleonic touch. He was an old man. Certainly, had his memory been fully active, he would never have denied knowledge of the United States Government's note to Britain in 1850 on the subject of liquor trading. Still, under very capable examination, he gave the public more information about the Company in the two days of his evidence than had been disclosed for more than a century.

The next witness was the Hon. C. W. W. Fitzwilliams, M.P., a member of the Committee who had travelled widely in America. He had found Vancouver Island good, and noted that among the three hundred white inhabitants there were some who did not like the Company's rule.

Alexander Isbister, born and schooled at Red River and a clerk in the service for three years, testified against the Company, mostly on the grounds that under a fur trade monopoly Indians and half-breeds did not get justice. He believed there was ample room for agricultural expansion in the west.

Sir John Richardson, C.B., one of the stout old Franklin school of Arctic explorers, gave a lucid picture of all he had seen in Canada during seven years' residence and three expeditions. He completely endorsed the Company government, though he thought Red River and Vancouver Island might be set aside for Crown colony administration.

Rear-Admiral Sir George Back, also of the navy school of Arctic leaders, had been twice with Franklin and once on his own account in the far north. "I saw nothing but the utmost kindness to the Indians and fairness in dealing. . . . I have seen strong instances of great benevolence on the part of Hudson's Bay officers." Within his own experience Indians would several times have starved had not men in the forts provided for them at personal sacrifice.

James Cooper, a former sea captain in the Company service but latterly a settler on Vancouver Island, protested against the absence of adequate defence against Indians, and of a proper court. If the island were under Crown colony rule, a trade treaty could be arranged for the disposal of agricultural products.

William Henry Draper, Chief Justice of Upper Canada, was an important witness. He had come with a watching brief from the Canadian Government, but was prevailed upon to give his own views, which he did with the admirable clarity of one familiar with public hearings and the rules of evidence. Canada was vitally interested in the west; first, to have settled colonial boundaries; second, to have it remain British; third, to have the right to settle freely west of the Great Lakes.

"I conceive that the Hudson's Bay Company are a Company conducting their Government in a manner consonant with their interests as a trading company and conducting it in that view most admirably. I do not think that the interests of a trading company can ever be considered as compatible with the settlement of the province," said the Chief Justice. The right to explore and survey should be given to Canada. He favoured British colonial administration of Red River with Canadian co-operation by means of transportation; as settlements became established they should be taken under Canadian Government; the Hudson's Bay Company should continue to hold the Indian territories to keep the peace. In this matter of peace, the memory of the old North West–Hudson's Bay strife and the shadow of the contemporary Indian wars in the United States were never far from the thoughts of those who advocated the wiping out of Company privileges.

Draper's answers were carefully calculated and carefully qualified. There were no extreme or extravagant statements. The boldest forecast he allowed himself, interjecting it with apologies, became in less than thirty years a reality: "I hope you will not laugh at me as very visionary, but I hope to see the time, or my children may live to see the time, when there is a railway going all across that country and ending at the Pacific."

Dr. David Anderson, Bishop of Rupert's Land, told the committee that the Church maintained twenty clergymen, nineteen native teachers, and spent six thousand pounds annually in the territories under Hudson's Bay rule. The Company had done much for the Indians and "assisted me largely in many ways," but was not interested in educating the natives. Bishop Anderson believed the Indians should be prepared to meet the inevitable rise in settlement; the use of rum should be stopped.

Joseph Maynard, solicitor to the Company, appeared briefly to file copies of the exclusive licences to trade west of Rupert's Land, one of 1821 and one of 1838.

A. R. Roche gave it as his opinion that most people in Canada wished to see the Company abolished and free trade restored in the Indian country. He filed a petition from six hundred residents of Red River objecting to almost everything in the method of government by the Company, but particularly their exclusion from the fur trade, and the prevailing system of land tenure.

Captain David Herd, who had served on Company ships for twenty-three years, reported on weather and ice conditions in Hudson Bay and Strait, and described the nature of cargoes. When asked if he knew anything of the country beyond the coast line at York Factory, his reply spoke for generations of shipmasters before and since that day. "The appearance of the country is so unfavourable that I never go out of my ship when I am there: I am glad to get there and glad to get away again."

J. McLaughlin, who had attempted to trade in furs in Rupert's Land, the most serious of civil offences under Company rule, told of his encounter with the Adventurers, largely through libel actions. He pointed to higher prices paid for furs in the United States, and protested against the restrictions exacted by the Company.

Richard Blanshard, first unhappy governor of Vancouver Island in 1849 and '50, gave an inkling of his troubles. The climate had been about the only agreeable element in his experience. The Crown had appointed him without salary, and the Company had agreed to set aside one thousand acres for the governor of the colony. Blanshard mistook this to be a gift to him personally, and there had been a quarrel with Chief Factor Douglas, who commanded Fort Victoria. There were about thirty settlers on the island at the time. His chief occupation had been settling disputes between the Company and disgruntled servants. The Company treated the Indians kindly.

Lieutenant-Colonel William Caldwell, commander of a corps of pensioners garrisoned at Fort Garry, and governor of Assiniboia from 1848 to 1855, said he was a "jack-in-office and did everything." In 1848 the inhabitants numbered five thousand, and the position of the head of both legislative and judicial bodies was extremely complicated. "I tried to do justly between man and man. That was my great object." The Company had done well by the Indians, but a monopoly was "no advance to any civilization."

Richard King, M.D., who had been with Sir George Back in 1833-36 as a naturalist, was enthusiastic about the agricultural future of the Saskatchewan Valley. He repeated old unconfirmed rumours of Company men having run foul of authority if they tried to grow field crops in certain territories. He also made extravagant statements about the decline of the beaver.

Simpson, Draper, and Ellice provided the committee with the pivotal evidence, Simpson as a practical fur trader who had lived among Indians; Draper as a judicially trained mind representing an ambitious colonial government; Ellice as an enlightened statesman who had lived in America and had, for more than fifty years, held substantial investments in the fur trade. "Bear" Ellice, he had been called by his London friends by reason of his association with the pelt business, but his career was never marked by any gross bearlike blundering. On the contrary, he was a cultured gentleman of excellent business judgment and finely tempered, diplomatic mind. He served many years on the Committee of the Hudson's Bay Company after the union in 1821, in which he had been a principal negotiator. His son, also named Edward, became deputy governor from 1858 to 1863. Both father and son were Members of Parliament, and at the time of the parliamentary investigation the son was a member of the committee of the Commons, while the father, a former secretary of the Treasury and now seventy-six years of age, was called as one of the key witnesses.

To a very attentive committee this grand old man told the story of fur trading in British North America as he had known it for more than half a century. Without malice or recrimination he recited the facts of the union of 1821, and revealed in passing that, when he had been in opposition to the Company thirty-odd years before, the validity of the Royal Charter had been selected as the vulnerable spot in the Hudson's Bay structure to attack, but the best legal opinions they could secure had warned them off this approach.

Ellice summed up concisely the earnings of the Company. At the union the stock was four hundred thousand pounds. This had been increased by payments in money or by profits carried to stock to five hundred thousand pounds, where it stood in 1857.

"I will tell you the profits of the Company that everybody may have all that we can tell them on the subject. The average profits for the last 17 years have been 65,573£. 2S. 7D. of which 39,343£. 5S. 1D. has been appropriated to the profit of the Company at home, and 26,229£. 5S. 1D. annually appropriated to the factors and traders in the interior. The general profits of the Company, since the formation of the Union, inclusive of this profit on the fur trade, have averaged about 12 per cent upon their capital and the share of profit given to the Chief Factors and traders averaged 617£. 13S. 2D. to each Chief Factor and 308£. 11S. 7D. to each chief trader."

The investigation was drawing to a close and Ellice was almost the last witness. His knowledge and experience of public affairs must have told him the time had come to make concessions. As a Northwester he had led the diehards out of what would have been a death struggle, to meet the enemy in a truce. Here before Parliament, where his wisdom was greater than Simpson's, he was leading the fur trade once more, and again he was adapting policy to changing conditions. He was asked by the chairman if it would be difficult to make an arrangement between the Canadian Government and the Company for the extension of settlement into Hudson's Bay territory.

Ellice made this significant reply:

"Not only would there be no difficulty in it, but the Hudson's Bay Company would be too glad to make a cession of any part of that territory for the purposes of settlement, upon one condition, that Canada shall be at the expense of governing it and maintaining a good police and preventing the introduction, so far as they can, of competition with the fur trade."

Mr. Labouchere (the chairman): "You think it would be advantageous to the Company to withdraw, as it were, to the more Northern part of their territory, and leave for gradual settlement the Southern portion of their country?"

Mr. Ellice: "I am of opinion that the existence and maintenance of the Hudson's Bay Company for the purpose of temporarily governing this country, until you can form settlements in it, is much more essential to Canada and to England than it is to the Company of Adventurers trading into Hudson's Bay."

The destiny of British North America was being gently and firmly shaped in the committee, on that June day of 1857.

During July, the committee held four meetings in camera to formulate its report to the House of Commons, and opinions divided sharply as members put forward various draft reports. Mr. Gladstone strongly advocated a prompt separation of all western lands fit for colonization from the Company's jurisdiction. The committee divided evenly on his motion and only the chairman's deciding vote defeated the proposal.

The final report was less than a thousand words in

length. In fourteen clauses policy was framed. It was a brilliant piece of directional work embodying those elements of administrative compromise which have been the genius of British parliamentary government, yet it guided towards a new course the whole relationship of the Crown, the government of Canada and the Hudson's Bay Company.

The settlers at Red River were given cause for real hope. The Company's part in British colonial affairs was recognized, but restrained with due regard to capital interests, and a central imperial purpose was definitely preserved.

Remembering that in ten years the Confederation of Canada was born, and that in twelve years the Company surrendered its charter rights to Rupert's Land, this committee's report of 1857 is an astonishingly skilful piece of preparatory work:

1. The desire of Canadian "fellow-subjects" for extension of settlement, the necessity of better government for Vancouver Island, and the state of the Red River Settlement, were noted.

2. The merits of Chief Justice Draper's evidence were appreciated.

3. In the interests of Empire solidarity it was essential to meet the "just and reasonable wishes of Canada" to enable her to annex for settlement such lands as she was prepared to administer, particularly the Red River and Saskatchewan valleys. The committee did not apprehend any troubles in a plan for the ceding of these districts by the Company to Canada, but left it to "Her Majesty's Government to consider . . . its details . . . before an Act of Parliament is prepared."

4. If colonial Canada was not ready to take over Red River soon, then some other provision should be made for its government.

5. The Company's rule of Vancouver Island should be terminated and that colony extended to include the lands west of the Rockies.

6. In all those territories where there was no prospect of permanent colonization, for the preservation of peace, for the protection of the natives against the evils of openly competitive fur trading, and for the conservation of fur-bearing animals, the Company should "continue to enjoy the privileges of exclusive trade." This was not to be regarded, however, as a confirmation of the validity of Charter rights.

7. In view of "the grave interests" at stake the committee concluded with the hope that all parties would approach the subject in a spirit of conciliation and justice.

It had been a long road since in that same borough of Westminster in the City of London, Charles II had signed the Charter of the Company of Adventurers. "The true and absolute Lords and proprietors" of the plains, the lakes, the forests, and the mountains were being brought into conformity with the new concepts of Empire.

Chapter XVII

THE SURRENDER

FROM the British parliamentary inquiry of 1857 it was plain that the sun of the royally chartered monopoly was setting. In the fur trade councils, the chief factors and chief traders met each outfit expectant of new imperial legislation to change the pattern of their lives. At Red River the colonists waited impatiently for representative government. And in the gloomy board-room of Hudson's Bay House, London, with its age-blackened furniture and portraits, the Governor and Committee sat tight and waited. Their position was stronger than they knew. Their profits had come from furs, and they failed to discern the trend of colonial events which year by year enhanced the value of their title to the vast territory of Rupert's Land.

Twelve years after the investigation, the only recommendation implemented had been the creation in 1858 of the Crown Colony of British Columbia. It was 1869 before the Hudson's Bay Company yielded up its feudal proprietorship of two hundred years.

In the last six years before this Deed of Surrender, the continuity of the Company's story was sharply dislocated and almost broken by a stock manipulation directed by a group of promoters. The Royal Charter itself, together with the proprietorship of 40 per cent. of net property by the commissioned officers, were the two elements in the structure which survived. Shareholder control changed hands in 1863, but the Charter lived on, and the partnership of officers under the Deed Poll continued just long enough to fix for many years to come the traditions of independence, dignity and hospitality in the fur trade service.

In its entirety it is a tortuous tale of statecraft and high finance, of capitalism compromising with colonial expansion in a solution which, painful to some, yet brought the greatest happiness to the greatest number.

The Company still ruled the west in 1860. By title to the soil and exclusive licence to trade, the Governor and Company were all-powerful under the Crown from the Rockies to the Bay and north to the Arctic, and in Labrador. The morale of the fur trade was high. There was peace in the land. The two hundred and eighty-six proprietors in England were content with many years of 10 and 15 per cent. dividends. Now the even tenor was to be broken; Parliament had said so, and in the far west the growing colony of British Columbia was gazing eastward, as in the east "the Canadas" were looking westward with courage.

Everything was ripe for the promoters' harvest. Swift, bold moves would be needed if shrewd men were to capture the corporation which rested so securely in its proprietorship over an area as great as European Russia. To own that Empire and then to hold for a price was the plan.

On July 31, 1862, the first feelers were put out and a letter from Downing Street was directed to Henry Hulse Berens, twentieth Governor of the Company:

"Sir, I am directed by the Duke of Newcastle to request that you will bring under consideration of the Hudson's Bay Company the enclosed copy of a letter from Thomas Baring, M.P., and other gentlemen relative to the formation of a Company for the purpose of opening a

U

route for Passenger Traffic and Telegraphic Communication across the Continent of British North America to the British Colonies on the Pacific. . . ."

A few days later old Berens, thirty years on the Committee and Governor for five years, replied to Downing Street:

"My Lord Duke, I have communicated with my colleagues. . . . They direct me to assure Your Grace of their readiness to co-operate with Her Majesty's Government in any measures they may be pleased to recommend for the improvement of the communication across the Territory of the Company, and for the settlement of the country. . . ."

Here was new policy, welcoming communication across British North America and the colonization of Rupert's Land. The Company was conforming to the times and prepared to yield to colonial office pressure. The colonial office in turn was impressed by the prospect of the Company being promoted by Mr. Baring and his associate, Edward Watkin. A highway and telegraphic communication across the plains and the mountains would strengthen imperial bonds at a time when North American destinies were rendered unpredictable by civil war in the United States. Newcastle eased the way for Baring, the banker, and Watkin, the Grand Trunk Railway promoter, to open negotiations with the Hudson's Bay Company.

Only the most confident and assured men could have withstood the interminable rebuffs with which the old worthies of Hudson's Bay House met the preliminary advances. By midsummer, 1863, they came to terms and Berens wrote to His Grace of the colonial office that "terms have been agreed upon by which the whole interests of the Hudson's Bay Company are to be transferred to the parties represented by Mr. Edward Watkin."

The proprietors received one and a half million pounds for their shares from the short-lived syndicate organized for the purpose of the transfer under the name of the

Annual supplies and mail being brought ashore at a Hudson's Bay Post in the Eastern Arctic

Group of commissioned officers held in Winnipeg, 1887

International Finance Society. The price of one hundred pounds Hudson's Bay stock had been less than two hundred pounds for several years; shareholders were now offered three hundred pounds a share, and most of them accepted. With the transfer went all the titles to the soil of Rupert's Land, all the authority of the Charter, and all the prestige won by stout-hearted men in the bloodless conquest of a wilderness.

A new committee was set up which included Sir Edmund Head, formerly Governor-General of Canada, as Governor of the Company; Curtis Miranda Lampson, Deputy Governor; Daniel Meinertzhagen, James Stewart Hodgson, John Henry William Schroeder, Richard Potter; Eden Colvile, son of the former Governor, and George Lyall were two retained from the old Committee.

The capital of the Company was promptly raised from five hundred thousand pounds to two million pounds. The International Finance Society as agent issued a prospectus offering the public one million nine hundred and thirty thousand pounds of stock at twenty pounds par value. The prospectus offered the investor participation in:

1. The assets (exclusive of Nos. 2 and 3 following) of the Hudson's Bay Company, valued by competent valuators at £1,023,500.

2. The landed territory of the Company held under the Charter and extending over an estimated area of more than 1,400,000 square miles or 896,000,000 acres.

3. A cash balance of £370,000.

Current net income was sufficient, said the prospectus, to provide a dividend exceeding 4 per cent. on the two million pounds of stock.

When the news of the huge transaction reached Canada and Rupert's Land, the Company's officers were profoundly shocked. At York Factory, at Fort Garry, at Norway House, and Edmonton, it was the only subject in the conversation of the mess, and as the word raced by express canoe to the forest posts of Upper Canada, to British

Columbia, and to the Mackenzie River, incredulity rose to indignation.

Chief Factor Donald Smith, at Rigolet on the Labrador, told long afterwards of the morning the Company ship arrived. As he read the news he trembled so he could scarcely stand. Men who had shown themselves a thousand times to be without fear, wilted before this breach of faith. "We have been sold out like cattle," wrote one. There was talk of a general resignation to set up a new fur trade company, but wiser heads advised everyone to wait and see.

These men and many of their fathers before them had served the Company for more than forty years as no corporation had ever been served before. Under the Deed Polls of 1821 and 1834, 40 per cent. of the net profits of the trade was distributed annually in eighty-five shares to the commissioned officers or partners. While Simpson had ruled, the cordiality and implicit confidence between the Governor and Committee and the men across the seas who spoke through their councils, had been absolute and unchallenged. Until only a few years before, all communications from London to the men of the fur trade had concluded with the phrase, "your loving friends."

That their interests and their services had been sold across a board-room table in London without consultation or warning, shook their loyalty to its very roots.

Had Simpson been alive, they wrote in angry letters, he would have protected their interests, but who were these new speculators with their flashy talk of highways and telegraph lines across a continent they had never seen? The officers had enjoyed their fur trade profits; but now apparently they were not to share in the rich potentialities of land sales about to be divorced from the fur trade.

The wintering partners saw too clearly the course of events. Alexander Grant Dallas, who had succeeded Simpson as governor-in-chief two years before, gave them no leadership. He was, in fact, in negotiation with Watkin before the deal had been consummated. Dallas was a man of some character and ability, who had been for several years the Company's agent on the Pacific Coast, though most of his career had been in mercantile affairs in China. Like several of his successors, he was appointed by the London Committee to direct their affairs in Canada with few of the qualities required in a successful Canadian governor.

The new executive moved quickly to assure the commissioned officers that all would be well. Dallas wrote them from Montreal, and Governor Head from London sent reassuring communications. Actually the Board had intended to find means of dissolving the Deed Poll and reducing expenses by putting the officers on salaries, but, confronted by the disastrous prospect of a general resignation, they hastened to placate the men of the fur trade. The Deed Poll would be maintained, wrote Governor Head, "and whatever collateral objects of a different character the Company may hereafter have in view, it is not the intention that these pursuits should interfere with the fur trade. . . ."

The wintering partners remained uneasy. They sensed they were being excluded from what they believed to be their rightful participation in the profits of the entire operations of the Company. Their discontent increased as the new Committee proceeded about the work of consolidating the Company's position to meet the changing affairs in Canada.

The Company next proposed that the Crown should take over government of the south-west portion of Rupert's Land. In the terms it was suggested the Crown should purchase the title to this land and the Company commence construction of the transcontinental telegraph across its own territories. Newcastle countered with alternatives, and a ponderously worded correspondence between Downing Street and Hudson's Bay House proceeded for a year.

In 1864 the government of Canada took a hand. Viewing with distrust the monopolistic character of the Company and its Charter, Canada impatiently held that it was "not to be entertained for a moment that half a continent should continue to be shut off from the world on the strength of a parchment title, however good." "Canada," stated the eloquent official dispatch to Downing Street, "looks forward with interest to the day when the valley of the Saskatchewan will become the back country of Canada, the land of hope for the hardy youth of the provinces when they seek new homes in the forest . . . when Canada will become the highway of immigration from Europe to those fertile valleys." But it was a matter for the Imperial Government to settle, concluded the colonial cabinet. The British Government, while sympathizing with the young colony's aspirations, was alert to the sacred property rights of the Company; there must be no ruthless uprooting of vested interests without due parliamentary enactments and compensation for British investors.

John A. Macdonald and George Etienne Cartier went to London, in 1865, to further the negotiations on behalf of Canada, and as the summer months dragged on in interviews and exchange of stiffly worded communications, two elements became dominant: first, the inevitable march of events towards the confederation of Canada; second, the powerful bargaining position of the Hudson's Bay Company. As the magnitude of their opportunity became increasingly apparent, the "electric telegraph" feature of the proposals faded out, and cash and land ownership became the objective which the new lords of the land draining into Hudson's Bay strove to attain.

Canada continued persistently to deny the existence of the Company's legal title to "that portion of the North Western Territory which is fit for cultivation and settlement," at the same time pointing to the Company's inability to cope with the probable immigration to the west of Americans—who might be "ignorant and regardless of the laws of England and perhaps hostile to the British Government."

On July 1, 1867, the Dominion of Canada was proclaimed

by authority of the British North America Act. Clause 146 of that statute made provision for the admission of Rupert's Land and the North-West Territories into the new Confederation.

Meanwhile, the basis of the transfer was still under dispute between the Company and the colonial office. The British Government, undoubtedly wearied to exhaustion by the whole affair, succeeded in placing the onus of settlement upon the Dominion in the Rupert's Land Act of 1868.

The Governor and Committee were unyielding in refusing to surrender their title to Canada until the terms had been settled. In this they received the support of the British Government. The Dominion hoped for a general agreement with the details to be worked out later; a speedy decision would have gained wide popular approval and won prestige for the new government, but the Company was prepared to play for time and specific conditions.

Once more a Canadian delegation came to London. Sir George Cartier and William McDougall arrived in October, 1868, and in the Westminster Palace Hotel they collaborated upon a series of communications which stand today as magnificent state papers. Conforming to the rigid formula of diplomatic usage these dispatches escape into the strength and forthrightness expressive of the nation newly born across the sea. Through the dreary winter the sparring continued, with the colonial office as intermediary. By March, 1869, the terms were agreed upon, and in November, by the instrument known as the Deed of Surrender, the Company of Adventurers of England trading into Hudson's Bay released its hold on the great central plains and the Arctic.

So it had come about at last. Simpson and his fur traders had foreseen it forty years before; Parliament had prepared the way in 1857, and the government facilitated it in 1868. It was probably the greatest single transfer of territory ever accomplished unheralded by war. In the British way, laborious but certain in direction, the transaction was concluded with the prerogatives of the Crown sustained, the aspirations of a people fulfilled, and the interests of capital protected.

When on the current of time great institutions, governments, churches, corporations, diverge from their historic courses, those who record the transition are prone to find the new way has broken completely with the old. Because the course has altered the stream cannot be the same. Historians examining the Canadian fur trade have written of the union of 1821 as the end of the old English Company. When the proprietorship changed in 1863, they declared that the Company of Rupert had departed for ever: nothing remained. The ceding of Rupert's Land to Canada in 1869 left only ashes; the very soul of the Company was its sovereignty. Historians have undertaken to demonstrate that a corporation selling general merchandise in great cities of the twentieth century can claim no true lineage with the Company of seventeenth-century adventurers.

Actually, the Company's Charter of 1670 survived as the instrument of incorporation until 1884. There have been four supplemental charters (1884, 1892, 1912, 1920) bearing the royal designation "By Warrant Under the King's (or Queen's) Manual," and, among other privileges, one excluding the Company from the terms of the Companies Act of Great Britain.

At the time of the Surrender, many in Rupert's Land who had fought the monopoly rule freely predicted the collapse of the Company. With responsible government in the new Manitoba, the fur trade thrown wide open to competition, stripped of special privilege the Company would withdraw sullenly to the forests of the north and there perish slowly, nourishing memories of departed power.

How the Company stepped from the pedestal of government and met competition on equal terms in fur trading and later in general merchandising to the rising cities of western Canada is the modern story.

Canada has never had cause to complain of the terms under which Rupert's Land was purchased.

1. The Canadian Government paid three hundred thousand pounds to the Company.

2. The Company retained a stated acreage around each of its one hundred and twenty forts or posts, varying from five to three thousand acres, in all forty-five thousand acres, much of which is held today, the remainder having become city real estate.

3. The Company during the ensuing fifty years might claim blocks of land set out for settlement within the Fertile Belt not exceeding one-twentieth of the total area. By this it received seven million acres, mostly in sections and half-sections throughout the prairie provinces. (It was 1928 before the final details of the transfer were wound up, and by that year the Company had sold all but two and a half million acres of its holdings.)

4. The Fertile Belt was defined as bounded on the south by the United States boundary, the west by the Rocky Mountains, the north by the North Saskatchewan River, the east by Lake Winnipeg, Lake of the Woods and the waters connecting them.

5. The Company was at liberty to carry on its trade without hindrance and no exceptional taxes were to be placed upon its land, trade, or its servants.

6. Canada was to take over at cost the several tons of telegraph construction materials which had been shipped from England to York Factory as a preliminary to the International Society's project.

While in London the destinies of Canada and the Company were being moulded, the fur trade partners continued to press anxious claims for more equitable participation in profits. Between 1848 and 1858 the share of profits received by officers under the Deed Poll averaged four hundred and forty-five pounds per share per annum. (The 40 per cent. of fur trade profits which came back to the chief factors and chief traders was divided

into eighty-five shares, each man receiving shares according
to his rank.)   From 1858 to 1868 this dropped to two
hundred and seventy-five pounds per share.   The hard
grip Simpson had kept on all detail of expenses was missing.
His successors, Dallas (1860–64) and William Mactavish
(1864–70), while strong, were incapable of applying the
sustained, relentless scrutiny to operations which Sir George,
knowing the fur trade from Labrador to Vancouver Island,
had brought to bear.   Moreover, conditions had altered
rapidly.   Costs of operation rose sharply under the influx
of free traders.   The vagaries of the buffalo hunt, essential
for supplies, the increase of wages to packers and voyageurs,
and the insurrection of the Metis at Red River cut deeply
into the earnings of Company traders.

Thinking of the future, the officers had slight hope of
any share in the three hundred thousand pounds paid their
Company by Canada.   In 1869, when the United States
made a first payment of forty-five thousand nine hundred
and eighteen pounds under the Oregon Treaty terms,
the English proprietors advanced strong views claiming
exclusive right to the sum.   It was the end of a twenty-year
legal battle interrupted by the Civil War.   When it was
settled the United States paid the Company four hundred
and fifty thousand dollars.   If the Governor and Committee
were to look to the sale of land for profits, and if, as Governor
Northcote intimated in 1871, there was money to be made
in selling supplies to the settlers streaming west to buy
farmlands, then the fur trade was to be eclipsed, and those
whose loyalty and toil had sustained the entire structure
for two centuries were to be relegated unrewarded to a
secondary department of a reorganized corporation.   Fur
traders could not be readily made over into shopkeepers or
land-agents, and Northcote was already talking of the need
for new blood.

In the Council Room at Norway House in July, 1870,
the Council of the Northern Department of Rupert's Land
met for the last time.   The burden of government was
about to be assumed by the Dominion and by Manitoba.

Problems of peace among savages, of schools and missions were not on the agenda. The full-bearded, sun-tanned men planned the work of the next outfit without the encumbrances of civil affairs. No longer were they absolute lords and proprietors. When the business of the council was concluded, they reassembled as a group of citizens to discuss how they might find some security in a way of life rendered unpredictable by forces of governments and investors far away.

Some who were there that day had sat at the same table with the Little Emperor: Chief Factors W. S. Christie, William McMurray, Robert Campbell, Robert Hamilton, James Stewart; Chief Traders Bernard Ross, Dr. William Cowan, Thomas Taylor, Samuel Mackenzie, Joseph Fortescue, Peter W. Bell, William H. Watt.

In Simpson's place sat bushy-browed, ruddy-bearded Donald A. Smith, chief factor from Labrador, manager of the Montreal District, and lately mediator from Canada to the Metis of Fort Garry. Smith was new to the west but already he had won the confidence of the proud men of the Northern Department. They appointed him their spokesman to go to London and press their claims. They could not afford the expense of a legal suit, and they knew that their lives had not equipped them to cope with men whose careers were spent in the wrangling and tortuous negotiation of the board-room. Indian traders, who could handle rebellious voyageurs on the portages, keep their accounts in order, and travel fast and hard in the wilderness, they knew their limitations in other fields. So "Mr. Labrador Smith," as some gentlemen of the London Committee called him, set out.

"Our immediate destiny is in your hands," an officer wrote Smith. "You know our life—you know how arduous our labours are. In nearly every instance they involved long servitude, separation from friends and relations, many hardships which we feel more sensitively as time wears away, and also family separations of a costly character, unless the alternative be accepted of permitting children to fall uneducated into the conditions of semibarbarism. In some cases to our knowledge, expenses of education have eaten up nearly the whole of the comparatively small emoluments obtained for service. Other hardships are occasional liabilities to starvation and much privation, insufficiency and poor description of food, exposure, increasing anxiety for the trade's success, and the maintenance of those committed to the charge of District and Post Managers. These might be, as they often are, borne cheerfully even for a long period, were the prospects of retirement on an adequate competency in sight; but failing this hope, they are almost insupportable. It is true there are exceptions where officers and clerks happen to be stationed where civilization exists; but these are not very numerous, while every regular servant of the Company is exposed, at least, to the possibility of being removed to the interior."

Donald A. Smith confronted the Governor and Committee with the demands, the hopes, and the aspirations of his colleagues, and secured a compromise. Northcote carried the case on to the proprietors at the General Court of June 28, 1871, and fought vigorously against shareholder greed, securing finally a sum of one hundred and seven thousand pounds to be divided among the officers, and a new Deed Poll. To the men this money meant relief from immediate distress. Though the conditions of the new Deed Poll were exacting, it contained a minimum guarantee of one hundred and fifty pounds per share which eight years later was increased to two hundred pounds a share. New ranks were created, and shares were divided as follows: inspecting chief factor, three shares; chief factors, two and a half shares; factors, two shares; chief traders, one and a half shares; junior chief traders, one share.

Smith won a personal victory, and came back to Canada with promotion in his pocket, making him an object of suspicion to many of the old guard. Several stated frankly they believed he had not pressed their full claim and that he had "sold out" for his own advancement.

The wintering partners, on the other hand, accepted the cash settlement thankfully, and most of them agreed to the new Deed Poll which excluded them from land profits. The fur trade lost for ever something which only a complete partnership could give.

This was the last phase of the partnership form of management. By 1894 the Governor and Committee, by the practice of filling senior posts in the fur trade with salaried men, had acquired without expense the 40 per cent. of profits which had been the true strength of the Company's operations in British North America.

Chapter XVIII

SMITH AND THE INSURRECTION

DONALD A. SMITH, Highland apprentice clerk, chief factor, successful speculator. Sir Donald Smith, politician, capitalist, and for twenty-five years Governor of the Hudson's Bay Company. Lord Strathcona and Mount Royal, empire-builder, philanthropist, and elder statesman. Canadian history has no stranger figure than this Scottish Smith whose career has suffered so acutely at the hands of biographers. A eulogistic official "life" published in 1915, a year after his death, and an unpleasant book published in 1914 by a political enemy, are the inadequate public records of this man's career.

This compressed outline of Donald A. Smith's life must necessarily be restricted to his association with the Hudson's Bay Company—a connection of seventy-six years. At the age of eighteen, he came to Canada in 1838 from the village of Forres in Elginshire, armed with letters of introduction from his uncle John Stuart. Uncle John had been a North-West partner, a Hudson's Bay chief factor, and had accompanied Simon Fraser in his descent of the Fraser River. Stuart Lake, British Columbia, carries his name today. He had favoured other fields for his nephew, but the suppression of the Papineau Rebellion having left an aftermath of instability in Lower Canada, young Smith chose the fur trade, and became an apprentice clerk under Sir George Simpson's eye at Lachine. Characteristically, the official biographer interjects at this point an anecdote of Simpson promptly ordering the youth to a basement to count musk-rat skins. Actually Simpson was in Europe throughout the first year of Smith's apprentice-

ship. Introduction from the chief factor uncle won no
preferment, for in 1841 the nephew was sent to Tadoussac
on the lower St. Lawrence at the mouth of the deep and
gloomy Saguenay River. For seven years he lived the
cramped, cheerless life of a fur trade clerk at the bleak
posts of Godbout, Seven Islands, Bersimis, and Mingan—
notoriously the dullest and least desirable district in the
service even to this day. Cold, damp summers, windswept,
bitter winters with only Indians for company and few
luxuries for food. He graduated from this training school
to spend twenty years on the Labrador Coast.

At North West River, twelve hundred miles from Montreal
where the continent shoulders east into the Atlantic, was
some slight semblance of civilization. To Smith the life
was neither dull nor lonely. Carefully planning each
day's work in advance, applying minute care to detail, he
wrested satisfaction from complete mastery of his job—
though his successors complained that his accounting was
unorthodox if not eccentric.

It was a self-disciplined apprenticeship of twenty years,
from which most men would have emerged encrusted
with rigid habits of intellect and body, crabbed in spirit
and immune to wider ambition. The young Scot made
it a conditioning for a great career. He read prodigiously
into arts, sciences and philosophy, and formulated a
realistic attitude to life curiously tempered by superstition
and a Highland belief in "second sight" which he never
lost.

When Smith went to Labrador his superior was Chief
Trader Richard Hardisty, who had been with the com-
missariat of Wellington's army in the Peninsular campaign
and at Waterloo. Isabella Hardisty, his daughter, had
made an unfortunate marriage with a fur trader named
Grant, a marriage in the Scottish–Hudson's Bay Company
manner, without clergy (since there were none) and with
only the pledges of both in the presence of witnesses.
Beckles Willson in his *Life of Strathcona* writes that this
was "duly annulled and a few months later on March 9,

1853, she married Mr. Smith." In another forty-four years she became the Baroness Strathcona and Mount Royal, and their only daughter succeeded to the title in her own right.

In his marriage year, Donald A. Smith succeeded Hardisty in charge of the district. Fur trading alone could not absorb his activities, and as the years moved swiftly, the semi-annual mails carried out to Montreal reports of novel activities at Eskimaux Bay, North-West River. Donald Smith was farming and keeping cattle on the Labrador Coast. He had seven acres of land under cultivation, including some under glass. He built roads, an unprecedented accomplishment for a fur trader who scrupulously left the trails and portages in agonizing condition to defeat his competitors. But most impressive of all, he was improving the trade and showing profits in Labrador salmon. Gradually those who found their way to his domain, naval officers, scientists, explorers, brought out word of a remarkable man who lived and entertained like a gentleman on the Labrador Coast, and who counted and sorted the nails as they came out of the packing cases. Moreover, it was said that despite his isolation he had a strong, shrewd sense of the drift of world affairs. An active correspondence with colleagues in all parts of the north, including six Hardisty brothers-in-law in the service, added to the growing conclusions respecting his sagacity.

Before Simpson's death, in 1860, Smith's letters revealed something of insight into the trend of events which is extraordinary in the light of his own career.

"I myself am becoming convinced that before many decades are past the world will see a great change in the country north of Lake Superior and in the Red River country when the Company's licence expires or its Charter is modified. . . . You will understand that I, as a Labrador man, cannot be expected to sympathize altogether with the prejudice against settlers and railways entertained by many of the western commissioned officers. At all events, it is probable that settlement of

Lord Strathcona, Governor of the Hudson's Bay Company (1889—1914) and High Commissioner for Canada in Great Britain

From a painting by Charles Comf

The last dog teams leaving Lower Fort Garry, on the Red River, 19c

the country from Fort William Westward to the Red River, and even a considerable distance beyond, will eventually take place and with damaging effect to the fur trade generally."

And later, but still ten years before the Deed of Surrender:

"Although destiny has sent me to the east . . . I have never made a secret of the fact that my heart—or a large part of it—was in the west. . . . As I pen this a map of Rupert's Land hangs on the wall before me. So I beg you to hesitate before putting me beyond the pale as a mere Labrador man."

Smith was still a Labrador fur trader when he was forty-two years old. He had become a chief factor, enjoying two of the eighty-five shares held by the wintering partners. This meant about three hundred and fifty pounds a year, plus all living expenses. There was little temptation to extravagance at Eskimaux Bay, and Smith saved with all the fervour of an ambitious Scotsman.

In 1863 came the disturbing news of the sale of the Company to the International Finance Society. A year later, on his furlough, Smith visited England for the first time in twenty-six years, and made it his business to establish relations with the new Governor and Committee. He made a highly favourable impression on the directorate, and drew the private conclusion that the wintering partners need not expect too much at the hands of the new shareholders.

Returning to Labrador via Montreal, in 1866, he caught glimpses of new horizons of wealth. His young cousin, George Stephen, was the junior in a family drapery business in Montreal, and Smith tasted something of the adventurous business life his handsome cousin was leading. George Stephen carried the air of assured success. With perhaps some condescension he introduced the Labrador fur trader to his friends in the Bank of Montreal and in the shipping circles. From that summer onward, Donald Smith's pace quickened.

x

For many years the Company had acted as banker for
its officers. These men, with their living provided and
little chance to spend, were thrifty almost by compulsion.
It was common for officers without family obligations to
allow their three or four hundred pounds per year to
accumulate for long periods at the comfortable interest
rates available through the "Officers and Servants Account."
The earnings of the commissioned officers of course varied
each year with the Company's success; in the profitable
"outfit" of 1836, chief factors earned eight hundred and
twelve pounds and chief traders four hundred and six
pounds. As trust funds they were conservatively invested
by the Company—too conservatively for Donald Smith,
who now knew enough of the inner circle of Montreal
business to convince him that twenty years of savings
would be more profitably placed in industrial stocks and
mortgages. His success from the outset quickly drew about
him a group of fellow officers who annually entrusted him
with their savings and portions of their earnings. So in
June, 1869, when Smith came out of the wilderness to
take over the Montreal District, he controlled the investment of a sum sufficiently large to make him a citizen of
more than average interest to the powers of the Bank of
Montreal.

The rôle of agent-investor for the men of the fur trade
was the beginning of a colossal personal fortune. The
circle widened quickly; there were losses to some, but
for hundreds of Hudson's Bay men, Donald Smith made
money. As late as 1908 scores of post managers and officers
were regularly assigning portions of their salaries "to Lord
Strathcona for investment."

Smith was barely in Montreal a few months when the
slow-moving course of events in far-off Rupert's Land
was dramatically animated by civil strife, and the Montreal
manager found himself projected into the political life
of Canada. The bluster and confusion of the Riel Insurrection (1869-70) carried his career forward with
startling suddenness.

Out in that territory where the northern Ontario forests thin into scrub and give way to the prairie of the true west, known variously as Red River, Assiniboia, and soon to be shaped into the province of Manitoba, lived 11,500 persons. Of these 5,757 were French half-breeds called Metis, the offspring of voyageurs. The rest were Hudson's Bay Company families, Selkirk settlers' descendants, English and Scottish half-breeds, and new settlers from Canada. Each group had its own reasons for favouring or distrusting the transfer of the district from the administration of the Company to the state of an infant province in the young Dominion whose confederation had just occurred in 1867.

In 1869 the Metis were at the peak of their power, race proud and jealous of the freedom they had enjoyed under the paternalism of the Company. They were acutely conscious of their racial position, aware, without malice, of the loosely defined but real social barriers between them and the prospective governing authority. A few had risen to rank in the Company's service.

From Indian maternity they inherited their nomadic spirit. They grew up in the life of the hunt. From the French they were heirs to centuries of song and the telling of tales, and amenability to Mother Church. Many of them avoided the restraints of farming, and were happiest on the plains of the buffalo hunt. Improvident, cheerful and God-fearing, like a lost tribe they had lived leaderless and without direction until the surrender of Rupert's Land to the new Dominion struck alarm to their hearts and galvanized them into swift action under the boy leader, Louis Riel.

The Metis knew no easy life. As the hewers of wood and the carriers of water under a monopoly, their burdens had been heavy. At the paddles in the canoes, on the heavy sweeps of the York boats, or struggling over portages, they toiled for meagre wages. Their capacity for physical endurance and their unflagging sense of song have been commented on by every traveller who crossed the fur

empire and wrote a book. Occasionally they rebelled
at the portages; then it was a matter for the officer commanding the brigade to cope with the voyageurs by bribery,
persuasion, or sometimes a blow. The life was hard, but
in old age there was a cabin and patch of land by the
Red River for the asking and enough pension to provide
tobacco, with a dram of rum at the "Big House" in the
fort on holidays. No one starved and no one expected to
be wealthy.

For more than a decade an English-speaking minority
bearing the label of "The Canadian Party" had been
the most articulate political faction of the Red River
Colony. Its membership was drawn mostly from settlers
who had come west from Ontario, and included the store-
keepers and free traders. They all chafed under the
restraints of Hudson's Bay Company rule. When Parliament inquired into the state of the Company in 1857,
their petition was heard with interest. In the report of
that committee they saw hope of an early opening up
of the west, and their restlessness grew under the long
delay in the implementing of the great purpose. The
Nor'wester, the sole newspaper of the settlement, was their
oracle; in flights of soaring editorials it cried from the
prairie to all the world to witness the iniquities of Company government, and jeered at the officers when the
International Finance Society bought out the London
ownership: they had been sold "like dumb driven cattle."
Incoming settlers and small merchants were good recruits
to the Canadian Party, responding readily to the agitation
for the speedy transfer of Rupert's Land to the Crown.
The leaders became zealots in the cause of British democracy.
With the quick emotions of pioneers, the Canadian Party
welcomed boisterously the news that on December 1, 1869,
Rupert's Land was to be proclaimed part of the Dominion
of Canada. To the Metis, this minority Canadian Party
group typified the forces which threatened to change all
the old order.

In the central position, between these conflicting interests, was the local government, the Hudson's Bay Company. The little principality of Assiniboia, roughly delineated as a fifty-mile radius around Fort Garry, had been administered since 1858 by Chief Factor William Mactavish (who in 1864 became also governor of Rupert's Land) and his appointed council of seventeen men in addition to the governor, judge and two bishops. This council had been made truly representative of all elements in the settlement, but it could hardly escape the status of oligarchy, and its work of maintaining elementary public services or the settlement of minor domestic controversies in an almost crimeless area was not heavy. It was, however, monopoly's best endeavour to provide adequate government without conceding undue measures of democracy which might encroach upon sacred privileges of the fur trade.

Mactavish was one of the old school of officers whose allegiance had suffered with the London "selling out" of 1863. The events at Red River moved towards a climax in the autumn of 1869, and found Mactavish an ill, aged governor, worn out in the conscientious carrying out of his duties. Failure of crops and fisheries had brought the colony close to starvation the preceding year. Depressed and discouraged over his own private affairs, exhausted physically, Mactavish was unable to cope with the insurrection. Moreover, he had been snubbed at Ottawa when he had personally undertaken to warn the authorities of impending trouble, and he resented the brusque manner in which the Canadian Government was now moving into his domain.

The centre of this world was Fort Garry, where the council met. Its stone walls enclosed the governor's residence, storehouses, men's quarters, workshops, a sales shop, and a rarely used jail. In the past it had been garrisoned, but now only a nightwatchman kept guard. The settlement was strung out through the woods along the Red River, and across from the fort was the cathedral village of St. Boniface. Outside the walls, twenty-five buildings, including two hotels, a butcher's shop and a saloon, were sprawled about. West along the Assiniboine and north along the Red were the cabins of the Metis and the comfortable farm homes of the settlers from Ontario and retired officers of the Company. Anglican, Presbyterian and Wesleyan churches served the English-speaking Protestant minority. The French village, St. Boniface, was dominated by the grey stone Roman Catholic cathedral.

On November 29, 1869, Sir John A. Macdonald summoned Donald A. Smith to Ottawa. There was trouble at Red River. Canada's machinery for taking over Rupert's Land had been wrecked by the Metis. William McDougall, whom Canada had sent out to be lieutenant governor of the new province, had travelled by way of Chicago and St. Paul, and upon entering the territory on November 2 had been met by armed Metis and obliged to retire humiliated to the American side of the international boundary. All this, the Prime Minister told Mr. Smith, was "serious business." He added, with some anger, that it appeared Hudson's Bay officers at Fort Garry had tacitly abetted the rebels in obstructing the carrying out of the transfer agreed upon by Canada and the Company.

In his dilemma Macdonald had turned naturally to Montreal to look for help in a matter involving the Hudson's Bay Company, probably unaware he was talking only to a district manager. So removed from the life of older Canada had been the Company's operations that Sir John assumed Montreal, where Simpson had lived, was still the Company headquarters. The busy Prime Minister, having surmounted all the apparent obstacles in the long negotiations for the acquisition of Rupert's Land, had anticipated neither a new racial problem nor internal complications within the Company. The birth of a new self-governing Dominion had been an all-absorbing task.

Donald Smith, manager of the Montreal District, had never been west. Now he was to proceed to the scene with all haste as the special commissioner of the Canadian Government and endeavour to smooth out the trouble.

Two days after Christmas he arrived at Fort Garry, having travelled by rail to St. Paul and finished the journey by sleigh across six hundred miles of prairie.

Fort Garry, since November 13, had been in the hands of young Louis Riel and his armed Metis. A provisional government had been established. Chief Factor Mactavish, governor of Assiniboia and of Rupert's Land, was gravely ill, "nightly coughing much blood," and virtually a prisoner of Riel in the fort. The Metis, having rejected the lieutenant governor sent out from Canada, put Commissioner Smith under arrest. He submitted, and settled down to three weeks of a waiting game. Allowed to communicate with the people of the settlement, he said little and studied every aspect of the trouble.

Resentment and fear were emotional elements of the half-breed rising. Resentment against the London management of the Company for having sold to another authority the soil which was their native land. Resentment against the hasty assertiveness of this new purchaser in sending surveyors to Red River months before the transfer was to take place. Fear of the loud promises of this government of Canada to flood the land with agricultural settlers. Fear of impending hordes of speculators, carpetbaggers and land promoters. Fear of an invasion of Orange Protestantism from Ontario.

The Canadian Government had bungled the whole affair badly. The acquisition of Rupert's Land and the throwing open to settlement of the land of hope were to have been a powerful, popular stroke for Sir John Macdonald's Government, and the cabinet had assumed that after settling with the Hudson's Bay Company proprietors the setting up of an administration at Red River was an executive detail. Ottawa sensed nothing of the strength or the importance of the Metis, and apparently knew nothing of the attitude of the commissioned officer-partners to the Governor and Committee of the Company. These officers, whose integrity had sustained peace and civil authority in the land, were still smarting under the change in ownership of the Company, and were only further provoked by the surrender of Rupert's Land. They saw Canada pay the Company three hundred thousand pounds, and they knew that, in the clamour of shareholders for a division of these spoils, the likelihood of the active partners receiving any portion was slight. And now, from the east and from the south they might expect the land-hungry multitudes. They were dispirited men.

During his taciturn weeks in Fort Garry in January, 1870, Smith gathered up the threads of the story. The alarm of the Metis had flashed into action the preceding autumn when the surveyors from Canada began to run lines across the small farm plots of the half-breeds along the Red River banks. Fear had quickened into alarm. This, they said, was the trespassing of interlopers and the beginning of oppression. As free men they armed to resist the new power, and the movement fused rapidly about their leader Riel.

Louis Riel was the son of half-breed parents, educated by the Church for nine years in Montreal. Volatile, persuasive in oratory, and with the gift of leadership, he led five hundred men in August of 1869. By the number of guns in their hands they held the Canadian Party subdued. Riel did not consider his uprising as rebellion against the Crown. It was, at the outset, a successful attempt to prevent the entry of the lieutenant governor from Canada until terms could be made on behalf of the Metis race.

The Canadian Government had instructed McDougall to proceed to Fort Garry and there issue the Queen's Proclamation on December 1, 1869. On the same day the Proclamation would be signed at Ottawa by the governor-general. In the interval between McDougall's arrival at the boundary on October 30 and the tentative date of the Proclamation, the cabinet at Ottawa, startled by the unexpected insurrection, postponed the official transfer until July 15, 1870. McDougall knew nothing of this, and from the cramped discomfort of his quarters at Pembina issued with assurance the now unauthorized Proclamation in the Queen's name, also two others on his own, belligerent in tone, setting up a paper government in the hope that the Canadian Party at Red River would rise to his support. But Riel's predominance of men and guns had that situation covered. It was weeks before the news filtered in that the Ottawa Proclamation had not been signed, leaving the absurd figure of McDougall dangling on the Minnesota boundary line with his petty retinue, including aide-de-camp, secretary and attorney-general designate, proclaiming worthless documents to the frosty air.

These things Donald Smith learned during his three weeks in Fort Garry. It was for him to pull Canada's chestnuts from the fire and then to extinguish the blaze. The work, which the Canadian Government should have been about, months before, of winning the understanding of the half-breeds, now devolved upon him.

Riel was first president of a "national committee." This had been followed by a "provisional government" with a flag of fleur-de-lis and shamrocks (there was an Irish O'Donoghue in Riel's council) flying over Fort Garry amid band music and speeches.

The young leader had taken the undefended fort on November 13. The actual circumstances have never been quite clear. Either the handful of Hudson's Bay men was unwilling to assume responsibility for bloodshed in defence of property, or they felt themselves merely unfortunate spectators in an affair between the people of Assiniboia and the authority which was expected daily from Canada. Despite frank anger with the management in London and with the government at Ottawa, substantiation has never been produced to support the rumour which has trickled down through hundreds of accounts that the Company's men gave tacit support to Riel. Riel displayed remarkable restraint in the seizure of the fort, and while he kept his men fed and armed from H. B. C. stores (the Company after fourteen years of litigation received £10,704 from Canada in settlement of rebellion losses) and paid his accounts with H. B. C. notes, there was little drunkenness and none of the outburst of violence which might have been expected from a people so close in blood ties to the fighting Indians of the plains.

The Metis were not killers, and while throughout ten months of insurrection there was a frenzy of gun-waving, galloping horsemen, oratory, proclamations and manifestos, the shooting was negligible and the deaths two. One was a fumbled shooting of an escaping prisoner, and the other a firing-squad court-martial of an obstreperous Canadian.

What had happened politically up to the time of Smith's arrival has been concisely stated by Father Morice in his critical history of the insurrection. "McDougall had launched the proclamation; Mactavish had stepped out, and Riel had followed in forming, finally with the co-operation of the whole settlement, a regular government." This was true, for Mactavish had by letter to McDougall advised him to withdraw and at the same time admitted his own inability to rule.

After conferences with Riel it was agreed that Donald Smith should be permitted to present to the people of Assiniboia his commission from the Canadian Government. A thousand citizens stood within Fort Garry's walls on January 19 to hear the man from Labrador and Montreal explain the good intentions of Canada towards the half-breeds of Red River. It was twenty degrees below zero, and for hours they stood, muffled heavily in buffalo coats or Hudson's Bay blanket *capots*, stamping with moccasined feet while the steam of their breathing was whipped by a north wind. That day was another step in the public career of Donald Smith, for he established his point, and out of his meeting the decision was reached to elect from the parishes of the settlement a convention of forty representatives of the entire community. The election was held; the convention met, chose Riel president, and the new provisional government became a legal entity.

Before proceeding with the election, the dying Mactavish was approached. Would he take the leadership?

R.M.S. *Nascopie*, the Company's ice-breaker supply ship, on her annual voyage to the Eastern Arctic

"Form a government, for God's sake, I have no power or authority," was his reply.

The convention struggled for days through the confusion of race and religious prejudice to prorogue, on February 10, with a Bill of Rights and the decision to send delegates to Ottawa. Smith's work as commissioner extraordinary was finished, and Riel was in the ascendant with his insistent declaration of his desire to hold office only until terms with Canada could be settled.

Throughout the midwinter he had been holding as prisoners a group of English-speaking men who had led an abortive attempt to overthrow his government. Several of the leaders had been sentenced to death, but with the setting up of the Council all were released except one, Thomas Scott, who was shot by a firing-squad against Fort Garry's wall. It was the act of a frenzied dictator who felt his power slipping, and it rudely dislocated the even tenor of events. It is not part of the Hudson's Bay Company story, and it is enough to record here the incendiary effect of the killing of Scott upon the Protestant population of Ontario. The absorption of Manitoba into confederation became entangled with demands from the east for retribution. Ottawa held to a steady course, and the Manitoba Act was passed by the House of Commons in May (with Donald Smith and Sir Stafford Northcote, Governor of the Company, sitting in the visitors' gallery).

The long negotiated transfer was complete. McDougall, who had gone west so viceregally in October, retired humiliated to political obscurity. Mactavish left Red River in May to die just after he landed in England. Throughout the summer of that eventful year, Riel and a handful of his men continued to occupy the fort, and peace reigned in the settlement. In the far fastness of the lakes and forests fur trading went on, and the men wondered what the surrender of the monopoly would hold for them.

Donald Smith, now aged fifty, was on the threshold of his career. Confidant of the government, intimate with Montreal financial interests, and on friendly terms with the Governor and Committee, the long years of Labrador fur trading were very far away.

In August, 1870, just a year after he defied the Canadian surveyors, Riel was swept from the scene in an inglorious dénouement. On the 23rd of the month a military force of twelve hundred from Canada, bedraggled by ninety-six days of travel, approached Fort Garry. They had come not to enforce sovereignty but to sustain civil power in the new Manitoba. A spirit of vengeance had been fanned into flame among the boy volunteers from Ontario during their months of travel. In a drenching rain eight hundred Canadian militiamen and four hundred imperial regulars floundered through the adhesive Red River mud and approached Fort Garry in skirmishing order.

Riel had fled to Dakota. "It was to save ourselves and them from bloodshed," he wrote to Donald Smith, a few days afterwards. Riel insisted that he had hoped until the last, as the head of the provisional government recognized by Canada, to receive the new civil government with a salute and an address of welcome. Instead, Canada had sent troops first, and reports of the inflammatory temper in the ranks had made it unwise in the interests of peace for him to remain. The flight has been given the label of cowardice. Fifteen years later he came back to lead his people in a mad rebellion that cost Canada men and money before Riel was hanged.

Smith's courage and decision in the winter of 1869–70, coupled with his success as an investor in Montreal, gave him immediate prestige among Company officers in the Northern Council. His selection as their advocate before the Governor and Committee, and his emergence from that encounter with a compromise settlement for the officers and promotion for himself, have already been told.

Most of the fur traders were grateful for the cash he secured for them, and the opportunity for retirement without utter poverty. Some believed he had gone over to the proprietors, and had been bought off by advancement to the new post of chief commissioner for the Company

in Canada. It was so throughout his career. Few men
have been so heartily hated, and yet he carried with him
a vast circle of friends. Enemies he met with untiring
vindictiveness, while friends were constantly, throughout
his life, receiving tokens of generous thoughtfulness.

So brilliantly had his star shone in that tumultuous year
of 1870, when he faced the confusion at Fort Garry and
the Hudson's Bay shareholders in London, that Canada
offered him the lieutenant governorship of the frontier
province of Manitoba. But Smith had seen horizons in
the west too wide and far too glowing to find any comfort
in the restrictions of viceregal office. The old Company,
shorn of its monopoly, still offered liberties of action and
still held potential rewards too rich to be thrown away for
a term of civil honours.

Red River people had warmed to Smith for the judicious
handling of his part in coping with Riel. Foreseeing
richer plums in public affairs than a mere lieutenant
governorship, he found friends who readily placed his
name before the free and independent voters of the new
constituency of Lisgar in Manitoba. Hudson's Bay clan-
nishness and the support of fur trade families helped to
assure his victory. Donald Smith, three years out of
Labrador, was duly elected to the Canadian House of
Commons in 1871.

This was a new public rôle for a chief factor of the
secretive old Company, but Sir Stafford Northcote, the
Governor, had approved. Sir Stafford, with a boldness
unprecedented among governors, had crossed the Atlantic
in 1870 and travelled as far west as Ottawa. He went
no further; the prospect of facing the resentment and
anger of the officers in the west probably deterred him
from shattering the aloof tradition of two hundred years
of trading into Hudson Bay without a visit from the head
of the Company.

Smith's obscure life in Labrador and his success as
Canada's advocate at Red River made him the centre of
widespread curiosity at Ottawa. He became a celebrity

at the Capital, while at Fort Garry he was the politician and senior officer of the Hudson's Bay Company and not above exploiting his authority in the interest of political advancement.

At election time strange orders went out from the Commissioner's office to transport half-breed voters from one constituency to another—at the Company's expense. And the fur traders, with the implicit obedience of their training, carried out instructions, accepting it all with amusement as part of new duties under a new régime. His election in 1878 from the Manitoba constituency of Selkirk was stormy, close-in fighting, for Smith had broken with Sir John Macdonald six years before and had refused in the Commons to support his leader in the "Canadian Pacific Scandal." That action had brought a fresh host of enemies, and his '79 election was upset on the ground of corrupt practice. The Supreme Court of Canada confirmed the decision. He attempted to win the riding again and was defeated. But Donald Smith did not allow the scar to embarrass him. Events were moving too swiftly. Already he had profited by western Canada's first land boom, and after the panic of '73 he was a member of a syndicate which bought up the depreciated bonds of the St. Paul, Minneapolis and Manitoba Railway. The mere fur trade could hold him no longer, and in 1874 he resigned to take the office of land commissioner for the Company, reporting directly to London.

Quietly, through these years he was buying shares in the Company until, in 1884, the Committee found it advisable to admit him to the inner circle of proprietorship. In 1889 he became Governor of the Hudson's Bay Company.

Smith's association with the Canadian Pacific Railway has a generous part in the history of the corporation. Unostentatiously he was a member of the syndicate formed in 1881 to see the long-hoped-for project through. During the Canadian Pacific's first great construction year Smith was made a director. In 1885, as the steel was being

driven through the mountain passes and the whole enterprise was on the brink of financial collapse, Donald Smith
and his cousin George Stephen, the first president of the
road, endorsed a five months' note for one million dollars
to keep the company going. It was a year of hope and
despair until the last spike was driven at Craigellachie in
the mountains by Smith himself.

Here is a brief chronology of this man who was sixty
years of age in 1880: 1886—knighted and elected to
parliament from Mount Royal constituency, Montreal;
1889—elected twenty-sixth Governor of the Hudson's Bay
Company and Chancellor of McGill University ; 1896—
appointed High Commissioner for Canada in London;
1897—elevated to the peerage as Lord Strathcona and
Mount Royal; 1900—equipped and maintained at his
own expense a cavalry regiment of five hundred and forty
Canadian officers and men (Lord Strathcona's Horse) for
service in the South African War.

More than a little of Strathcona's power lay in his capacity
for silence. His imperturbable composure in negotiation
and in all the tension and excitement of the animated
Canadian scene of the '90's, gave him the supreme advantage
of weighty last words when the committees or directors
had worn themselves out with wrangling. Those who sat
with him, when dissensions seemed to tear all finality of
decision beyond hope of repair, have told with admiration
of his taciturn withdrawal behind the benign Presbyterian
elder-like beard and countenance, only to emerge with a
quiet-spoken pronouncement which carried the day.

In what might be called the old Hudson's Bay manner,
he never felt obliged to explain his motives. Just as the
Company's business was no one else's affair, so Smith
moved to decisions nourishing his own purposes. In a
world which responded readily to the flamboyant in newspaper interviews and in political oration, his intentions
were inevitably mistrusted. He survived more vitriolic
public denunciation than most Canadian public men and
lived to enjoy the latter day glow of an empire-builder.

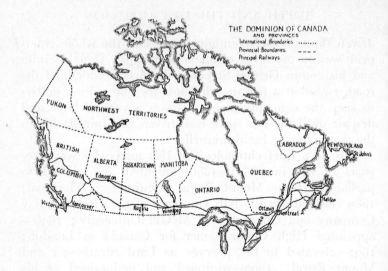

THE DOMINION OF CANADA
AND PROVINCES
International Boundaries ....
Provincial Boundaries ----
Principal Railways ----

CHAPTER XIX

THIS CENTURY

UNDER Strathcona's governorship the Hudson's Bay
Company did not keep pace with Canada. It was
the blind spot in his deep faith in the country that, believing
implicitly in the Canadian Pacific Railway, he failed to
see any future for the Hudson's Bay Company other than
the diminishing asset of land. As an opportunist he diverted
energy into the land business, neglecting the fur trade and
the retail expansion which later swung the Adventurers
back to prosperity and renewed vitality.

Strathcona was sixty-nine when, as the largest shareholder, he became twenty-sixth in the long line of governors
since Prince Rupert. He was wealthy and his interests
were highly diversified. He believed the fur trade doomed,
and that in land sales lay the true wealth, despite depressing
recoil of the west from its first real estate boom. His
policy was to coast easily until land values were restored,
though shareholders clamoured at dividends of only 3, 4,
or 5 per cent.

336

THE HUDSON'S BAY COMPANY'S RETAIL STORES
(Upper) Vancouver, British Columbia
(Lower) Winnipeg, Manitoba

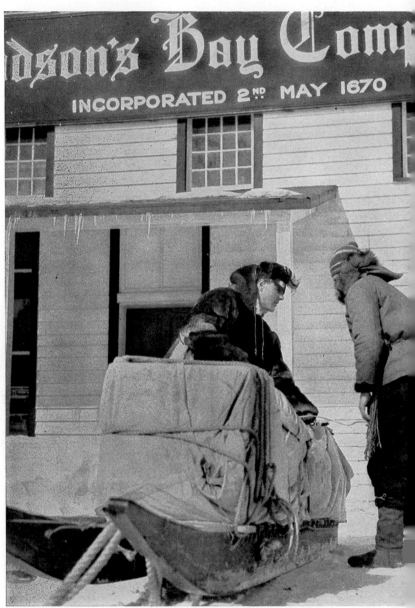

True North where winter transportation still depends upon men and do

"The twentieth century is Canada's century," Sir Wilfrid Laurier, the Prime Minister, was telling Canadians as the Company entered the two hundred and thirtieth year of its history. In 1904 dividends rose to 15·9 per cent.; in 1905 to 29 per cent.; and in 1906 to 40 per cent. Proprietors were happy again, and the eighty-four-year-old Governor content. On the estate at Glencoe and at the London house, hospitality was lavish. The white-bearded man from Labrador was conspicuous, carrying his peerage with ease through the succession of luncheons, dinners and receptions as Canada's representative in the heart of the Empire.

Out in the Canadian west, where the railways were depositing tens of thousands of farmland purchasers, the Company was selling hundreds of thousands of acres at mounting prices. It was quick and relatively easy money. In brassy, arrogant young cities of the west, the old posts evolved into "sales shops," curiously transplanting to the prairie the dingy gentility of the drapery establishment of English provincial towns. In the north, fur trade went on, with neglected personnel borne upon the momentum of centuries. Here and there the old pride and zeal survived, flashing out like a Jacobite loyalty in the twentieth century. The thread never quite snapped. If there are virtues in implicit loyalty, if there is anything admirable in facing the world with a united front, then the wintering partnership of the nineteenth century gave the Hudson's Bay Company an unparalleled example of self-discipline.

It is looked back upon with interest, not merely as an obsolete code and a lost loyalty, but with sadness that commercial enterprise will not again command the same deep, absolute and unwavering devotion. Perhaps the business of this century has no place for such *esprit de corps*, yet through all the sagging morale of the years following the crushing out of the Deed Poll, some men in the fur trade carried on the tradition.

Though he had been present at the death of the partnership system, Strathcona did nothing to rebuild the fur

trade personnel. Some of the old men clung to their rank
to the last; others retired under the terms of the old Deed
Poll; later there was the pitiable spectacle of Smith giving
private pensions to aged veterans who had suffered under
his settlement in 1871.

The apprenticeship plan of bringing out boys to spend
years learning the business had no place in the rapidly
changing west. Where jobs were available everywhere,
spirited youngsters would not contract themselves to the
long isolation.

His loss of faith in the fur trade was only one of Strathcona's errors in business judgment, but as money rolled
in from land sales, all other activities were eclipsed, and
to the absentee proprietors their Governor was a pre-
eminent success. His appointments to senior posts in
Canada carried a flavour of politics, and the filling of a
responsible position was often a trading in some of his
Lordship's other activities. In remote districts, posts frequently went for years without competent inspection;
buildings drooped into a state of half decay; men sometimes remained at their posts for a lifetime, sinking into a
shabby, contented, if eccentric routine of life, ruling their
little forest principalities with rude, effective paternalism.
In the Fertile Belt where homesteaders were turning prairie
sod, the Hudson's Bay men found themselves elected to
office in new communities, and a few were sent to Ottawa,
though it is not recorded that they found happiness playing
public parts.

Lulled by the revenues of land selling (reaching a peak
of three hundred and fifty thousand acres at more than
five dollars an acre in 1903) even the "sales shops" lost
the natural leadership which was theirs by inheritance.
London management could not grasp the reality of cities
rising swiftly from tent towns. After ten years of the new
century had gone, the old Company found itself surpassed
by aggressive young retail merchant organizations.

Moreover, there was growing resentment against the
Company's long record of having taken wealth from the

country while contributing not even the impressive buildings which boards of trade in ambitious cities regard as "a stake in the community." To this was added the more active irritant of selling town lots in competition with thousands of citizens speculating feverishly themselves. "What has the Hudson's Bay Company ever done for Canada?" these people asked, dimly aware of two centuries of monopoly, and acutely conscious of current profits from farmlands and city real estate.

And the Company, roused at last, finding itself increasingly unpopular with the public and despised by competitors as hopelessly antiquated, rushed into expansion plans. Great department stores for the cities of the west were blue-printed in 1910–11–12.

In Vancouver and Calgary modern department stores were built in 1913; the Victoria store in 1914; additions were made to the Edmonton store in 1914. (In 1915, with a fine indifference to historical association, the old stockaded fort at Edmonton was swept away to smooth out the lawns and lands around the Alberta parliament buildings.)

In the smaller towns of MacLeod, Lethbridge, Vernon, Yorkton and Kamloops, new buildings were bought or built as part of the belated effort to catch up with the march of Canada. Three million immigrants had arrived between the opening of the century and the outbreak of war in 1914.

At the General Court of the proprietors on June 13, 1913, Strathcona, aged ninety-three, presided, and a resounding dividend of 50 per cent was paid to more than seven thousand shareholders. In January, 1914, he died, rich in honours, leaving a personal estate estimated at nearly five million pounds after enormous benefactions to philanthropic and educational institutions: King Edward's Hospital Fund, two hundred thousand pounds; Royal Victoria Hospital, Montreal, two hundred thousand pounds; McGill University, four hundred and ten thousand pounds; Yale University, one hundred thousand pounds; and others, as well as a lengthy private pension list of old friends of fur trade days, and even some impoverished Eskimo families on the Labrador.

War in 1914 arrested the next phase in the attempt to recover lost ground in the field of retailing, and the blue prints were shelved while the London head office revealed an unexpected flexibility by expanding into war service as overseas purchasing agent for the French Government.

Between 1915 and 1919, through an elaborate maze of subsidiaries and overseas agencies, the Company arranged credits for the French military administration throughout the world, organized steamship services, purchased and transported foodstuffs, fuel, timber and munitions. More than thirteen million tons were transported for France, and in 1918 this work achieved a volume of eleven thousand tons of freight discharged daily in the ports of France. The Bay Steamship Company, a wartime subsidiary, comprised a fleet of two hundred and twenty-five thousand tons deadweight, of which enemy submarines sank more than two-fifths. Including vessels under charter, the Company at one period had under its management more than one million tons of shipping. The long experience in northern navigation was utilized in transport to north Russian ports. At Archangel, through four years of changing Russian governments, there was an H. B. C. agency which was only abandoned when all British citizens were recalled by the home government.

In this Arctic work ships were blown up, crushed in ice, and sunk by enemy action. Every voyage was tense with the hazards of war added to the dangers of ice fields and frozen seas, and except when seamen yarn together, most of the tales of these high adventures are still untold.

The most celebrated vessel of this wartime Armada is R.M.S. *Nascopie*, named after the Indian tribe of the Labrador interior. An icebreaker-freighter of fifteen hundred tons, her voyages into the European Arctic in war and her subsequent annual voyages to the eastern

Canadian Arctic have made her a storied ship of the British merchant marine. Each year she leaves Montreal in early July with mail and supplies for Arctic trading posts as well as those of the Royal Canadian Mounted Police and the missions. Scientists, policemen, missionaries and fur traders of the eastern Arctic have a deep affection for the stout little ship.

The war took five hundred and twenty men from the Company to the fighting services, and of these seventy-eight were killed.

Peace came, and dividends of 40 and 45 per cent. in 1918 and 1919. The profits of the French Government contracts were supplemented by unprecedented land sales. Under "two-dollar wheat" in 1918, almost four hundred thousand acres of farmlands were sold, at an average of better than fifteen dollars an acre. The fur trade, by reason of conspicuous individual leadership in the Labrador and eastern Arctic districts, cashed in smartly with huge catches of white fox, which brought top prices at the London auction. The aggressive extension of the fur trade in the area of Hudson Strait and the east coast of Baffin Island, as well as along the western Arctic Coast, made a latter-day epic. It was a minor wilderness conquest in a land even more desolate and forbidding than the western shores of Hudson Bay, and it disclosed an unsuspected vitality in an otherwise lethargic division. The building and expansion programme of the retail stores, deferred by the war, was resumed in the desire to overtake the tempo of life in cities maturing rapidly in metropolitan character.

The curtain of the two hundred and fiftieth anniversary of incorporation was lifted on May 2, 1920, with a flourish of street parades, Indian pageantry, and a visit to Canada by Sir Robert Kindersley, twenty-eighth Governor. With a somewhat awkward reluctance, the Company was stirred to interest in its own past. To be able to look back on two and a half centuries in a country which marked antiquity by a mere hundred years, suddenly seemed an

unexploited asset. But history and department-store
promotion require extremely skilful blending if they are
to serve a useful publicity purpose. These things do not
mingle readily, and the Company soon turned to the safer
policy of understatement in matters relating to its own
history.

A sprinkling of memorial tablets, cairns, a gift book,
and several thousand feet of motion-picture film lying in
a vault, are not the only salvage from the two hundred
and fiftieth anniversary.

From the first voyage of the *Nonsuch* to Hudson Bay
in 1668, all Hudson's Bay officers kept journals and business
records. Literally mountains accumulated; their first
usefulness over, they lay neglected in London garrets,
Winnipeg warehouse basements, and in the outbuildings
of a hundred odd posts between Ungava and Vancouver
Island. The Company was incredibly, wholeheartedly,
and somewhat arrogantly indifferent to the stuff of history.
The Great Seal, dinner-plate size, was once rescued by a
curious clerk from a refuse heap behind Hudson's Bay
House, London. Seventeenth-century letters were used as
insulating material in a northern post. Bales of journals
stowed under a wooden grandstand in Fort Garry were
inevitably destroyed by fire. Still, a common legend
persisted that in the records were secrets so dark and
ominous as to shake the foundations of men and nations.
Students of Canadian history were not allowed to browse
(in the state of the records, it could not be called search)
among the littered accumulations in London. Under the
Strathcona régime two or three were given the privilege
of working under strict limitations.

The work of establishing archives commenced in 1920,
and is not yet finished. In 1923 all departments and
branches in Canada were house-cleaned for historical
material. Several tons of papers were assembled in
Winnipeg and shipped to London, and in the general
sweeping up enough relics appeared to furnish two museums.
With expert advice, the services of an archivist and staff,

a competent cataloguing of the records has proceeded systematically. The archives are now freely available to accredited workers in the field of history. As students have probed deeply, no skeletons have yet clattered out of cupboards nor have nations been rocked.

Instead, as orderly scholarship assembles the pattern of the past, the fabric of history appears. Here and there the thread is broken; now and then there is a stain; but it is a whole cloth, woven by the active minds and toiling hands of men, with occasional brilliant strands upon a field of hodden grey. A long and honest piece, and every thread is a story of men and their money, their ships, their guns, their women and children, their furs, their ambitions, failures, their courage and cowardice, all in the service of a great Company.

Now that the whole design can be examined, the Company, appreciating its historic importance, has undertaken a plan for the publication of letters and journals of its men. This material, which is not to be issued with any view to profit, will be edited and prepared for publication by historians whose reputations will place the whole project above any suggestion of censorship or bluepencilling by the owners.

The fulfilment of this plan will enrich the annals of Canadian life and mark a new liberal, enlightened attitude on the part of the Company towards its past. So, out of the alarums and excursions, the cinema and street parades of the two hundred and fiftieth anniversary year, this worthy effort was launched by a Company which one of its enemies a century earlier declared "had not a soul above a beaver skin."

The temptation to append a description of the course since 1920, and to link in neat analogies the policies of post-war years with decisions of far away and long ago, must be resisted. Two hundred and fifty years should be enough. The significant statistics of the 1920's and '30's may be seen in the financial pages of the daily press. If the study of corporations can produce one unassailable generalization it is the complete inability of a company to appraise its place in contemporary history—or for any outsider to do it.

It is reasonable, though, to report without prejudice the state of the Company in 1936 as a rounding out of this narrative.

Today some thirteen thousand persons hold shares, nearly all of them in Great Britain. A governor, deputy governor and committee compose the directorate. The committee consists of nine members elected by the proprietors at the annual general court, three members being retired each year. The Governor and Committee meet regularly in Hudson's Bay House, London, in a magnificent board room hung with portraits of Rupert, James II, Charles II, Simpson, Pelly and others.

The Governor and Committee in 1931 deputized a substantial measure of their authority to a Canadian Committee, with headquarters at Hudson's Bay House, Winnipeg, but, as the elected representatives of the proprietors, retained control of matters of major policy and finance.

The present Governor, and the thirtieth, is P. Ashley Cooper, Esquire. Since his election in 1931 he has frequently visited Canada, inspecting not only retail stores but using aeroplane and ship to reach northern fur trade posts.

In 1928 the present Hudson's Bay House, Bishopsgate, London, was opened. In 1925 Beaver House, Trinity Lane, London, was established, where since 1928 the fur sales have been held. From 1670 to 1682 Company meetings convened in such historic places as The Tower, The Mint, Prince Rupert's lodgings in Whitehall, Garraway's Coffee House, and the Excise Office. In 1682 they moved to Scriveners Hall, then to Culver Court. (Next door, in the Elephant Inn, Hogarth is said to have done murals in the taproom, one being *The Hudson's Bay Company Porters Going to Dinner*.) In 1794 they purchased Numbers 3 and 4 Fenchurch Street, remaining there for a century and then

Photo, Max Sauer

"No. 1 Northern"

he Dominion Government's 2,500,000 bushel grain elevator at Churchill,
on Hudson Bay

leasing Number 1 Lime Street, old silk warehouses of the Honourable East India Company.

The major operation in London is the warehousing and auctioning of furs. Beaver House is completely equipped for the highly specialized operations of receiving, sorting, grading, storing, and auctioning of pelts. At specified dates auctions are held with buyers attending from the United States and all parts of Europe to bid for furs from all the world. An international reputation for integrity has sustained the prestige of the Company since the first sales in Garraway's Coffee House in 1669, and Hudson's Bay grading is accepted as standard in the trade everywhere.

In Canada the executive authority is the Canadian Committee, responsible to the Governor and Committee in London. Since 1884 groups in various forms attempted to centralize the Company's operations in Canada, but at no time before 1931 were they more than advisory to the Governor and Committee. They could guide and recommend, but the decisions of infinite detail rested ultimately thousands of miles away. The Canadian Committee occupies today a unique function in corporate administration, doing the duties of an active directorate, being entrusted with the conduct of the Canadian business, yet not directly responsible to the shareholders. Its chairman is an elected member of the London Committee.

The Canadian Committee, meeting weekly at Hudson's Bay House, Winnipeg, the head office in Canada, is composed of men whose knowledge of western life and commerce is brought to the service of the Company in a realistic administration. A general manager and small group of executives make up the headquarters, known as the Canadian Committee Office. Spreading out across Canada from this office, mostly westward, are the three major departments, fur trade, retail stores, and land, as well as two small departments, wholesale, and wines and spirits.

In their relative earning power the three dominant branches have fluctuated in reaction to local and world economics during the last fifty years, with the chain of department stores (three thousand employees) coming into current leadership. The last unit to be modernized was the present Winnipeg store, opened in 1926, designed, built and equipped with an open-handedness that seemed partly planned to silence for ever the old public grumble against penny-pinching in the midst of prosperity. Of the six large stores (Winnipeg, Vancouver, Calgary, Edmonton, Victoria, Saskatoon) three evolved from century-old fur trade forts through the "sales shop" phase, while Calgary, Vancouver and Saskatoon were born as general mercantile establishments, set up in growing communities. Visitors to western Canadian cities may be disappointed to find few evidences of the antiquity of the stores' origin—a flag, a coat-of-arms over a door, or perhaps a museum in a remote corner are all that suggest seventeenth-century adventuring. But it is in the very conformity to the best modern retail standards that the management takes pride. The astonishing adaptability of this very old Company, its recurrent resiliency, its undefeatable buoyancy, and its strength in throwing off the deadweight of outmoded custom, disclose its inherent power. To the consumer, "the Bay" is a merchandising institution; a few may regret the passing of more casual days, but some also find intangible satisfaction even in the purchase of modest household necessities from a company so intimately and vitally close to Canada from the beginning.

The retail stores represent fixed assets of twenty-seven million dollars. Total sales increased from four million, five hundred and ninety-two thousand dollars in 1911 to thirty-five million, eight hundred and ten thousand dollars in 1930. After the lean years of 1931-34 they demonstrated vigorous recovery.

The fur trade as the senior branch gives continuity to the long story. Until the Deed of Surrender it is all fur trade history. Then the chronicle must spread itself out through the broadening commercial life of Canada. The fur trade survived in spite of the solemn predictions of its

death by the real estate speculators and retired railroad
contractors of the '80's and '90's. It weathered the influx
of free traders, the decline of morale and the fluctuations
of fashion. It was not so much by an aggressive fight
for trade as by deep-rooted prestige and authority with
natives and, in the years before the war, by the opening
of the Arctic.

In 1936 fur trading to a remarkable extent operates
according to the old formula, but the old ways have been
accelerated to these times; Red River carts and York
boats are museum pieces in Outfit 266, while in 1935
men of the service logged seven hundred hours of flying
time. This division employs six hundred people and
maintains two hundred and twenty posts in the northland.
Trade in remote districts is by barter in the old, old
manner. Further south, white trappers and Indians sell
for cash, and at scores of posts the Company is general
merchant to frontier villages or brisk mining camps. At
places bearing such ancient names as Fort St. James and
Moose Factory, the white, red-roofed buildings are really
general stores where fresh fruit, nationally advertised
goods and soft drinks are displayed in chain-store manner
and sold by young apprentice clerks in white jackets. In
the same stores are dog harness, parkas, blankets, traps
and beads, for the Company is still "trading into Hudson's
Bay," though adjusting itself to advancing civilization.
This modern diversity has brought with it a quickening of
pace, and in the post-war years drastic altering to changing
conditions.

How participation in the development of mining has
been avoided seems strange. With posts sprinkled across
the pre-Cambrian shield, and men living and travelling
in the area for centuries, it is extraordinary that someone
did not turn to prospecting as a relief from fur trade routine.
Even in the last fifty years, while some of the great mining
fields of the world opened beside posts, the Company was
content to enjoy the benefits of having miners as well
as trappers for customers. Possibly it was restraint rather

than apathy, for it is a truism that whenever the Company departed from the natural course of its trading life—whether it was attempting business in Honolulu or shipping reindeer to Baffinland or drilling oil wells in Alberta—its efforts were dogged by misfortune. In any event, in the changing north (the New North, as newspapers and magazines call it) the fur trade keeps to the business of trading.

The old unquenchable prediction of the wiping out of fur-bearing animals has never come true. Hudson's Bay Company and government authorities have co-operated, except in some bygone irritating incidents, to conserve fur-bearing life and to maintain a means of livelihood for white trappers as well as natives. With due allowance for errors, the endeavour has succeeded. Today near East Main, on the east coast of James Bay, a significant and in some ways typical conservation project is operating. Under nominal lease from the Quebec Government, seventeen thousand square miles of otherwise waste, swampy forest has been turned into a beaver preserve, with Indians as rangers and controlled trapping to restore the natural wealth of the land. A similar experiment is proceeding in an area of one thousand square miles adjacent to Cumberland House in Saskatchewan. In miniature it revives old monopoly practice: an odd commentary on the basic soundness of this economic principle, so repugnant to democracy, that in solution of the fur-bearing and native trading problems, government has turned back the clock.

The production of fur from domestically-bred animals is cutting across the old pattern of trapping and trading. Those whose business it is to study the industry as a whole are cautious about predicting the ultimate effect of fur farming on the trade. The Hudson's Bay Company maintains fur farms in Prince Edward Island, Quebec and Manitoba, thus participating in production as well as collection of furs. Fur farming today accounts for more than 30 per cent. of the annual value of Canadian pelts.

The relation between fur trader and native in the exploration and development of North America is a subject begging the treatment of some ethnologist-historian. It is a rich field, with absorbing bypaths into economics, politics, and the humanities. Even in the more limited field of the Company, the effect of association upon Indians and Eskimo deserves far deeper examination than it has yet received.

The Indian and the Eskimo are now wards of the Dominion of Canada. They cannot be allowed to starve and their health must be watched. Their ability to maintain themselves economically must be fostered. In all these things the Company works with the federal authority.

As primitive people thrust back upon the hinterland or confined to reservations they have suffered racially, recoiling from the first impact with white civilization in a confusion of epidemics, notably smallpox and measles. As ordered administration was brought to their care, they came back slowly, until today the Indian population (one hundred and twelve thousand) is increasing. After painful errors, the Canadian Indian emerges comparatively well in the sad story of subject races.

The Eskimo came under white influence much later than the Indian. Whalers worked in Baffin Bay on the east and Alaska on the west long ago, and left the ruin of venereal disease and tuberculosis, but the Arctic Coast Eskimo remained virtually untouched until this century, when the Company went north for white fox and established posts. Here again the government has the co-operation of the trading company in efforts to foster healthy independence among the 5,959 Eskimo. It is a subject of considerable controversy which cannot be pursued here, though it would seem that the course now being followed is humane and in the best interest of the natives.

Just as the treatment of Indians must be adapted to suit each tribe, so does fur trade in the eastern Arctic differ from the western. Eskimo east and west of the Mackenzie River mouth are aggressive and businesslike, owning motor schooners and trading like petty capitalists. (In 1934 they formed a combine and held out successfully for better terms to load a boat for the Royal Canadian Mounted Police.) Their kin north of Hudson Bay and on Baffin Island are generations behind them in these matters but they learn rapidly. Racially they are cheerful, clever nomads.

Dependent upon the life cycle of animals, the public auctions in London, New York and Leipzig, the whims of fashion designers on two continents, fur trading is strangely different from the orthodox form of commercial experience. Primarily it is based on men living strenuously in lonely places where individual resourcefulness and courage are part of the day's routine. While men live and work in the north under these conditions there will always be city-bred, urban-bound millions who regard that way of life with curious interest and some envy, searching for escape in vicarious adventures of the forests or the Barren Lands. It would be unfair to set about destroying that illusion. Despite the shopkeeping in drab squalor of Indian villages, the unrelieved monotony of the North Atlantic smashing eternally on grey rock, the months of Arctic night, the deep, damp chill of mountain valleys, the complete isolation from faces and voices of friends, the endless round of petty chores—there are men who find it good. In the few score posts of the high north which are neither village chain stores nor supply depots of shabby hamlets, there is a tradition of independent masculine living. Sometimes completely alone, and sometimes with a missionary and a policeman for company, the men create a busy, contented existence with their dogs and their boats. After the day's work there are books, the blessing of radio, and always the journal to be kept. Annually the ship arrives with mail and supplies, and now at some Arctic posts the aeroplane brings a welcome shattering of the silence. When the ship and the plane depart the post settles back thankfully into the cold quiet; the seasons and the years swing past; the fur trader

emerges for his long furlough into a world singularly complex
and tortured by man.

So, fur trading survives, and in some years flourishes, in
its own unique way a link between luxury and lonely
toil.

The third department of the Company sells land. It
also administers the gigantic estate of two million acres,
residue of the seven million acquired by the Deed of
Surrender. The department has been selling land for
more than sixty years, encompassing booms, panics, prosperity, and depression, acquiring a maturity of experience
in farm and city property rarely encountered in the
vagaries of the real estate business. Like the retail and
fur trades, the land department headquarters is in Hudson's
Bay House, Winnipeg. A head office staff includes
engineers, draftsmen, accountants and statisticians, while
throughout the Fertile Belt field men and sales solicitors
are engaged in the administration as well as the sale of
land.

Some years the department has earned millions of dollars:
in the dreary stretches of lean times it has staggered under
huge taxation. For areas suffering from a succession of
parched seasons, these taxes have often been the only
dependable source of revenue to maintain essential public
services. City and town holdings include warehouses,
office buildings, residences, a golf course and suburban
lots. Some are part of the acreage that surrounded the
walls of the old forts. Under the provocative heading of
"sundry lands and abandoned fur trade posts," come such
oddments as a group of twenty-eight islands in the lower
St. Lawrence River, a spot of an island in the Pacific, and
a stone fort, complete with bastions, on the Red River
eighteen miles from Winnipeg—the flotsam of trading in
three centuries.

The very scale of operation make mistakes inevitable,
and errors in land policy during some of the feverish,
speculative phases were in proportion to the project. In
some cities, notably Edmonton, when the structure of

fantastically inflated values crumpled, the Company was left with paved roads and boulevards through scrub and bush. When, after years, it wearied of tax-paying on this sub-divided waste and the land fell back on the hands of the municipality, public relations were unhappy. An individual would have let go long before, but for a corporation these things are difficult and only time eradicates the blot.

The two minor divisions at Hudson's Bay House are the Wholesale, and Wines and Spirits departments. The former handles tea and coffee and tobacco under the H. B. C. brand, and the celebrated Hudson's Bay Point blankets, an article of merchandise associated with the Company's name for almost a century and a half which has gathered about it a rich lore. The florid days of spirits and the Indian trade have already been described. The restraints which the Company brought to the trade in liquor in Simpson's day have prevailed. In a business not conspicuous in North America for its ethical practices, the Hudson's Bay Company has carried on with integrity and moderation.

The story of the Hudson's Bay Company cannot be terminated neatly in phrases of finality. It lives today— a merchant trader so full-blooded, so animated, that the final pages must be left open. Contemporary Adventurers regard the past with an interest only slightly more than academic, the present with vital realism, and the future with a happy, almost youthful, eager concern. Any honest attempt to tell the story even in the general outline undertaken here, must conclude upon open pages, if only to symbolize a great tomorrow.

APPENDICES

Appendix A

A SELECTED BIBLIOGRAPHY

ADAM, MERCER G.—*The Canadian North-West, its history and its troubles from the early days of the fur trade to the era of the railway and the settler; with incidents of travel in the region and the narrative of three insurrections.* Toronto, 1885.

ANDERSON, Rev. DAVID, Bishop of Rupert's Land.—*Notes of the Flood at Red River.* London, 1852.

BACK, Sir GEORGE.—*Narrative of the Arctic Land Expedition to the Mouth of the Great Fish River, and along the shores of the Arctic Ocean in the years* 1833, 1834 *and* 1835. London, 1836.

BALLANTYNE, R. M.—*Hudson's Bay or Every-Day Life in the Wilds of North America.* Edinburgh and London, 1848.

BEGG, ALEXANDER.—*The History of the North-west.* 3 vols. London, 1895.
History of British Columbia. Toronto, 1894.

BELL, C. N.—*Journal of Henry Kelsey.* (1691–1692.) Maps 44 pp. Winnipeg, 1928.

BISHOP OF RUPERT'S LAND.—*The Net in the Bay; or A Journal of a Visit to Moose and Albany.* London, 1854.

BRITISH AMERICAN JOINT COMMISSION.—*Hudson's Bay vs. United States. British and American Joint Commission for the Settlement of the Claims of the Hudson's Bay and Puget's Sound Agricultural Companies. Memorial and Argument on the part of the Hudson's Bay Company.* Montreal, 1868.

BRYCE, GEORGE, M.A., LL.D.—*The Remarkable History of the Hudson's Bay Company.* London, 1910.
Brief Biographies of Selkirk, Simpson, Mackenzie, Douglas in the Makers of Canada. Oxford University Press, 1927.
1906 edition has Bryce's biographies of Mackenzie, Selkirk and Simpson; 1910 edition adds a brief biography of Douglas; 1927 edition has a volume on Lord Strathcona by John Macnaughton.

355

The Remarkable History of the Hudson's Bay Company, including that of French Traders of North Western Canada and of the North West, XY, and Astor Fur Company. London, 1900.

Sketch of the Life and Discoveries of Robert Campbell, Chief Factor of the Hudson's Bay Company. The Historical and Scientific Society of Manitoba, Transactions No. 52. Winnipeg, 1898.

Manitoba: Its Infancy, Growth and Present Condition. London, 1882.

The Romantic Settlement of Lord Selkirk's Colonists. Toronto, 1909.

BURPEE, L. J.—*The Search for the Western Sea: The Story of the Exploration of North Western America.* 2 vols. Toronto, 1908. *On the Old Athabasca Trail.* Toronto, 1926.

BUTLER, Col. (later General Sir) WILLIAM F.—*The Great Lone Land.* London, 1872. *The Wild North Land.* 1874.

CAMERON, WILLIAM BLEASDELL.—*The War Trail of Big Bear.* Toronto, 1926.

CAMPBELL, RODERICK, F.R.G.S.—*The Father of St. Kilda; Twenty Years in Isolation in the Sub-Arctic Territory of the Hudson's Bay Company.* London, 1901.

CAREY, C. H.—*History of Oregon.* Chicago, 1922.

CHEADLE, W. P.—*Cheadle's Journal of a Trip Across Canada, 1862–1863.* With Introduction and Notes by A. G. Doughty and Gustave Lanctot. Ottawa, 1931.

CLARKE, S. A.—*Pioneer Days of Oregon History.* 2 vols. Portland, 1905.

COATS, Captain W.—*The geography of Hudson's Bay: Being the Remarks of Captain W. Coats in Many Voyages to that Locality Between the Years 1727 and 1751.* Edited by John Barrow, F.R.S., F.S.A. London, Hakluyt Society, 1852.

COATS, R. H., and R. E. GOSNELL.—*Sir James Douglas. The Makers of Canada.* Toronto, 1908.

COCHRANE, CHAS. NORRIS.—*David Thompson, the Explorer.* Toronto, 1924.

COCKING, MATTHEW.—*Journal of Matthew Cocking from York Factory to the Blackfeet Country,* 1772. Toronto, Royal Society of Canada, 1908. Edited with Introduction and Notes by Lawrence J. Burpee.

COWIE, ISAAC.—*The Company of Adventurers.* Toronto, 1913.

COX, ROSS.—*Adventures on the Columbia River.* 2 vols. London, 1831.

CROUSE, NELLIS M.—*The Search for the Northwest Passage.* Columbia University Press, New York, 1934.

DAVIDSON, GORDON CHARLES.—*The North West Company.* University of California, Publications in History, vol. 7. Berkeley, 1918.

DOBBS, ARTHUR.—*An Account of the Countries Adjoining to Hudson's Bay in the North-West part of America.* London, 1744.
Remarks upon Captain Middleton's Defence. London, 1744.
A Reply to Captain Middleton's Answer. London, 1745.

DODDS, JAMES.—*The Hudson's Bay Company, Its Position and Prospects.* The substance of an address delivered at a meeting of the shareholders in the London Tavern on January 24, 1866, by James Dodds. London, 1866.

DOUGLAS, DAVID.—*Journal Kept During His Travels in North America,* 1823–1827. London, 1914.

DOUGLAS, T.—*A Narrative of Occurrences in the Indian Countries of North America since the connexion of the Right Hon. the Earl of Selkirk with the Hudson's Bay Company and his attempt to establish a colony on the Red River, with a detailed account of His Lordship's military expedition to and subsequent proceedings at Fort William in Upper Canada.*

DUGAS, Abbé G.—*The Canadian West: Its Discovery by the Sieur de la Verendrye: Its Development by the Fur-Trading Companies, Down to the Year* 1822. Translated from the French. Montreal, 1905.

DUNN, JOHN.—*History of the Oregon Territory and British North-America Fur Trade.* London, 1844.

DYE, Mrs. EVA E.—*McLoughlin and Old Oregon.* Chicago, 1900.

ELLIOTT, T. C.—*Peter Skene Ogden, Fur Trader.* Published in the Oregon Historical Quarterly, September, 1910, and reprinted privately by the author.
David Thompson, Pathfinder, and The Columbia River. Washington, 1911.

ELLIS, HENRY.—*A Voyage to Hudson's Bay by the Dobbs Galley and California, in the years* 1746 *and* 1747, *for Discovering a North West Passage.* London, 1748. Dublin, 1749.

ERMATINGER, EDWARD.—*Ermatinger's York Factory Express Journal. Being a record of journeys made between Fort Vancouver and Hudson Bay in the years* 1827–1828. With Introduction by Judge C. O. Ermatinger, and Notes by Judge C. O. Ermatinger and James White. Toronto. Transactions of the Royal Society of Canada, 1912.

Evidence and Argument for the United States in the matter of the Claim of the Hudson's Bay Company, pending before the British and American Joint Commission for the final settlement of the Claims of the Hudson's Bay and Puget's Sound Agricultural Companies. Washington City; 5 vols. in 1867 and 1 in 1868. The Claimant's evidence appeared in 1 vol. in 1865.

FITZGERALD, JAMES EDWARD.—*An examination of the Charter and Proceedings of the Hudson's Bay Company with reference to the Grant of Vancouver's Island.* London, 1849.

FRANKLIN, Captain JOHN.—*Narrative of a Journey to the Shores of the Polar Sea in the years* 1819–20–1–2. London, 1824.
Narrative of a Second Expedition to the Polar Sea in the years 1825, 1826 *and* 1827. London, 1828.

FREMONT, DONATIEN.—*Pierre Radisson.* Winnipeg, 1934.

FULLER, GEORGE W.—*A History of the Pacific Northwest.* New York, 1931.

GARRIOCH, Rev. A. C.—*The Far and Furry North.* Published by the author, 1925.
A Hatchet Mark in Duplicate. 1929.

GARRY, NICHOLAS.—*The Diary of Nicholas Garry,* 1821. Transactions of the Royal Society of Canada, 1900.

GIBBON, JOHN MURRAY.—*Steel of Empire, the romantic history of the Canadian Pacific, the Northwest Passage of today.* Indianapolis, 1935.

GODSELL, PHILIP H.—*Arctic Trader, the Account of Twenty Years with the Hudson's Bay Company.* New York, 1934.

GOSNELL, R. E.—*The History of British Columbia.* Toronto, 1901.

GRAHAM, ANGUS.—*The Golden Grindstone. The Adventures of George M. Mitchell.* Oxford University Press, 1935.

GREENBIE, SYDNEY.—*Frontiers and the Fur Trade.* New York, 1929.

GUILLET, EDWIN C.—*Early Life in Upper Canada.* Toronto, 1933.

GUNN, Hon. DONALD and CHARLES R. TUTTLE.—*History of Manitoba from the Earliest Settlement*. Ottawa, 1880.

HAMMOND, M. O.—*Confederation and Its Leaders*. Toronto, 1917.

HANNAY, DAVID.—*The Great Chartered Companies*. London, 1926.

HARGRAVE, JOSEPH JAMES.—*Red River*. Montreal, 1871.

HARMON, DANIEL WILLIAMS.—*A Journal of Voyages and Travels in the Interior of North America*. Andover, 1820.

HEALY, W. J.—*Women of Red River: Being a Book Written from the Recollections of Women Surviving from the Red River Era*. Winnipeg Women's Canadian Club, Winnipeg, 1923.

HEARNE, SAMUEL.—*A Journey from Prince of Wales's Fort in Hudson's Bay to the Northern Ocean*. With Maps and Plates. London, 1795. Another edition Dublin, 1796; a French translation published in Paris, 1799; new edition published by Champlain Society, Toronto, 1911, with Introduction and Notes by J. B. Tyrrell.

Hearne, Samuel and Philip Turnor, the Journals of.—Edited with Introduction and Notes by J. B. Tyrrell. Champlain Society, Toronto, 1934.

HEMING, ARTHUR.—*Spirit Lake*. New York, 1907.
The Drama of the Forests. Romance and Adventure. New York and Toronto, 1921.

HENRY, ALEXANDER (Senior).—*Travels and Adventures in Canada and the Indian Territories, 1760–1776*. New York, 1809; new edition by James Bain, Toronto, 1901.
Manuscript Journals of Alexander Henry, Fur Trader of the Northwest Company, and of David Thompson, Official Geographer and Explorer of the same company, 1799–1814. Edited by Elliott Coues; 3 vols. New York, 1897.

HILL, ROBERT B.—*Manitoba: History of Its Early Settlement, Development and Resources*. Toronto, 1890.

HOLMAN, F. V.—*Dr. John McLoughlin, the Father of Oregon*. Cleveland, Ohio, 1907.

HOWAY, F. W.—*British Columbia: The Making of a Province*. Toronto, 1928.

HOWAY, Judge F. W.—*The Raison d'Etre of Forts Yale and Hope*. Royal Society of Canada, 1922.

HUDSON'S BAY COMPANY.—*Charters, Statutes and Orders in Council relating to the Hudson's Bay Company.* London, 1931.

HUDSON'S BAY COMPANY.—*Index to the Reports and Proceedings of the General Courts of Proprietors of the Hudson's Bay Company,* 1866–1928.

HUDSON'S BAY COMPANY.—*Canada's Fur Bearers; containing notes on the principal animals of Canada, trapping and the preparation of furs for the market.* Winnipeg, 1934.

HUDSON'S BAY COMPANY.—*Correspondence between Her Majesty's Government and the Hudson's Bay Company.* London, 1869.

HUDSON'S BAY COMPANY.—*Letter from the Colonial Office to the Governor of the Hudson's Bay Company, dated March 9th,* 1869. London.

HUDSON'S BAY COMPANY.—*Extent and Value of the Possessory Rights of the Hudson's Bay Company in Oregon, South of the Forty-ninth Degree.* Undated pamphlet.

HUDSON'S BAY COMPANY.—*Trading into Hudson's Bay. A Narrative of the Visit of Patrick Ashley Cooper, Thirtieth Governor of the Hudson's Bay Company, to Labrador, Hudson Strait and Hudson Bay in the Year* 1934. *From the Journal of R. H. H. Macaulay.* Published by the Hudson's Bay Company, Winnipeg, 1934.

HUDSON'S BAY COMPANY.—*A Brief History.* Sixty-eight pages and Illustrations, with a section on fur-bearing animals. London, 1935.

HUGHES, KATHERINE.—*Father Lacombe: The Black-Robe Voyageur.* Toronto, 1920. First edition, Toronto, 1911.

INNIS, H. A.—*Peter Pond, Fur Trader and Adventurer.* Toronto, 1930.
    The Fur Trade in Canada. New Haven, Conn., 1930.
    The Fur Trade of Canada. Toronto, 1927.

IRVING, WASHINGTON.—*Astoria: or Enterprise Beyond the Rocky Mountains.* London, 1836.

IRVING, WASHINGTON.—*Astoria. Rocky Mountains: Scenes, Incidents and Adventures in the Far West.* Two vols.; Maps. Philadelphia, 1837.

ISBISTER, A. K.—*A few Words on the Hudson's Bay Company, with a statement of the grievances of the natives and half-caste Indians, addressed to the British Government through their delegates now in London.* London.

Jeremie's Narrative. Twenty Years of York Factory, 1694–1714. Translated from the French edition of 1720. With Notes and Introduction by R. Douglas, M.A., and J. N. Wallace, D.L.S. Ottawa, 1926.

JOHNSTON, ROBERT C.—*John McLoughlin, Patriarch of the North West.* Portland, Oregon, 1935.

KANE, PAUL.—*Wanderings of an Artist Among the Indians of North America, from Canada to Vancouver Island and Oregon through the Hudson's Bay Company's Territory and Back Again.* London, 1859. Also a limited edition by the Radisson Society of Canada, 1925.

KELSEY, HENRY.—*The Kelsey Papers.* With an Introduction by A. G. Doughty, Dominion Archivist, and Prof. Chester Martin. Archives of Canada, 1929.
Journal of Henry Kelsey (1691–1692). With Notes by Charles N. Bell. Winnipeg, 1928.

KEMP, R. H.—*Hudson's Bay : A Half-Breed Dance and Other Far Western Stories.* Spokane, 1909.

KENNEDY, H. A.—*The Book of the West.* Toronto, 1925.

KENNEY, JAMES F.—*The Career of Henry Kelsey.* Royal Society of Canada, 1929.

KING, RICHARD, M.D.—*The Franklin Expedition from First to Last.* London, 1855.

KINGSTON, W. H. G.—*Snowshoes and Canoes, or the Early Days of a Fur Trader.* London, 1892.

KNIGHT, JAMES.—*The Founding of Churchill; Being the journal of Captain James Knight, Governor-in-Chief of Hudson Bay from 14th July to 13th of September,* 1717. Edited by James F. Kenney, Director of Historical Research, Public Archives of Canada. Toronto, 1932.

LANDMANN, GEORGE.—*Adventures and Recollections.* 2 vols. London, 1852.

LAUT, AGNES.—*Pathfinders of the West.* 1918.
The Conquest of the Great Northwest. New York, sixth edition. Toronto, 2 vols.
The Adventurers of England. Chronicles of Canada, vol. 18. Toronto, 1914.

LEACOCK, STEPHEN.—*Adventurers of the Far North. Chronicles of Canada*, vol. 20. Toronto, 1914.

LEITH, C. K. and A. T.—*A Summer and Winter on Hudson Bay.* Published privately by the authors at Madison, Wisconsin, 1912.

LEWIS, WILLIAM S., and PHILLIPS, PAUL C.—Editors of the *Journal of John Work, a chief trader of the Hudson's Bay Company during his expedition from Vancouver to the Flatheads and Blackfeet of the Pacific Northwest.* Cleveland, 1923.

LONG, J.—*Voyages and Travels of an Indian Interpreter and Trader, describing the Manners and Customs of the North American Indians; with an account of the posts situated on the River St. Lawrence, Lake Ontario, etc.* London, 1791.
New edition edited by R. G. Thwaites in Early Western Travels, vol. ii. Cleveland, 1904.

LUGRIN, N. DE BERTRAND.—*Pioneer Women of Vancouver Island,* 1843–1866. Edited by John Hosie. The Women's Canadian Club, Victoria, B.C., 1928.

MACBETH, R. G.—*Sir Augustus Nanton.* Toronto, 1931.

MACDONALD, RANALD.—*The Narrative of His Early Life on the Columbia Under the Hudson's Bay Company's Régime; of His Experience in the Pacific Whale Fishery; and of His Great Adventure in Japan; with Sketch of His Later Life on the Western Frontier,* 1824–1894. Edited by William S. Lewis and Navjiro Murakami. Spokane, Wash., 1923.

MACDONELL, Capt. MILES.—*Selkirk Settlement: Letter Book of of Captain Miles Macdonell,* 1811 *and* 1812. Canadian Archives, Report for 1886, pp. 187–226.

MACFARLANE, R., Chief Factor of the Hudson's Bay Company.— *Notes on Mammals Collected and Observed in the Northern Mackenzie River District, Northwest Territories, with Remarks on explorers and explorations of the Far North.* Washington, 1905.

MACKENZIE, ALEXANDER.—*Voyages from Montreal on the River St. Lawrence Through the Continent of North America to the Frozen Ocean and the Pacific in the years* 1789 *and* 1793. London, 1801.

MACOUN, JOHN.—*Manitoba and the Great Northwest.* 1882.

MAIR, CHARLES.—*Through the Mackenzie Basin. A narrative of the Athabasca and Peace River Treaty Expedition of* 1899, *containing maps and photographs, also notes on the mammals and birds of Northern Canada by Roderick MacFarlane, Retired Chief Factor of the Hudson's Bay Company.* Toronto, 1908.

MARQUIS, T. G.—*The " adventurers " of Hudson's Bay.* A section of forty-three pages in vol. 1, Canada and Its Provinces. Toronto, 1914.

MARTIG, RALPH RICHARD.—*The Hudson's Bay Company Claims,* 1846–69. Urbana, Illinois, 1934. Pamphlet, 12 pages.

MARTIN, ARCHER.—*The Hudson's Bay Company's Land Tenures and the Occupation of Assiniboia by Lord Selkirk's Settlers; with a list of Grantees under the Earl and the Company.* London, 1898.

MARTIN, CHESTER.—*Lord Selkirk's Work in Canada.* Oxford Historical and Literary Studies, vol. 7. Oxford, 1916.

MARTIN, R. M.—*The Hudson's Bay Territories and Vancouver's Island; with an Exposition of the Chartered Rights, Conduct, and Policy of the Honble. Hudson's Bay Corporation.* London, 1849.

MASSON, L. R.—*Les Bourgeois de la Compagnie du Nord-Ouest.* 2 vols. Quebec, 1889–90.

McCAIN, CHARLES W.—*History of the S.S.* Beaver, *Being a graphic and vivid sketch of this noted pioneer steamer and her romantic cruise for over half a century on the placid island-dotted waters of the North Pacific.* Vancouver, 1894.

McDONALD, Chief Factor ARCHIBALD.—*Peace River; A canoe voyage, Hudson's Bay to the Pacific by the late Sir George Simpson in* 1828. *Journal of the later Chief Factor Archibald McDonald (Hon. Hudson's Bay Company) who accompanied him.* Edited by Malcolm McLeod. Ottawa, 1872.

M'GILLIVRAY, DUNCAN.—*Journal of Duncan M'Gillivray of the Northwest Company at Fort George, on the Saskatchewan,* 1794–95. Edited by Arthur S. Morton. Toronto, 1929.

McKEEVOR, THOMAS.—*A Voyage to Hudson's Bay During the Summer of* 1812. London, 1819.

McKENZIE, N. M. W. J.—*The Men of the Hudson's Bay Company, Winnipeg.* Fort William, Ontario, 1921.

McLean, John.—*Notes on a Twenty-five Years' Service in the Hudson's Bay Territory.* 2 vols. London, 1849. Reprinted by the Champlain Society, 1932; edited by W. S. Wallace.

McWilliams, Margaret.—*Manitoba Milestones.* Toronto, 1928.

Merk, Frederick.—*Fur Trade and Empire; George Simpson's Journal, 1824–25.* Cambridge, Mass., Harvard Historical Studies, vol. 31, 1931.

Metcalfe, J. H.—*The Tread of the Pioneers.* Toronto, 1932.

Middleton, Christopher.—*A Reply to Mr. Dobbs's Answer to a Pamphlet Entitled Forgery Detected.* London, 1745.
A Reply to the Remarks of Arthur Dobbs. London, 1744.
A Vindication of the conduct of Captain Christopher Middleton. London, 1743.
Forgery Detected. London, 1745.

Milton, B., Viscount, and W. Cheadle.—*The Northwest Passage by Land. Being the narrative of an expedition from the Atlantic to the Pacific undertaken with a view to exploring a route across the continent to British Columbia through British Territory by one of the northern passes in the Rocky Mountains.* London, 1865.

Moberley, H. J., and W. B. Cameron.—*When Fur Was King.* Toronto, 1929.

Montgomery, Richard G.—*The White-Headed Eagle; John McLoughlin, Builder of an Empire.* New York, 1935.

Moore, Charles.—*The North-west Under Three Flags, 1635–1796.* New York, 1900.

Morice, Rev. A. G., O.M.I.—*The History of the Northern Interior of British Columbia (formerly New Caledonia), 1660–1880.* Toronto.

Morice, A. G.—*A Critical History of the Red River Insurrection.* Winnipeg, 1935.

Murray, Alexander Hunter.—*Journal of the Yukon, 1847–48.* Edited with Notes by L. J. Burpee. Publication of the Canadian Archives, No. 4. Ottawa, 1910.

Nute, Grace Lee.—*The Voyageur.* New York, 1931.

Ogden, Peter Skene.—*Traits of American-Indian Life and Character by a Fur Trader.* London, 1853. The authorship is disputed.

OLIVER, EDMUND H.—*The Canadian Northwest, Early Development and Legislative Records.* Public Archives of Canada, 2 vols., 1914, 1915.

PINKERTON, ROBERT E.—*The Gentlemen Adventurers.* Toronto, 1931. Published in England and U.S.A. under the title, *Hudson's Bay Company.*

POND, PETER and OTHERS.—*Five Fur Traders of the Northwest; Being the Narrative of Peter Pond and the Diaries of John Macdonell, Archibald N. McLeod, Hugh Faries, and Thomas Connor.* Edited by Charles M. Gates, with an Introduction by Grace Lee Nute. University of Minnesota Press, 1933.

PRESTON, W. T. R.—*Life and Times of Lord Strathcona.* Toronto, 1914.

PUGET'S SOUND AGRICULTURAL COMPANY VS. UNITED STATES.—*British and American Joint Commission for the Settlement of the Claims of the Hudson's Bay and the Puget's Sound Agricultural Companies. Memorial and Argument on the part of the Puget's Sound Agricultural Company.* Montreal, 1868.

RADISSON.—*Voyages of Peter Esprit Radisson: Being an Account of His Travels and Experiences Among the North American Indians, from 1652 to 1684.* Boston, 1885.

RAE, JOHN.—*Narrative of an Expedition to the Shores of the Arctic Sea, 1846–47; with an Appendix on the Natural History of the District.* Dedicated to Sir George Simpson. London, 1850.

REED, CHARLES BERT, M.D.—*Masters of the Wilderness.* Chicago Historical Society, 1914.

REPORTS AND ANONYMOUS PUBLICATIONS—
Opinions and Award of the Commissioners under the Treaty of July 1, 1863, Between Great Britain and the United States, for the Final Settlement of Claims of the Hudson's Bay and Puget Sound Agricultural Companies, Pronounced September 10, 1869. Montreal, 1869.

Relations of the Voyages of Pierre Esprit Radisson in 1682-3-4. Canadian Archives, Report for 1895, pp. 1–83.

Reports of the Proceedings Connected with the Dispute Between the Earl of Selkirk and the North West Company at the Assizes Held at York in Upper Canada, October,

1818, from Minutes Taken in Court. Published Montreal and London, 1819.

Report from the Select Committee on the Hudson's Bay Company, Together with Proceedings of the Committee.

Minutes of Evidence, Appendix, and Index. Ordered by the House of Commons to be printed, 1857.

Report from the Committee appointed to enquire into the state and conditions of the countries adjoining to Hudson's Bay Company, and of the trade carried on there, together with Appendix. London, 1749.

Calendar of Papers Relating to Hudson's Bay. Canadian Archives Report for 1895.

Transactions Between England and France Relating to Hudson's Bay, 1687. Canadian Archives Report for 1883.

Return to an Address of The Honourable the House of Commons dated 26 May, 1842, for copy of the existing Charter or grant by the Crown to the Hudson's Bay Company; together with copies or extracts of the correspondence which took place at the last renewal of the Charter between the Government and the Company or individuals on behalf of the Company; also the dates of all former charters or grants to the Company. Ordered by the House of Commons to be printed, 8 August, 1842.

A Short Narrative and Justification of the Proceedings of the Committee Appointed by the Adventurers to Prosecute the Discovery of the Passage to the Western Ocean of America. London, 1749.

The Hudson's Bay Company, What is It? London, 1864.

A Short State of the Countries and Trade of North America Claimed by the Hudson's Bay Company. London, 1749.

ROBINSON, H. M.—*Great Fur Land; or, Sketches of Life in Hudson Bay Territory.* 1879.

ROBSON, JOSEPH.—*An Account of Six Years' Residence in Hudson's Bay, From* 1733 *to* 1736 *and* 1744 *to* 1747. London, 1752.

ROSS, ALEXANDER.—*The Red River Settlement: Its Rise, Progress, and Present State.* London, 1856.

Fur Hunters of the Far West. A Narrative of Adventures in the Oregon and Rocky Mountains. 2 vols. London, 1855.

ROURKE, LOUISE.—*Land of the Frozen Tide.* London, 1929.

RUSSELL, ALEX. J.—*The Red River Country, Hudson's Bay and North-West Territories, considered in relation to Canada.* Ottawa, 1869.

RYERSON, Rev. JOHN.—*Hudson's Bay, or, A Missionary Tour in the Territory of the Hon. Hudson's Bay Company.* Toronto, 1855.

SAGE, WALTER N., M.A., Ph.D.—*Sir James Douglas and British Columbia.* University of Toronto Press, 1930.

SCHOLEFIELD, E. O. S., and R. E. GOSNELL.—*British Columbia: Sixty Years of Progress.* Vancouver, 1913.

SCHOOLING, Sir WILLIAM, K.B.E.—*The Hudson's Bay Company,* 1670–1920. Hudson's Bay Company, London, 1920. Published by the Company in commemoration of its 250th anniversary. Copies already rare. Useful.

SCRIVEN, GEORGE P.—*The Story of the Hudson's Bay Company.* Washington, D.C., 1929.

SELKIRK, Earl of.—*A Sketch of the British Fur Trade in North America, with Observations Relative to the Northwest Company of Montreal.* London, 1816.

SHORTT, ADAM, and A. G. DOUGHTY.—*Canada and Its Provinces.* 23 vols. Edited by Messrs. Shortt and Doughty. Toronto, 1914.

SIMPSON, ALEXANDER.—*Life and Travels of Thomas Simpson, The Arctic Discoverer.* London, 1845.

SIMPSON, Sir GEORGE.—*Narrative of a Journey Round the World During the Years* 1841 *and* 1842. London, 1847.

SIMPSON, THOMAS.—*Narrative of the Discoveries on the North Coast of America effected by the Officers of the Hudson's Bay Company during the years* 1836–39. London, 1843.

SKINNER, CONSTANCE LINDSAY.—*Adventurers of Oregon.* Chronicles of America. New Haven, 1920.
Beavers, Kings and Cabins. London, 1933.

SOUTHESK, Earl of.—*Saskatchewan and the Rocky Mountains. A diary and narrative of travel, sport and adventure during a journey through the Hudson's Bay Company's territories, in* 1859 *and* 1860. Maps and Illustrations. Toronto, 1875.

Statement respecting the Earl of Selkirk's Settlement on the Red River in North America; its destruction in 1815 *and* 1816 ; *and the massacre of Governor Semple and his party. With observations upon a recent publication entitled " A Narrative of Occurrences in the Indian Countries."* London, 1817.

STEVENS, W. E.—*The Organization of the British Fur Trade,* 1760–1800. From Mississippi Valley Historical Review, vol. 3, No. 2, 1916.

SULLIVAN, MAURICE S.—*The Travels of Jedediah Smith. A Documentary Outline including the journal of the Great American Pathfinder.* Santa Ana, California, 1934.

SUTTON, G. M.—*Eskimo Year.* Toronto, 1934.

TACHE, Mgr. ALEX.—*Vingt Années des Missions dans le Nord Ouest de L'Amerique.* Montreal, 1886.

THOMPSON, DAVID.—*David Thompson's Narrative of His Explorations in Western America,* 1784–1812. Edited by J. B. Tyrrell. Champlain Society, Toronto, 1916.

TREEPORT, ANDREW.—*The Case of the Hudson's Bay Company in a letter to Lord Palmerston.* London, 1857.

TROYED, DE.—*Journal de l'expedition du chevalier de Troyed à la baie d'Hudson, en* 1686. Edité et annoté par l'abbé Ivanhoe Caron. Beauceville, 1918.

TUCKER, S.—*The Rainbow in the North. A short account of the first establishment of Christianity in Rupert's Land by the Church Missionary Society.* London, 1851.

TYRRELL, J. B.—*Documents Relating to the Early History of Hudson Bay.* Edited by J. B. Tyrrell. Toronto, 1931. Champlain Society publication, vol. 18.

TYTLER, PATRICK FRASER, and R. M. BALLANTYNE.—*The Northern Coasts of America and the Hudson's Bay Territories.* London, 1854.

UMFREVILLE, EDWARD.—*The Present State of Hudson's Bay; Containing a Full Description of That Settlement and the adjacent country and Likewise of the Fur Trade, with Hints for its Improvement.* London, 1790.

VANDIVEER, CLARENCE A.—*The Fur Trade and Early Western Exploration.* Cleveland, Ohio, 1929.

VOORHIS, ERNEST.—*Compiler of Historic Forts and Trading Posts of the French Régime and of the English Fur Trading Companies.* Department of the Interior, Ottawa, 1930.

WADE, MARK S.—*The Thompson Country. Being notes of the history of Southern British Columbia and particularly of the City of Kamloops, formerly Fort Thompson.* Kamloops, 1907.

WALES, WILLIAM, and DYMOND, JOSEPH.—*Astronomical Observation Made by Order of the Royal Society at Prince of Wales' Fort, on the North-West Coast of Hudson's Bay. Communicated to the Royal Society 16th November,* 1769. London, 1770.

WALLACE, J. N.—*The Wintering Partners on Peace River; from the earliest records to the union in* 1821. *With a summary of the Dunvegan Journal,* 1806. Ottawa, 1929.

WALLACE, W. STEWART.—*Documents Relating to the North-West Company.* Toronto, Champlain Society, XXII, 1935.

WARRE, Captain HENRY J.—*Sketches of the Journey Across the Continent of North America from Canada to the Oregon Territory and Pacific Ocean.* London, 1848.

WATSON, ROBERT.—*Lower Fort Garry, Hudson's Bay Company,* 1928. *The Hudson's Bay Company* (short school history reader). Toronto, 1928.

WEST, REV. JOHN.—*The Substance of a Journal During a Residence at the Red River Colony, British North America; and frequent excursions among the North-West American Indians in the years* 1820, 1821, 1822, 1823. Maps and illustrations. London, 1824.

WILLSON, BECKLES.—*The Great Company; Being the History of the Honourable Company of Merchants Adventurers Trading into Hudson's Bay.* London, 1900.
Life of Lord Strathcona and Mount Royal. London, 1915.

WISLIZENUS, F. A., M.D.—*A Journey to the Rocky Mountains in the Year* 1839. Translated from the German. St. Louis, Missouri Historical Society, 1912. 500 copies.

WOOD, LOUIS AUBREY.—*The Red River Colony. Chronicles of Canada,* vol. 21, 1915.

WORK, JOHN.—*The Journal of John Work, a chief trader of the Hudson's Bay Company, during his expedition from Vancouver to the Flatheads and Blackfeet of the Pacific Northwest. Edited, and with account of the fur trade in the Northwest, and life of Work,* by William S. Lewis and Paul C. Phillips. Cleveland, Ohio, 1923.

WYETH, Captain NATHANIEL J.—*Correspondence and Journal of Capt. Nathaniel J. Wyeth, 1831–36; A Record of Two Expeditions for the Occupation of the Oregon Country.* Edited by F. G. Young. Eugene, Oregon, 1899.

GOVERNORS OF THE HUDSON'S BAY COMPANY

Prince Rupert	1670–1682
James, Duke of York	1683–1685
John Churchill (Duke of Marlborough)	1685–1692
Sir Stephen Evance	1692–1696
Sir William Trumbull	1696–1700
Sir Stephen Evance	1700–1712
Sir Bibye Lake, Bart.	1712–1743
Benjamin Pitt	1743–1746
Thomas Knapp	1746–1750
Sir Atwell Lake, Bart.	1750–1760
Sir William Baker	1760–1770
Bibye Lake	1770–1782
Samuel Wegg	1782–1799
Sir James Winter Lake, Bart.	1799–1807
William Mainwaring	1807–1812
Joseph Berens, Junior	1812–1822
Sir John Henry Pelly, Bart.	1822–1852
Andrew Colvile	1852–1856
John Shepherd	1856–1858
Henry Hulse Berens	1858–1863
Sir Edmund Walker Head, Bart.	1863–1868
The Earl of Kimberley	1868–1869
Sir Stafford H. Northcote, Bart., M.P., Earl of Iddesleigh	1869–1874
George Joachim Goschen, M.P.	1874–1880
Eden Colvile	1880–1889
Donald A. Smith, Baron Strathcona and Mount Royal	1889–1914
Sir Thomas Skinner, Bart.	1914–1916
Sir Robert Molesworth Kindersley	1916–1925
Charles Vincent Sale	1925–1931
Patrick Ashley Cooper	1931–

DEPUTY GOVERNORS OF THE HUDSON'S BAY COMPANY

Sir John Robinson	1670–1675
Sir James Hayes	1675–1685
Sir Edward Dering	1685–1691
Samuel Clarke	1691–1701
John Nicholson	1701–1710
Thomas Lake	1710–1711
Sir Bibye Lake, Bart.	1711–1712
Captain John Merry	1712–1729
Samuel Jones	1729–1735
Benjamin Pitt	1735–1743
Thomas Knapp	1743–1746
Sir Atwell Lake, Bart.	1746–1750
Sir William Baker, Bart.	1750–1760
Captain John Merry	1760–1765
Bibye Lake	1765–1770
Robert Merry	1770–1774
Samuel Wegg	1774–1782
Sir James Winter Lake, Bart.	1782–1799
Richard Hulse	1799–1805
Nicholas Caesar Corsellis	1805–1806
William Mainwaring	1806–1807
Joseph Berens, Junior	1807–1812
John Henry Pelly	1812–1822
Nicholas Garry	1822–1835
Benjamin Harrison	1835–1839
Andrew Colvile	1839–1852
John Shepherd	1852–1856
Henry Hulse Berens	1856–1858
Edward Ellice, M.P.	1858–1863
Sir Curtis Miranda Lampson, Bart.	1863–1871
Eden Colvile	1871–1880
Sir John Rose, Bart., G.C.M.G.	1880–1888
Sir Donald A. Smith, G.C.M.G.	1888–1889
The Earl of Lichfield	1889–1910
Sir Thomas Skinner, Bart.	1910–1914
Leonard D. Cunliffe	1914–1916
Charles Vincent Sale	1916–1926
Sir Frederick Henry Richmond	1926–1931
Sir Alexander Murray	1932–

Appendix C

NUMBER OF PROPRIETORS OF THE HUDSON'S BAY COMPANY EVERY FIFTIETH YEAR FROM 1670 TO 1820, AND ALSO IN 1863, 1913 AND 1936

1670 (2nd May)	18 Proprietors		
1720 ,, ,,	50	,,	
1770 ,, ,,	109	,,	
1820 ,, ,,	77	,,	
1863 (1st July)	286	,,	
1913 ,, ,,	4,000–4,500	,,	(Ordinary)
	3,000	,,	(Preference)
1936 ,, ,,	12,500–13,000	,,	(Ordinary and Preference)
	3,000	,,	(Preference)

N.B.—The numbers in this table for 1913 and 1936 are only approximate.

With regard to 1913, the total number of proprietors cannot be computed, as some of the 3,000 Preference Shareholders were no doubt also possessors of Ordinary Shares.

There are now (1936) 12,500–13,000 Proprietors in all, this number including 3,000 Preference Shareholders.

Appendix D

LIST OF DIVIDENDS PAID BY THE COMPANY:
1670–1863

Date Payable		Capital	Dividend	Bonus
23rd April	1684	On original stock of £10,500	50%	
11th July	1688	,,	50%	
11th Oct.	1689	,,	25%	
Oct.	1690	On increased stock of £31,500	25%	
	1691–1717	,,	No dividend	
15th Nov.	1718	,,	10%	
25th Dec.	1719	,,	6%	
27th June	1721	On increased stock of £103,950	5%	
3rd April	1722	,,	10%	
17th April	1723	,,	8%	
26th March	1724	,,	12%	
22nd April	1725	,,	10%	
26th April	1726	,,	10%	
24th April	1727	,,	10%	
24th April	1728	,,	10%	
29th April	1729	,,	10%	
27th April	1730	,,	10%	
30th April	1731	,,	10%	
18th April	1732	,,	10%	
20th April	1733	,,	10%	
26th April	1734	,,	10%	
25th April	1735	,,	10%	
10th May	1736	,,	10%	
27th May	1737	,,	8%	
27th May	1738	,,	8%	
30th April	1739	,,	10%	

Date Payable		Capital	Dividend	Bonus
15th April	1740	On increased stock of £103,950	10%	
11th May	1741	,,	10%	
21st April	1742	,,	10%	
25th April	1743	,,	10%	
9th April	1744	,,	10%	
24th April	1745	,,	10%	
28th April	1746	,,	8%	
13th April	1747	,,	8%	
18th April	1748	,,	8%	
22nd May	1749	,,	7%	
26th April	1750	,,	7%	
15th April	1751	,,	8%	
6th April	1752	,,	8%	
9th April	1753	,,	8%	
8th April	1754	,,	8%	
7th April	1755	,,	8%	
12th April	1756	,,	8%	
4th April	1757	,,	8%	
3rd April	1758	,,	8%	
9th April	1759	,,	8%	
9th April	1760	,,	8%	
6th April	1761	,,	8%	
7th April	1762	,,	8%	
11th April	1763	,,	10%	
9th April	1764	,,	10%	
11th April	1765	,,	10%	
9th April	1766	,,	10%	
6th April	1767	,,	10%	
7th April	1768	,,	10%	
6th April	1769	,,	10%	
5th April	1770	,,	10%	
10th April	1771	,,	10%	
8th April	1772	,,	10%	
7th April	1773	,,	10%	
7th April	1774	,,	10%	

Date Payable		Capital	Dividend	Bonus
6th April	1775	On increased stock of £103,950	10%	
11th April	1776	,,	10%	
8th April	1777	,,	10%	
9th April	1778	,,	10%	
6th May	1779	,,	8%	
12th April	1780	,,	8%	
18th April	1781	,,	8%	
15th April	1782	,,	8%	
	1783	,,	No dividend	
	1784	,,	,,	
	1785	,,	,,	
12th June	1786	,,	5%	
23rd April	1787	,,	5%	
21st April	1788	,,	5%	
20th April	1789	,,	5%	
12th April	1790	,,	6%	
18th April	1791	,,	7%	
16th April	1792	,,	8%	
15th April	1793	,,	8%	
1st May	1794	,,	8%	
13th April	1795	,,	6%	
28th April	1796	,,	6%	
10th April	1797	,,	6%	
18th July	1798	,,	6%	
17th April	1799	,,	6%	
5th June	1800	,,	6%	
3rd Aug.	1801	,,	4%	
28th June	1802	,,	4%	
30th June	1803	,,	4%	
9th May	1804	,,	4%	
10th April	1805	,,	4%	
2nd April	1806	,,	4%	
23rd April	1807	,,	4%	
28th April	1808	,,	4%	
	1809–1814		No dividend	
1st May	1815	,,	4%	

Date Payable		Capital	Dividend	Bonus	Rate per cent. for the Year
13th May	1816	On increased stock of £103,950	4%		
26th May	1817	,,	4%		
1st June	1818	,,	4%		
2nd June	1819	,,	4%		
2nd June	1820	,,	4%		
4th June	1821	,,	4%		
6th June	1822	,,	4%		
5th June	1823	,,	4%		
7th June	1824	,,	4%		
7th June	1825	£400,000	10%		
13th June	1826	,,	10%		
22nd Jan.	1827	,,	5%		10%
10th July	1827	,,	5%		
10th Jan.	1828	,,	5%	10%	20%
8th July	1828	,,	5%		
9th Jan.	1829	,,	5%	10%	20%
10th July	1829	,,	5%		
11th Jan.	1830	,,	5%	10%	20%
9th July	1830	,,	5%		
11th Jan.	1831	,,	5%	10%	20%
9th July	1831	,,	5%		
12th Jan.	1832	,,	5%	10%	20%
10th July	1832	,,	5%		
10th Jan.	1833	,,	5%	6%	16%
10th July	1833	,,	5%		
10th Jan.	1834	,,	5%		10%
10th July	1834	,,	5%		
10th Jan.	1835	,,	5%	5%	15%
9th July	1835	,,	5%		
9th Jan.	1836	,,	5%	13%	23%
9th July	1836	,,	5%		
10th Jan.	1837	,,	5%		10%
11th July	1837	,,	5%		

Date Payable		Capital	Dividend	Bonus	Rate per cent. for the Year
9th Jan.	1838	£400,000	5% ⎫		
5th April	1838	,,	⎬	5%	25%
10th July	1838	,,	5% ⎭	10%	
10th Jan.	1839	,,	5% ⎫	3%	23%
9th July	1839	,,	5% ⎭	10%	
9th Jan.	1840	,,	5% ⎫		15%
8th July	1840	,,	5% ⎭	5%	
9th Jan.	1841	,,	5% ⎫		15%
8th July	1841	,,	5% ⎭	5%	
10th Jan.	1842	,,	5% ⎫		15%
8th July	1842	,,	10% ⎭		
9th Jan.	1843	,,	5% ⎫		10%
8th July	1843	,,	5% ⎭		
8th Jan.	1844	,,	5% ⎫		10%
8th July	1844	,,	5% ⎭		
10th Jan.	1845	,,	5% ⎫		15%
10th July	1845	,,	10% ⎭		
8th Jan.	1846	,,	5% ⎫		10%
9th July	1846	,,	5% ⎭		
8th Jan.	1847	,,	5% ⎫		10%
8th July	1847	,,	5% ⎭		
10th Jan.	1848	,,	5% ⎫		10%
10th July	1848	,,	5% ⎭		
8th Jan.	1849	,,	5% ⎫		10%
9th July	1849	,,	5% ⎭		
10th Jan.	1850	,,	5% ⎫		10%
9th July	1850	£440,000	5% ⎭		
9th Jan.	1851	,,	5% ⎫		10%
10th July	1851	,,	5% ⎭		
8th Jan.	1852	,,	5% ⎫		10%
8th July	1852	£462,000	5% ⎭		
10th Jan.	1853	,,	5% ⎫		10%
9th July	1853	,,	5% ⎭		

Date Payable		Capital	Dividend	Bonus	Rate per cent. for the Year
9th Jan.	1854	£500,000	5% ⎫		10%
10th July	1854	,,	5% ⎭		
8th Jan.	1855	,,	5% ⎫		10%
9th July	1855	,,	5% ⎭		
8th Jan.	1856	,,	5% ⎫		10%
9th July	1856	,,	5% ⎭		
8th Jan.	1857	,,	5% ⎫		10%
8th July	1857	,,	5% ⎭		
8th Jan.	1858	,,	5% ⎫		10%
8th July	1858	,,	5% ⎭		
10th Jan.	1859	,,	5% ⎫		10%
8th July	1859	,,	5% ⎭		
9th Jan.	1860	,,	5% ⎫		15%
9th July	1860	,,	10% ⎭		
8th Jan.	1861	,,	5% ⎫		10%
9th July	1861	,,	5% ⎭		
8th Jan.	1862	,,	5% ⎫		10%
9th July	1862	,,	5% ⎭		
8th Jan.	1863	,,	5% ⎫		11·94%
1st July	1863	,,	£6.18.9% ⎭		

Appendix E

DIVIDENDS AND RETURN OF CAPITAL PAID BY THE HUDSON'S BAY COMPANY:
1864-1936

Date	Return of Capital (p. Share)	Capital	Dividend per Share	Bonus per Share	Rate per cent. for the Year
Jan. 1864 Interim		£2,000,000 (£20 p. Share)	5/-		
July Final		,,	13/-		4½%
Jan. 1865 Interim		,,	8/-		
July 1865 Final		,,	10/-		4½%
Jan. 1866 Interim		,,	8/-		
July 1866 Final		,,	14/-		5½%
Jan. 1867 Interim		,,	8/-		
July 1867 Final		,,	10/-		4½%
Jan. 1868 Interim		,,	8/-		
July 1868 Final		,,	4/-		3%
Jan. 1869 Interim		,,	6/-		
July 1869 Final		,,	8/-		3½%
Jan. 1870 Interim		,,	4/-		
July 1870 Final	£3	,,	Nil		1%
Jan. 1871 Interim		£1,700,000 (£17 p. Share)	6/-		
July 1871 Final		,,	6/-		3·53%
Jan. 1872 Interim		,,	5/-		
July 1872 Final		,,	12/-		5%
Jan. 1873 Interim		,,	8/-		
July 1873 Final		,,	12/-		5·88%
Jan. 1874 Interim		,,	6/-		
July 1874 Final		,,	14/-		5·88%

EMPEROR ALEXANDER I IN 1805

Date	Return of Capital (p. Share)	Capital	Dividend per Share	Bonus per Share	Rate per cent. for the Year
Jan. 1875 Interim		(£17 p. Share)	8/– }		6·76%
July 1875 Final		,,	15/– }		
Jan. 1876 Interim		,,	8/– }		4·41%
July 1876 Final		,,	7/– }		
July 1877		,,	None		
July 1878		,,	None		
July 1879		,,	8/–		2·35%
July 1880		,,	9/–		2·65%
July 1881		£1,700,000	14/–		4·11%
July 1882	£2	,,	14/–		4·11%
July 1883	£1	£1,500,000 (£15 p. Share)	12/–		4%
July 1884	£1	£1,400,000 (£14 p. Share)	22/–		7·86%
July 1885		£1,300,000 (£13 p. Share)	None		
July 1886		,,	15/–		5·77%
July 1887		,,	17/–		6·54%
July 1888		,,	None		
July 1889		,,	14/–		5·38%
July 1890		,,	14/–		5·38%
July 1891		,,	6/6		2½%
July 1892		,,	6/6		2½%
July 1893		,,	12/–		4·61%
July 1894		,,	10/–		3·84%
July 1895		,,	12/–		4·61%
July 1896		,,	13/–		5%
July 1897		,,	13/–		5%
July 1898		,,	13/–		5%
July 1899		,,	13/–	7/–	7·69%
July 1900		,,	15/–	10/–	9·61%
July 1901		(£13 p. Share)	15/–		5·77%
July 1902		,,	15/–	7/6	8·65%
July 1903	£2	,,	22/6		8·65%
July 1904	£1	£1,100,000 (£11 p. Share)	35/–		15·91%

Date	Return of Capital (p. Share)	Capital	Dividend per Share	Bonus per Share	Rate per cent. for the Year
Jan. 1905 Interim		£1,000,000 (£10 p. Share)	10/–⎫		29%
July 1905 Final		,,	48/–⎭		
Jan. 1906 Interim		,,	10/–⎫		40%
July 1906 Final		,,	70/–⎭		
Jan. 1907 Interim		,,	20/–⎫		42½%
July 1907 Final		,,	65/–⎭		
Jan. 1908 Interim		,,	£1⎫		30%
July 1908 Final		,,	£2⎭		
Jan. 1909 Interim		,,	15/–⎫		25%
July 1909 Final		,,	35/–⎭		

Date	Capital	Dividend per Share or Rate of Divd.	Bonus per Share	Land Distribution	Bonus per Share	Rate per cent. for the Year
Jan. 1910 Interim	£1,000,000			15/–⎫		40%
July 1910 Final	,,	32/–		33/–⎭		
Jan. 1911 Interim	,,			£1⎫		40%
July 1911 Final	,,	30/–		30/–⎭		
Jan. 1912 Interim	,,			£1⎫		40%
July 1912 Final	,,	£2		£1⎭		
Jan. 1913 Interim	,, (£1 per Share)			10%⎫		50%
July 1913 Final	,,	20%		10%⎭	10%	
Jan. 1914 Interim	,,			15%⎫		40%
July 1914 Final	,,	Nil		25%⎭		
1915	£1,000,000	Nil		Nil		Nil
1916	,,	15%		5%		20%
Jan. 1917 Interim	,,	10%				30%
July 1917 Final	,,	5%		15%		
Jan. 1918 Interim	,,	10%				40%
July 1918 Final	,,	5%	5%	20%⎭		

Date	Capital	Dividend per Share or Rate of Divd.	Bonus per Share	Land Distribution	Bonus per Share	Rate per cent. for the Year
Jan. 1919 Interim	£1,000,000	10%				
July 1919 Final	,,	5%	10%	20%		45%
Jan. 1920 Interim	,,	10%				
July 1920 Final	,,	5%	10%	15%		40%
Jan. 1921 Interim	,,	10%				
July 1921 Final	,,	5%	10%	15%		40%
Jan. 1922 Interim	,,	10%				
July 1922 Final	,,	10%	15%	10%		45%
Jan. 1923 Interim	,,	10%				
July 1923 Final	,,	5%	2½%	2%		19½%
Jan. 1924 Interim	,,	10%				
July 1924 Final	,,	5%	5%	Nil		20%
Jan. 1925 Interim	,,	10%				
July 1925 Final	,,	5%	5%	Nil		20%
Jan. 1926 Interim	,,	10%				
July 1926 Final	,,	5%	5%	3½%		23½%
Jan. 1927 Interim	£1,500,000	10%				
July 1927 Final	,,			10%		20%
Jan. 1928 Interim	£2,000,000	7½%				
July 1928 Final	,,	7½%		10%		25%
Jan. 1929 Interim	,,	7½%				
July 1929 Final	,,	7½%		10%		25%
Jan. 1930 Interim	,,	7½%				
July 1930 Final	,,	2½%		7½%		17½%
1931–1935	£2,492,224	Nil		Nil		Nil
1936–	,,	4%				4%

Appendix F

PRICES OF HUDSON'S BAY STOCK: 1692–1700

	Year	Price per £100 of Stock
Mar.	1692 . . .	260
May (early)	1692 . . .	250
May 9th	1692 . . .	215
May (end)	1692 . . .	215
June	1692 . . .	245
Jan.	1693 . . .	190
Feb. and Mar. (early)	1693 . . .	180
Mar. (end)	1693 . . .	185
Apl.–July	1693 . . .	175
Aug. 18th	1693 . . .	150
Oct. (middle)	1693 . . .	190
Oct. 22nd	1693 . . .	200
Oct. 27th	1693 . . .	220
Nov.	1693 . . .	220
Dec.	1693 . . .	205
Feb.–Apr.	1694 . . .	190
May 23rd–June 13th	1694 . . .	150
July 4th–23rd	1694 . . .	130
Aug. 22nd	1694 . . .	150
Sept. 22nd	1694 . . .	185
Last quarter of	1694 . . .	Between 170 and 185
Dec. (end)	1694 . . .	175
Feb. 1st	1695 . . .	155
Mar. 1st	1695 . . .	155
June 14th	1695 . . .	230
June–Aug. 16th	1695 . . .	220
Nov. (end)	1695 . . .	130
Jan.	1696 . . .	130
June 26th	1696 . . .	98
July	1696 . . .	100
July–Dec.	1696 . . .	105
Jan.–Feb.	1697 . . .	80 for payment in cash or 95 in bank-money

PRICES OF HUDSON'S BAY STOCK:
1692–1700

	Year				Price per £100 of Stock
Oct.	1697 .	.	.		130
Nov. 24th	1697 .	.	.		130
Dec. 24th	1697 .	.	.		115
	1698, 1699, 1700 .	.	.		100–110

Note.—After 1700 the newspapers ceased to record quotations.

(Scott, W. R.)—"The Constitution and Finance of English, Scottish and Irish Joint Stock Companies to 1720"—Vol. II—Pp. 228–237. (London, Cambridge University Press, 1910.)

Year	Date of Highest Price	Prices	Date of Lowest Price
1692	March to April 18	260–215	May
1693	Oct. 27 to Nov. 17	220–150	Aug. 18
1694	June 5–12	205–130	July 4–25
1695	June 14	230–130	Dec.
1696	Jan. 3–17	125– 98	June 26, July 3
1697	Oct. 6–13	130– 95	Feb. to Aug.
1698	Jan. 6–26	110–100	Feb. 10–23
	Mar. 16–April 30		
1699	(nominal)	110–105	
1700	(nominal)	110–105	

(Scott, W. R.)—"The Constitution and Finance of English, Scottish and Irish Joint Stock Companies to 1720"—Vol. II, Pp. 228–237. (London, Cambridge University Press, 1910.)

Appendix G

TABLE SHOWING FLUCTUATIONS IN PRICE OF HUDSON'S BAY COMPANY'S STOCK: 1821–1837

Date		Price of Stock
April	1821	£100%
May	1821	99⅞%
July	1821	100%
Aug.	1821	96%
Dec.	1821	98%
Jan.	1822	100%
Feb.	1822	99½%
March	1822	155%
April	1822	150%
July	1822	150%
Jan.	1823	176%
Feb.	1823	176%
March	1823	176%
April	1823	175½%
June	1823	170%
July	1823	170%
Oct.	1823	160%
Jan.	1824	160%
July	1824	160%
Sept.	1824	160%
Oct.	1824	210%
Dec.	1824	212%
Jan.	1825	212%
May	1825	260%
Dec.	1825	235%
Jan.	1826	No transfers
July	1826	„ „
Jan.	1827	„ „
July	1827	210%
Jan.	1828	210%

386

Date		Price of Stock
June 1828	. . . . .	£235%
Aug. 1828	. . . . .	235%
Jan. 1829	. . . . .	225%
Aug. 1829	. . . . .	230%
Jan. 1830	. . . . .	240%
July 1830	. . . . .	250%
Dec. 1830	. . . . .	250%
Feb. 1831	. . . . .	250%
July 1831	. . . . .	240%
Jan. 1832	. . . . .	242%
July 1832	. . . . .	245%
Jan. 1833	. . . . .	246%
July 1833	. . . . .	240%
Jan. 1834	. . . . .	245%
July 1834	. . . . .	250%
Jan. 1835	. . . . .	260%
July 1835	. . . . .	250%
Jan. 1836	. . . . .	251%
July 1836	. . . .	No transfers
Dec. 1836	. . . . .	255%
Jan. 1837	. . . .	No transfers
May 1837	. . . . .	255%

This table has been compiled from information supplied by the Secretary of the Company to a Proprietor, John Forsyth of 40 York Terrace, Regent's Park, London; dated 26th May and 1st June 1837.

Appendix H

NOTES ON RELATIONS BETWEEN HUDSON'S BAY COMPANY AND THE CROWN

On the foundation of the Company, a presentation of three hundred pounds in the original stock and adventure was made to H.R.H. James, Duke of York, brother of Charles II, who had granted the Charter to the Company. When the Duke of York became king in 1685, as James II he continued to hold his stock. On July 11, 1688, when a dividend of "fifty pounds p Cent" was declared, the King's dividend was paid in 150 "Guinneys but his Ma^{tle} directed his Divident should bee paid into the Exchequer and soe His Honour the Deputy Governor had paid onely £150: into the Exchequer for such his Ma^{tle} Divident and had a Tally for it and his Honour the Deputy Governor is to bee charged with the change of the Gold in his accompt."

Presentation of the dividend to James II took place only a short time before William of Orange landed at Torbay on November 5, 1688.

On the accession of William III in 1689, the stock held by the abdicated James II was held by the Governor and Committee to have "rightly devolved" upon King William. At a meeting of the Committee in September, 1690, it was resolved that the King's dividend of seventy-five pounds due in 1689 (a twenty-five per cent dividend) and a further sum of two hundred and twenty-five pounds for another dividend of twenty-five per cent now due on the stock which had recently been trebled, be paid to the King in golden guineas.

The presentation was made by Sir Edward Dering, the Deputy Governor, accompanied by Messrs. Clarke, Pitts, Hayward and Cudworth of the Committee and by several other members of the Company, all introduced into "His Maj^{tles} Clossett by the Right Hono^{ble} the Earle of Portland."

The Deputy Governor's address, in part, follows:

"May it Please your Matie.

Your Maties most Loyall & Dutifull Subjects, the Hudsons Bay

Comp^a begg leave most humbly to Congratulate y^r Maties Happy Returne Home with Honour & Safety. And wee doe Daily pray to Heaven (that Hath Soe Wonderfully preserv^d your Royall person) that in all your Undertakeings yr. Matie may bee as Victorious as Cæsar, as Beloved as Titus, and (after all) have the glorious long Reigne & Pecefull End of Augustus.

"On this Happy Ocasion wee desier allso most humbly to Present to your Matie a divedend of three hundred Guines Upon Three Hundred pounds Stock in the Hudsons Bay Comp^a now Rightfully devolved to your Matie. And altho, wee have been the greatest Sufferers, of any Comp^a from those Common Enemies of all mankind the French, yet when your Maties Just Armes shall have given Repose to all Christendome, Wee also Shall Enjoy our Share, of those great Benefitts, & doe not doubt but to appeare often with this golden fruite in our hands Under the Happy Influence of your Maties Most Gracious protection over Us & all our Concernes which wee most Humbly begg."

According to the London *Gazette*, the King received the deputation "very Graciously, and was Pleased to assure them of His Protection and Royal Favour upon all Occasions."

The reigning monarch continued to hold the stock originally presented to James, Duke of York, for many years. From 1690 to 1718 there were no dividends, but after that dividends were regularly paid to His Majesty until 1764. The personal presentation was not continued, but the King signed a warrant deputing some one to receive the dividend on his behalf. In 1735 the warrant was signed by Queen Caroline.

In 1812 a claim was made by the Commissioners of His Majesty's real and personal estate for the payment of arrears of dividends since 1674. It was then decided by the Governor and Committee to take counsel's opinion as to whether the stock first held by James II had ever rightfully descended to William III; that is whether it had been the property of the Crown or personal property of James II. A number of legal points were involved, the Company's very practical argument being that in 1720, when a call of ten per cent was made, the Crown had not responded.

No further claim for dividends was made by the Crown after 1813. When the Company's finances were reorganized in 1824, a resolution was passed by the Committee and confirmed by the General Court that the £2,970, the King's stock, to which "no person had shewn any Title for very many Years," be placed in an account to be called "unclaimed stock," and "be debited with the Call and Interest thereon, and, from time to time, credited with Dividends, till the same is repaid."

Appendix I

STANDING RULES AND REGULATIONS
1835

RESOLVED · · · THAT the following be the TARIFF for advances throughout the Northern and Southern Departments.

" · · · 1st. COMMISSIONED GENTLEMEN. The Depôt Inventory Tariff for all Goods supplied them during the Summer, and 25 per Cent. thereon for all subsequent advances, without distinction, whether taken at the Depôt or inland; wines and spirits excepted, to be at 100 per Cent. on the Depôt Inventory Tariff; but leather and all other country produce to be at the Depôt Inventory Tariff, or actual cost, throughout the year.

" · · · 2nd. CLERKS and SERVANTS' TARIFF 50 per Cent. on the prime cost of all imported goods, and $12\frac{1}{2}$ per Cent. on the Depôt cost of all country made articles, supplied during the summer at the Depôt, wines and spirits excepted, to be continued at fixed prices, viz. Madeira wine 20s., Port and all other wines 16s., Shrub, Gin and Brandy 16s., Spirits reduced to proof strength 12s. per gallon; and all subsequent advances without distinction of articles, whether taken at the Depôt or inland, to be charged 50 per Cent. on the York or Moose Inventory Tariff, with the exception of wines and spirits, to be sold at 50 per Cent. on the Depôt summer Sale Tariff to Servants; and all country produce, consisting of dressed and parchment leather, Buffalo Robes, provisions, &c. &c. will be sold throughout the year at 50 per Cent. on Depôt Inventory prices. It is however understood that, in consideration of the peculiar living and mode of journeying at the Bay side Settlements, wines and spirits will be allowed to continue at the Depôt summer Sale Tariff throughout the year.

RESOLVED 3rd. THAT it is however understood, that the foregoing Tariffs are intended for the ordinary saleable articles, as those classed unsaleable or considered as such, it is left discretionary with those, superintending Districts or Posts, to dispose of at a price corresponding with their estimated value.

„ 4th. THAT all Commissioned Gentlemen, Clerks and Servants, be charged 10 per Cent. on the last average nett Sales, for any Furs supplied from the Stores during the current outfit for personal or family use in the country, and 20 per Cent. if supplied for any other purpose.

„ 5th. THAT all Freemen, Half-breed and Iroquois Trappers, having no other means of paying for their supplies than with their hunts, be treated on the footing of Indians, unless when specially provided for by Council; and that freemen trappers having funds in the Company's hands, and unable to pay their supplies with Furs, be charged 200 per Cent. on the District Inventory prices; and that no money in payment of Furs or other articles be allowed either class without directions from Council, but the Furs of those owing balances in money to the Company, will be taken in payment thereof at the rate of 4s. 6d. sterling per each made Beaver.

„ 6th. THAT all Furs killed by, or in the possession of, the Company's Officers and Servants, be considered the Company's property, and paid for in Goods at the Indian standard of the place, except to those on special agreements, fort hunters, &c. &c.

RESOLVED 7th.   THAT no Commissioned Gentlemen be allowed to purchase or dispose of Horses, Cattle or Dogs on private account, but that all such dealings be for and on account of the Company, each Commissioned Gentleman to be permitted however, to keep a saddle horse or a train of dogs for his own use, when considered necessary, on paying the surplus cost thereof, over and above the established Indian or Inventory price of the District; and that Clerks and Servants be permitted to purchase such horses as may be absolutely necessary to enable them to do their duty, from the Company only, at Inventory prices, it being understood in the event of removal or retirement of the individuals, that the Company will assume such horses at the cost price.

„   8th.   THAT all country produce, &c. subject to valuation on Inventories or in Transfers, be priced as follows, viz.

Birch Bark, per bottom	.	fath.	1s	6d
side	. .	„	—s	9d
Barley, rough	. . .	bush.	3s	—d
hulled	. . .	„	4s	—d
Boats, not less than 24 feet keel	. . . .	ea.	300s	—d
Canoes, large North	. .	„	100s	—d
small fishing	. .	„	20s	—d
Corn, Indian, rough	. .	bush.	3s	—d
hulled	. .	„	4s	—d
Fat or Grease	. . .	lb.	—s	3d
Flour	. . . .	Cwt.	s	d
Geese, fresh or salted	. .	ea.	—s	4d
Gum or Pitch	. . .	lb.	—s	2d
Meat, pounded	. . .	lb.	—s	3d
dried or piece	. .	„	—s	2d
fresh	. .	„	—s	1d
salted	. .	„	—s	2d
Oil, Sturgeon	. . .	Gall.	2s	—d
Pimican, fine or common	.	lb.	—s	3d
per bag of 90 lbs.	. .	ea.	22s	6d

Rice, Indian . . .	bush.	4s	—d
Robes, Buffalo, prime . .	ea.	5s	—d
common .	,,	2s	6d
Salt	bush.	8s	—d
Shagganapie, per pack cords	lb.	—s	2d
Snow Shoes	,,	—s	4d
Shoes, Indian . . .	pair	—s	6d
Sinews	lb.	—s	2d
Skins, dressed, Buffalo .	ea.	2s	6d
Red Deer, large	,,	3s	—d
small	,,	1s	—d
Rein Deer, large	,,	2s	—d
small	,,	1s	—d
Moose, large	,,	4s	—d
small	,,	2s	—d
parchment Moose, large	,,	2s	—d
small	,,	1s	—d
Red Deer, large	,,	2s	—d
small	,,	1s	—d
Rein Deer, prime	,,	1s	—d
Sugar, Maple . . .	lb.	—s	4d
Tents, Mooseskin, not used on the voyage, but brought out in bales	ea.	25s	—d
Tongues, Buffalo . .	,,	—s	9d
Red Deer or Moose	,,	—s	9d
Rein Deer, prime .	,,	—s	6d
Wheat . . .	bush.	4s	—d
Dogs, when transferred .	ea.	10s	—d
Horses do. .	,,	40s	—d
Horned Cattle, full grown male or female, when transferred . . .	,,	60s	—d
Calves or Pigs, whether male or female, when transferred	,,	20s	—d
Sheep, Ewes, when transferred	,,	40s	—d
Lambs, do.	,,	10s	—d
Rams, do.	,,	40s	—d

RESOLVED 9th. THAT Buffalo Robes, dressed and parchment leather, brought out to Norway House and the Depôt, or transferred to other Districts, be charged at Inventory prices; and that the same articles when sold to Settlers at Red River be charged at 100 per Cent. on Inventory prices, to cover the freight and risk attending the transport thither, and that no provisions, excepting at a Depôt or required for transfers, be valued on Inventories.

RESOLVED 10th. THAT all imported Goods returned to the Depôt, be considered on the account and risk of the District transferring the same.

Serious inconvenience having been experienced of late years from the circumstance of Gentlemen in charge of Brigades leaving the Factory with craft not fully laden, thereby occasioning a loss of freight; it is

,, 11th. THAT the lading of Boats belonging to all Districts in the Northern Department, leaving the Depôt, be 70 pieces goods of full weight or measurement, exclusive of the usual allowance for passengers, viz.: 10 pieces for each Commissioned Gentleman, 5 pieces for first class Clerks, 3 pieces for junior Clerks and Postmasters; THAT one-half of the above allowances be made to cover the freight of private orders for the same classes remaining inland: and that each servant remaining inland be allowed the freight of $1\frac{1}{2}$ pieces to cover his private order, which shall be considered cargo; but that the private luggage of the crew be over and above the cargo; and that in all cases where a loss of freight is occasioned by neglect of this Resolve, the same be chargeable to the private account of the Commissioned Gentleman conducting the Brigade.

And with reference to the foregoing Resolutions, in order to regulate the charge for freight of private property conveyed inland exceeding the fixed allowance; it is

RESOLVED 12th.   THAT the same be charged to private account
of the parties as follows, viz.:

From York factory to Mc. Ken-
    zie's R. District .   .   . 50s per piece.
    Athabasca   .   .   . 40s   ,,
    Sask^n·, Eng: River, Lac la
      Pluie, Upper Red River
      and Swan River .   . 30s per piece.
    Red River Settlement, and
      the Winipeg Posts . 18s   ,,
    Norway House   .   . 14s   ,,
    Oxford and Nelson River 10s   ,,
    Churchill and Severn . 2s   ,,

From Norway House to Mc.-
    Kenzie's R. District .   . 36s per piece.
    Athabasca   .   .   . 26s   ,,
    Sask^n·, Eng: River, Lac la
      Pluie, Upper Red River
      and Swan River .   . 16s   ,,
    Red River Settlement, and
      the Winipeg Posts . 4s   ,,
    Oxford and Nelson River 2s   ,,
    York Factory .   .   . 5s   ,,

From Moosefactory to New
    Brunswick   .   .   . 10s per piece.
    Lake Superior Dist. . 17s   ,,
    Lake Huron .   .   . 20s   ,,
    Old Albany Factory . 3s   ,,
    Rupert's River, and East
      Main .   .   . 3s   ,,
    Albany inland   . . 20s   ,,
    Rupert's River inland . 20s   ,,
    Abbetibe   .   . 15s   ,,
    Temiscamingue and Grand
      Lac .   .   . 20s   ,,
    Kenogumissie Dist: . 15s   ,,

,,   13th.   THAT the freight to be allowed to Districts, for
the transport of pieces, be as follows, viz.:
From—

York Factory to Red River   .   1s per piece.
York Factory to Norway House 14s   ,,
York Factory to Oxford House 10s   ,,
Oxford Ho. to Norway House   4s   ,,
Norway Ho. to Red River   .   4s   ,,
Red River to Norway House .   1s   ,,
Norway Ho. to Oxford House   2s   ,,
Oxford Ho. to York Factory .   3s   ,,

RESOLVED 14th. THAT all Chief Factors and Chief Traders, for whom no special mode of conveyance is provided, accompany their loaded craft to and from the Depôt; and the better to prevent loss of freight, that those in charge of loaded Boats from the Depôt previous to their departure give in to the person appointed for that purpose correct Bills of lading thereof, which must be conformable to the provisions of the 11th Resolve.

The better to insure co-operation and efficiency between those superintending and those co-operating in Districts, to which two or more Commissioned Gentlemen are appointed; it is

,,   15th. THAT the person appointed as superintendent thereof by Council be authorised to assume the direction of affairs, and to issue such orders and instructions for the good government and successful management of the posts and trade thereof as to him may from time to time appear expedient, to which every attention and conformity are required from those to whom such orders and instructions are addressed or have reference.

Serious inconvenience to the service having in many instances arisen of late from the circumstance of Clerks in distant parts of the country applying to the Governor and Council for permission to visit the Depôt or withdraw from the District, without having previously consulted the Commissioned Gentlemen superintending the District, and to guard against a recurrence of such inconvenience; it is

RESOLVED 16th. THAT no such permission be granted in future, unless the applicant first submit his request in writing to the Gentleman superintending the District to which he belongs, who is hereby directed to report on the same for the information of the Governor and Council; and that any Clerk coming to the Depôt without such permission be considered as retiring from the service.

In order to guard against irregularities and expenses, arising from little favouritisms and partialities which occasionally discover themselves; it is

„ 17th. THAT all appointments to the offices of Postmasters, Interpreters, Apprentice Tradesmen or Sailors, in the service, be made by the Governor and Council, by whom also the wages of the parties are to be regulated, and that no individual be permitted to make such appointments, or to increase, reduce or determine such wages. And that the wages of Postmasters shall not hereafter exceed £50 per annum, except in cases where parties are at present in the enjoyment of higher wages.

„ 18th. THAT no Guide or Interpreter, whether at the Factory Depôt or inland, be permitted to mess with Commissioned Gentlemen or Clerks in charge of Posts; but while at the Depôts they will be allowed per week four days ordinary Rations as issued to Engagés, besides two loaves of Bread, 3 lbs. Pork, $\frac{1}{4}$ lb. Tea, 2 lbs. Sugar, and 1 pint Rum, and have an allowance delivered to them on departure for the voyage inland of 1 lb. Tea, 6 lbs. Sugar, 10 lbs. Biscuit, and 10 lbs. Beef or Pork, besides an extra allowance for the wintering grounds of 25 lbs. Flour, 20 lbs. Sugar, and 10 lbs. Grease, in addition to the ordinary rations of engagés at the place where they winter.

In looking over the list of servants in each District, it is much to be regretted that the number and classification determined on by the Resolutions of Council are not generally adhered to, which is productive of irregularity and unnecessary expense; it is therefore

RESOLVED 19th. THAT no Gentleman be permitted in future to deviate from the number and classification of people determined on in Council to be employed in the business of the District.

As it appears by the accounts from several Districts that the established scale of wages is not duly observed, it is

„ 20th. THAT, in order to prevent all misapprehension on that subject in future, the existing scale of wages be attended to, as follows, viz.:

For all Districts in the H. B. Territories:

Steersmen	£22
Bowsmen	20
Middlemen	17

For Athabasca and Mc. Kenzie's River:

Steersmen	£24
Bowsmen	22
Middlemen	19

For the Columbia:

Boutes	£22
Middlemen	17

For New Caledonia, Millbank, Nass & Stikine:

Boutes	£24
Middlemen	19

together with an augmentation of £3 to those who may be employed on the voyage from the west side the mountains to York factory and back again; Guides never to exceed £5 in addition to the wages of Steersmen of the District, and not to be exempted from the ordinary duties of a Steersman, nor allowed an extra man in their boats, with the exception of the Athabasca Guide, and the Guides of the hired transport brigades; no more Bowsmen or Steersmen to be employed in any District than absolutely required for the management of the craft belonging thereto.

Boat builders not to exceed £30 per annum wages.

Interpreters not to exceed £25 per annum wages.

Wages of Mechanics at the Depôt to be regulated and varied according to circumstances; and those of Blacksmiths inland not to exceed the wages of Steersmen of the District.

In order to guard against misapprehensions, and to check irregularities in regard to servants wages; it is

RESOLVED 21st. THAT all Servants engaged in England, in Canada, or in the country, be considered for the term of their first contracts as being disposable for general service at the wages stated in their engagements, unless "prix du Poste" be distinctly specified, in which case the wages of the District to which the party is attached to be allowed. But in all cases where the Engagements are renewed in the country, the wages of the District for which the servant is engaged to be allowed accordingly.

The items of gratuities and extra service money have encreased to such a degree as to render it necessary to check them; it is therefore

Resolved 22nd. That no Gratuity or extra service money be allowed to any Servant or person whatsoever (except the usual gratuities to Indians in consideration of good hunts, &c., &c.) unless such gratuities or extra service monies be authorized by a formal resolve in Council.

To prevent misapprehension and abuse; it is

„ 23rd. That all Commissioned Gentlemen having distinct charges be permitted to employ on the voyage or inland one of the people appointed to the District, in the capacity of cook or servant in addition to his ordinary duties, and that for such extra service he be allowed the sum of £3 in addition to his regular wages, to be put to the credit of his account at the end of the year, provided the contract wages of such servant do not exceed those of a common labourer of the District.

And in order to insure due respect and attention to the foregoing resolutions; it is

„ 24th. That parties deviating from the instructions contained in the Resolutions on the subject of servants, wages, gratuities, &c., be held liable for the amount of expenses incurred by such irregularities, which the accountants of the several Depôts are hereby authorised to charge to their accounts immediately, from whence it cannot be withdrawn, nor can the charge be remitted, without special authority from the Governor and Council first duly asked and obtained.

„ 25th. That in renewing all contracts it be distinctly specified that the person hired be at the rate of so much per annum, wages and duty to commence and be computed from the 1st June, if hired in the country, and if hired in Britain or in Canada, the same to commence and be computed from the date of his embarkation

2 C

thence, and in either case both to be continued to his re-embarkation and departure from the Depôt, subject however, if under the rank of a Clerk, to work his passage from thence when required, in any of the Company's craft or vessels, whether light or laden, without any compensation, till his arrival in England or in Montreal, where his engagement will cease. Also that a clause be inserted therein requiring the person hired to give a year's notice of his intention of retiring at the expiration of his agreement, otherwise he will be retained and considered disposable for the current at the salary of the preceding year's outfit.

RESOLVED 26th. THAT the originals of all contracts with Clerks and Servants, together with notices of retirement, be deposited with the Accountant at the Depôt, for the purpose of being registered.

„ 27th. THAT no indebted servant be permitted to have advances in the course of the year exceeding three-fourths of his current wages, viz.: about half at the Depôt and one-fourth inland.

„ 28th. THAT no Servant be sent from one District to another without being accompanied with a satisfactory statement of his account, and that no advances excepting bare essentials be made such servant, while absent from his District, without a special order; and that no servant be transferred from one District to another, or exchanged for another, except at the Depôt, and with the knowledge of the principal Accountant.

„ 29th. THAT no transfers of money from one account to another be allowed in the general accounts, but that such be permitted in the sale shops.

Much irregularity, and in many cases considerable loss, having arisen from the circumstance of the accounts of retiring servants not being transmitted to the Depôt the year of their retirement; it is

RESOLVED 30th. THAT all Gentlemen in charge of Districts be directed to deliver or forward every summer to the Gentleman in charge of the Depôt complete lists of all Servants, freemen, or their families, retiring from their respective Districts, whether to England, Canada, or Red River Settlement, together with complete statements of the inland accounts of these people, in order that the Accountant may transmit correct and final pay-lists with them to their several destinations; that no servants be allowed to retire without going to the Depôt, except under particular circumstances; and that Gentlemen in charge of Districts be liable for any loss arising from neglect of this Resolution.

  ,,   31st. THAT persons retiring from the service, likewise "Goers and Comers," be permitted to take with them not exceeding 20 pairs Indian shoes, or 2 skins dressed leather; that the baggage of craft going to Canada be examined at Norway House and Michipicoton; that the baggage of all persons going to Europe be examined at the Depôt on the coast, and in the event of any articles of furs, which have not been regularly purchased and paid for agreeably to the 4th Resolve, or in the event of any shoes or leather being found among such baggage, exceeding the quantities allowed, the same to be forfeited.

To prevent misapprehension on the part of Clerks or Servants in regard to pecuniary matters; it is

RESOLVED 32nd. THAT those having funds or balances due to them by the Fur Trade, and who may be desirous of making payments in England or Canada, be directed to authorize the Governor officially, in writing, to take the necessary steps for that purpose, as no other mode of application will be attended to.

„ 33rd. THAT all supplies and advances furnished by one District or Post, for account of Officers, Servants and others attached to another District or Post, be charged at the established sale prices, detailed among the other Book Debts of the place, and the amount thereof entered in the statement of advances and Book Debts of the District supplying the same, and by which District alone they are to be charged and taken notice of.

„ 34th. THAT in Districts to which only one Commissioned Gentleman is appointed, he be directed to furnish annually complete accounts of the business thereof to the Accountant at the Depôt, and in Districts to which two or more Commissioned Gentlemen are appointed, that each be directed to furnish accounts of the business under their respective management, the same to be annually transmitted to the person superintending such District, and through him to the Accountant at the Depôt, likewise a journal of occurrences, with correct copies of all official correspondence, and a report conveying every requisite information in regard to the state and mode of conducting the trade, exhibiting a comparative statement of the closing and immediately preceding outfits, together with such suggestions in regard to the improvement of the trade as may occur, such report also to contain an abstract of the Indian population, exhibiting the number of men, women and children of both sexes; and that all Clerks in charge of Posts be directed to furnish similar accounts and statements.

With a view to save Interest on Inventories inland; it is

RESOLVED 35th. THAT they be hereafter classed, commencing with those of June, 1835, under three principal and distinct heads, and priced as follows, viz.:

> 1st. Trading Goods to comprise all those not damaged, intended for trade or sales to servants, to be priced at the established schedule of advance of the District.

> 2nd. Damaged and unsaleable, to comprise all of that description, to be priced as heretofore at a fixed value.

> 3rd. Country produce, to comprise leather and such other produce as the minutes of Council authorise being valued, to be at fixed prices.

No Stores or unproductive property of any description, whether new or in use, such as Utensils (Fort or Culinary), allowances, stationery, medicines, to be valued, of all which property every Commissioned Gentleman is directed to take in from the Depôt merely what is required for the use of the current Outfit.

,,   36th. THAT Gentlemen in charge of Districts and Posts be directed to furnish annually, with the Inventories, a list of the articles in use at each Post, distinguishing them according to their condition as good, half worn, much worn; also a list of cattle or other live-stock, and the number of acres in cultivation, and quantity of seed sown for the next crop, with quantity reaped the preceding summer. The cattle should be distinguished Bulls, Cows, of the several ages, calves, one year old, two years old, three years old, and upwards, without any valuation affixed.

RESOLVED 37th. THAT regular and correct accounts of all supplies furnished along the communication, or of property transferred from one Post or District to another, be delivered or forwarded accompanying such supplies, or transfers of property, otherwise no charge thereof can afterwards be brought by the District furnishing against the District receiving the same.

„   38th. THAT a list of the Indian and half breed and freemen trappers, considered as appertaining to each District, be made out and settled on annually by the Gentleman in charge of neighbouring Districts, and that who hunts in payment of supplies advanced by one Post or District, be taken or received by another Post or District, excepting for account or on behalf of the place furnishing such supplies, and in all doubtful cases that such matters be determined and settled on by the parties concerned on a fair and liberal principle.

„   39th. THAT the Indians be treated with kindness and indulgence, and mild and conciliatory means resorted to in order to encourage industry, repress vice, and inculcate morality; that the use of spirituous liquors be gradually discontinued in the few Districts in which it is yet indispensable, and that the Indians be liberally supplied with requisite necessaries, particularly with articles of ammunition, whether they have the means of paying for it or not; and that no Gentleman in charge of Districts or Posts be at liberty to alter or vary the standard or usual mode of trade with the

Indians, except by special permission of Council.

In order gradually to wean the Indians all over the country from the use of spirituous liquors, to which they are so much addicted, it is

RESOLVED 40th. THAT none of that article, either for trade, sales, or gratuitous indulgence to servants, or allowances to officers, be imported into English River, Athabasca or Mc. Kenzie's River Districts, and that such deficiency on the outfit be made up by a proportionate increase in the supplies of ammunition and tobacco.

The subject of nursing the country with a view to the preservation of Beaver not being sufficiently understood or attended to; it is

,, 41st. THAT all Gentlemen in charge of Districts and Posts, except such as are exposed to opposition, exert their utmost influence in discouraging the hunting of Cub Beaver and of Beaver out of season, and that no Beaver traps or springs be issued from the Depôt of York, except for sale to the Piegan Indians, or those hunting foxes on the coast; and from the Depôt of Moose only for Lake Huron District, the Posts along Lake Superior, and to the Indians who hunt foxes on the Bay side; and that in any case where an unusual proportion of cub or unseasoned Beaver appears, the same to be particularly represented by the Gentleman superintending the Fur Stores, to the Governor and Council, for the information of the Honble Committee.

,, 42nd. THAT all Officers and Servants of the Company having women or children, and wishing to leave the same in the country on their retirement therefrom, be required to make such provision for their future maintenance, more particularly for that of the children, as circumstances may reasonably warrant, and the means of the individual permit; that all those desirous of withdrawing the same from the country be allowed every facility for that purpose; and that none hereafter be allowed to take a woman without binding himself down to such reasonable provision and maintenance for her and children, in the event of issue, as on a fair and equitable principle may be considered necessary, not only during his residence in the country, but after his departure therefrom.

REGULATIONS FOR PROMOTING MORAL AND RELIGIOUS IMPROVEMENT

RESOLVED 1st. THAT for the moral and religious improvement of the servants, and more effectual civilization and instruction of the families attached to the different Establishments, and of the Indians, that every Sunday divine service be publicly read, with becoming solemnity, once or twice a day, to be regulated by the number of people and other circumstances, at which every man, woman and child resident, will be required to attend, together with any of the Indians who may be at hand, and whom it may be proper to invite.

„ 2nd. THAT in course of the week due attention be bestowed to furnish the women and children such regular and useful occupation as is suited to their age and capacities, and best calculated to suppress vicious and promote virtuous habits.

„ 3rd. As a preparative to education, that the mother and children be always addressed and habituated to converse in the vernacular dialect (whether English or French) of the Father, and that he be encouraged to devote part of his leisure hours to teach the children their A. B. C., Catechism, together with such further elementary instruction as time and circumstances may permit.

THAT Chief Factors, Chief Traders and Clerks, in charge of Districts or Posts, be directed to take the proper measures for carrying these Regulations into effect, among the Company's Servants, families and Indians, attached to their respective charges.

INDEX